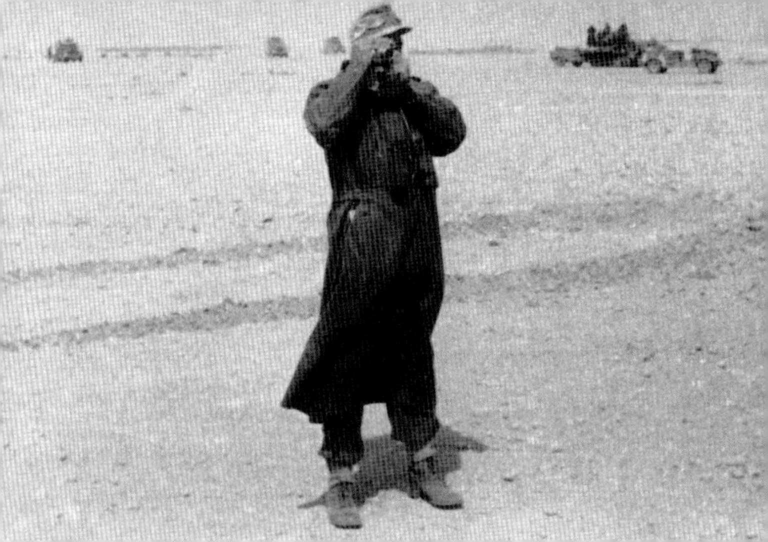

The Private Afrikakorps Photograph Collection of Rommel's Chief-of-Staff

Generalleutnant

FRITZ BAYERLEIN

P.A. Spayd & Fritz Dittmar-Bayerlein

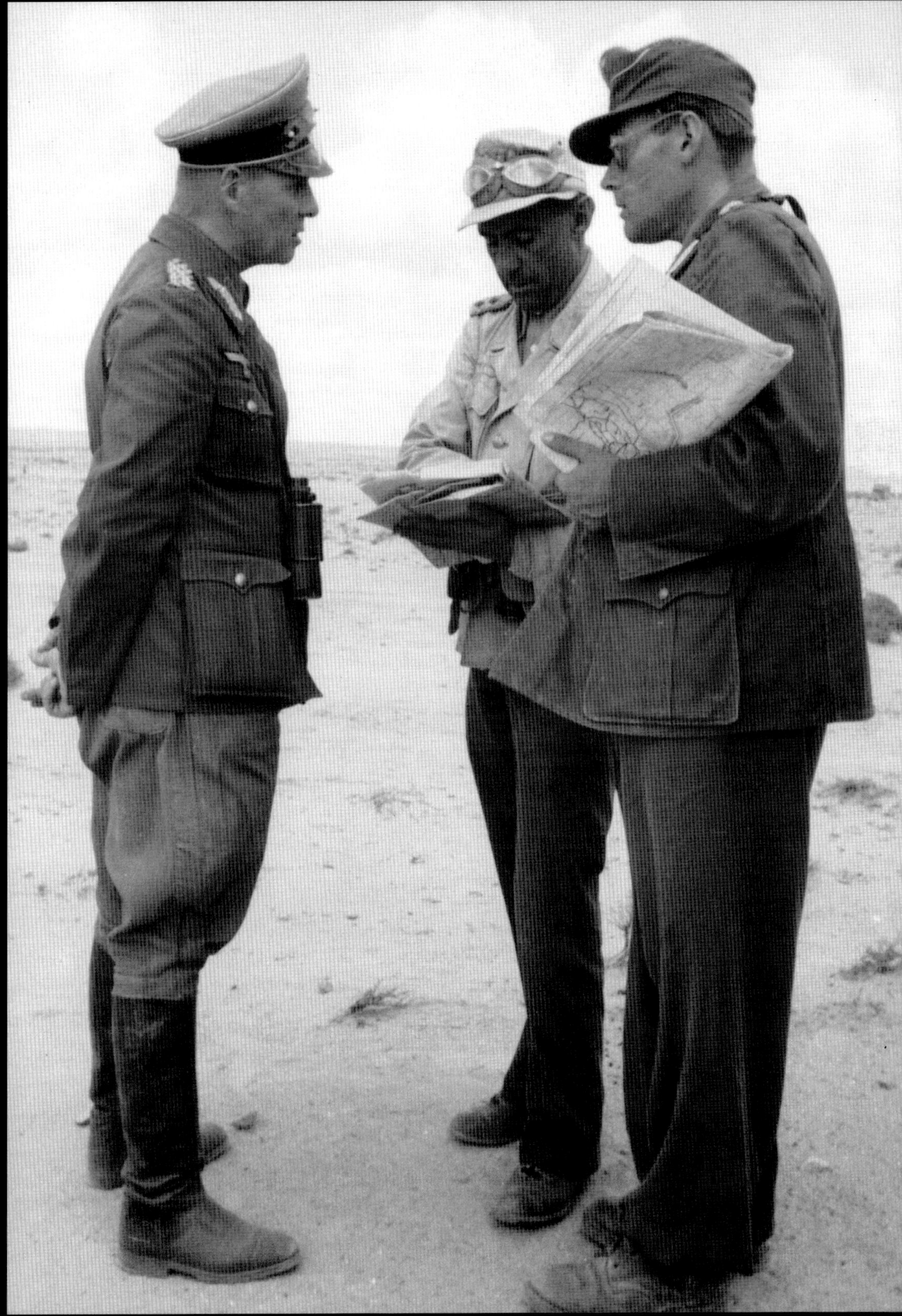

Schiffer Military History
Atglen, PA

Book design by Robert Biondi.

Library of Congress Catalog Number: 2004103127.

Printed in China.
ISBN: 0-7643-2065-3

We are always looking for people to write books on new and related subjects. If you have an idea for a book, please contact us at the address below.

Published by Schiffer Publishing Ltd.
4880 Lower Valley Road
Atglen, PA 19310
Phone: (610) 593-1777
FAX: (610) 593-2002
E-mail: Info@schifferbooks.com.
Visit our web site at: www.schifferbooks.com
Please write for a free catalog.
This book may be purchased from the publisher.
Please include $3.95 postage.
Try your bookstore first.

In Europe, Schiffer books are distributed by:
Bushwood Books
6 Marksbury Ave.
Kew Gardens
Surrey TW9 4JF
England
Phone: 44 (0)20 8392-8585
FAX: 44 (0)20 8392-9876
E-mail: Bushwd@aol.com.
Free postage in the UK. Europe: air mail at cost.
Try your bookstore first.

FOREWORD

I have had an interest in photos of the *Afrikakorps* for nearly fifty years. When I was a young thirteen year-old student in Australia an uncle who had served in the 9th Australian Infantry Division gave me a bag containing the war souvenirs from his time as a soldier in North Africa in World War II. Among his souvenirs was a small bundle of wartime photos (or snapshots). The photos were mostly German in origin but there were a few Italian photos and a couple that were obviously of Australian or other British Commonwealth soldiers. I already knew enough to divide the photos into these three categories but little else. Once I had separated the photos along national army lines I started to closely study the individual photos themselves.

So began what has been for me nearly a lifetime of learning about the German Army that fought in North Africa in World War II, and a continuing interest in photos from the period.

Patricia Spayd has done all students of the war in North Africa a great service in compiling the material for this book. It must also be stated that the book would not have been possible without the contribution of Fritz Dittmar-Bayerlein who generously opened his beloved uncle's private photograph collection to Ms. Spayd and then worked with her to ensure its preservation and publication.

The photos reproduced on these pages were taken by a photographer, who was himself, an important figure in shaping the events that made up the North African campaign. Through his photos we see those things that Fritz Bayerlein himself thought were important enough to make a photographic image of. We should also remember that because of who he was Fritz Bayerlein had a unique view of the war. He was the

Chief-of-Staff to Erwin Rommel. These photos therefore have an added significance for readers because they reflect not only the subject matter of the images snapped by the lens of Bayerlein's Leica but they are closely connected to who he was, where he was, what he was doing at that time, and who he was with.

Much of our understanding of history changes in time as each generation continues to study what happened and it is written and re-written about. This is natural because we each bring our own area of reference to see events of the period through. Our own reading and learning, our own points of view, and our own cultural and historical perspectives all go to shape our personal understanding of what happened and what it meant. However one thing in history that does not undergo change are the images that were made at the time by those who participated in the events that are recorded in those images. This book is full of images that are just as real and true today as the day when they were made. This is a book that will not date with time.

I believe this book and its photos will be just as interesting to the next generation of students of the North African campaigns as it is to the readers of today, and to the following generations yet to be born.

Dal McGuirk
Auckland
October 2003

CONTENTS

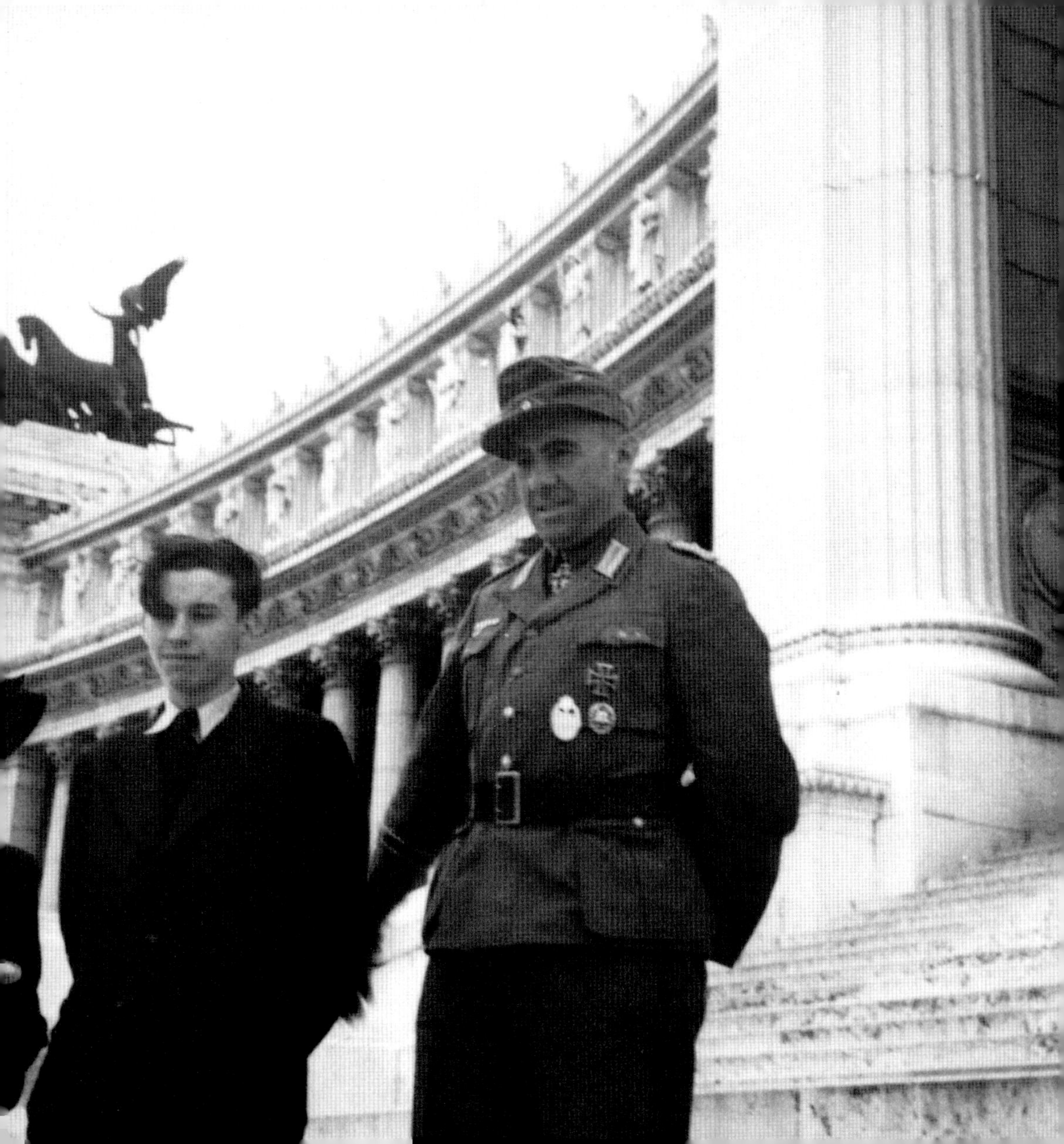

INTRODUCTION
"MY UNCLE AND I"
by Fritz Dittmar-Bayerlein

My uncle, *Generalleutnant* Fritz Bayerlein, was a career soldier serving in the Army from the last year of the Great War, and through to the very end of the Second World War. It was his dream to be a teacher of mathematics, but the realities of the first war, political conditions during the 1920s and 1930s, and ultimately World War II, that kept him from achieving his goal. By the time the war began in September 1939, our family was a small one. My parents, Uncle Fritz and I, along with several life-long friends, forged a close bond, dedicated to protecting each other throughout the terrors of a long and relentless war.

It was to my surprise – as well as my uncle's biographer, Patricia Spayd, and family friend, Helga Woods – that we found my uncle's complete collection of family and wartime photographs. My mother treasured and adored her older brother and had arranged these boxes of well-organized photographs. No one has seen these photographs in over twenty-two years. I uncovered them quite by accident, along with Ms. Spayd and Ms. Woods, as we visited in my uncle's apartment. Of course, it was with sadness that I viewed each photo, as the memories flooded back to me when my mother and uncle were alive. But I have the good memories to look back upon. The trials of the past change us forever.

We decided to present my uncle's collection from the African Western Desert that he photographed himself, or was photographed, with his Leica camera. This is the only theater of war that my uncle had extensively documented in his six years of fighting. We understand why he did this, it is the same reason we study this theatre still today after all of these years.

ACKNOWLEDGEMENTS

From Fritz Dittmar-Bayerlein:
I am fortunate to have a dedicated team who have devoted their time and energy to my uncle's *Afrikakorps* photograph project. My thanks to Mrs. Anna Schwarz, Ms. Helga Woods, Ms. Andrea Harris, and my uncle's biographer and my co-author, Ms. Patricia Spayd. I also wish to thank my personal friend of many years, Mr. Manfred Rommel, and his lovely wife, Lisalotte, for their help and support.

From Pat Spayd:
I am forever grateful to Fritz Dittmar-Bayerlein for his trust and confidence in me, for the many years of our working together and for our friendship. We now jointly bring a second book about the life of his beloved uncle, *Generalleutnant* Fritz Bayerlein, to completion. My thanks also to my fellow team-members, who with the greatest enthusiasm and dedication have helped Mr. Dittmar and I.

• • •

Many thanks from both of us to:
Robert W. Hasbrouck, Jr., for editing the final work, and we thank his wonderful German wife Astrid, who adds her wisdom and thoughts to our project.

Dal McGuirk, author of *Rommel's Army in Africa* and *AFRIKAKORPS - Self Portrait*, for help in identifying uniforms, field equipment and members of the

Afrikakorps, and for enlarging my own area of reference in helping me to place photos not captioned by Bayerlein with a time and place.

Gary Wilkins, friend and author of *The Collector's Guide to Third Reich Military Headgear*, and fellow Schiffer author, for his identification of rank, uniforms and explaining the unique ways the items were worn, plus his outstanding translations of Bayerlein's handwritten notes on the back of the photographs.

Thomas L. Jentz, fellow Schiffer author of many outstanding armor books, including his series *Panzertruppen*, for the identification of the armored vehicles shown in *General* Bayerlein's private photos.

Rex Trye, author of *Mussolini's Soldiers*, for identifying troops, the desert forts and ancient ruins of the Western Desert battlefield.

We both wish to extend our thanks for help in identifying *Afrikakorps* photographs, to *General* Bayerlein's comrades of the *Afrikakorps* veterans organization, the *Krieskameradschaft Afrikakorps Verband Deutsches Afrika Korps, Würzburg*, Herr Georg Richter, *Bundesvorsitzender*, Herr Eugen Grötz; Bernd Peitz of the *Kreiskameradschaft, Paderborn*; and the *Kameraden Zeitschrift* of Germany, Herr Friedbert Limmeroth, Frau Gisela Limmeroth, Götz "Boarcreek" Eberbach, and Claus Bittner.

And finally, thanks to Bob Biondi, our military editor at Schiffer Publishing, for his outstanding support of this new *General* Bayerlein book project. Without Bob these works would not be possible.

CHAPTER ONE

WINTER CAMPAIGN 1941-1942

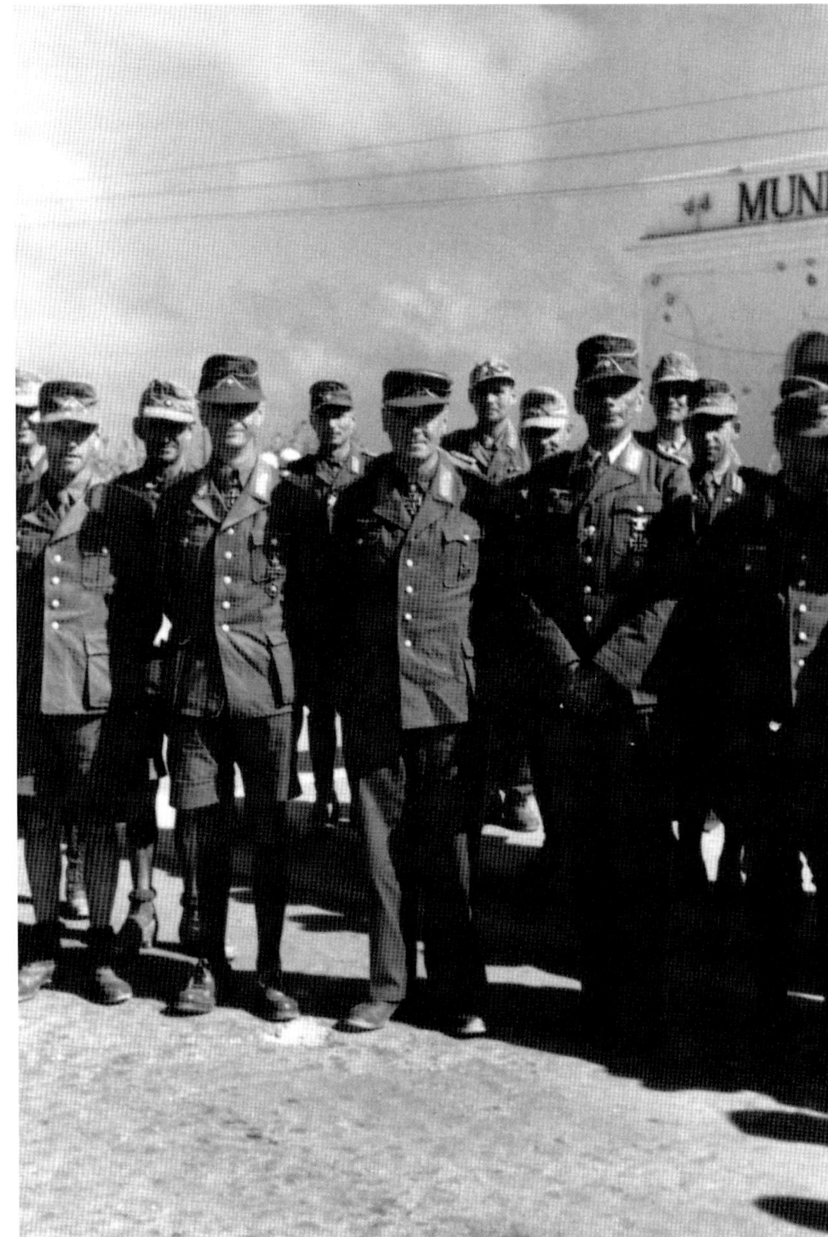

Right
Generalleutnant Ludwig Crüwell, commander of the Deutsches Afrikakorps, lines up with his new staff officers and visitors, all recent arrivals from Germany. A visiting general stands next to Crüwell, with the DAK staff.

Opposite
Wearing their new tropical issue uniforms, Oberstleutnant Bayerlein (2nd from right) lines up with the other new officers and visitors. Bayerlein arrived in Africa in early October 1941. Many of the men still have "white knees," indicating they were newcomers to the theater.

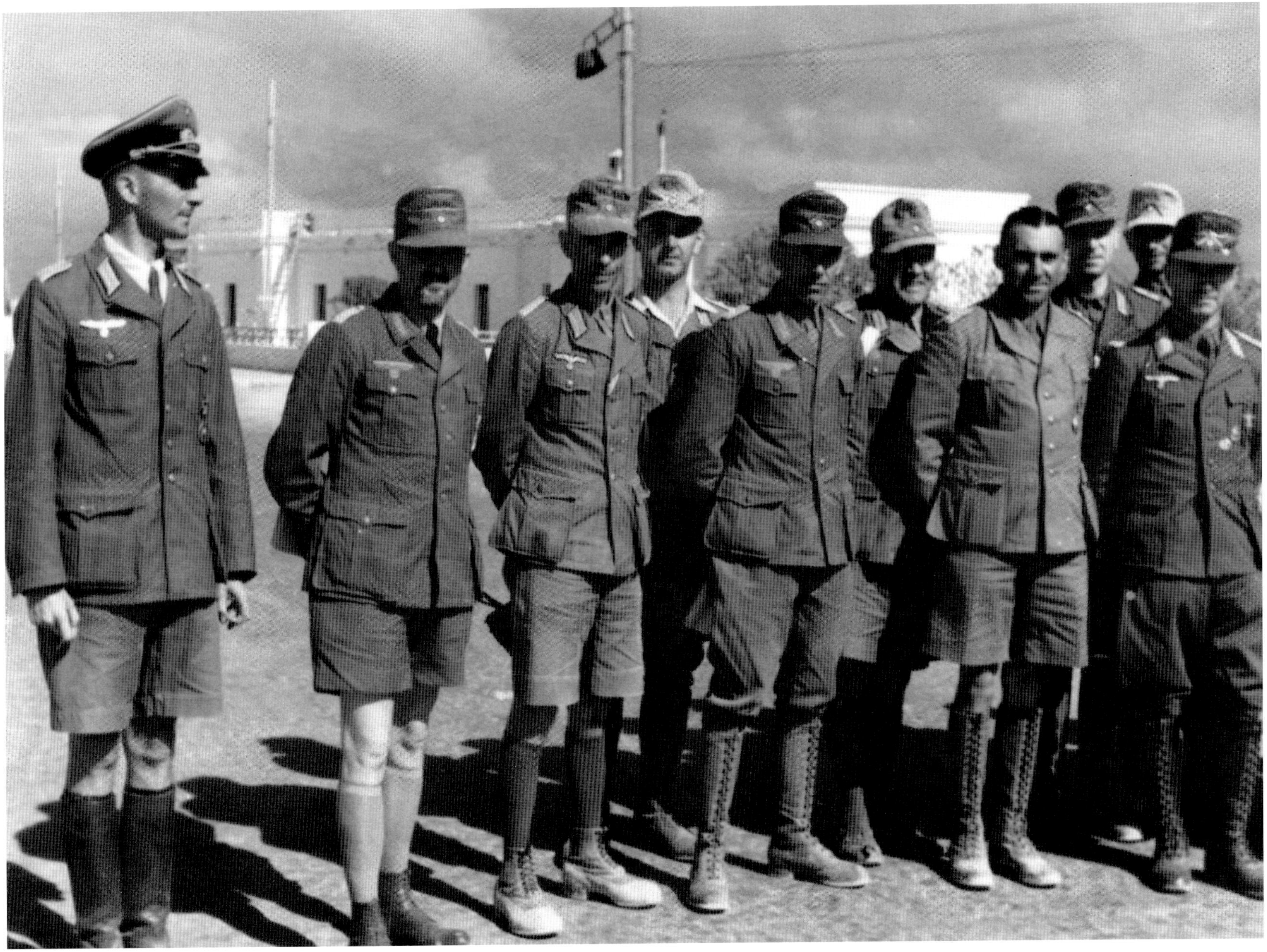

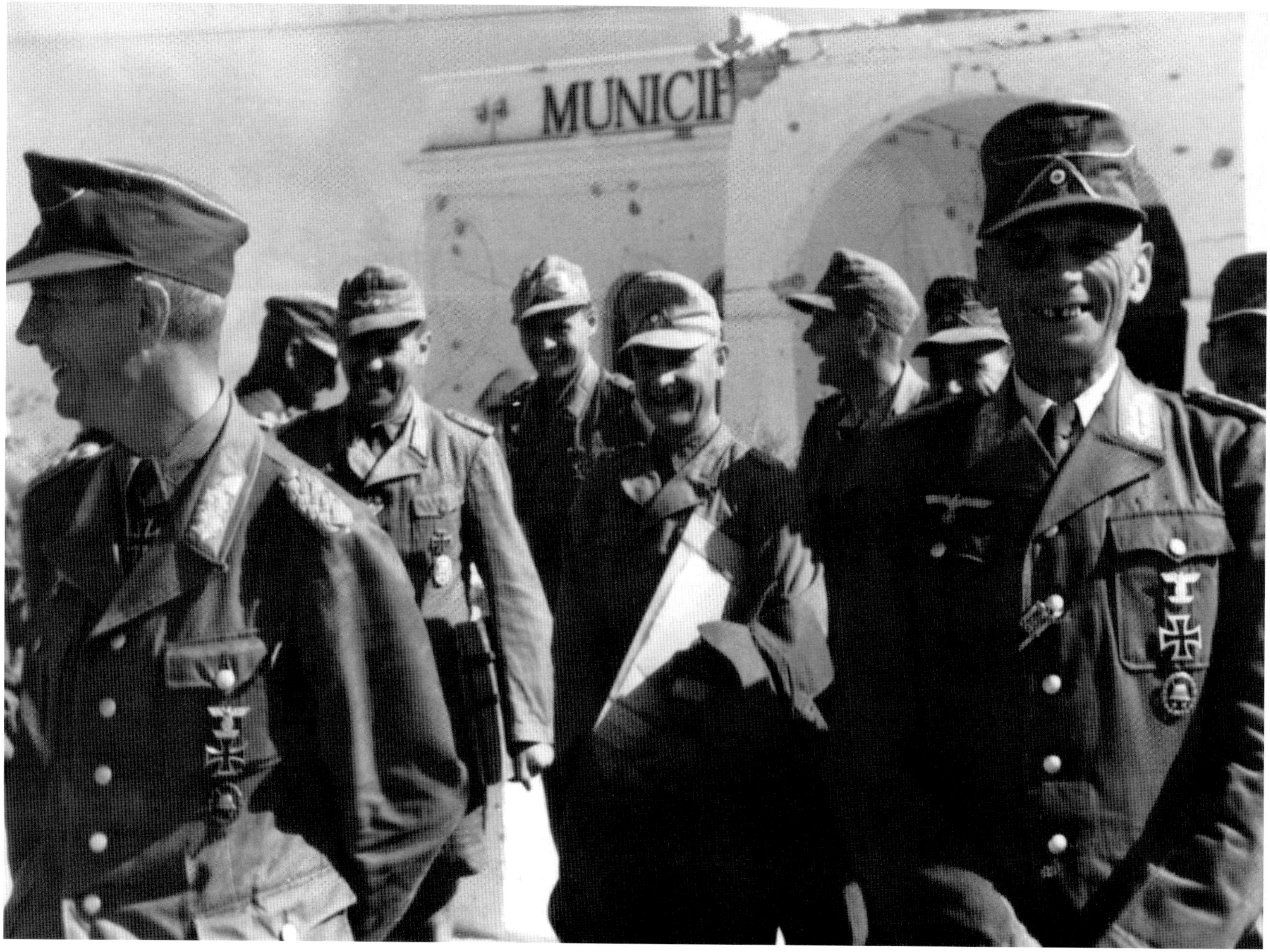
MUNICIP

Opposite
The formal line of officers disintegrates into laughter as visiting General von Rintelen – Chef des Verbindungskommando zur Italienischen Armee (communications) – sports a fake black eye and missing front tooth while joking for the camera. November 1941.

Right:
Generalleutnant Crüwell, his right hand bandaged from the recent fighting during the Totensonntag battle in November '41, reviews map locations with a young Hauptmann. Totensonntag is the German Memorial Day for those who died during World War I.

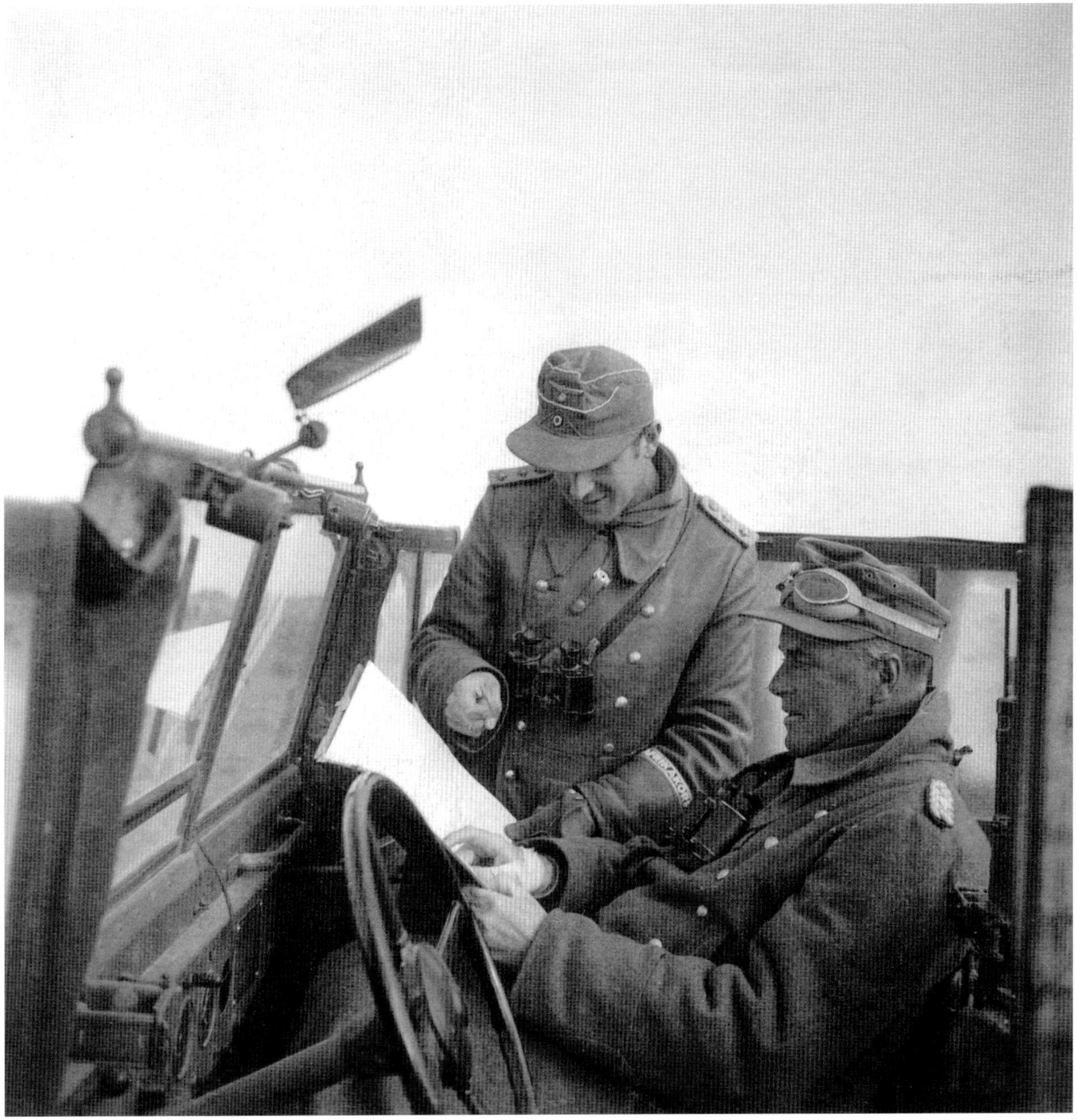

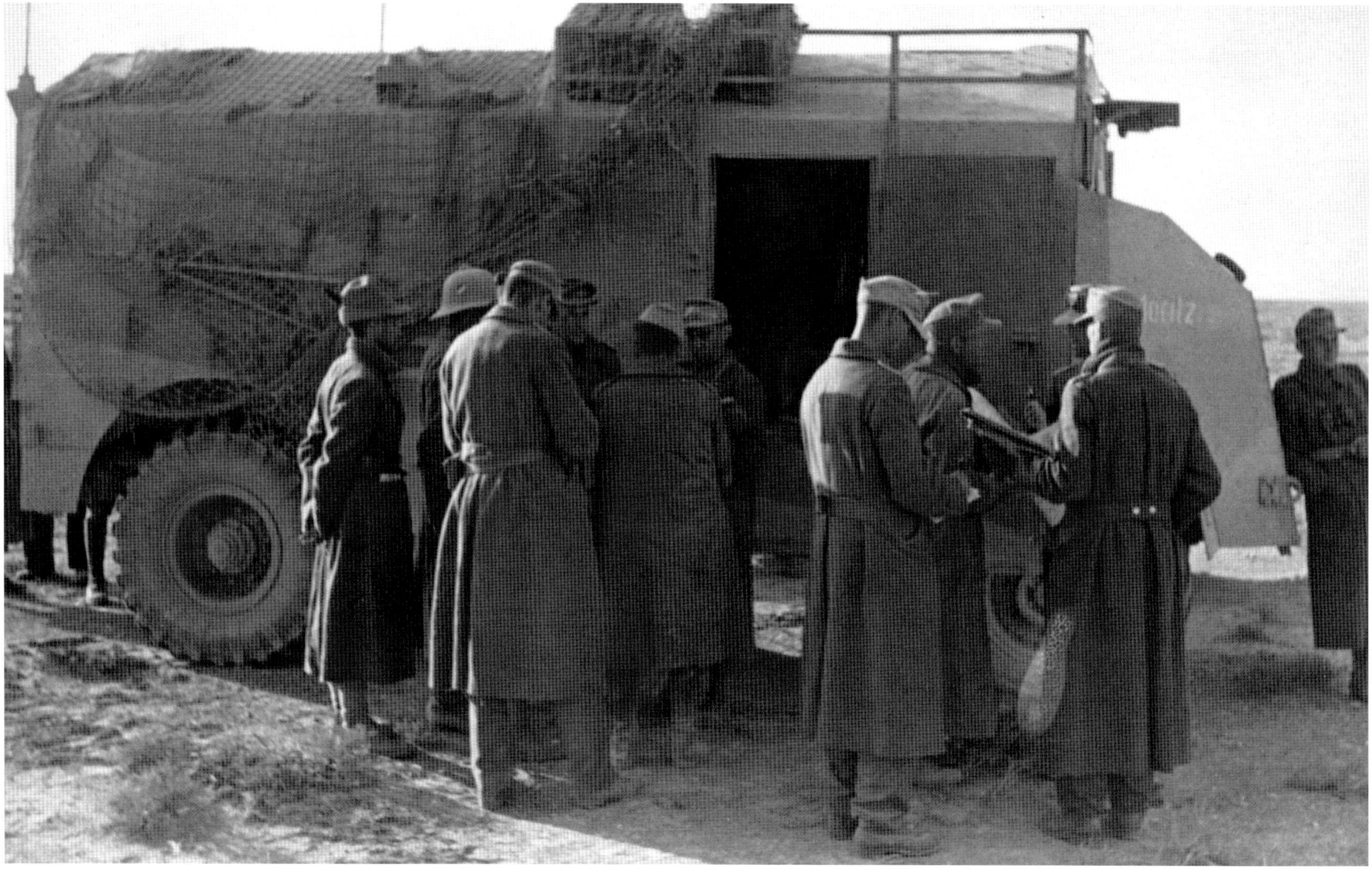

Officers cluster around General Crüwell beside his captured British command vehicle, nicknamed "Moritz" after the two German cartoon characters, "Max and Mortiz." The characters were two obnoxious boys who were always getting into trouble by playing malicious tricks on their neighbors. Generaloberst Rommel named the vehicles; "Max" was his. Oberstleutnant Bayerlein stands to the left of the doorway.

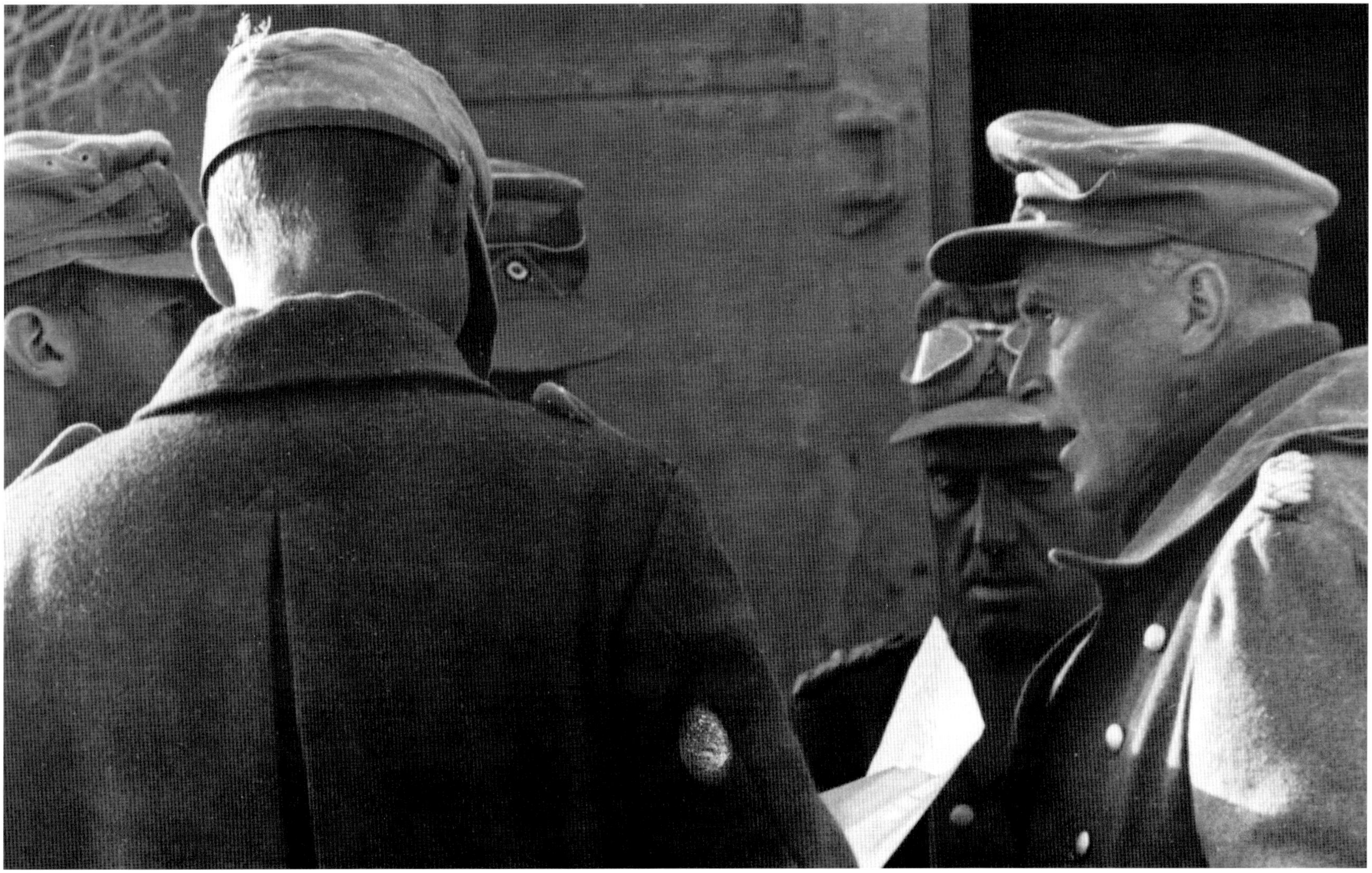

General Crüwell issues orders to his command staff. In "The Rommel Papers" Bayerlein describes the Winter Campaign of 1941-1942 and reports that Crüwell's, "whole headquarters staff together with almost the entire paraphernalia of command was surprised by the New Zealanders, who had come up from Sidi Azeiz unobserved, and taken prisoner after a heroic defense. General Crüwell and I escaped this fate by a hairsbreadth."[1]

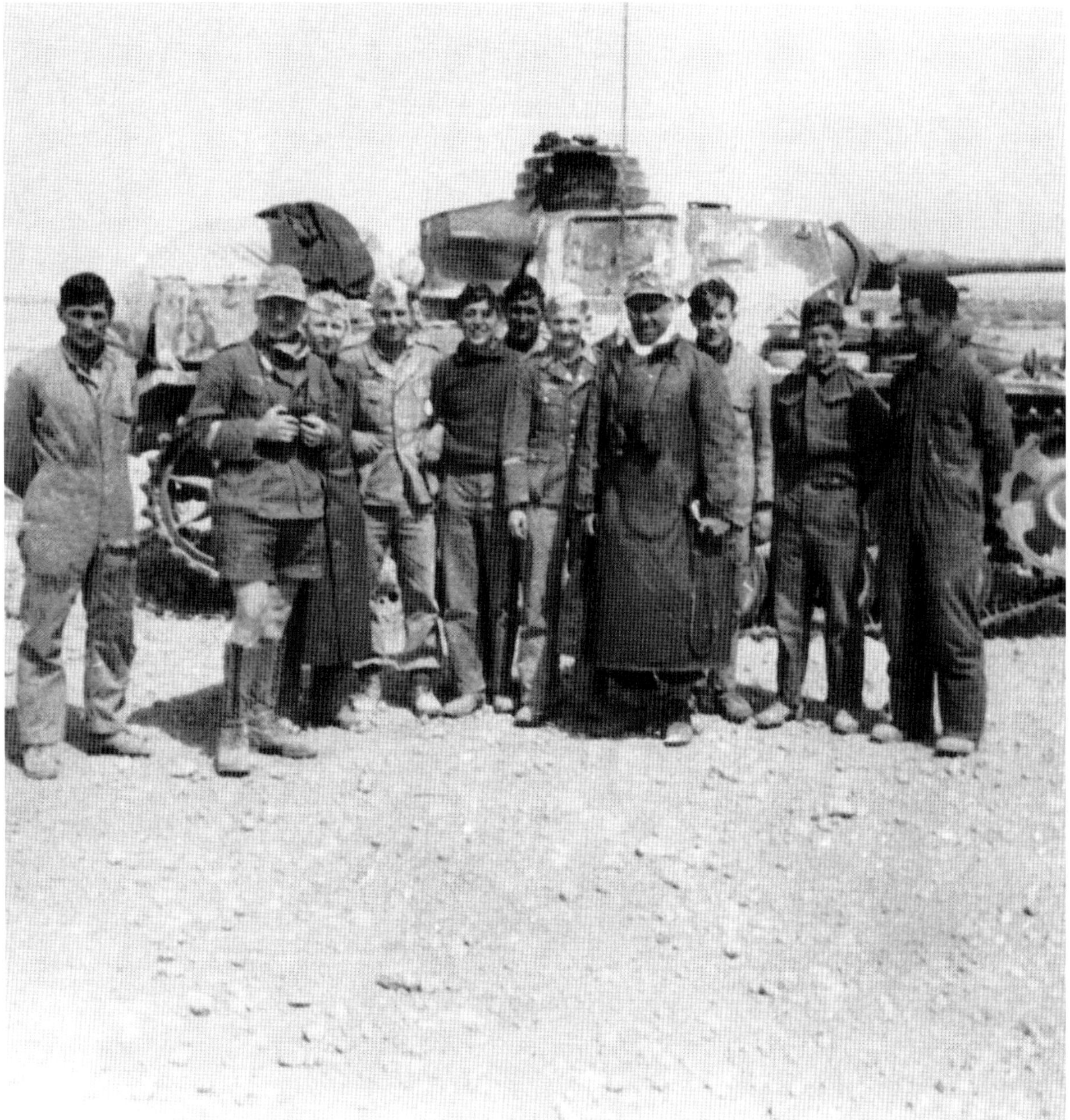

Bayerlein stands amid a panzer crew assigned to the DAK Headquarters escort group, the Begleit-kommando. Even the mechanics pose with the crewmembers and the sometimes short-tempered DAK Chief of Staff.

A different pose with part of the Begleitkommando group, a panzer crew temporarily assigned to General Crüwell's DAK Headquarters. In spite of having Oberstleutnant Bayerlein aboard, the crew is in a good humor. During tense battle situations, Bayerlein could be bad-tempered and irritable at times with the crew.[2]

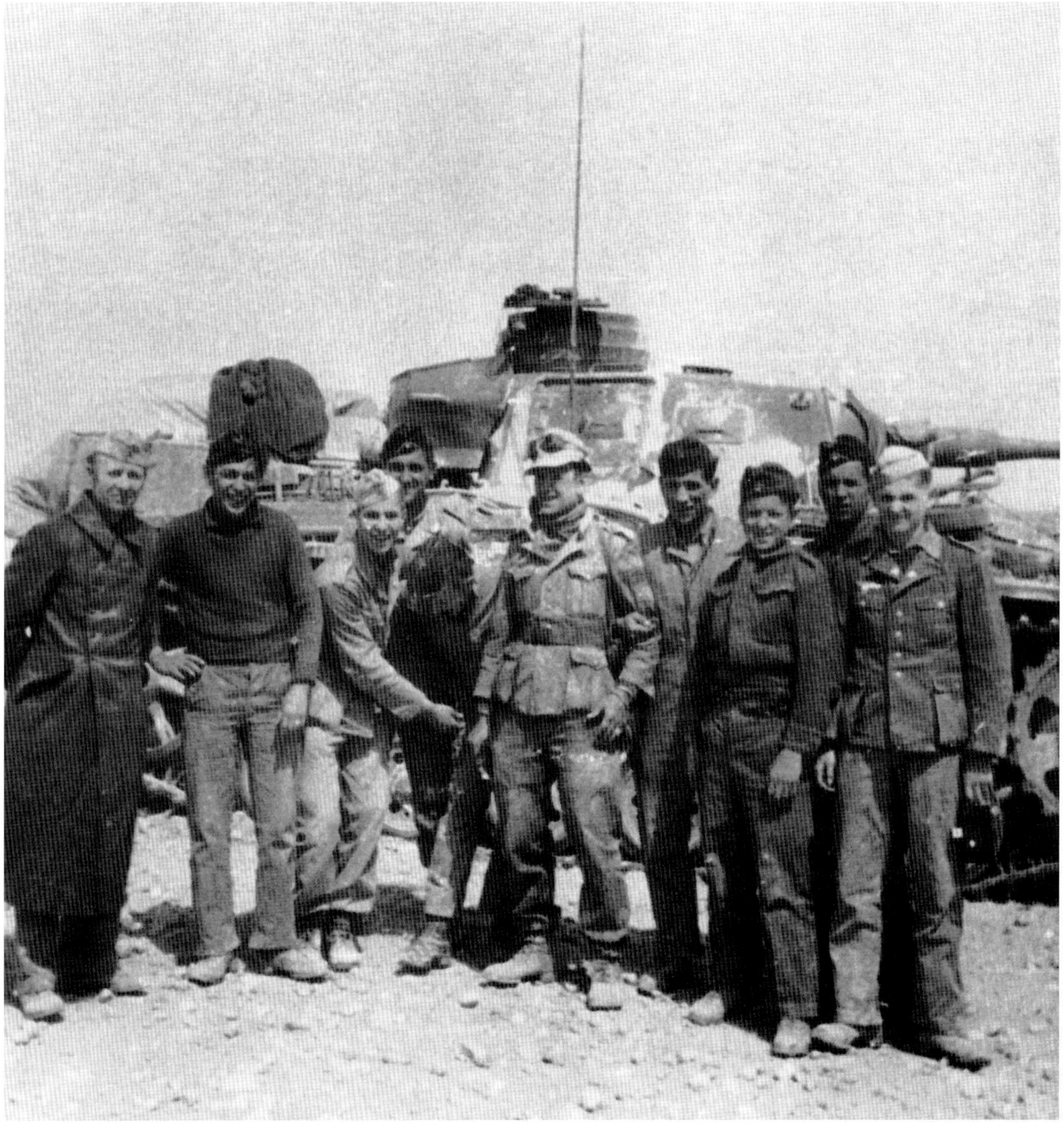

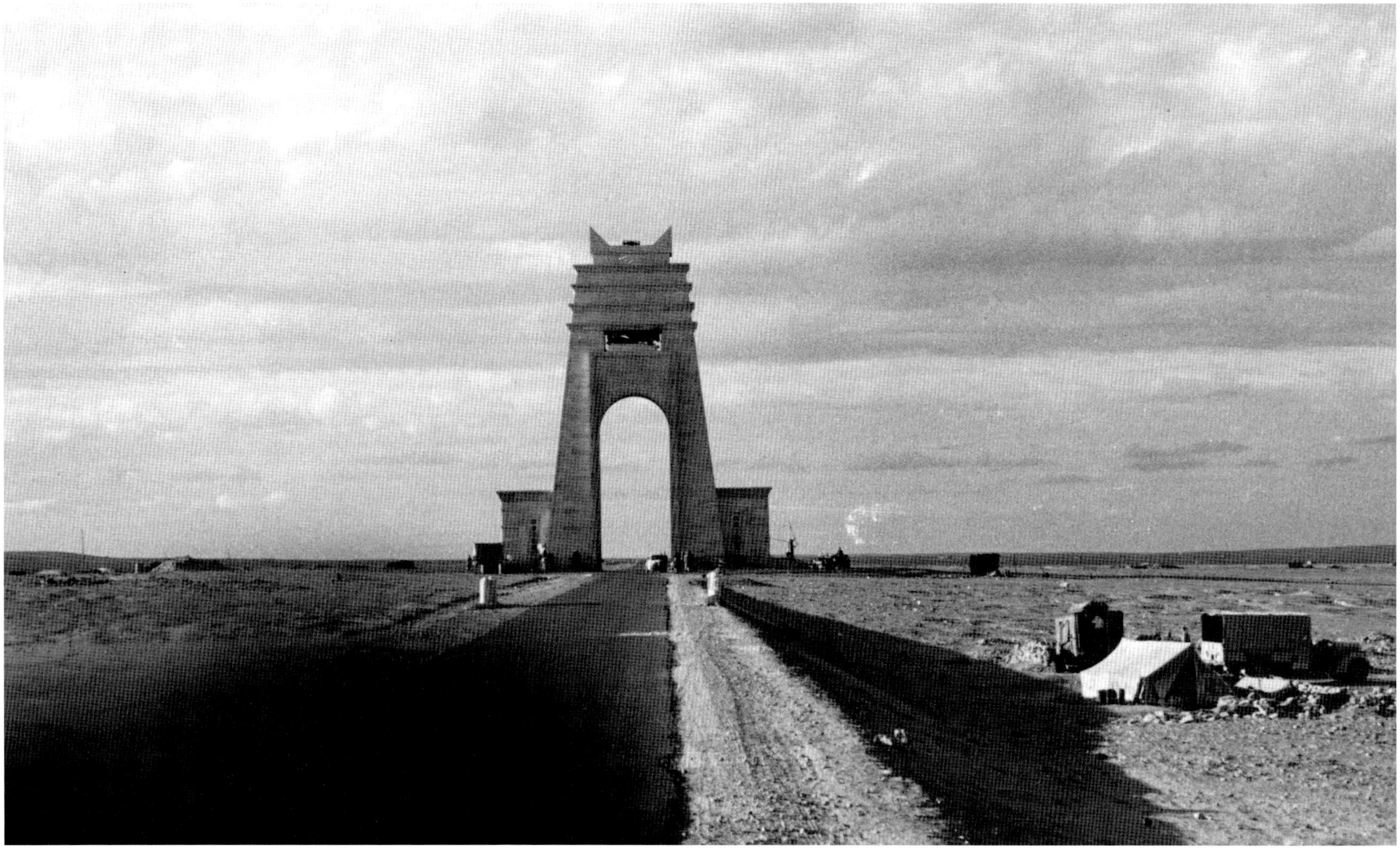

The massive entrance to the via Balbia, the Arco dei Fileni, marks the beginning of the coastal highway boundary between Tunisia and Cyrenaica. The monument and the road were both built and maintained by Italian engineers. A small camp sits on the right of the road, dwarfed by the scale of the monument. Bayerlein defended his DAK Headquarters movement along the via Balbia by fighting off a British attack against the soft-target supply and radio vehicles of his convoy. Pulling out the occasional panzer and 88mm anti-tank guns, Bayerlein commanded the group and fought off the British tank charge. Bayerlein was sure the British would not make a foolish old-fashioned-type horse cavalry charge into his formidable line of defense. To his surprise, British tanks charged, and Bayerlein's command group defeated them.[3]

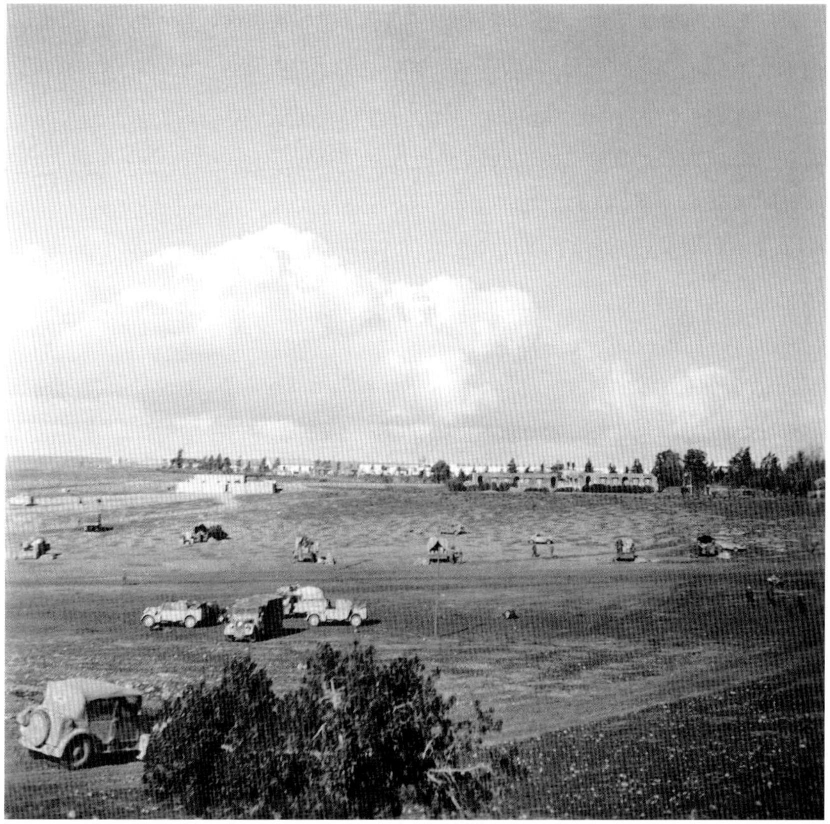

Bayerlein photographed his DAK Headquarters Group that had halted on the outskirts of a village with a desert fort in the distance. Maintaining prudent parking distance from the adjoining vehicles aided in surviving Allied air attacks and artillery barrages by the enemy. (Location unknown)

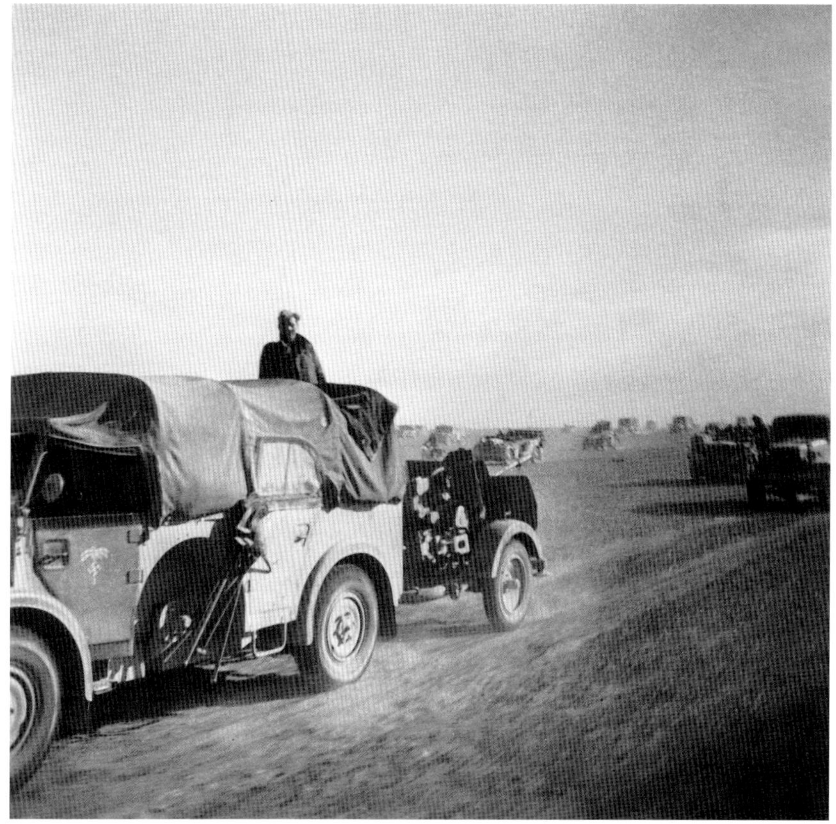

In a great camera shot from the back seat of his staff car, Bayerlein catches the battle group rapidly on the move. The Afrikakorps symbol of a palm tree and swastika is clearly visible on the door of the adjoining vehicle.

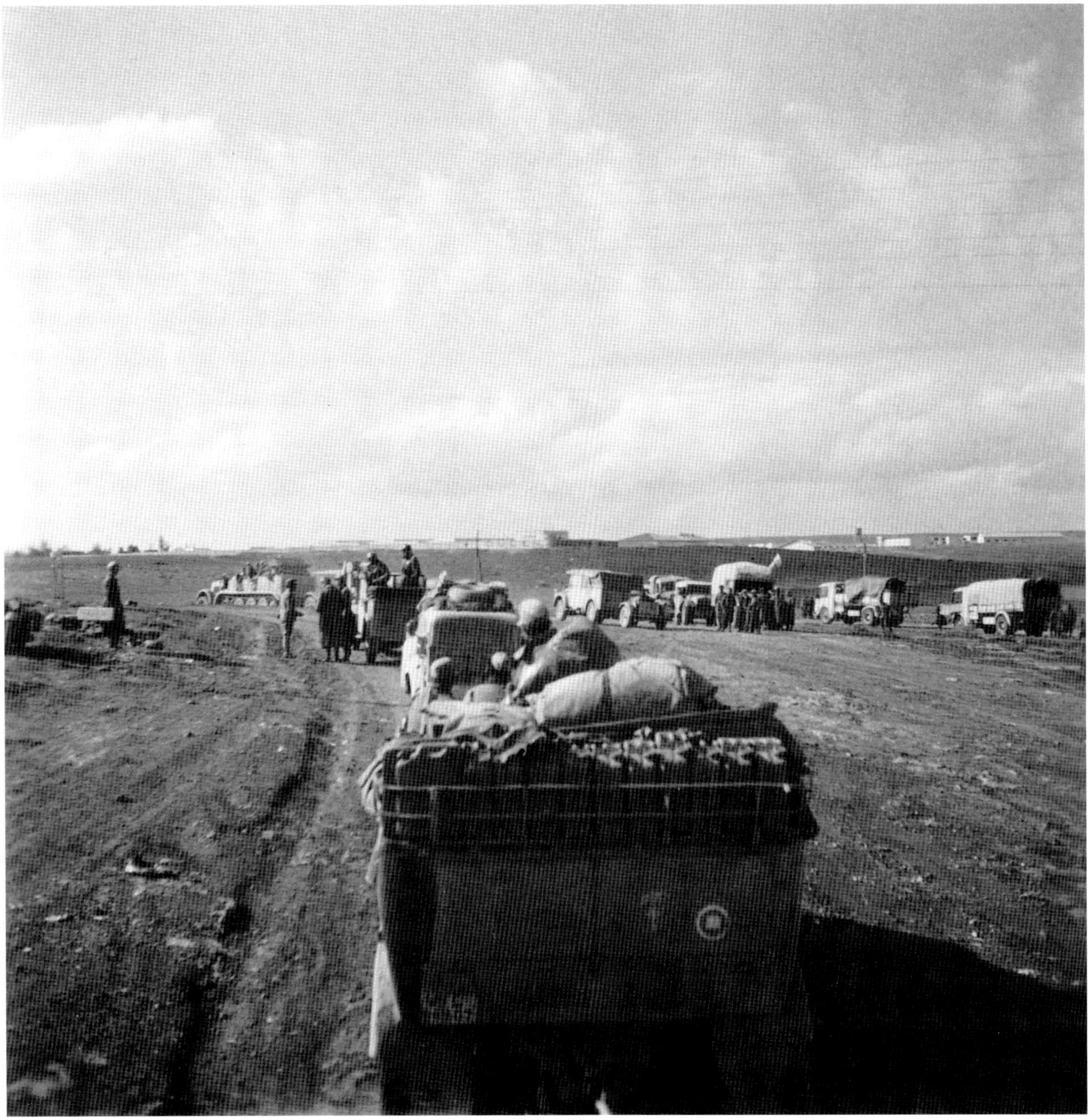

Momentarily halted in the desert, Bayerlein catches a roadside meeting in progress several vehicles in front of his car. An enormous old desert fort is visible in the distance to the right.

The Luftwaffe liaison (2nd from left) and an unshaven Bayerlein discuss reconnaissance operations as Oberst Eduard Crasemann (standing behind Bayerlein) listens in on their conversation. Crasemann was awarded the Knight's Cross on December 26th, 1941 – as was Bayerlein – while an Oberstleutnant and commanding officer of the 33rd Motorized Artillery in the 15th Panzer Division.

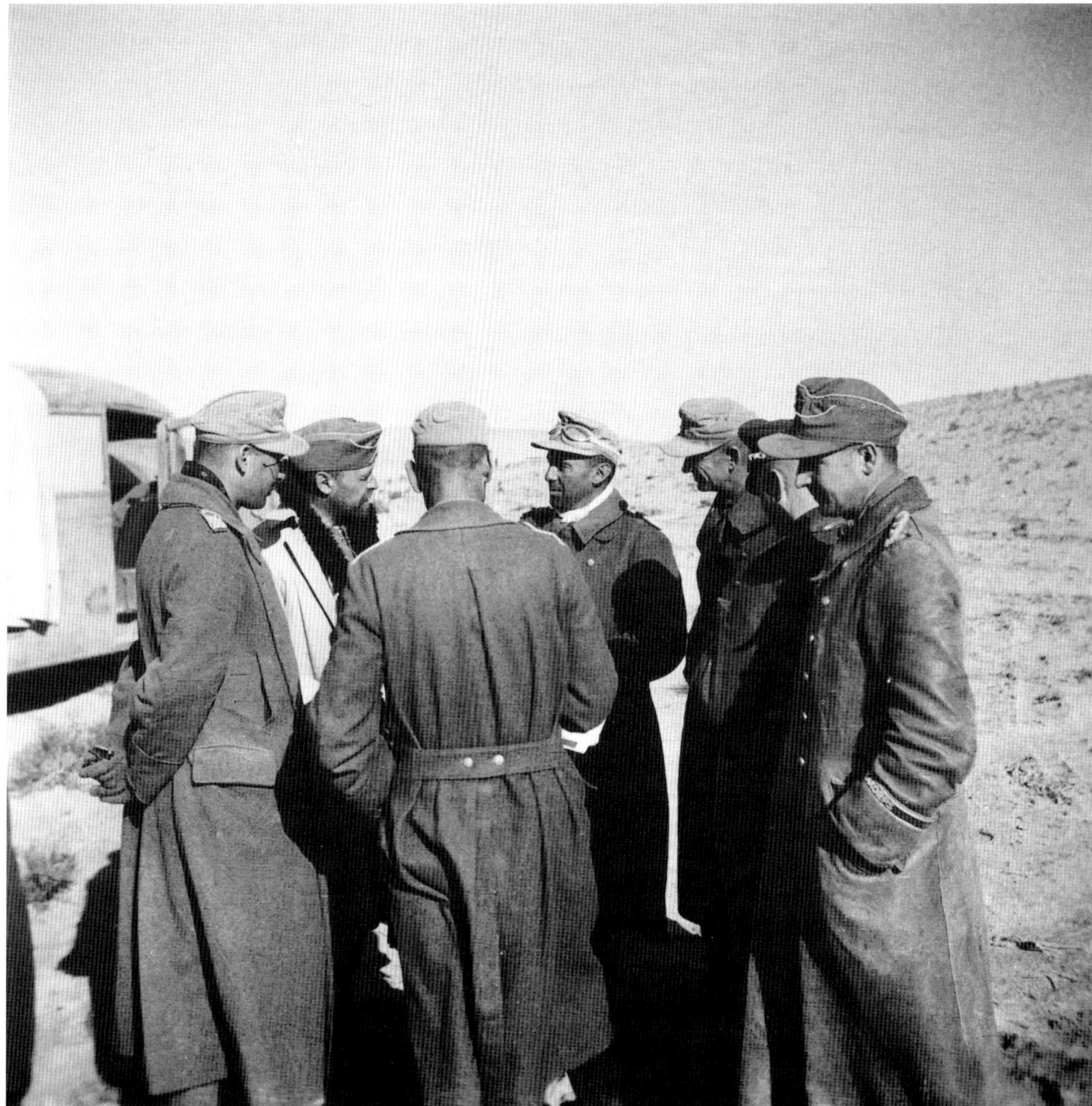

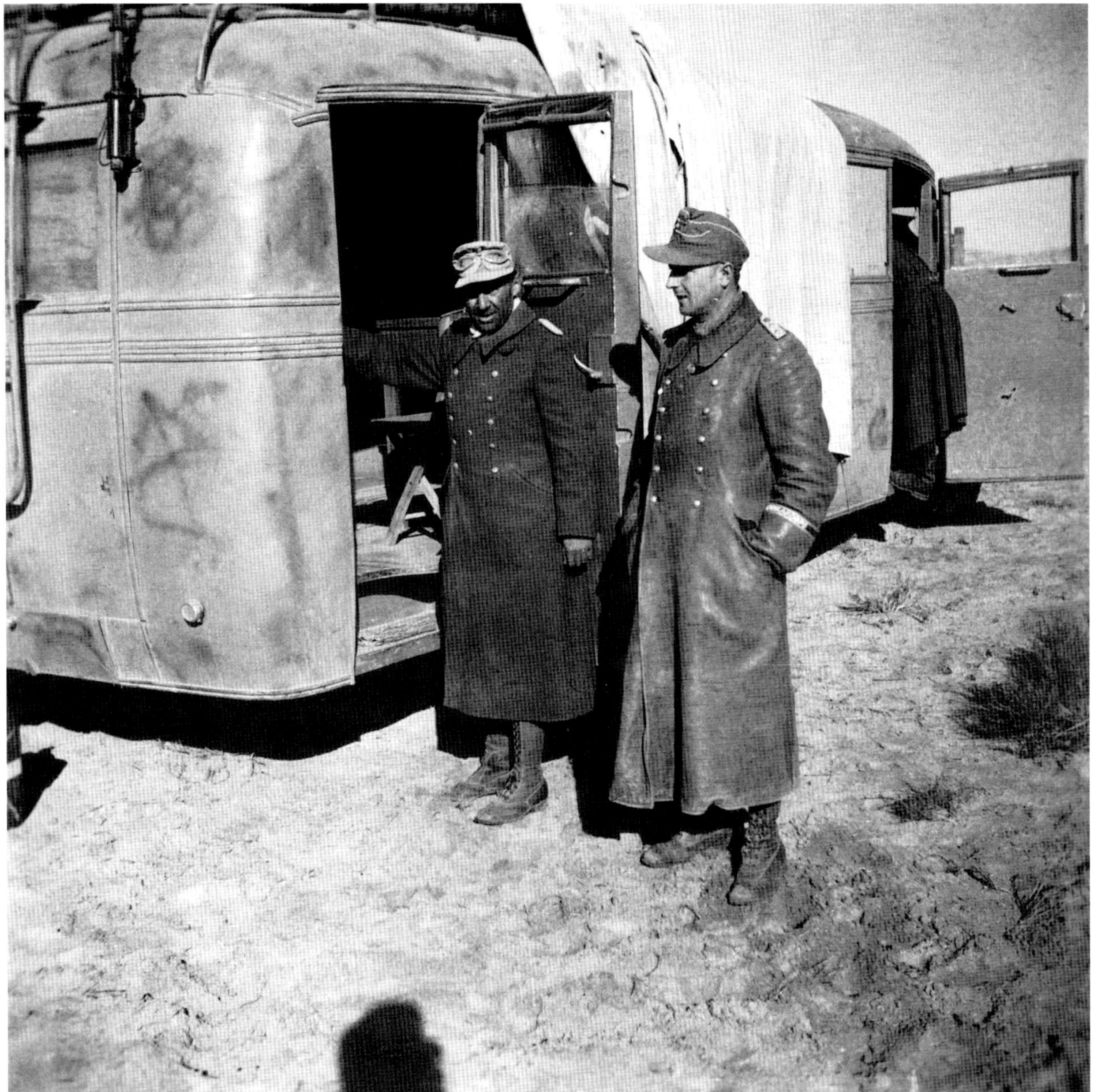

Meeting adjourned, Bayerlein returns to his "Chefs bus" – the command post and living quarters he shared with several other staff officers.

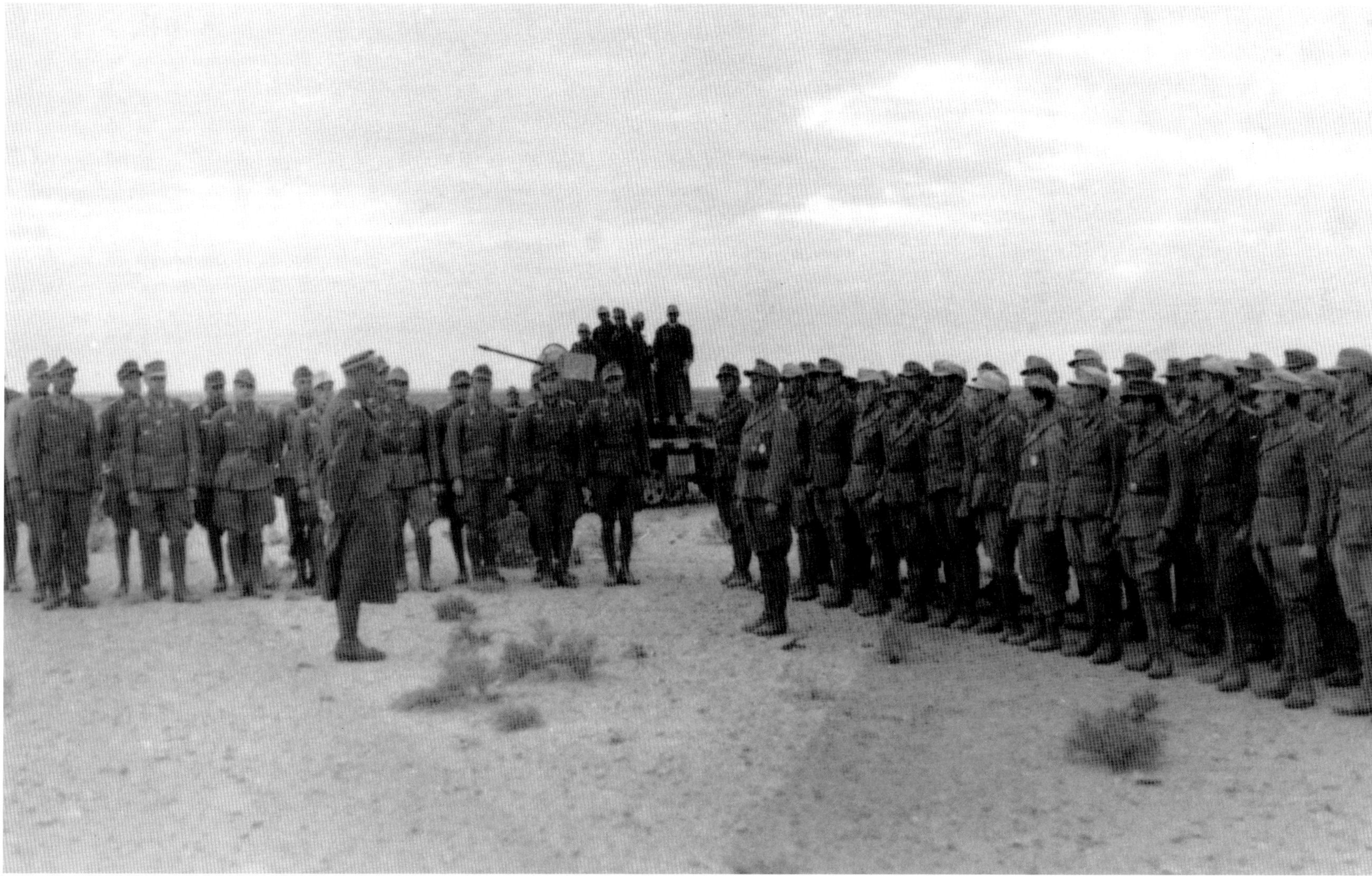

General Ludwig Crüwell awards his Deutsches Afrikakorps (DAK), Chief-of-Staff, Oberstleutnant Fritz Bayerlein, the Ritterkreuz on 26 December, 1941, for his actions during the Totensonntag battle in November around Sidi Rezegh and El Agheila, and for his successful fight with the British panzers on the via Balbia coastal road.

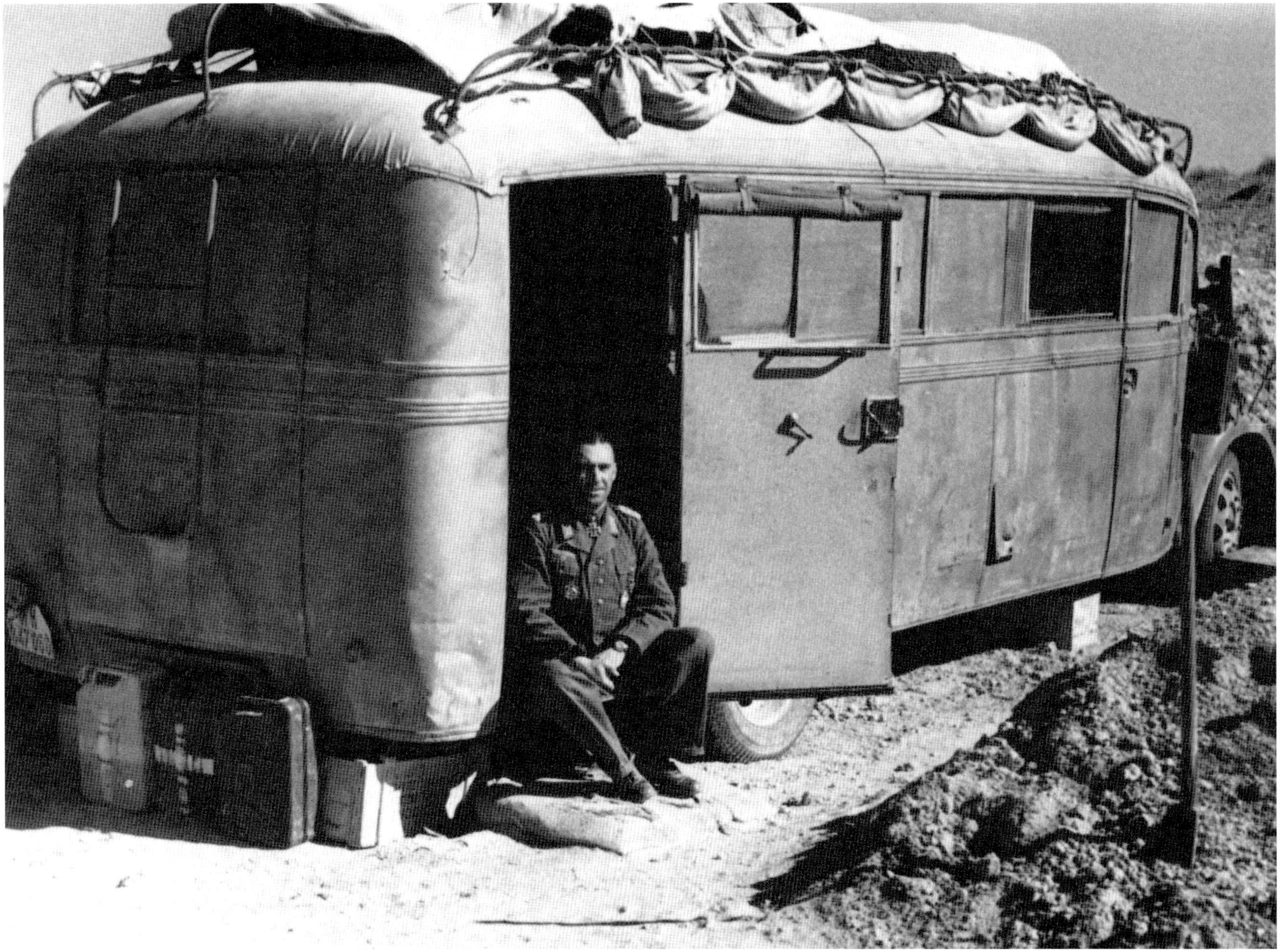

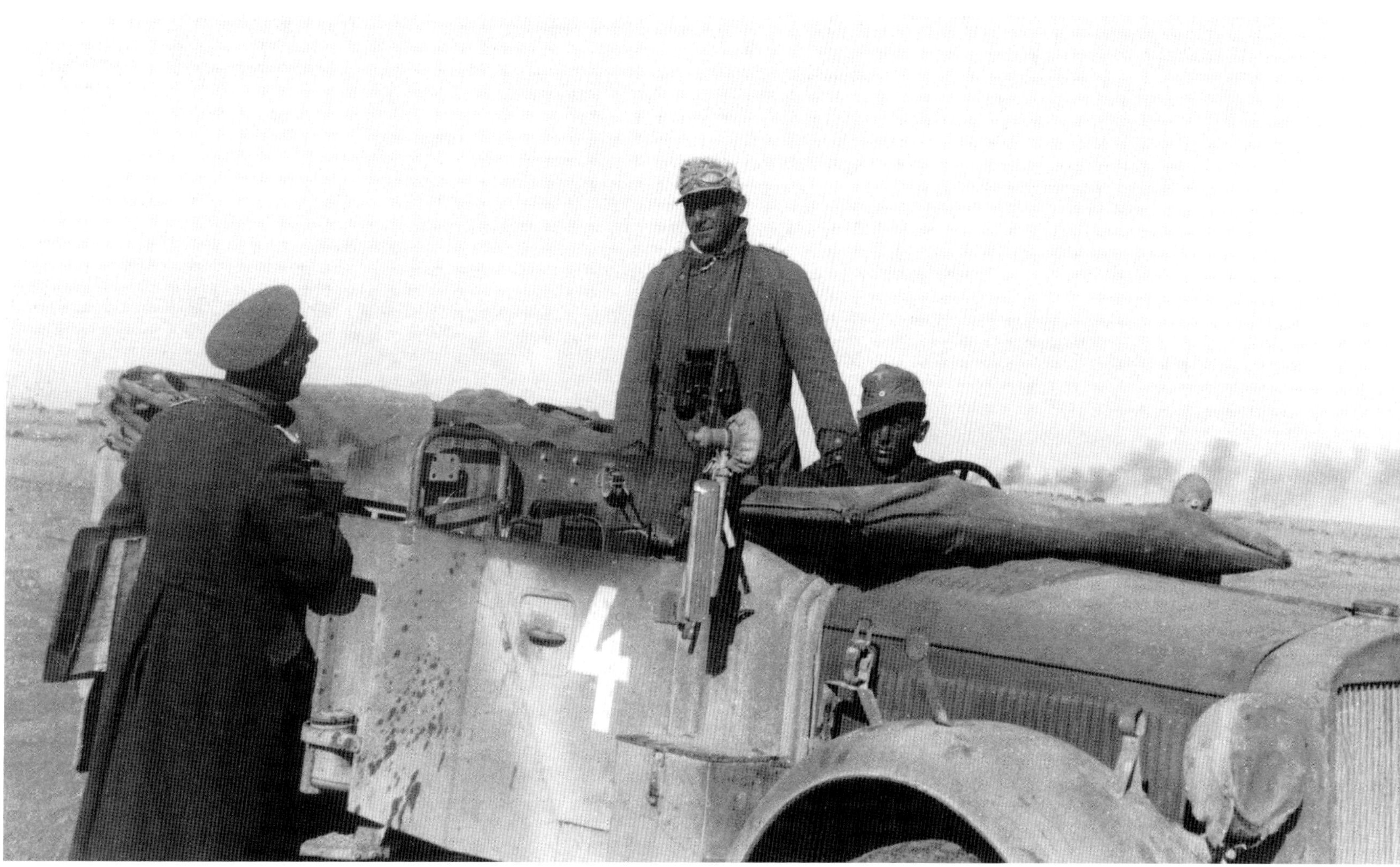

Opposite
The Chief-of-Staff, wearing his recently awarded Ritterkreuz, sits alone in the doorway of his Chefs bus. The windows were painted to eliminate glare from the sun, avoiding the attention of roving RAF fighter-bombers.

Above
Bayerlein listens to a battle report while a vehicle smolders black smoke in the background. From the pleased expression on his face, the report appears favorable.

The Luftwaffe liaison officer and a headquarters staff officer review the ground/air situation. It appears that this is a pre-battle coordination effort and not an active combat situation.

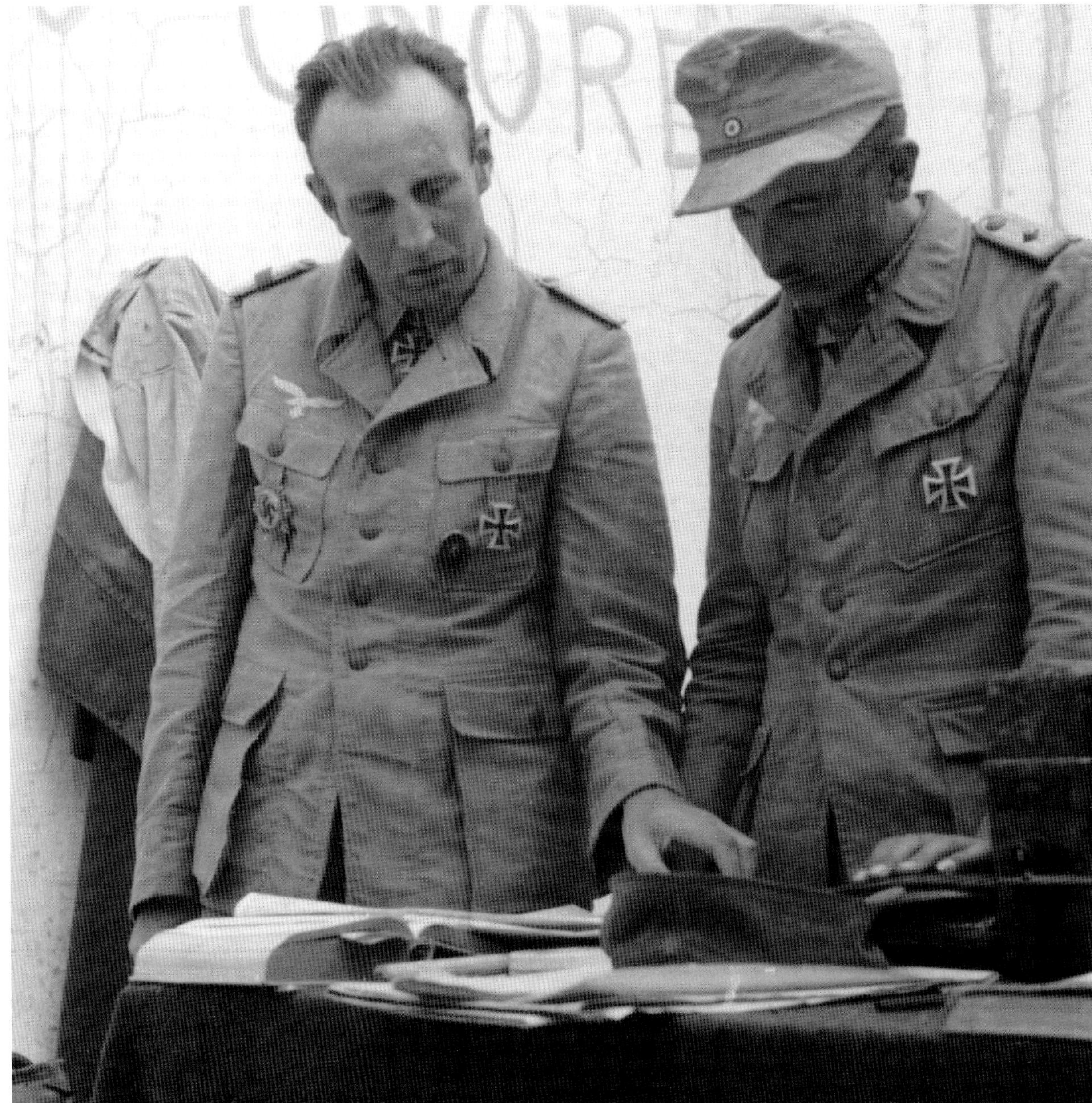

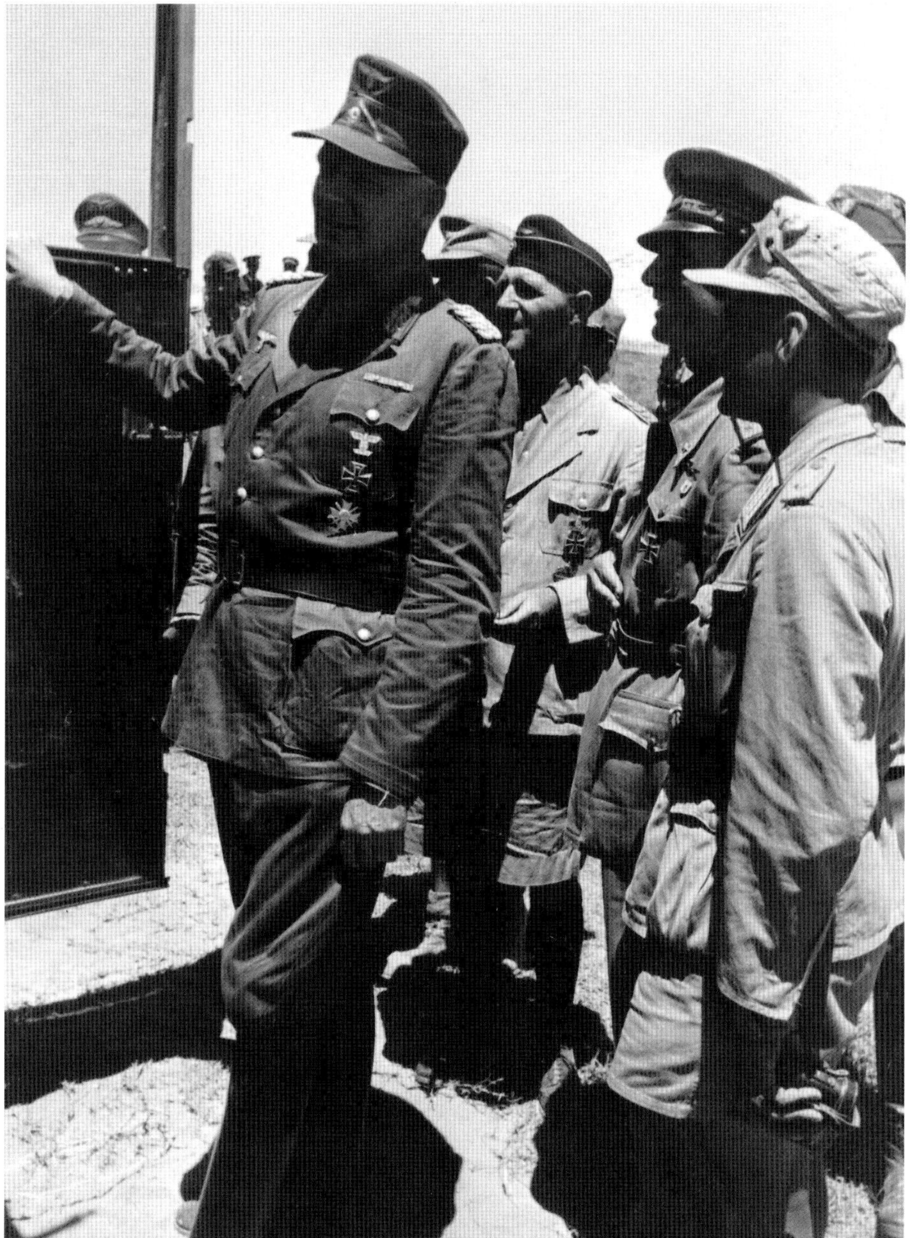

CHAPTER TWO

AFRIKAKORPS: SOLDIERS AND OFFICERS

Italian and German officers attend a pre-battle briefing.

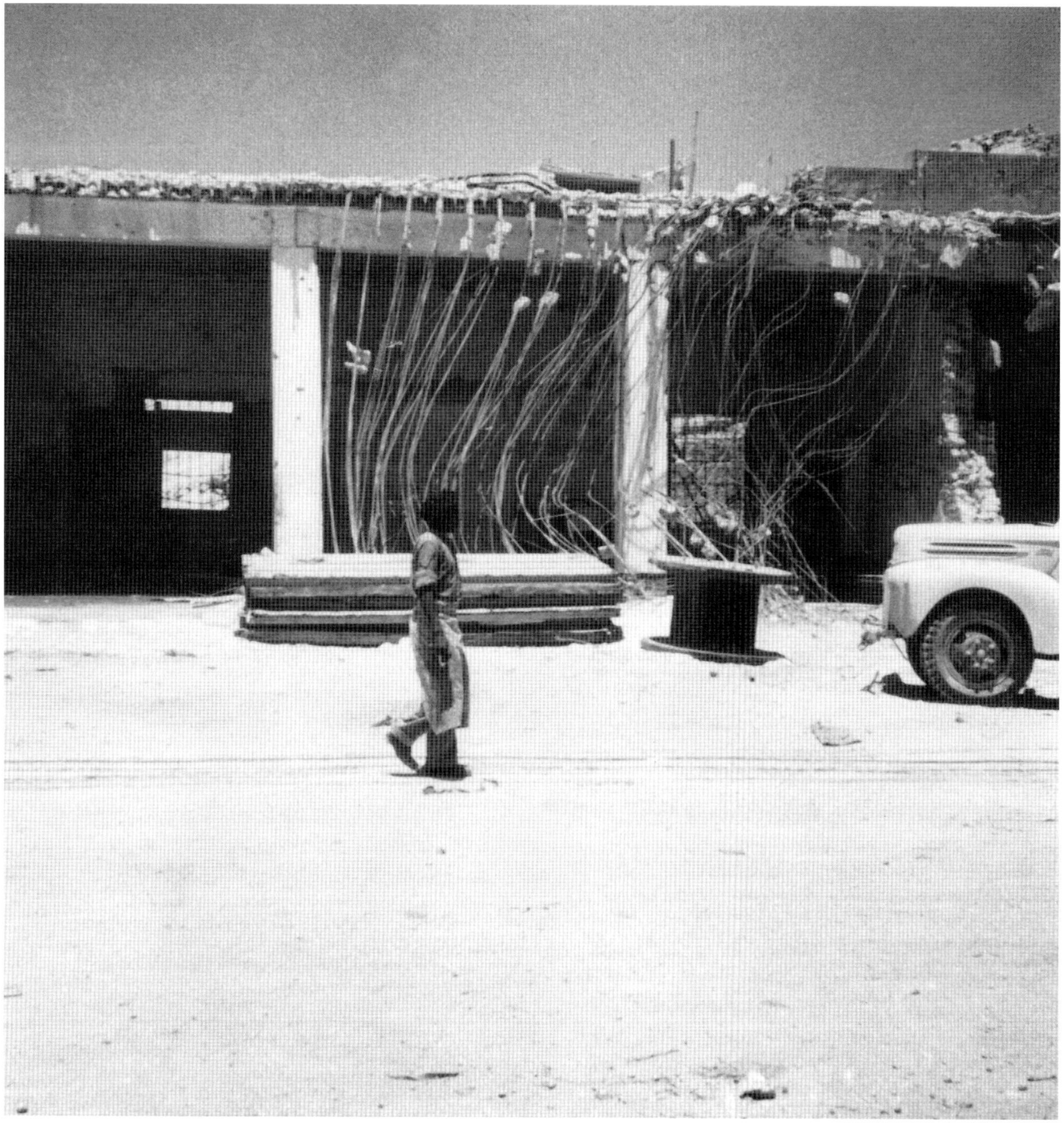

Left
An Italian soldier surveys a bomb-damaged building. The building appears to be a section of a train station (Bahnhof).

Opposite
"These soldiers are Ascari, Libyan Native troops belonging to the Royal Corps of Colonial Troops (RCTC). The troop was probably motorized, as they have the Model 38 Carcano carbine with folding bayonet and Model 1898 bandoleer. Photograph appears to be taken outside a barracks. The Non-commissioned Officer (NCO) on the second right is wearing boots, while the rest of the Truppa are wearing sandals. The officer on the right is an Italian." Per Rex Trye.[1]

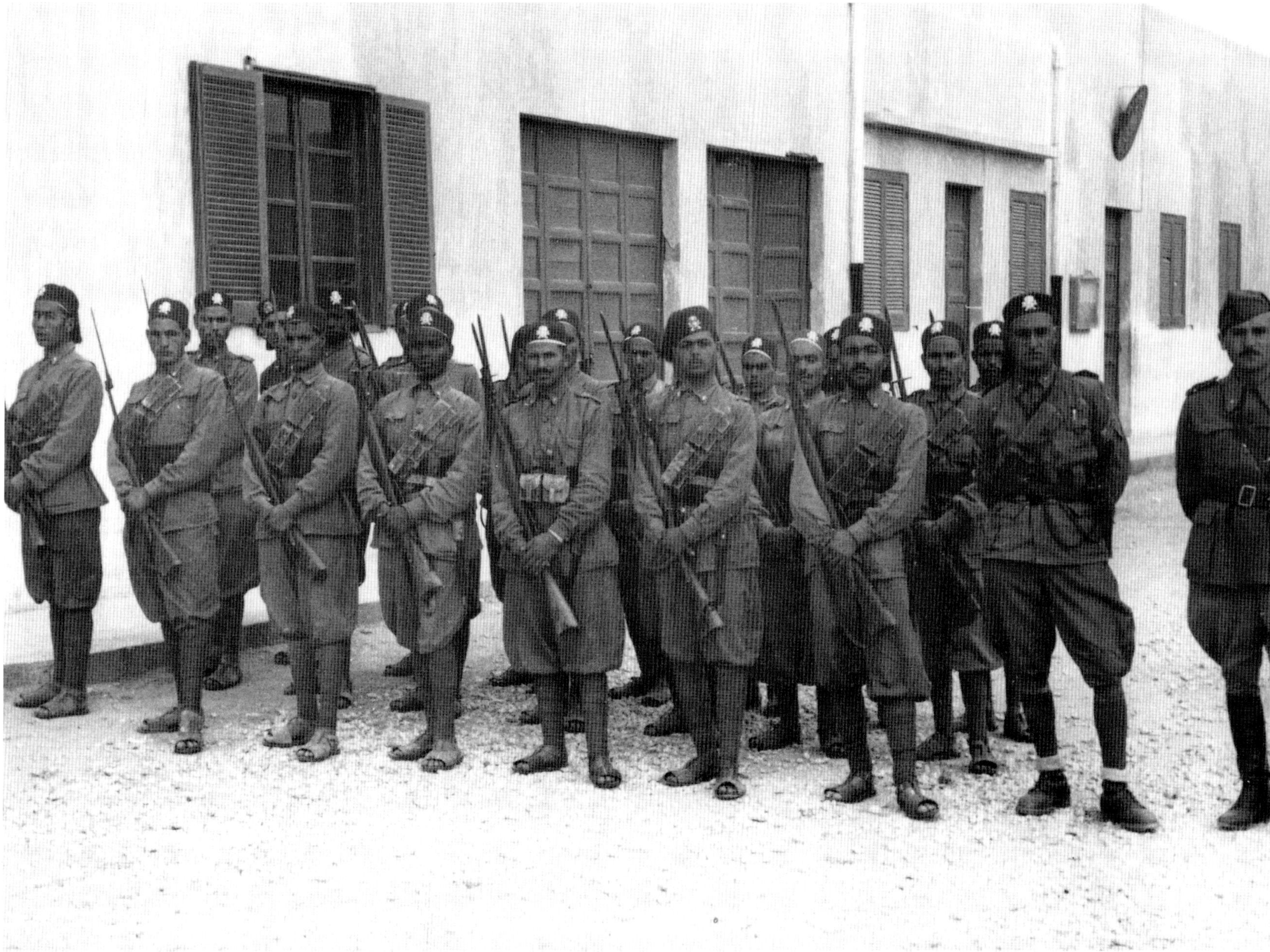

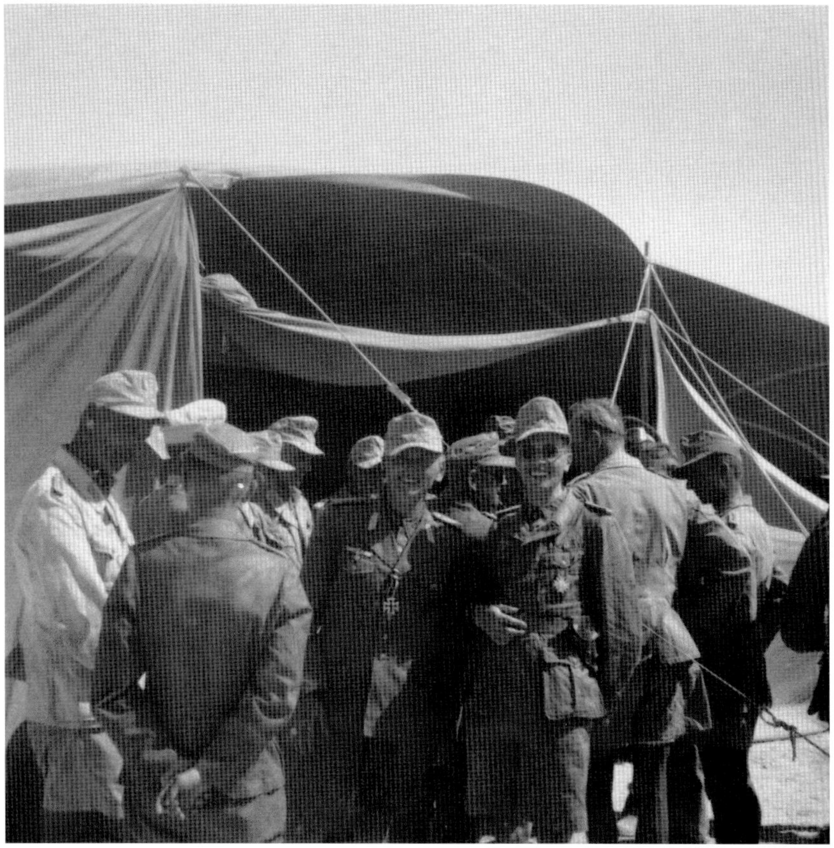

The queue for lunch – Bayerlein's friends pause and smile broadly for their Chief-of-Staff.

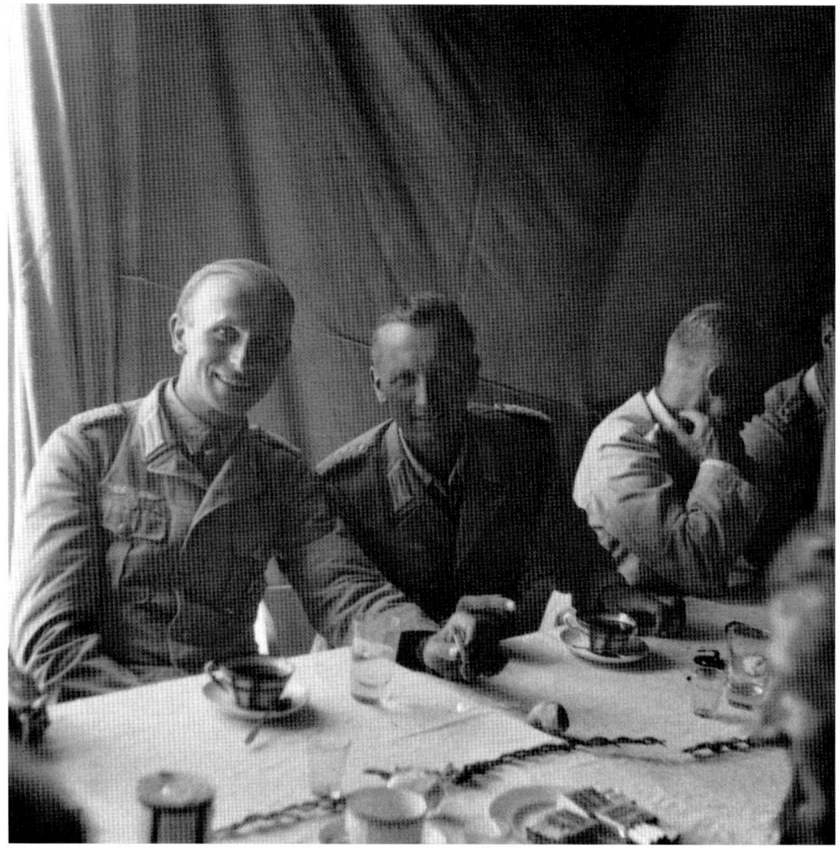

Staff officers take a break enjoying their coffee. Although difficult to make certain, the man on the left appears to be Major Hermann Schulte-Heuthaus, also a well-known member of Rommel's staff, coming on board during March 1942.[2]

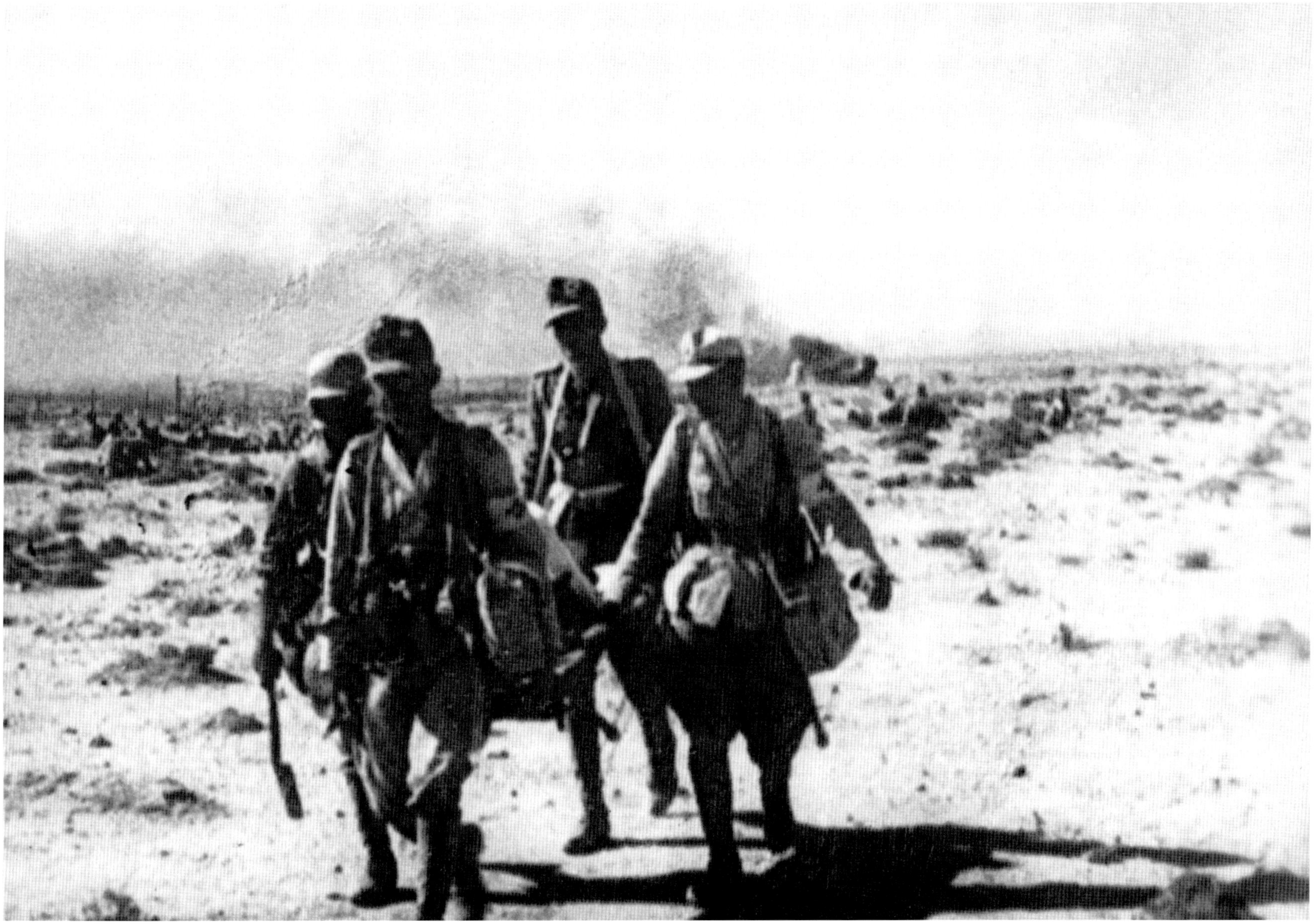

Soldiers trudge back from examining burning wreckage from a recent skirmish.

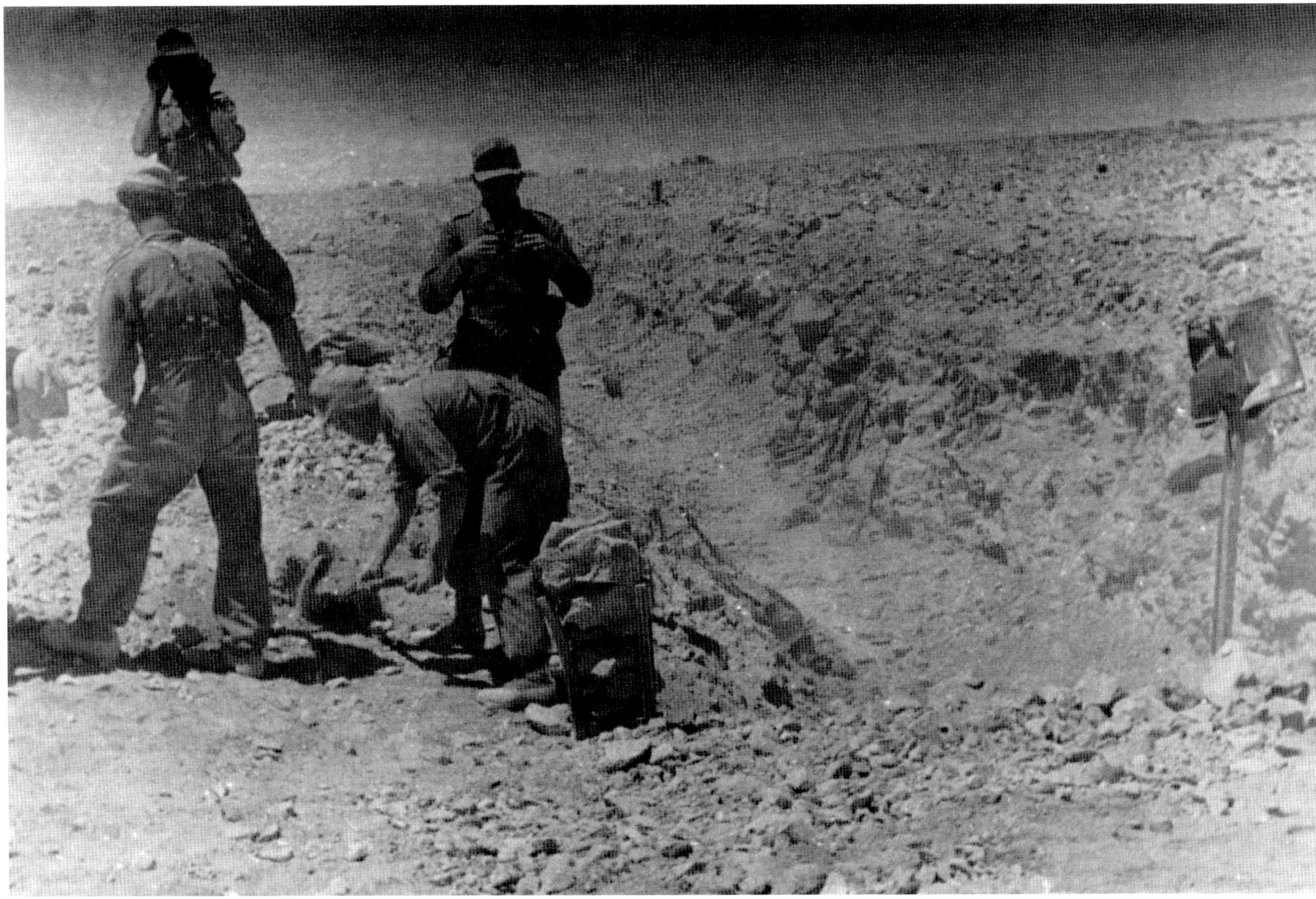

The men pause by a trench to arrange their gear.

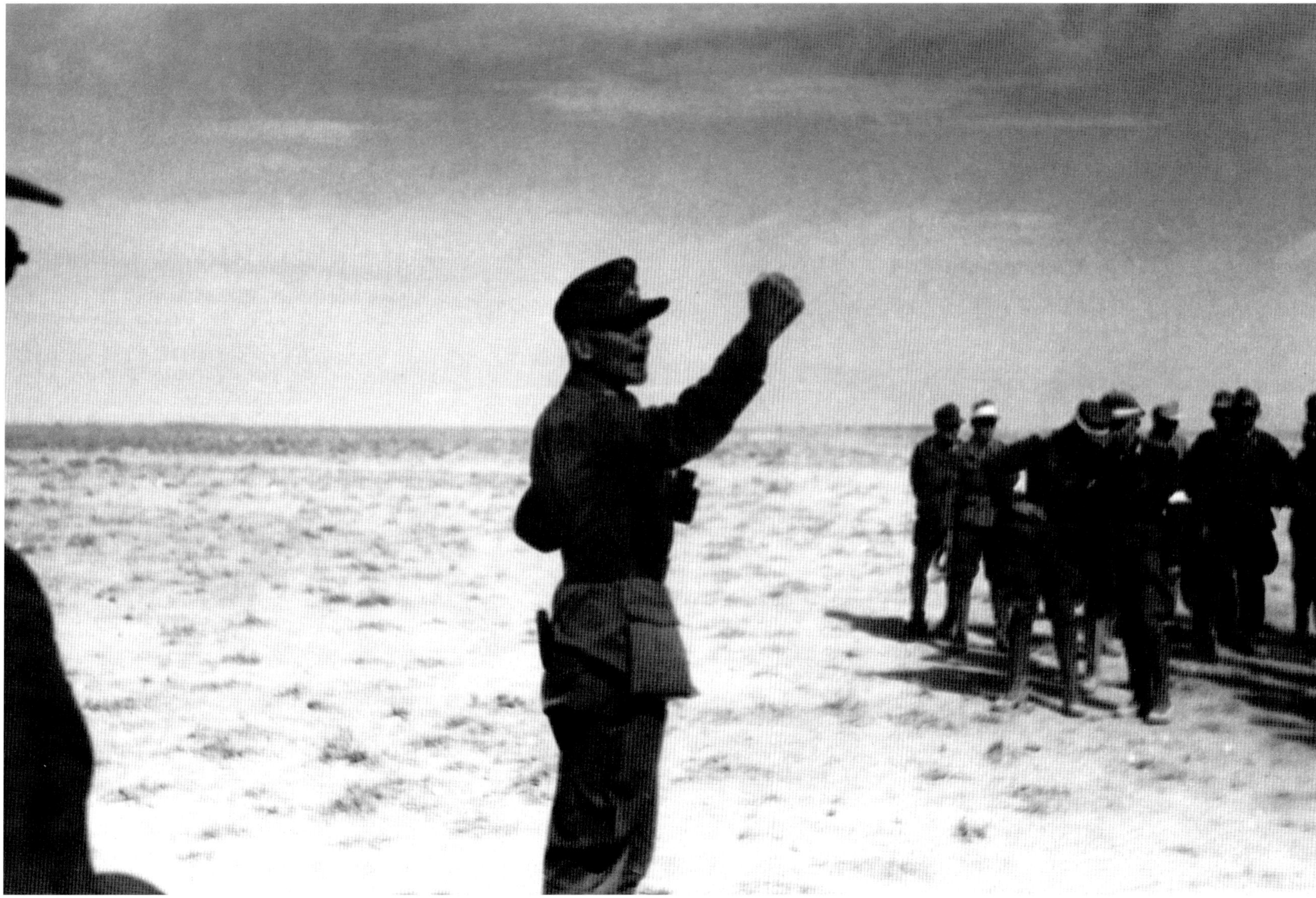

A young officer gestures for his men to gather for further orders.

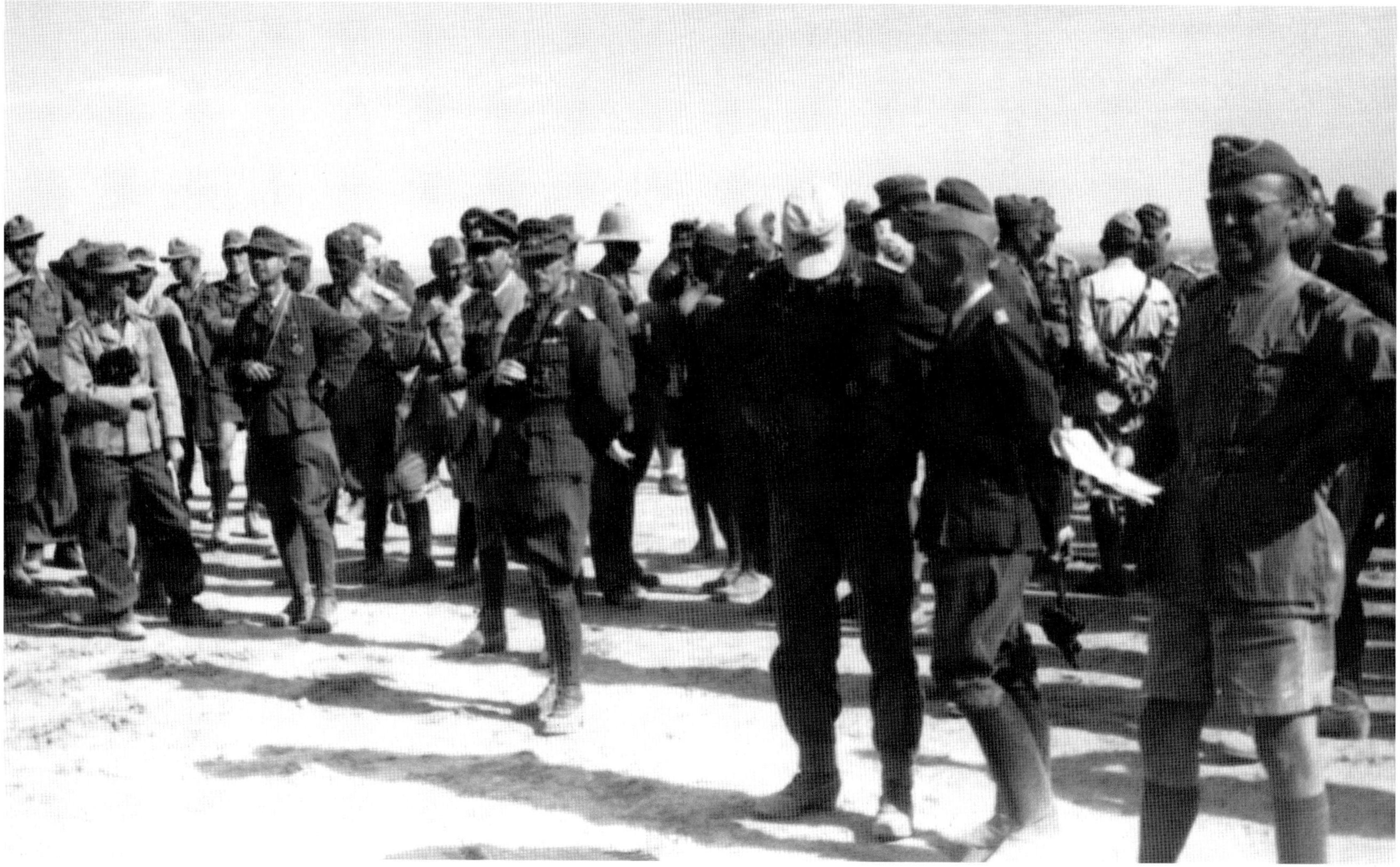

Above and Opposite
Two photos taken shortly after Bayerlein's arrival in Africa shows a group of German and Italian officers wearing a mixture of uniform combinations. Some are wearing uniforms of a darker color that indicates these had only recently been issued and had not suffered the fading older uniforms received from the bright sun and being washed in water laced with various chemicals. Visible in this photo are older and newer tropical field caps and Continental woolen officer sidecaps, shorts, breeches (worn with the high boots), trousers with bottoms 'bloused' or gathered over the ankle and worn with low boots, an Italian pith helmet, and one German officer wears his Continental service cap. The date of these photos may be the later part of 1941.[3]

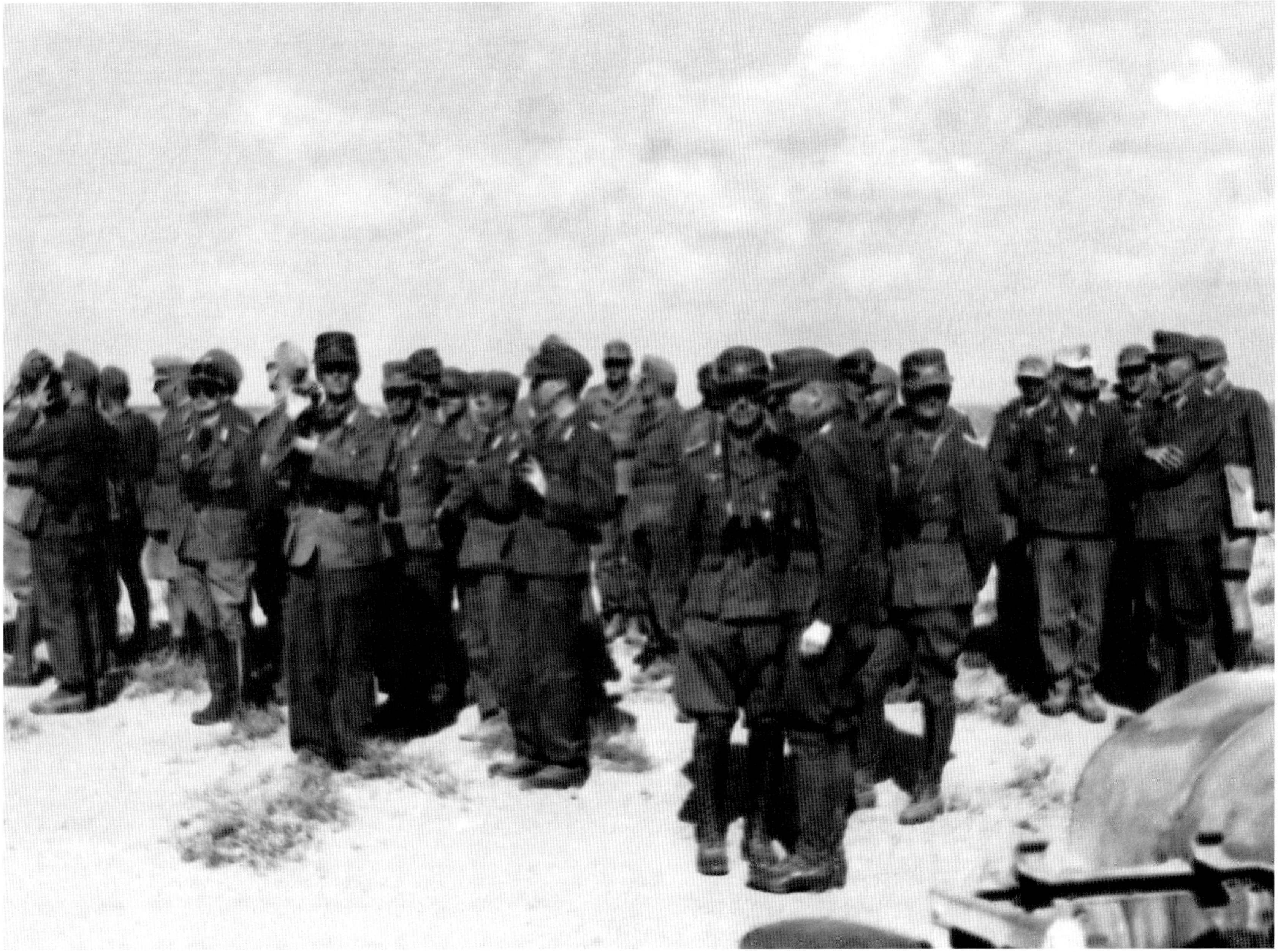

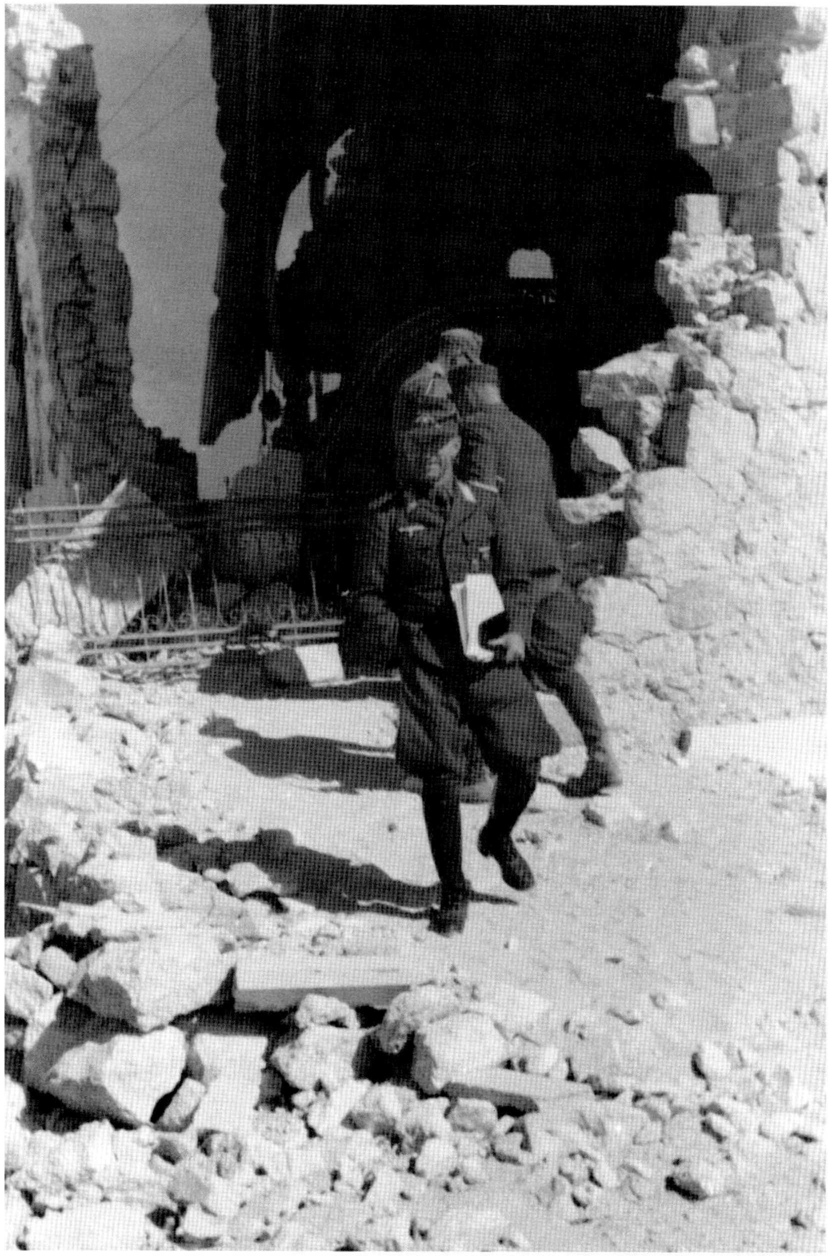

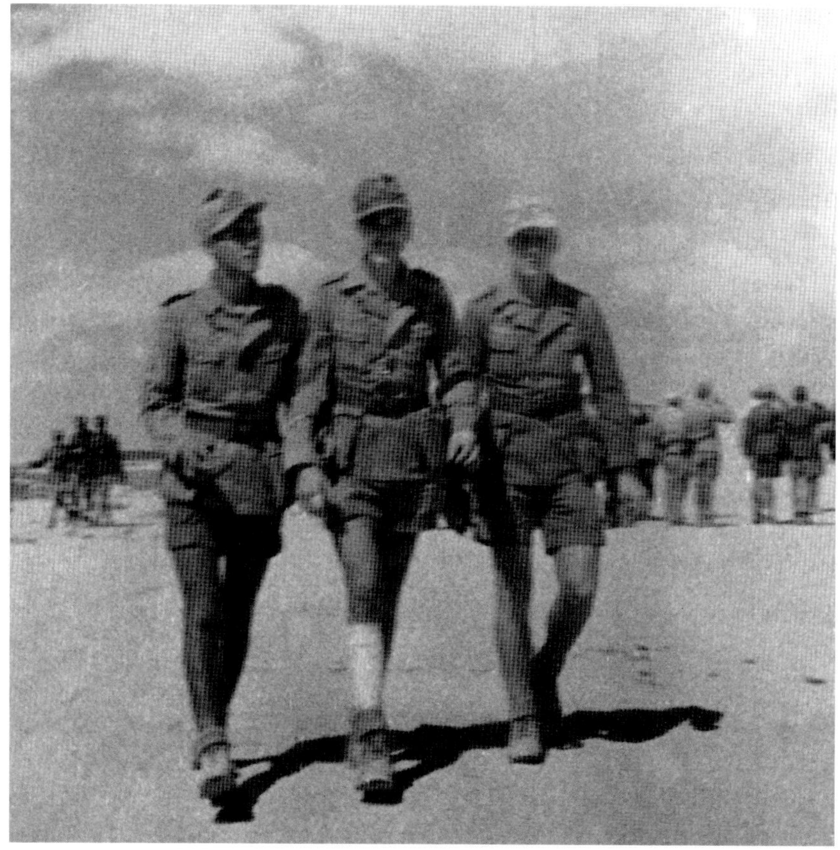

Left
The man in the photo appears to be Generaloberst Kurt Freiherr von Liebenstein, commander of the 164th Light Division, whose arrival in Africa was in early December 1942. Prior to his arrival in Africa, von Liebenstein had served as Chief-of-Staff to Guderian for Panzergruppe 2 in Russia in 1941. Bayerlein served as Operations Officer, Ia, of Panzergruppe 2 during the same time. Von Liebenstein and General Theodor Graf von Sponeck, who was commander of the 90th Light Division, along with Bayerlein fought well as a team in the retreat to Tunisia in the last months of the African war.[4]

Above
Three young soldiers from the headquarters escort group capture Bayerlein's attention.

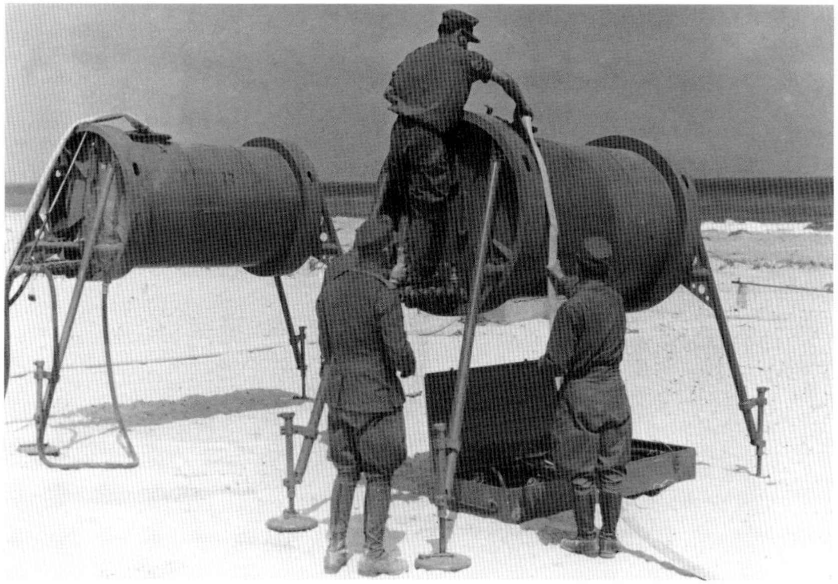

Right: Engineers work on fresh water wells. Above: Detailed photo of engineers at work on fresh water wells. The Mediterranean Sea is in the background. Below: The water works in progress. Bayerlein was a logistics officer before the beginning of the war, and he appears to be observing operations.

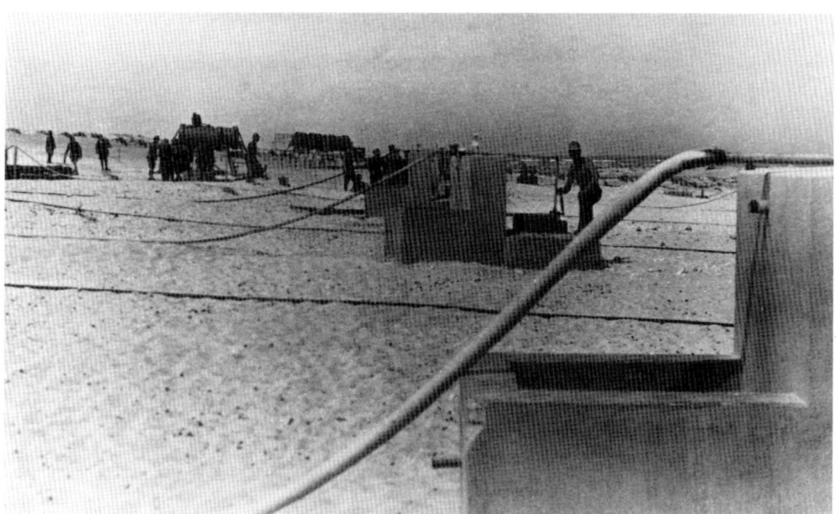

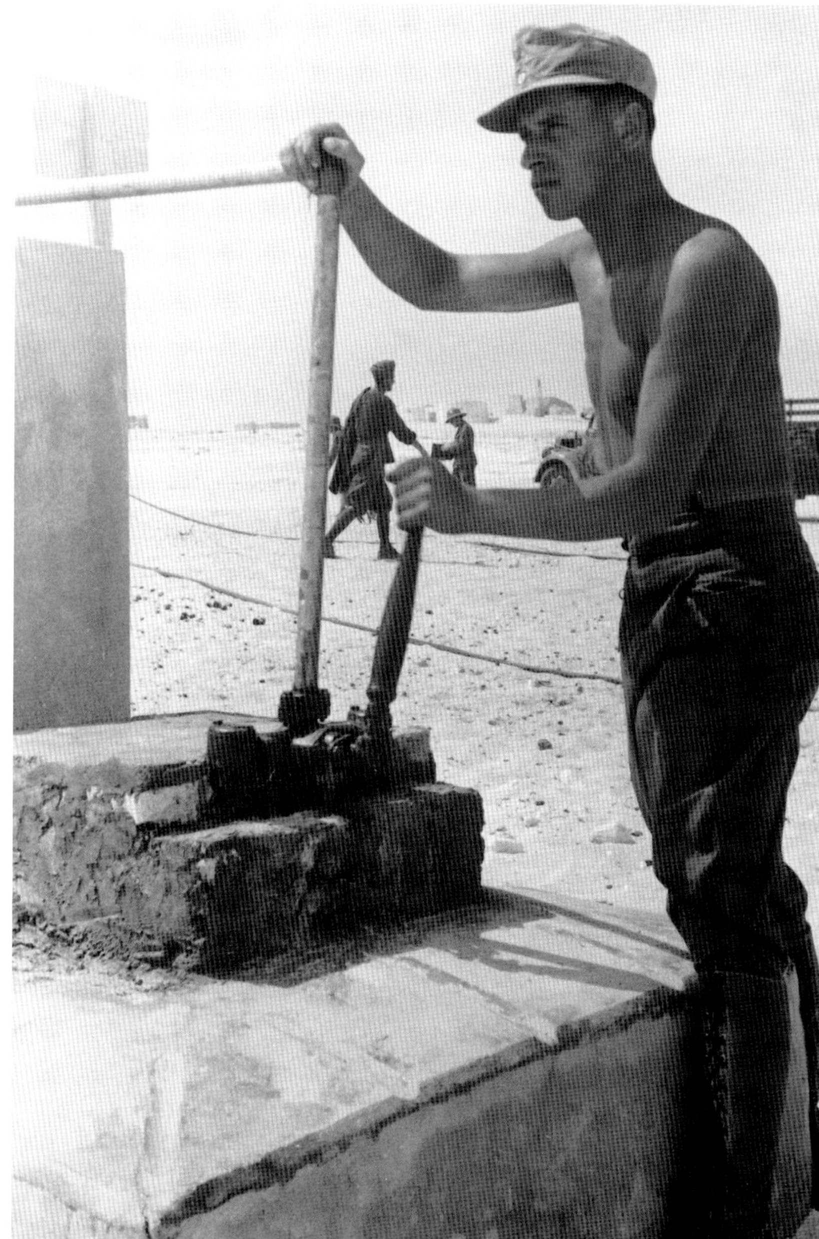

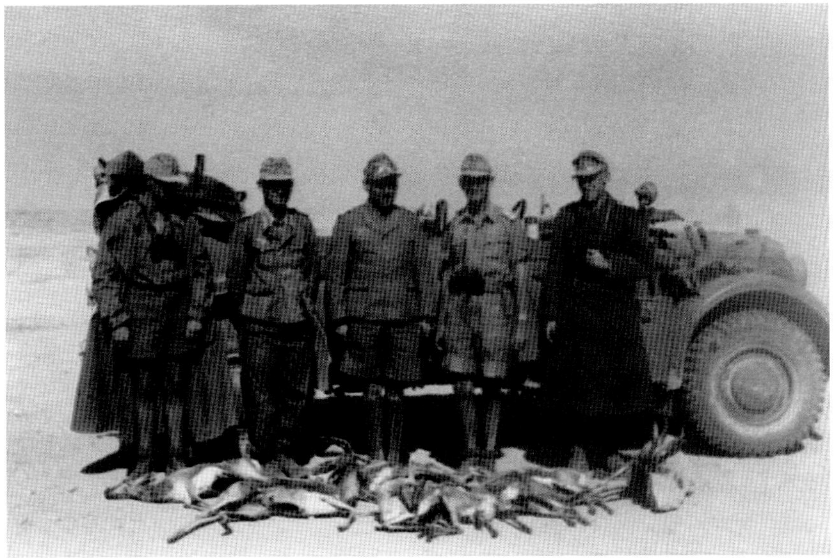

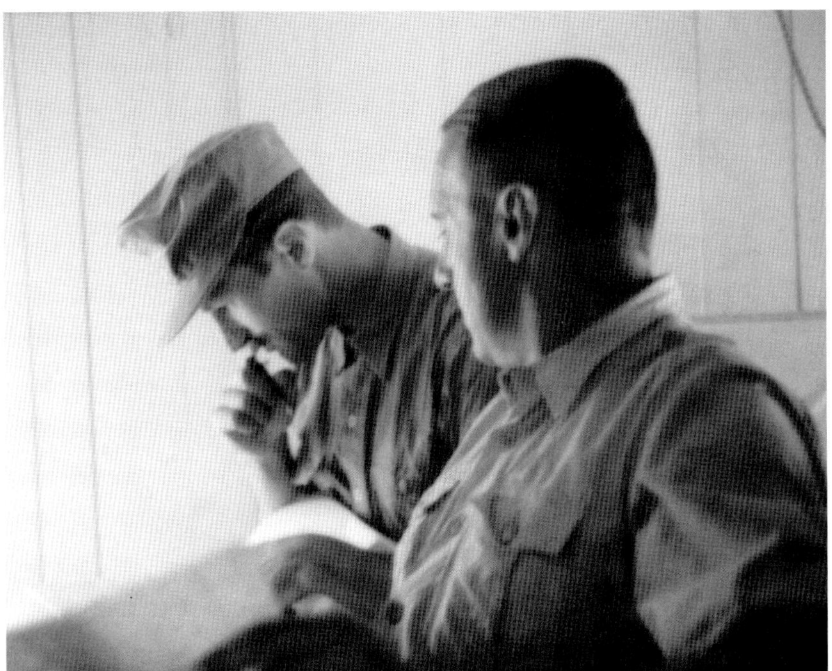

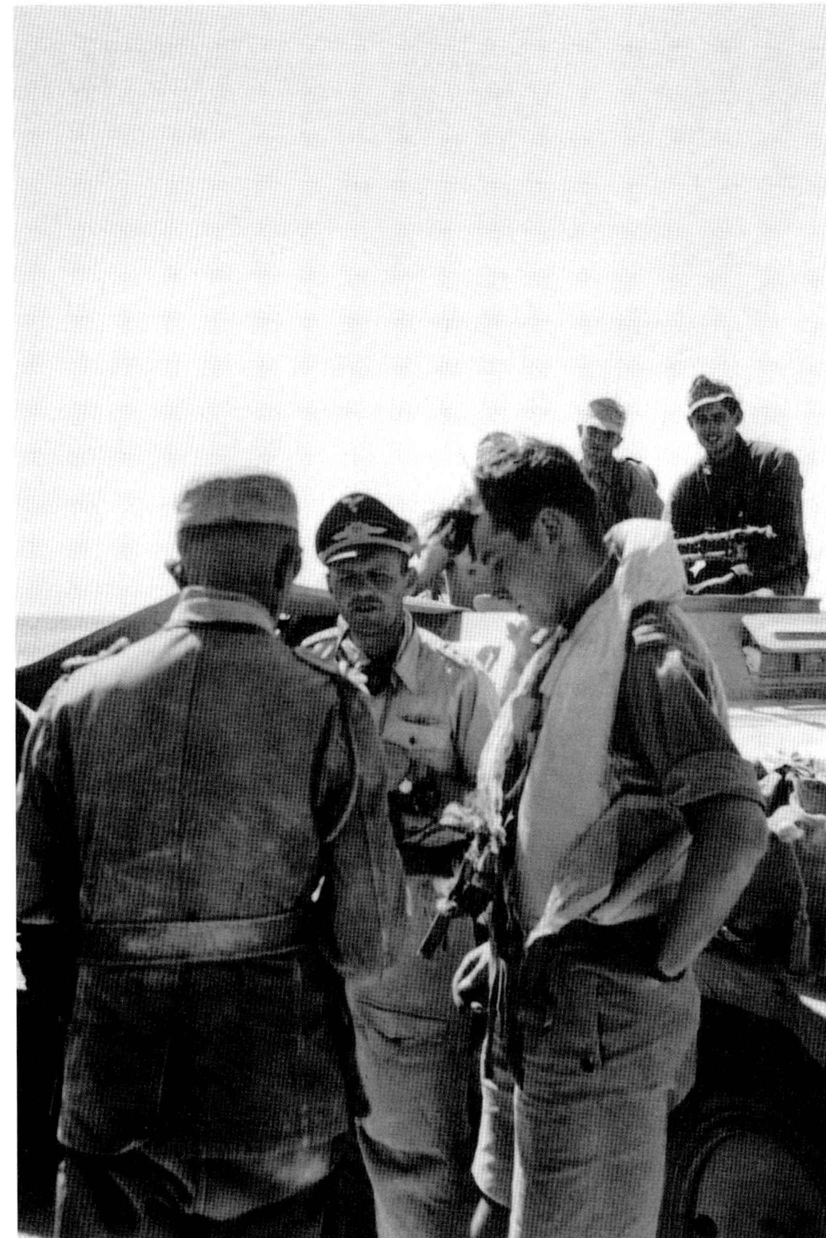

Opposite, top left
Headquarters staff and Chief-of-Staff Bayerlein (center, wearing shorts) stand over their trophy-gazelle dinner. Photo was taken shortly after Bayerlein's arrival in Africa as he is wearing the knee-length, lace up boots. He abandoned them shortly thereafter, choosing instead a low boot and long trousers. During the summer of 1942 the length of his short trousers rose to an alarming height above his knees.

Opposite, bottom left
Bayerlein's caption: "6 September. Northwest Qaret Seimeimat. Chef and Leibel in Mammut." Always the teacher, Bayerlein patiently instructs young Leutnant Leibel, who appears to be in deep thought over trying to solve a problem. Although he could erupt in a bad and irritable temper, Bayerlein normally was very patient and helpful with young officers and soldiers. His temper seemed to be directly linked to the stress of the particular combat situation – and whether he knew the answer or not. In one instance, asking Bayerlein a wrong question at the wrong time, his innocent panzer driver was, "engulfed in a tidal wave of Bavarian fury."[5]

Opposite, right
Bayerlein's caption reads: "Prisoner, British Flight officer." The man on the right, without a cap, leaning against the vehicle in the foreground, wearing a life vest is perhaps the British pilot, although it is strange he is wearing shorts while flying. One model of German life vest for pilots was smooth surfaced, and another German model had individual vertical ribs (each rib stuffed with a buoyant material called "Kapok"). Since this man is not wearing a Kapok vest and is the only one wearing flight gear at all, he is perhaps the British pilot Bayerlein is referring to on his note on the back of the photo.[6]

Right
Bayerlein's handwritten caption reads: "Deir el Gatani, 30 July 1942. Ia, Major Fruwirt."

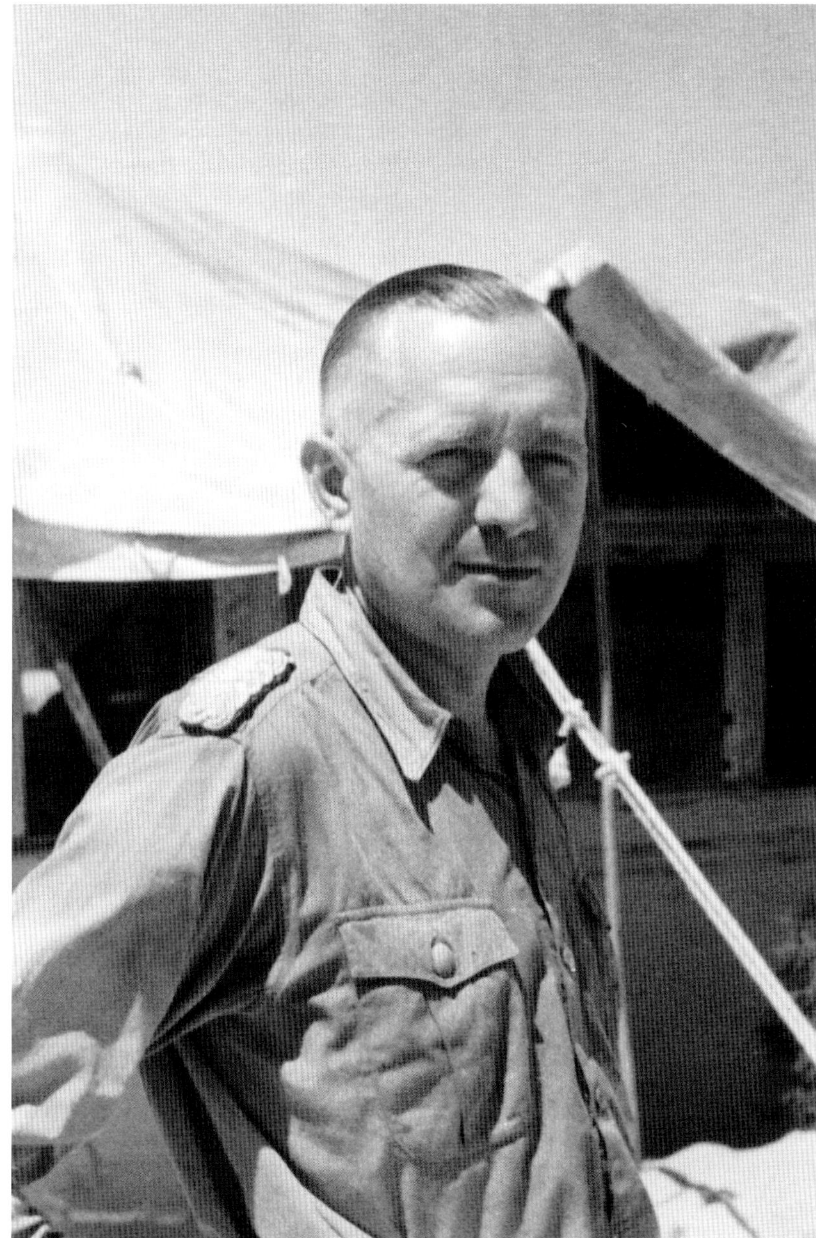

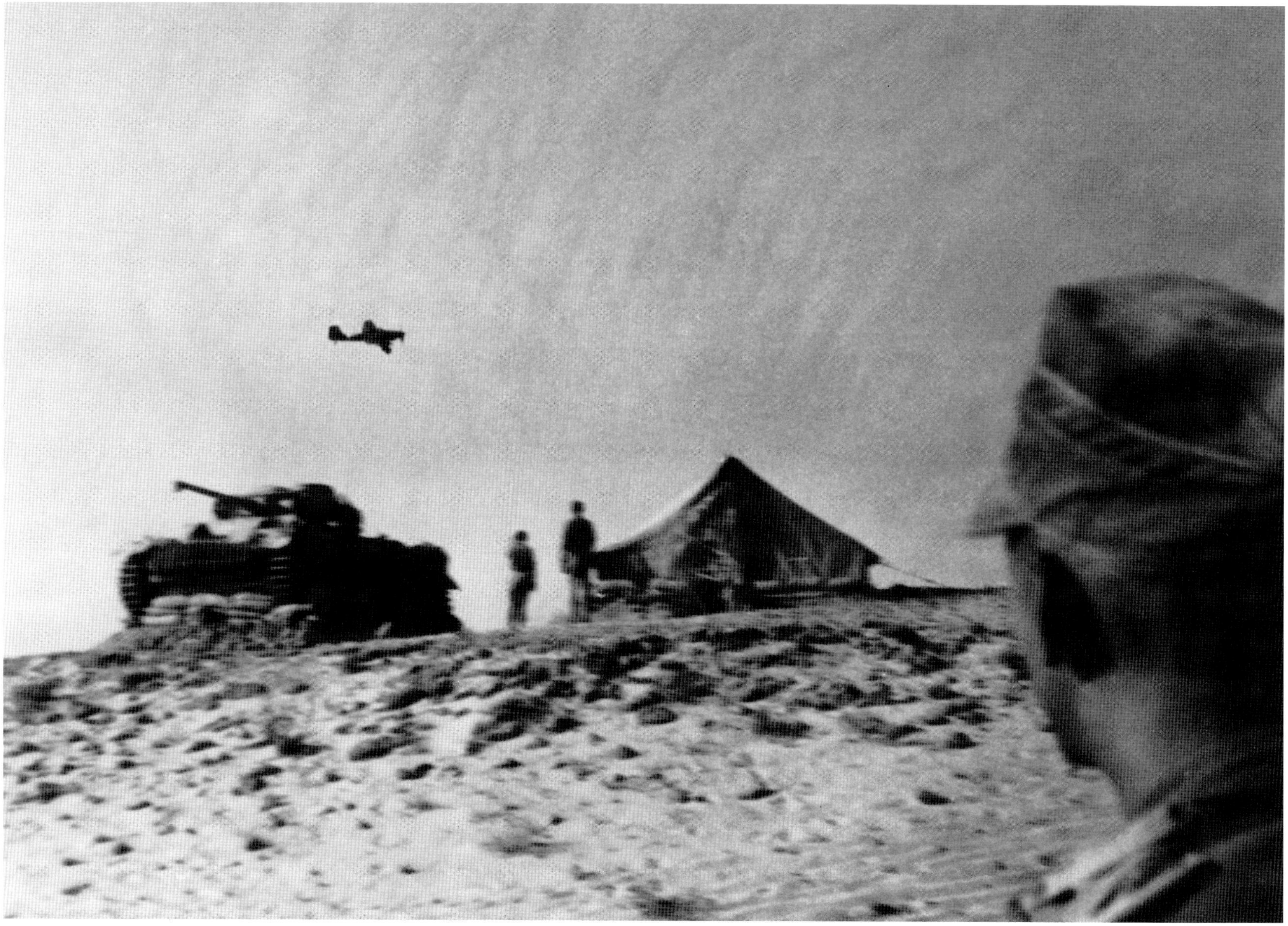

Bayerlein's original handwritten caption: "11 September, Qaret el Yidni, Fulka and Panzer." 1942.

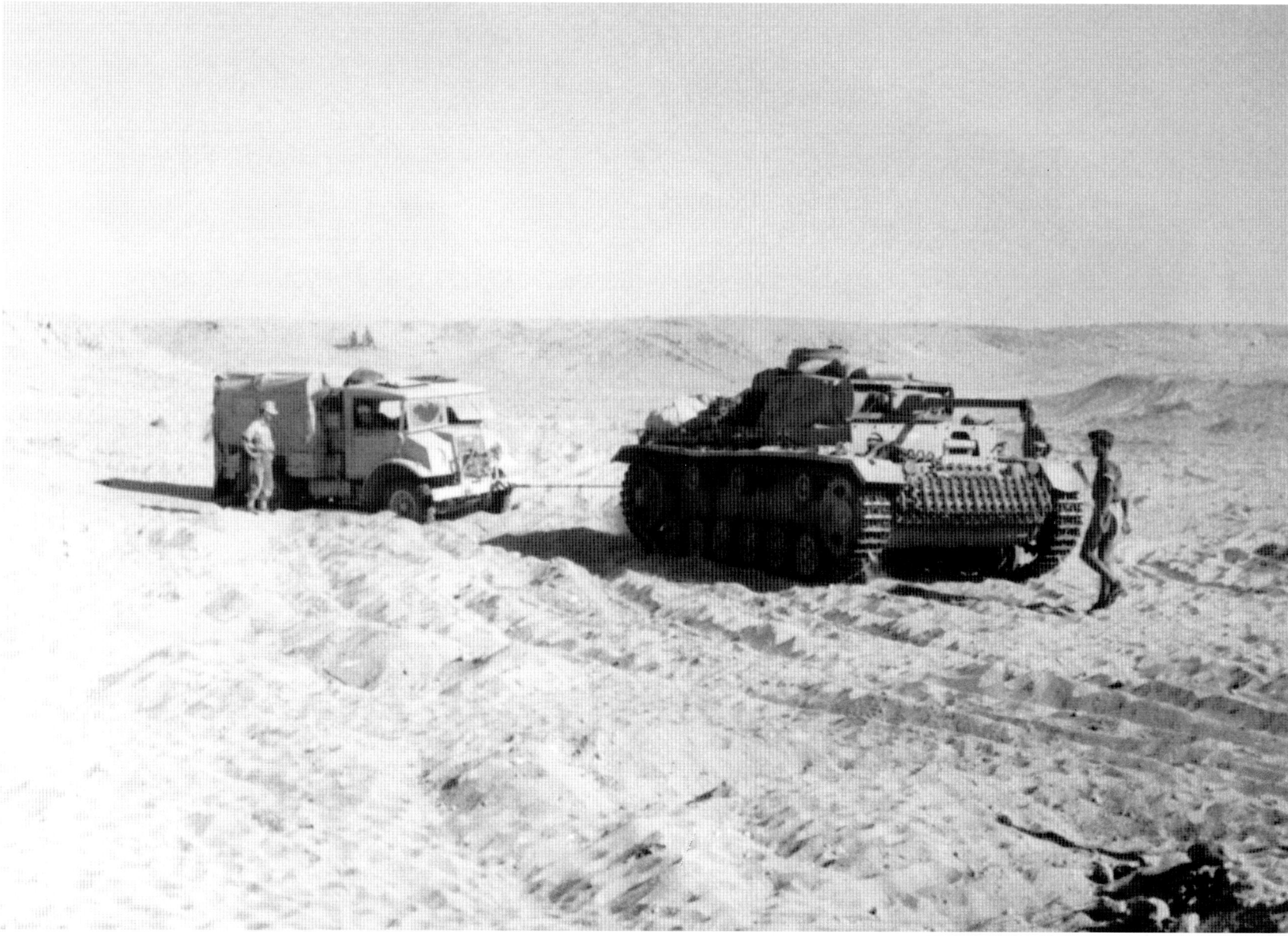

Bayerlein's caption: "7 September. Northwest Qaret Seimeimat. Chefs panzer towing the General's kitchen." 1942.

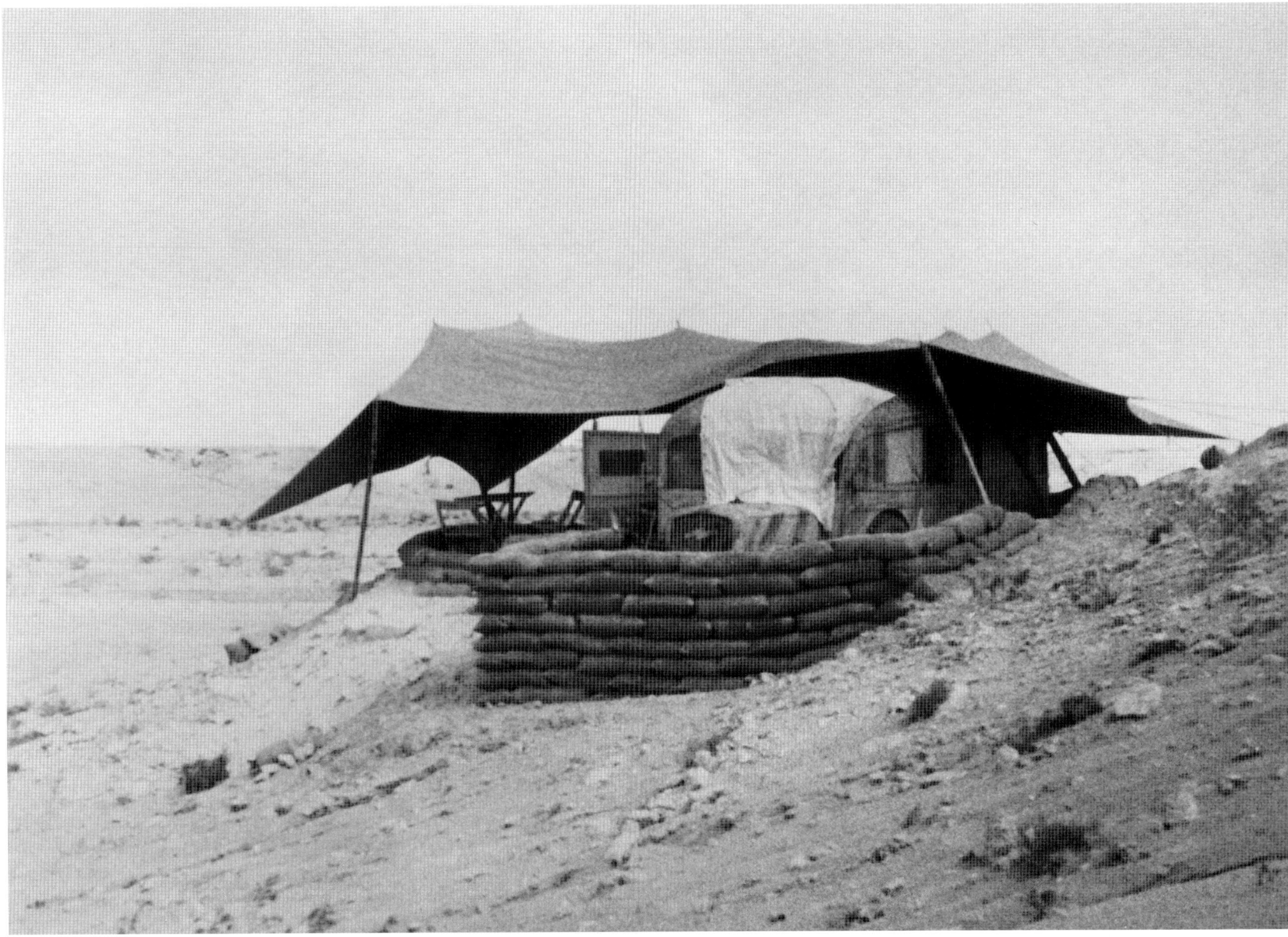

Bayerlein's caption: "4 October. Chef's bus. Manhz." The year would be 1942, and the village of Manhz.

Bayerlein's caption: "6 September. Major Fruwirt" the DAK Ia, Operations Officer.

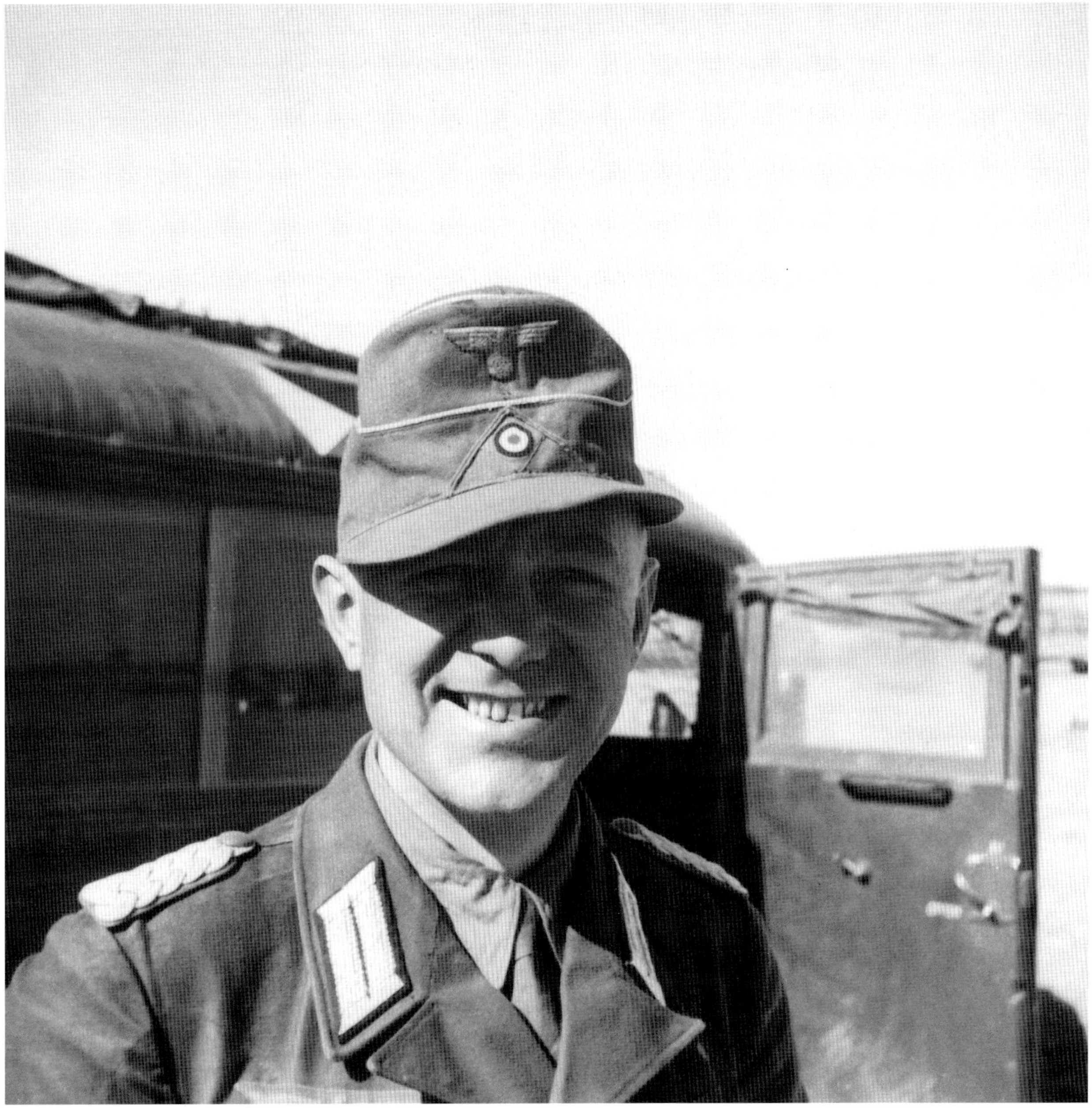

CHAPTER THREE

BAYERLEIN IN AFRICA

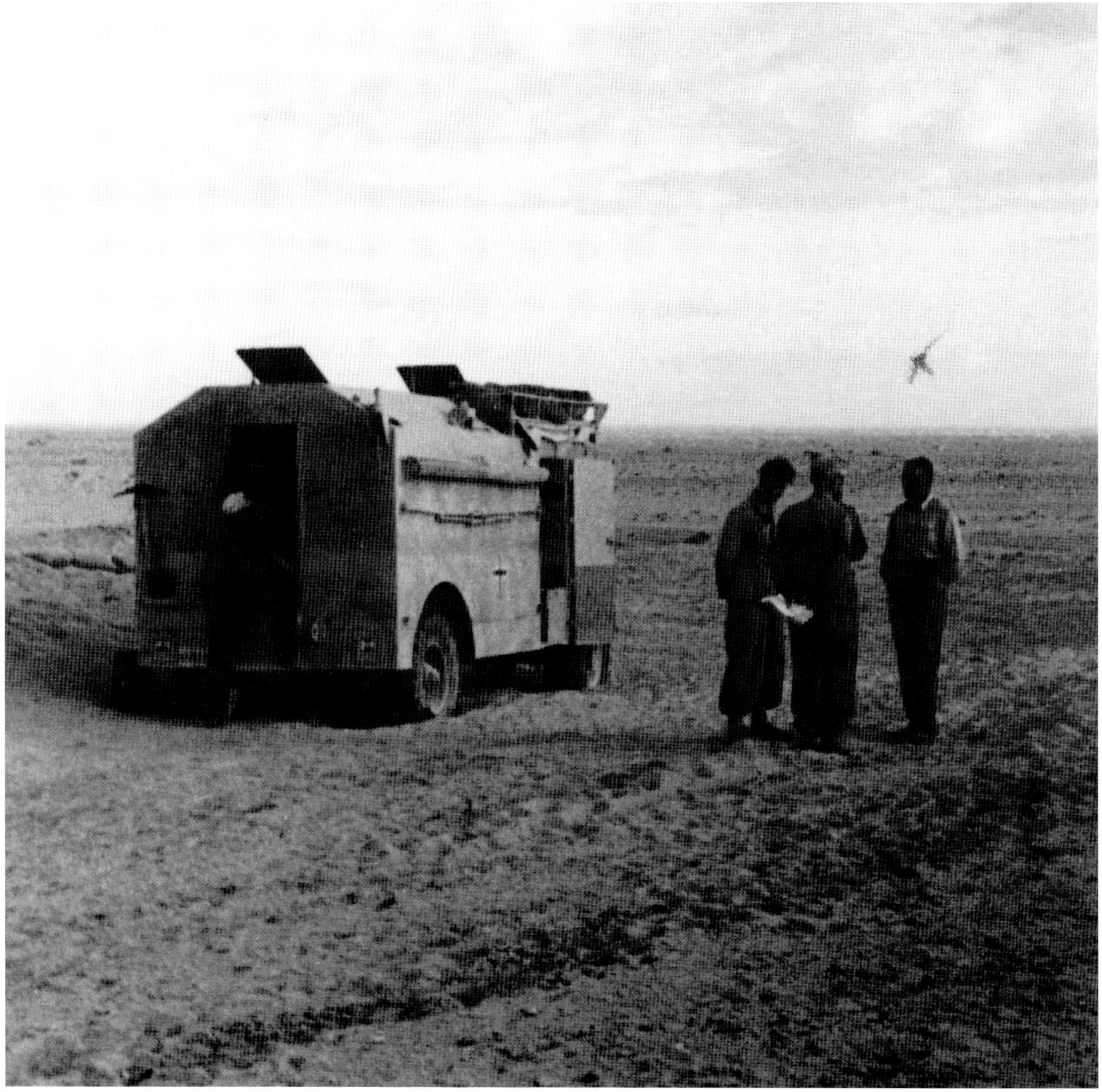

Oberstleutnant Fritz Bayerlein, with Oberleutnant Alexander Hartdegen and another staff officer, stand near their captured British command vehicle that Field Marshal Rommel humorously nicknamed "Moritz" after the 18th century troublesome cartoon characters "Max and Moritz". Rommel referred to the vehicles as a "Mammut" (mammoth). This photo was taken in June 1942. Hartdegen was transferred from Lisbon as an attaché in the African Desert. He and Bayerlein forged a close friendship that lasted their entire lives.

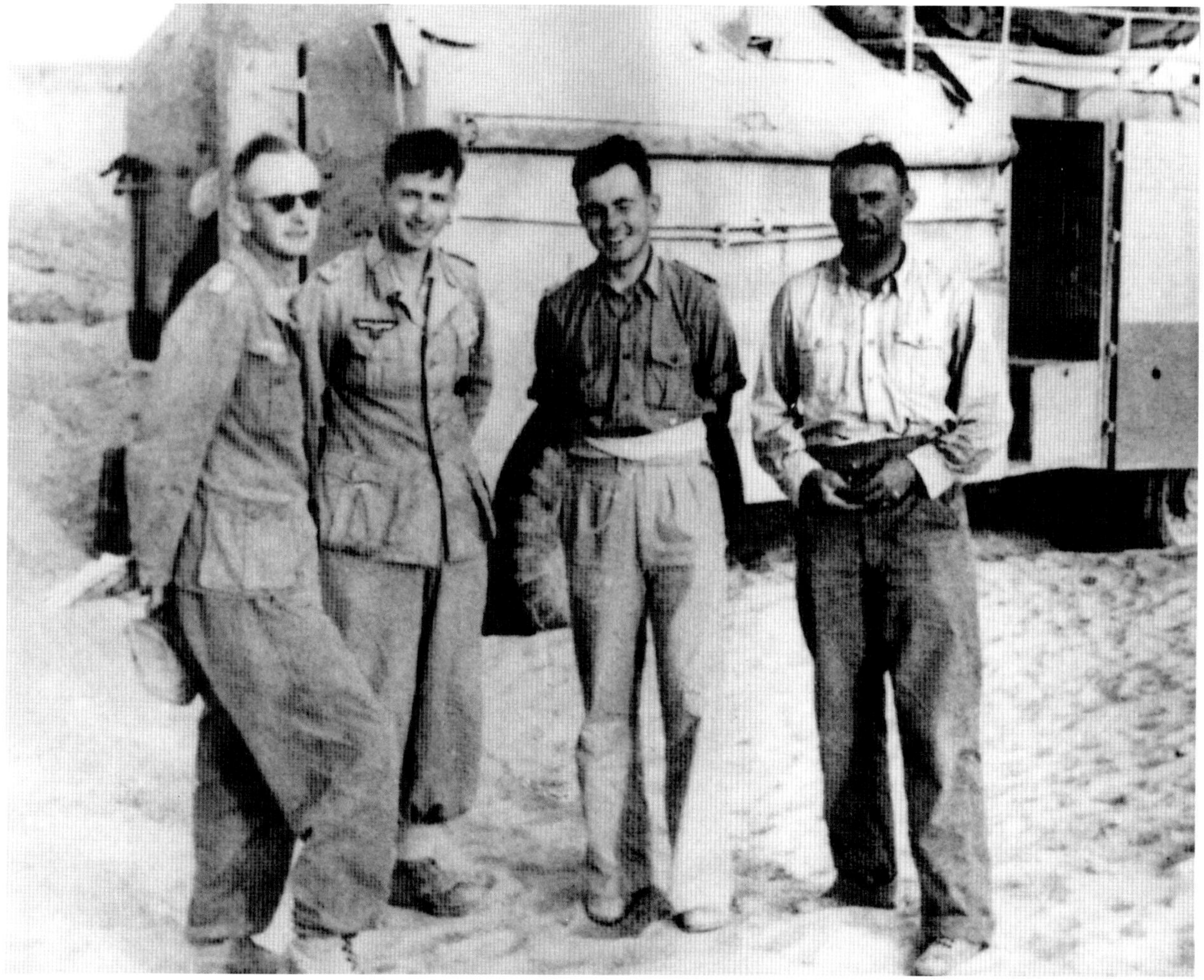

A close up of the men reveals a slightly less glamorous picture. The men and their clothing reveal a lack of water available in the desert fighting for washing. Bayerlein (right) and Alexander Hartdegen (second from left) had an instant liking for each other and mutual respect. Hartdegen was assigned to Bayerlein's command with 3rd Panzer, Berlin-Brandenburg Division in Russia from October 1943 through mid-January 1944. Subsequently, Hartdegen transferred with Bayerlein to the Panzer Lehr Division as his aide. Hartdegen's daughters relayed that their father viewed Bayerlein as an older brother, due to their age difference of fifteen years. The two men remained friends until Bayerlein's death in 1970.[1]

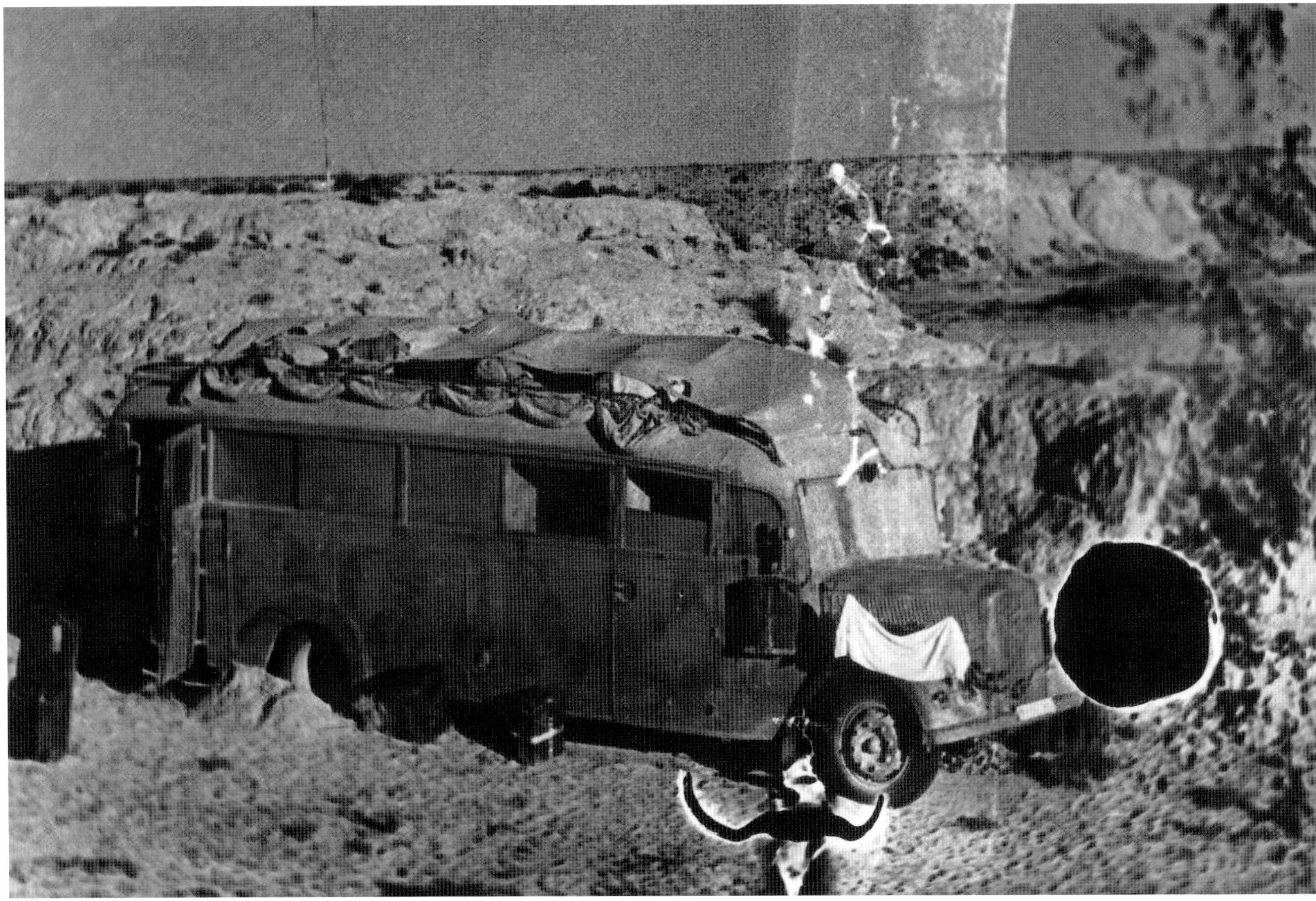

The "Chefs bus" (Chief's bus) as Bayerlein called his own command vehicle. General Crüwell usually claimed the captured British Mammut, "Moritz" for himself.

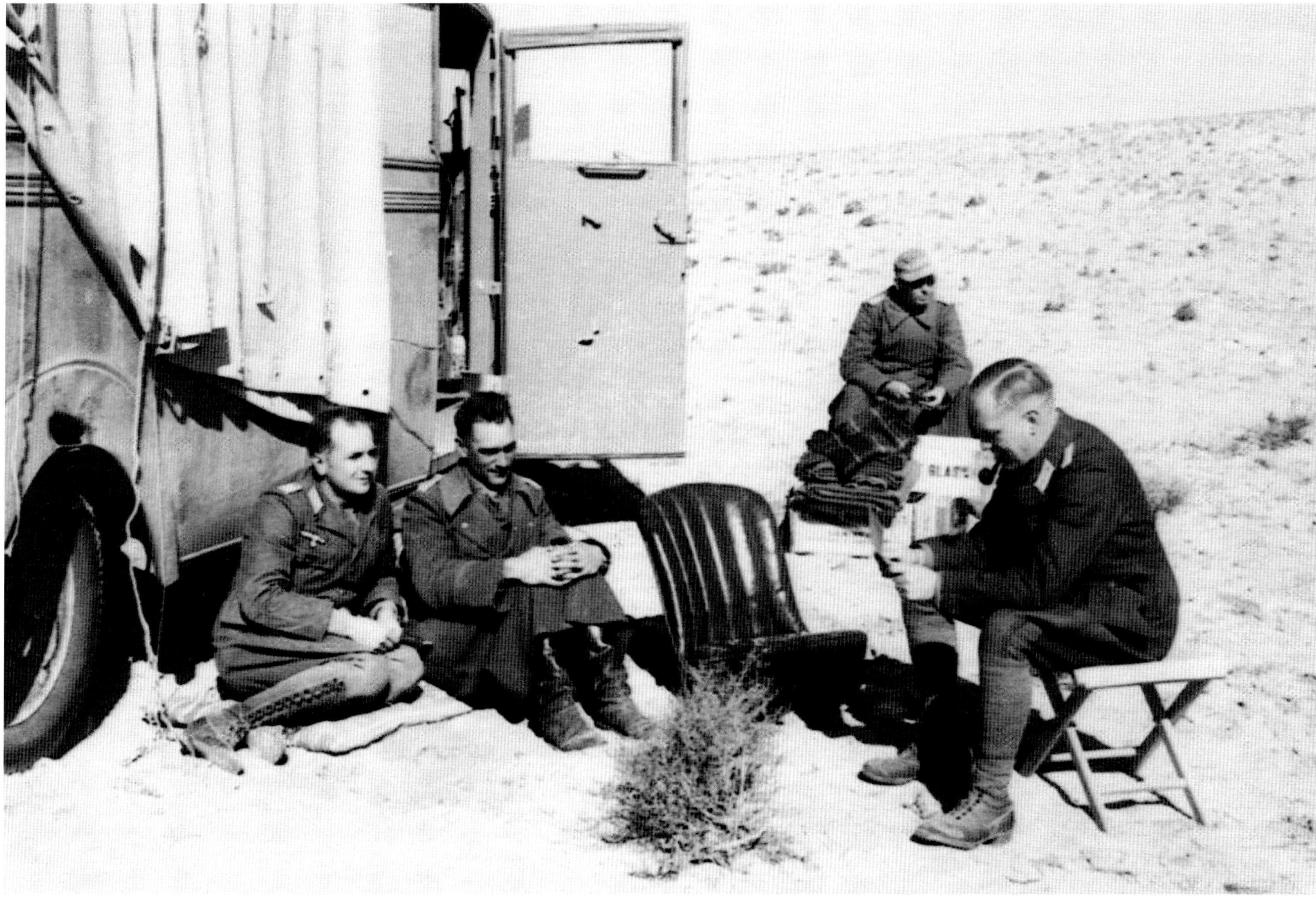

Sitting outside the Chefs bus, Sonderführer Walter Schmidt, a close friend of Bayerlein's from Würzburg, calmly smokes his pipe and converses with the other staff officers. Sonderführer Schmidt also helped Bayerlein to defend a helpless and sick Russian prisoner of war who was publicly beaten by a camp guard at the Würzburg Hauptbahnhof (train station) in September 1941, just prior to Bayerlein's transfer to Africa.[2] Schmitt was killed in the fighting at Tobruk.

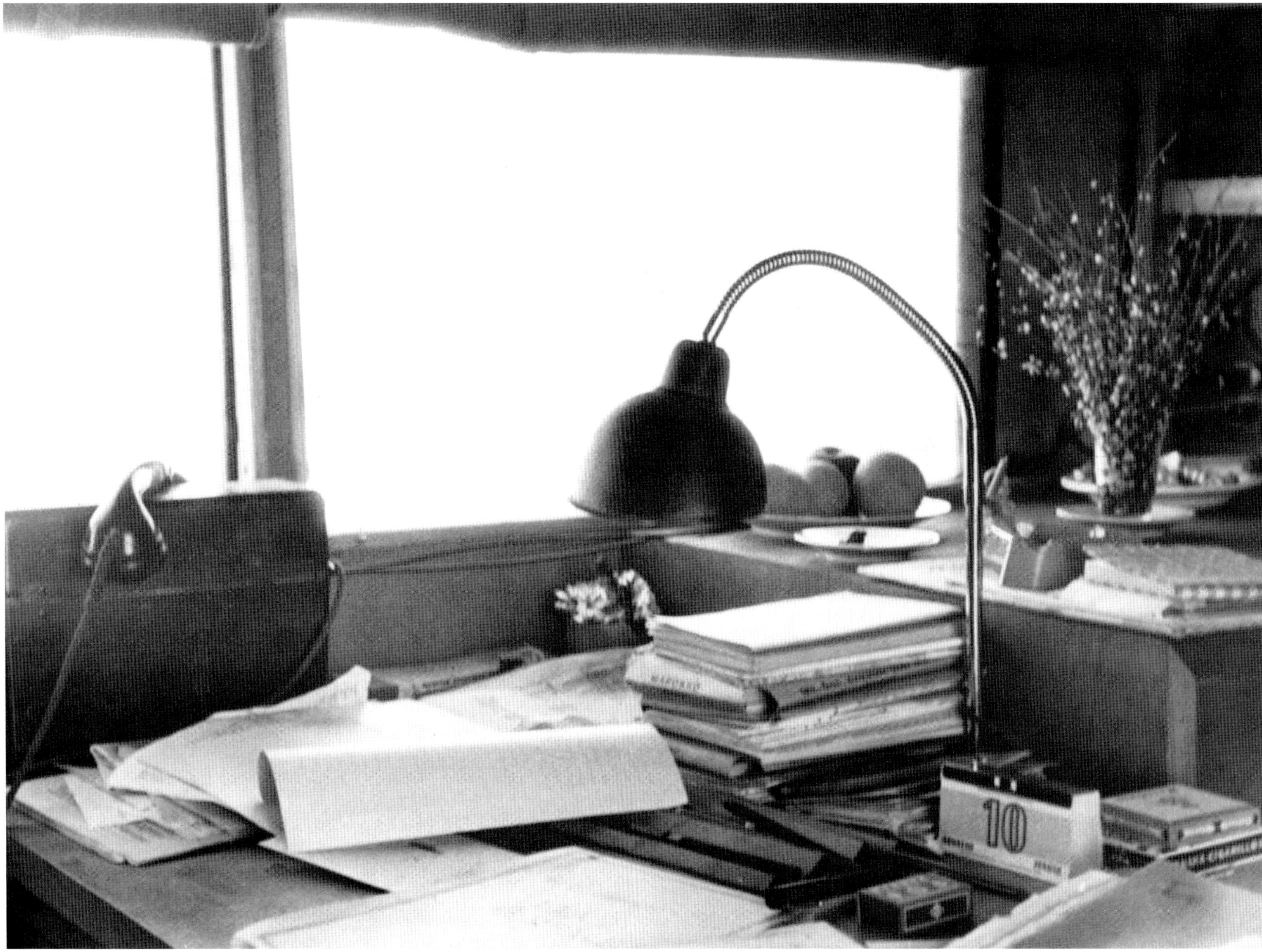
10

Opposite
The Chefs desk. Bayerlein set himself up a welcoming and comfortable working desk in his bus. The Chef had a fine eye and included a bowl of fruit and some dried desert flowers to break up the military monotony of his setting. His field phone sits to the side.

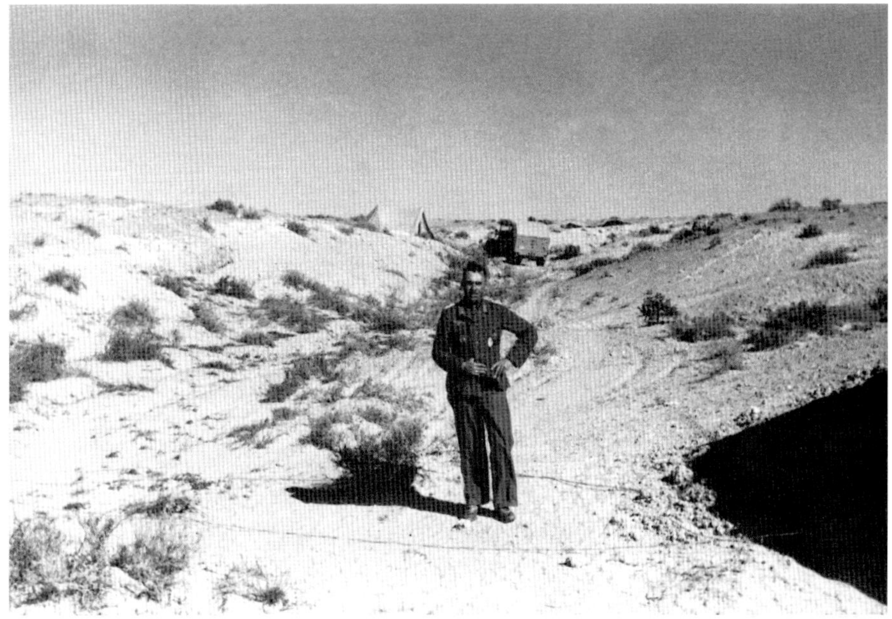

Right
Oberst Bayerlein stands alone, modeling the emptiness of the desert landscape. The photo can be dated to 1943, as identified by his purchase of a new tropical uniform and the Deutsche Kreuz in Gold on his right breast pocket, awarded in October, 1942.

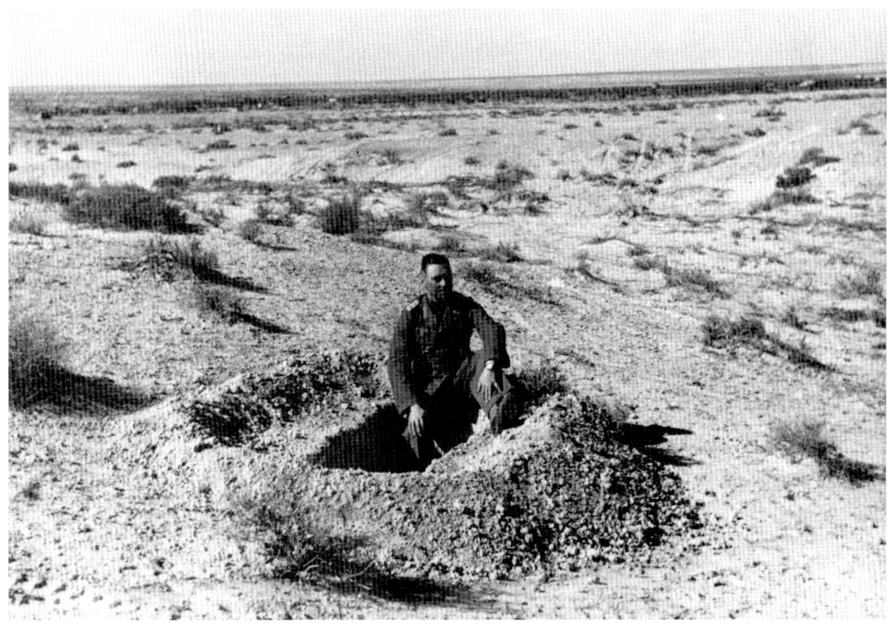

Right
Sitting in his shallow desert foxhole – no doubt dug by the Headquarters enlisted men – Oberst Bayerlein is a short distance from the other staff and vehicles. The distance is necessary to avoid mass casualties while under artillery shelling and attack by Allied aircraft.

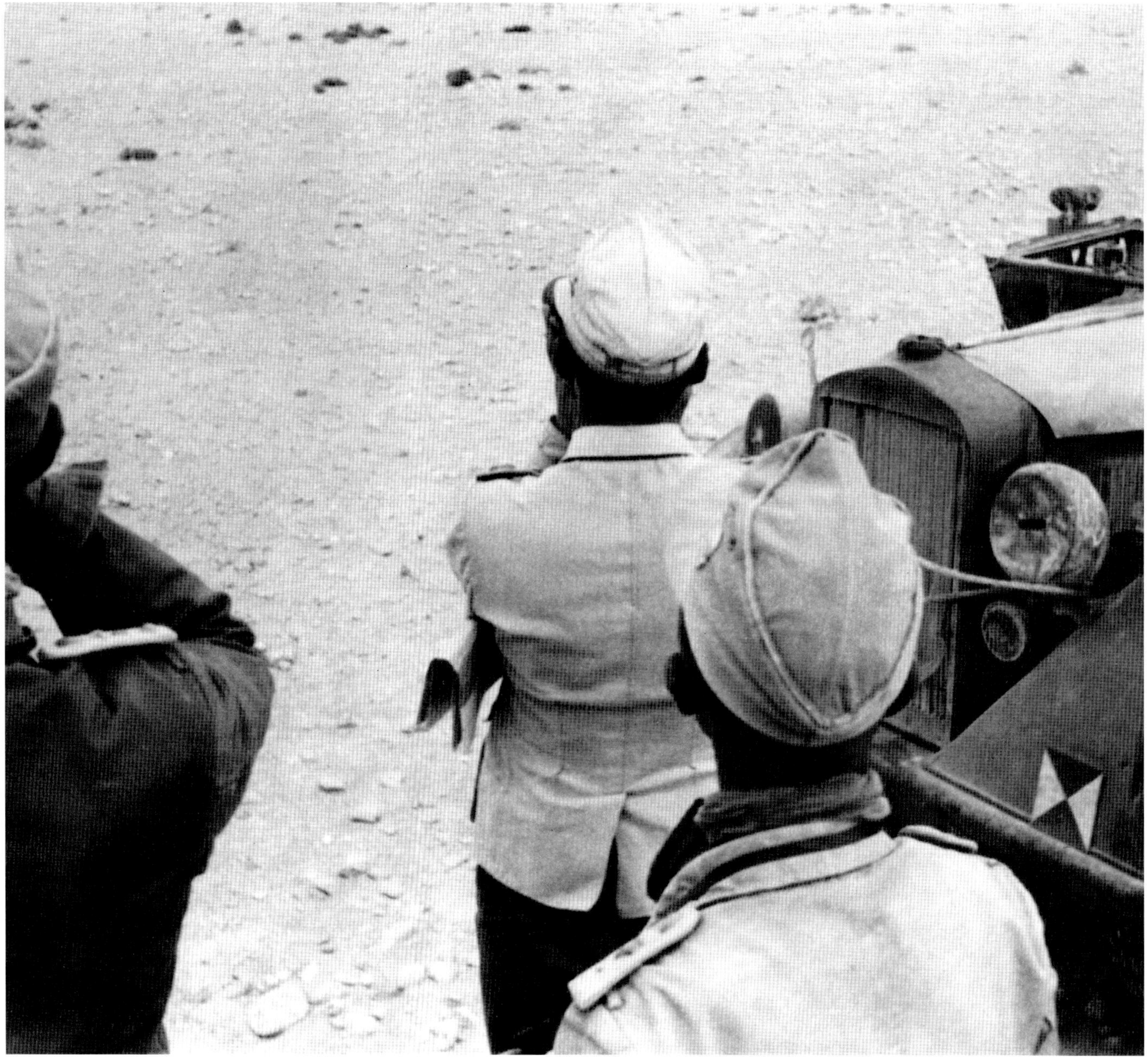

According to a short handwritten note on the photo, Bayerlein (back to camera, holding map) is looking toward the battle in progress at Fuka. He dated the photo 5 November 1942.

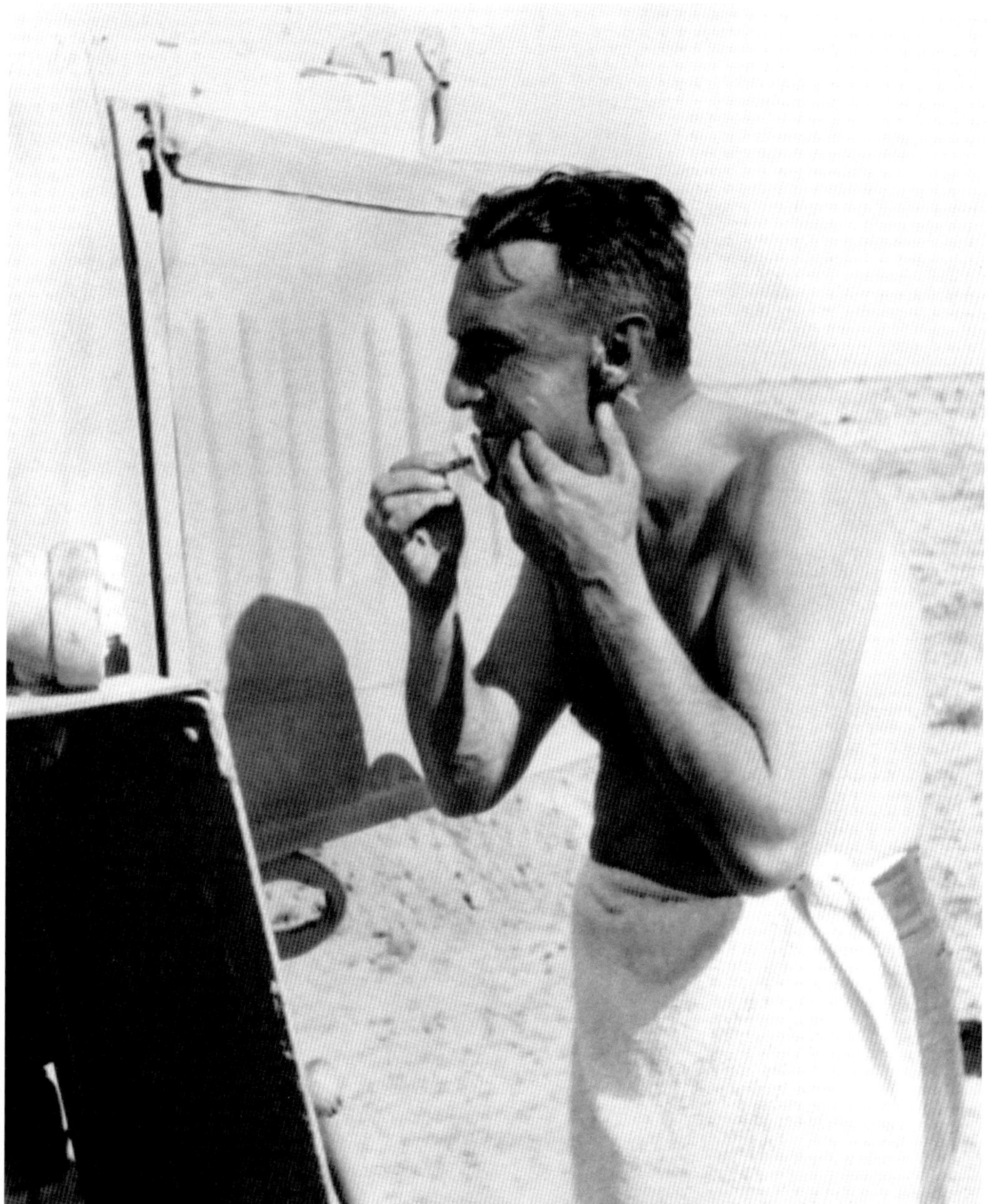

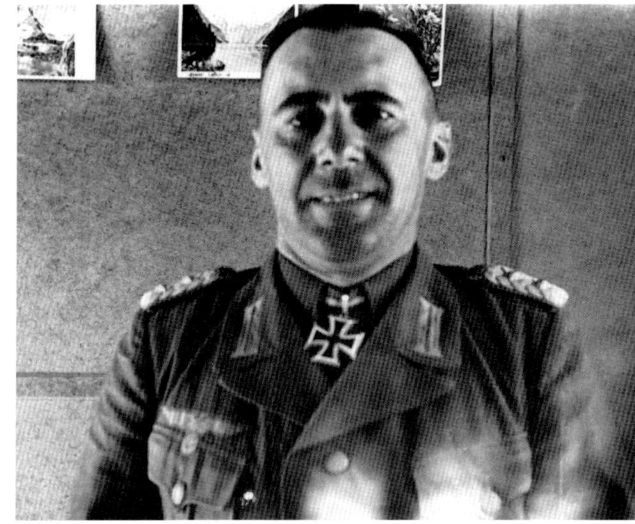

Left
An extremely rare photograph of Bayerlein shaving. The date he wrote on the back of the photo is 7 November 1942, identifying himself simply as "Chef".

Above
Seen here with a rather unsettling, nervous, forced smile, the newly promoted Oberst (Colonel) Fritz Bayerlein poses in front of his bulletin board on his bus, wearing his new epaulets. Flanked by postcards of his favored vacation spot to ski in the Bavarian Alps, the desert seems a distant nightmare compared to the differences in climate and terrain. The date of his promotion to Oberst was 1 April 1942.

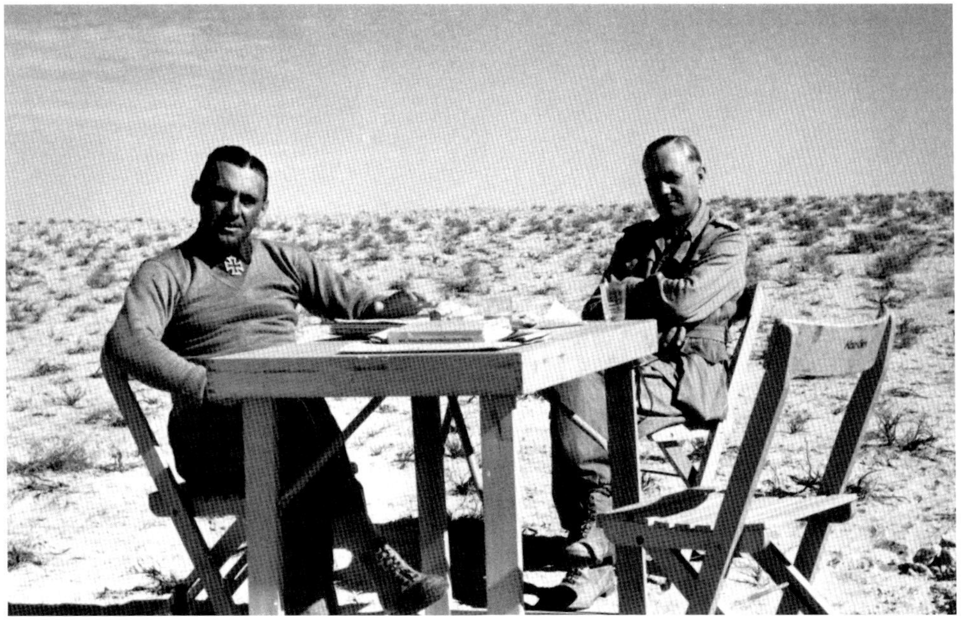

Left
Moving his desk from the sweltering bus to the outside air, Oberst Bayerlein and Major Fruwirt, the Ia Operations Officer, enjoy the tranquility of a day without fighting.

Opposite
Bayerlein and a headquarters staff officer enjoy a great day for conversation, map reading and sitting on boulders checking the surrounding terrain. Since Bayerlein is wearing his Deutsche Kreuz in Gold, awarded by Field Marshal Rommel on 23 October, the photo was probably taken in late October, early November 1942.

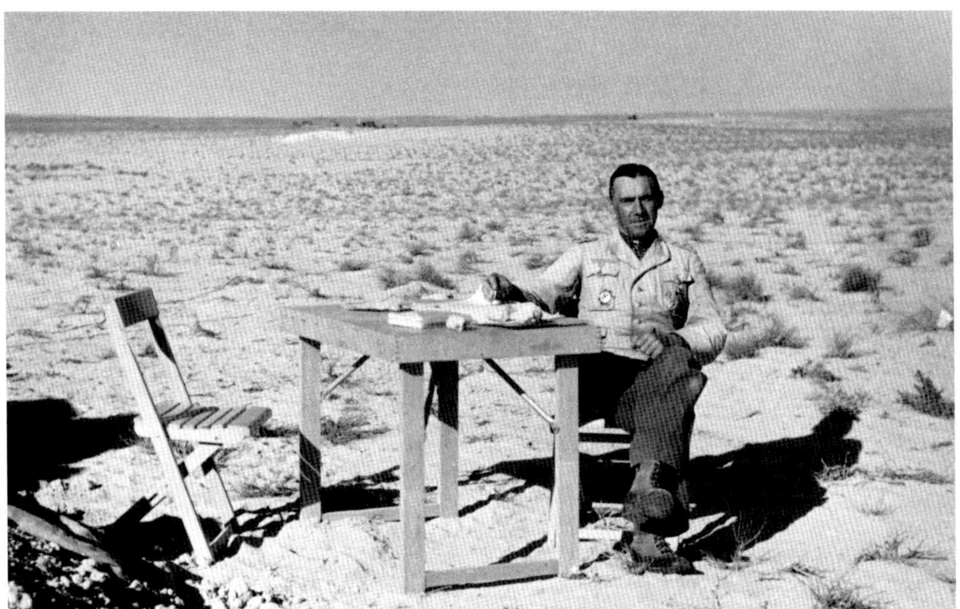

Left
Oberst Bayerlein, wearing his recently awarded "Deutsches Kreuz in Gold" enjoys another quiet, sunny day in his open-air office. The unflattering Kreuz was often referred to as the fried egg award due to its shape. Bayerlein gave the award to the First U.S. Army interrogator after his surrender in the Ruhr on 16 April, 1945. He commented that he disliked it.[3]

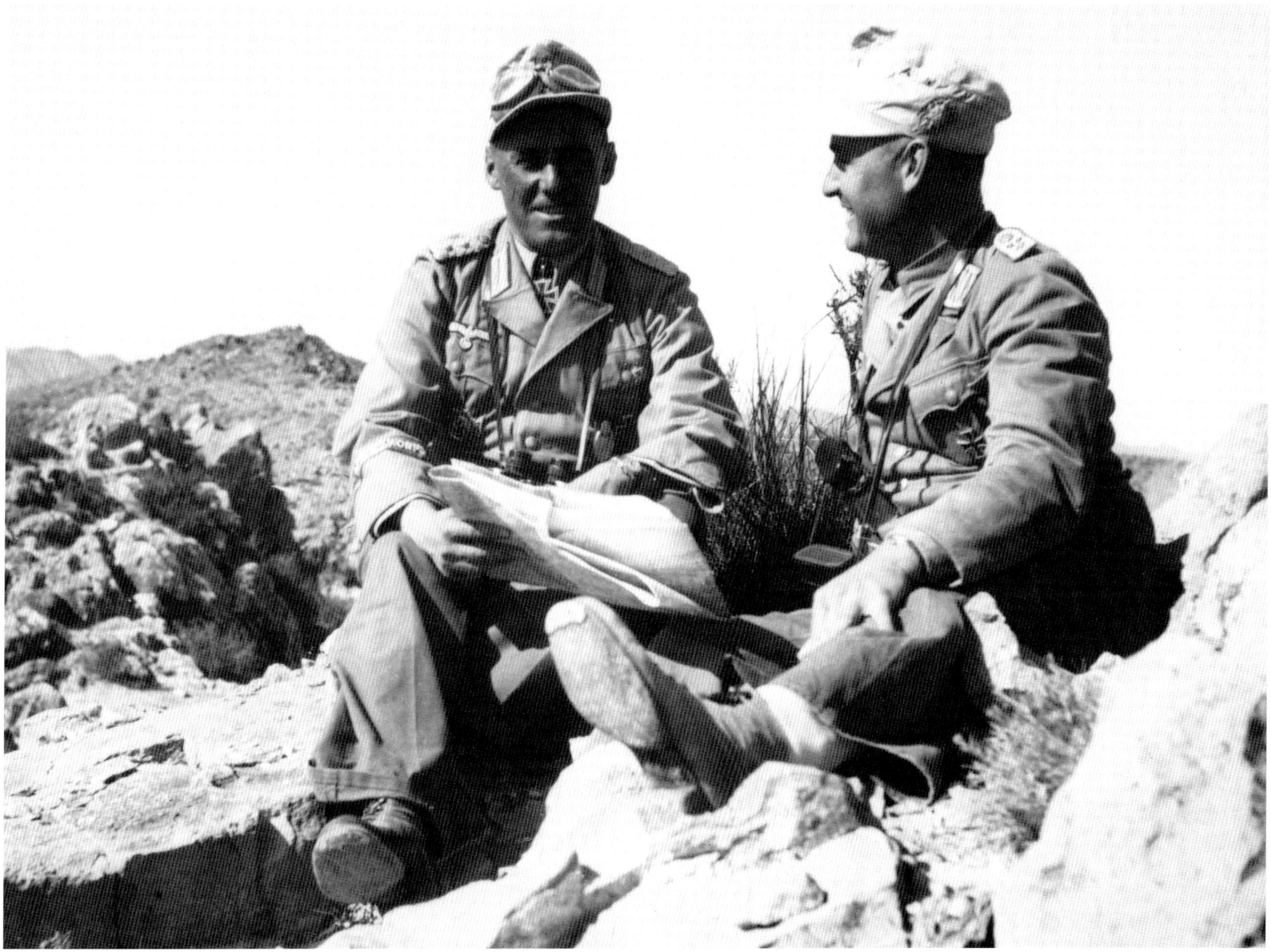

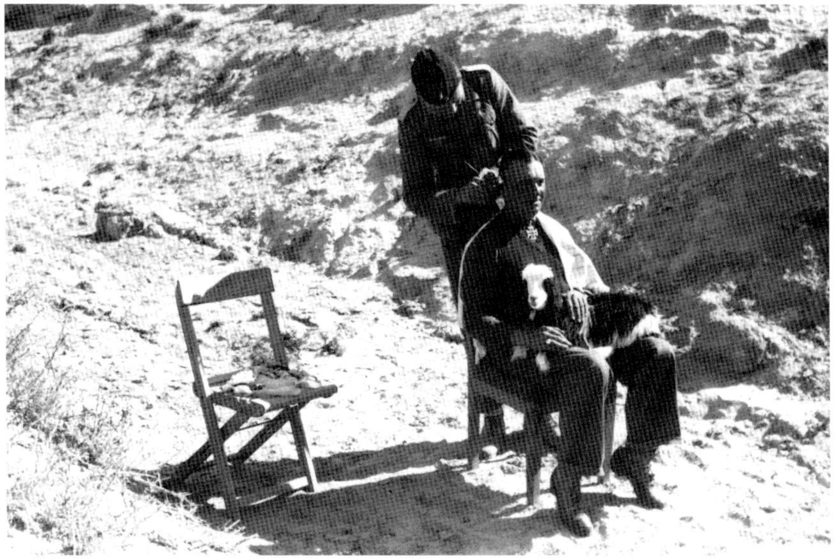

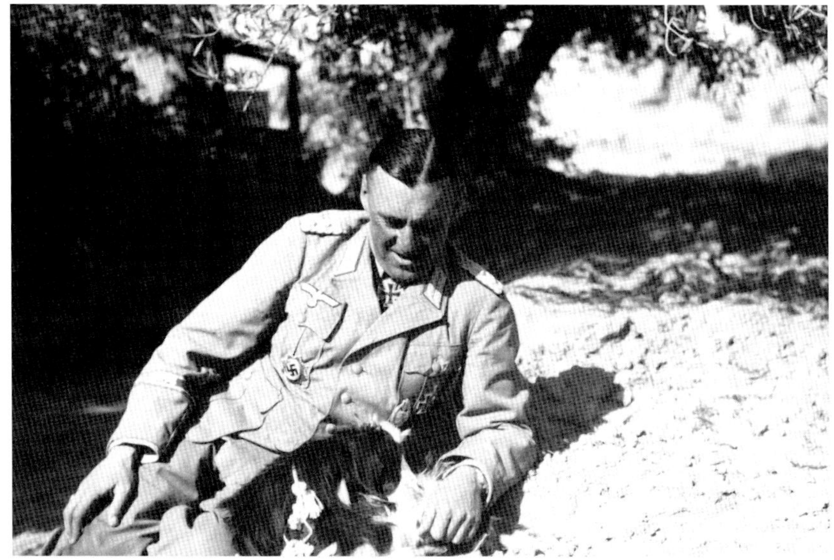

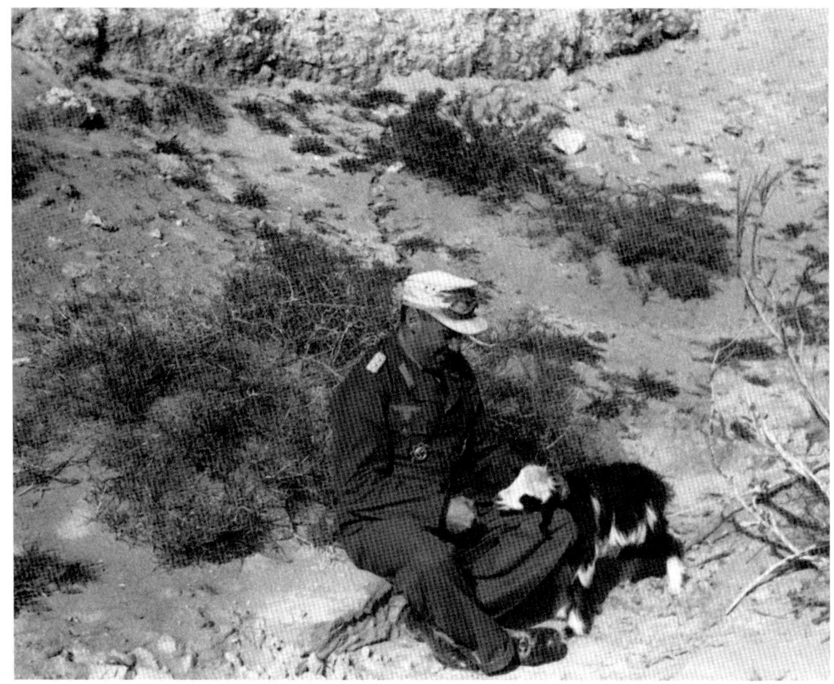

Above
The man and his goat. Bayerlein appeared to be quite taken with the little, young and colorful goat, a gift from the locals. No doubt intended for the stew pot, but Bayerlein made a pet out of it. The photo was taken in Tunisia, probably in January 1943 when Rommel's retreating armies were deploying in southern Tunisia.

Top right
Smiling and quite taken with his new pet, Oberst Bayerlein relaxes in the sun. Photo was taken in Tunisia, 1943.

Right
Wearing a new uniform and feeding his pet goat, Bayerlein forgets about the war for a short time. Photo taken in Tunisia, 1943.

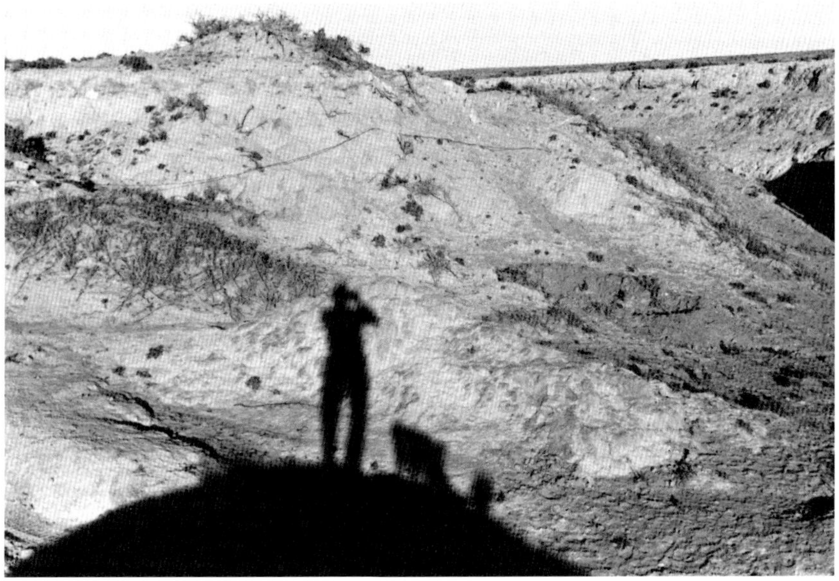

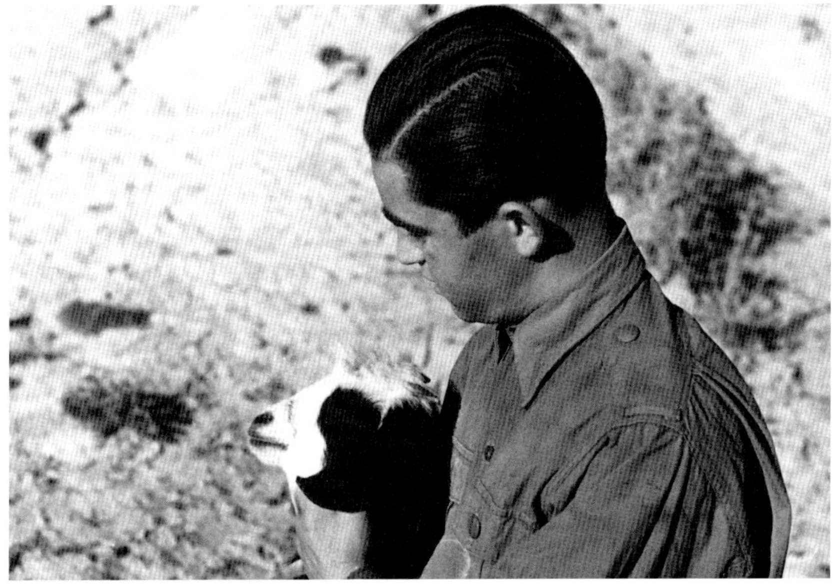

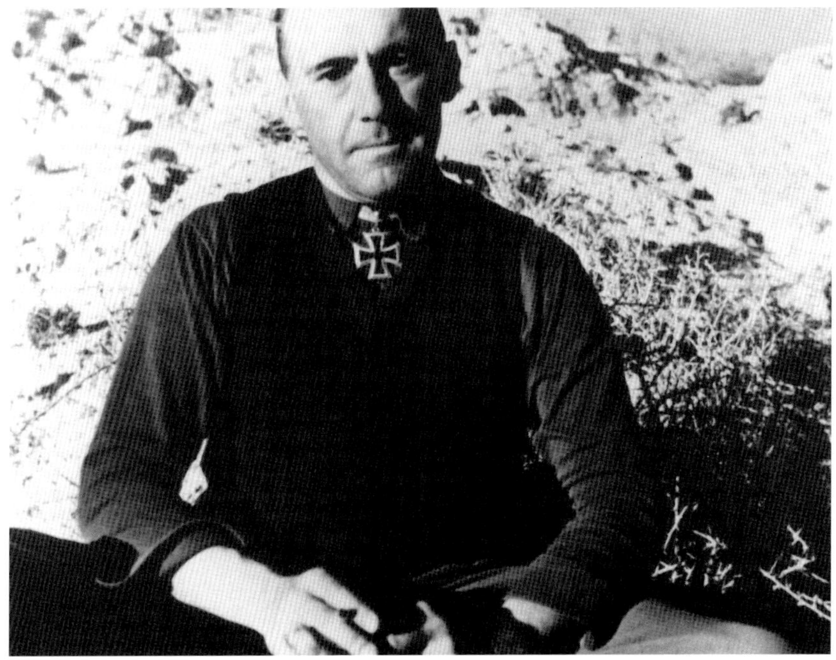

Above
Shadows outlined against the desert hillside, Bayerlein and his goat survey the landscape. Tunisia, 1943.

Top right
Oberleutnant Alexander Hartdegen, former aide to General Ritter von Thoma, petting the new little mascot. Tunisia, 1943.

Right
A reflective expression crosses Bayerlein's face, as Hartdegen catches of close-up photo of him. It is a rare photo taken of Bayerlein while smoking a cigarette, a habit that also aggravated his health problems. Tunisia, 1943.

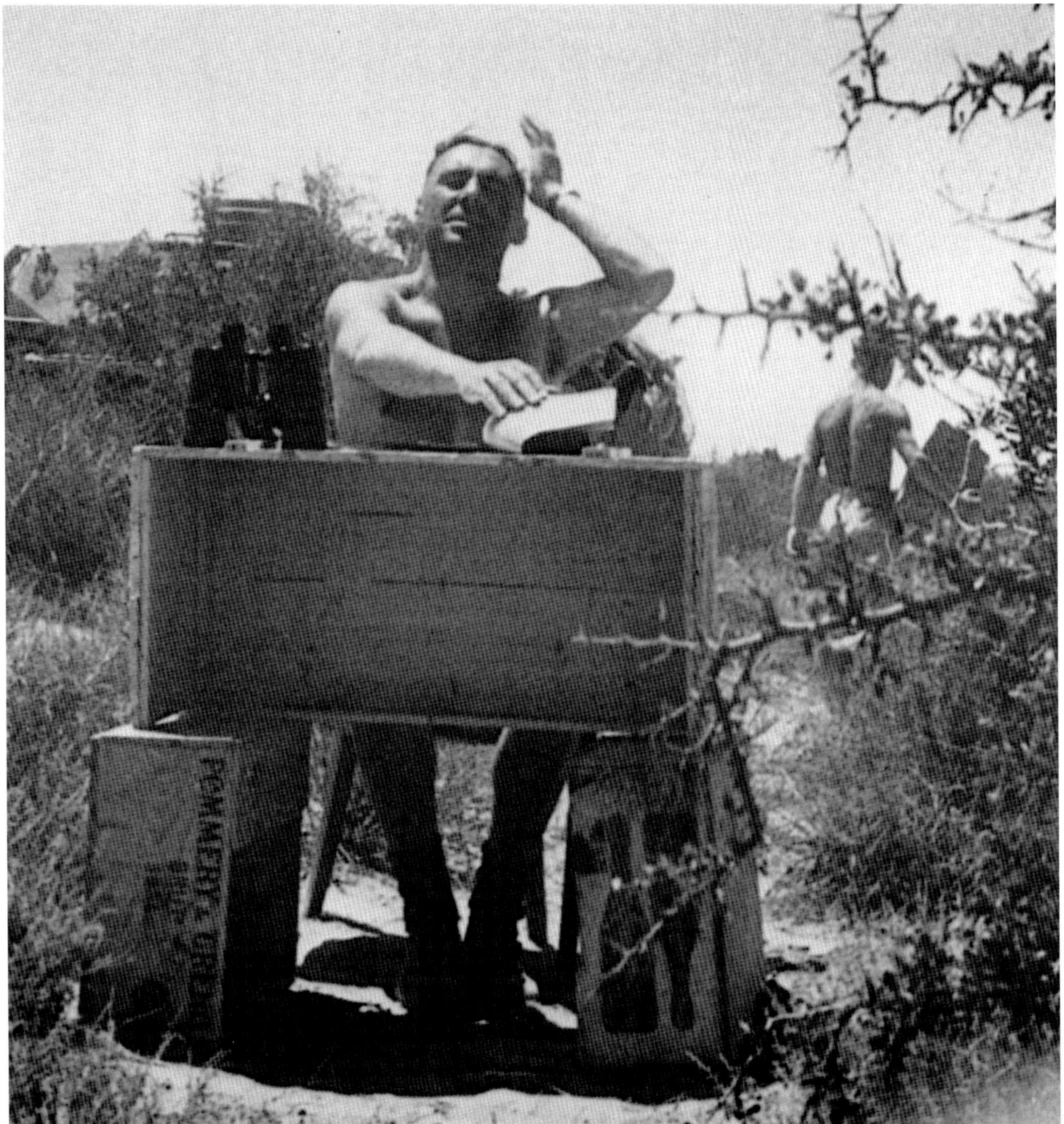

Left
With the camel thorn and a panzer as a backdrop, Bayerlein jokes around with the photographer.

Opposite
Bayerlein suns himself while reading at his makeshift wine-crate desk. His Chefs bus is parked nearby amid the camel thorn bushes. Tunisia, 1943.

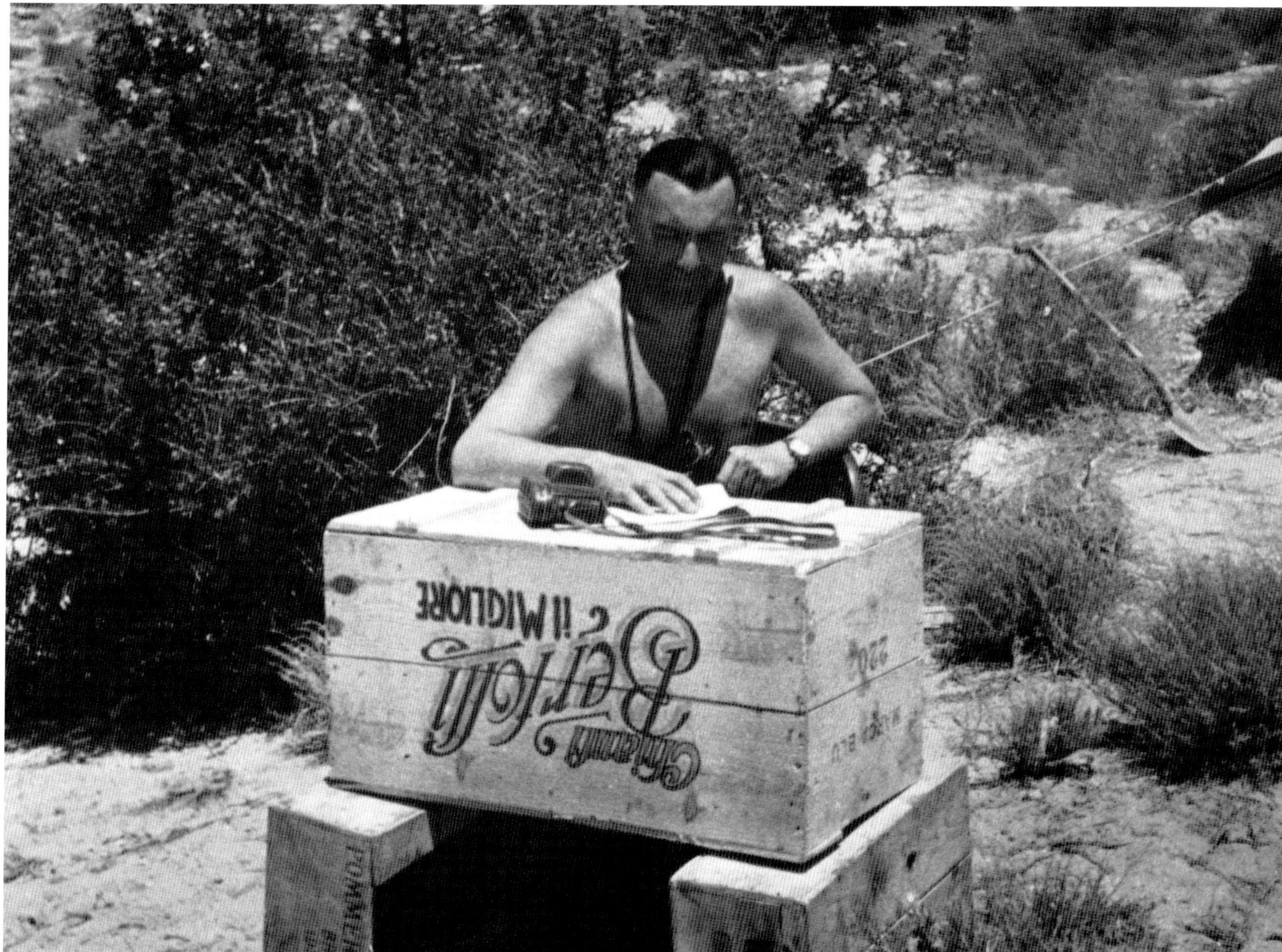

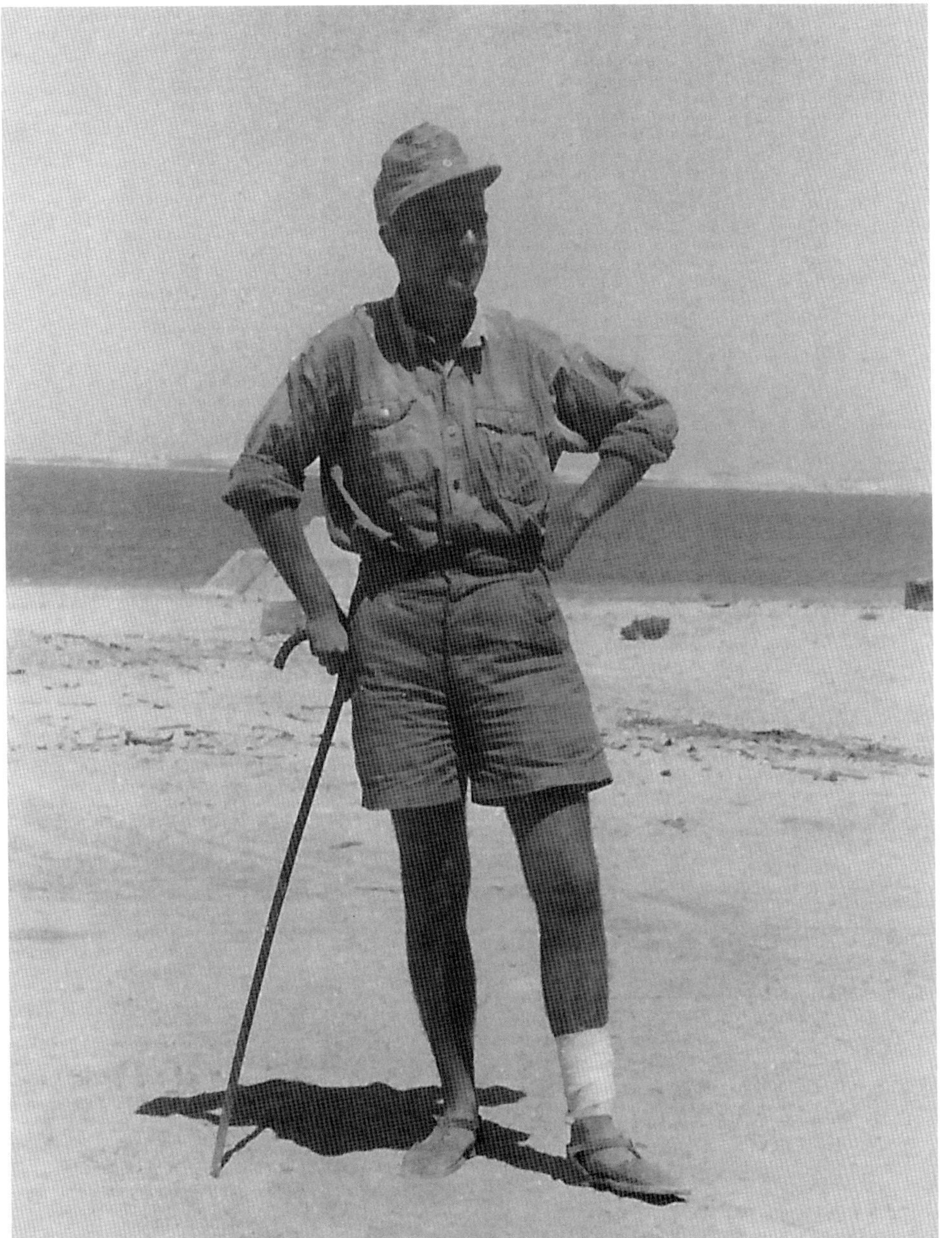

Opposite
Oberst Bayerlein with his friend and Ordannanzoffizier, Oberleutnant Alexander Hartdegen, who received his promotion to the higher rank on 1 June 1942. Photo captions reads: "Agedabia, November 1942" According to Mr. McGuirk, Agedabia was a very famous "watering hole" or "stopover" for the Afrikakorps. It is located on the famous coastal road (the Via Balbia) inland from the eastern end of the Gulf of Sirte. Agedabia was the site in 1941 and 1942 of a German rear area stores depot that supplied units passing units through with food and fuel and it also had such things as motor vehicle repair facilities. This photo was taken at the time when the Afrikakorps made it very last call at Agedabia. (Photo courtesy of the Hartdegen Family)[4]

Left
Oberleutnant Hartdegen, wounded in the summer of 1942, recovers at a base camp. "The sandals Hartdegen is wearing were commonplace, simply privately purchased examples of "leisure" footwear. Most were bought in the Arab bazaars, or from the Italian traders in the larger cities like Tripoli and Benghazi. These sandals were popular when not in the front line, where of course the soldiers would have had to follow whatever dress code was in force."[5] *According to Hartdegen's daughter, he was shot in the leg on July 21st, 1942.*[6] *(Photo courtesy of the Hartdegen family.)*

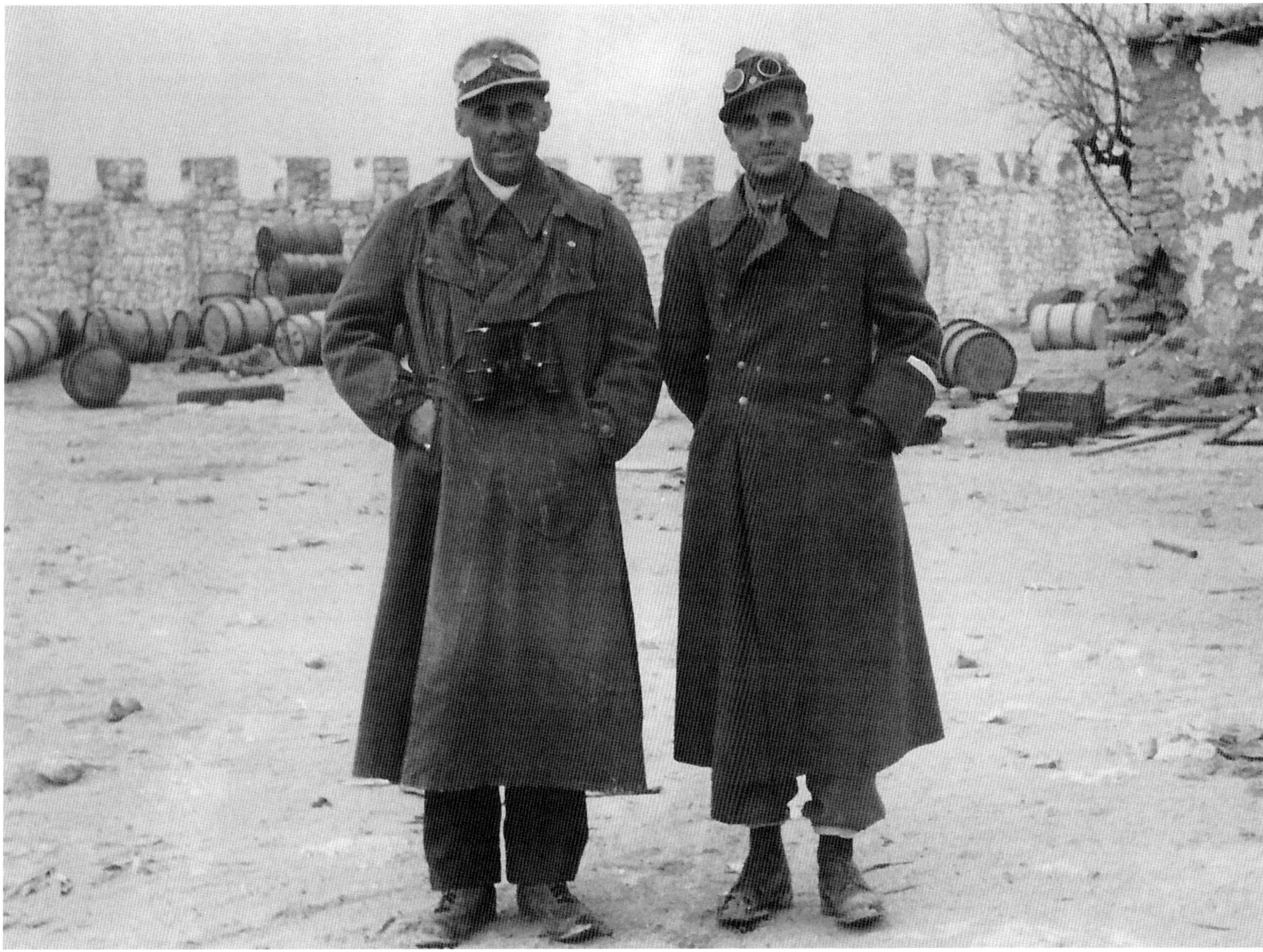

CHAPTER FOUR

THE FIELD MARSHAL

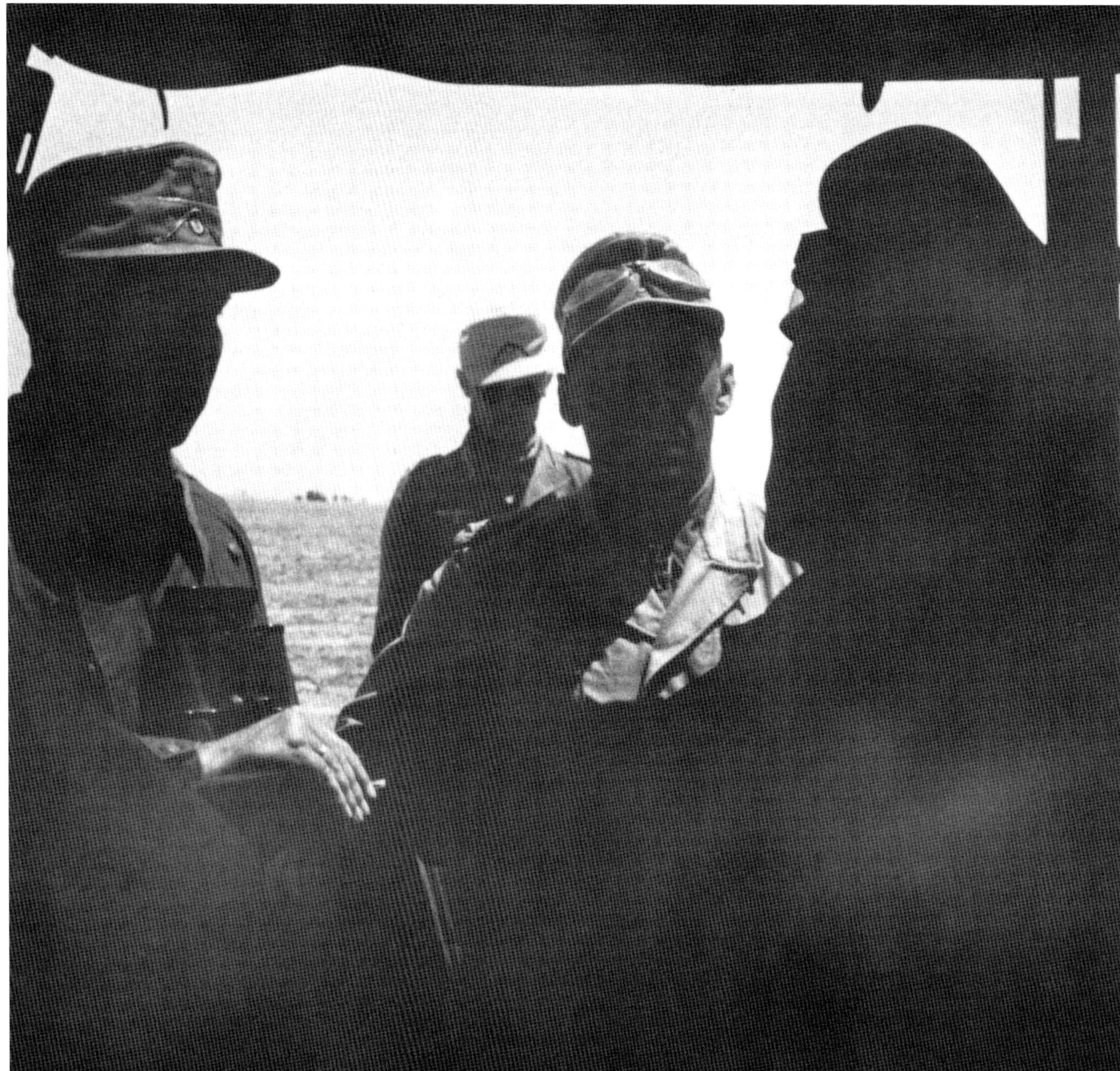

The unmistakable profile of Generalfeldmarschall Erwin Rommel. To his right, General Nehring, commander of the Deutsches Afrikakorps and his Stabschef (Chief-of-Staff) Oberst Bayerlein, consult with their commander.

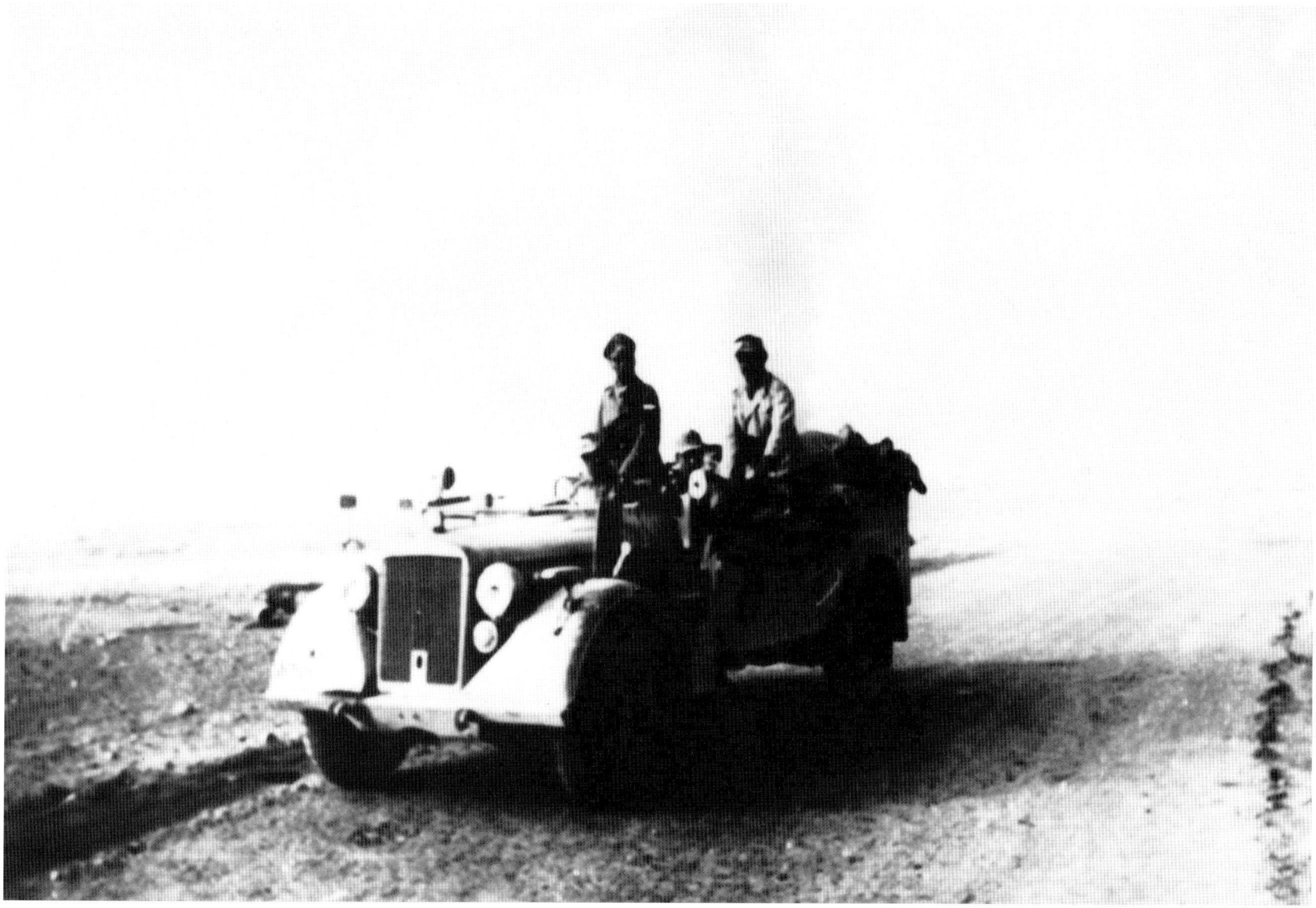

Rommel and Bayerlein in their staff car. Summer 1942.[1]

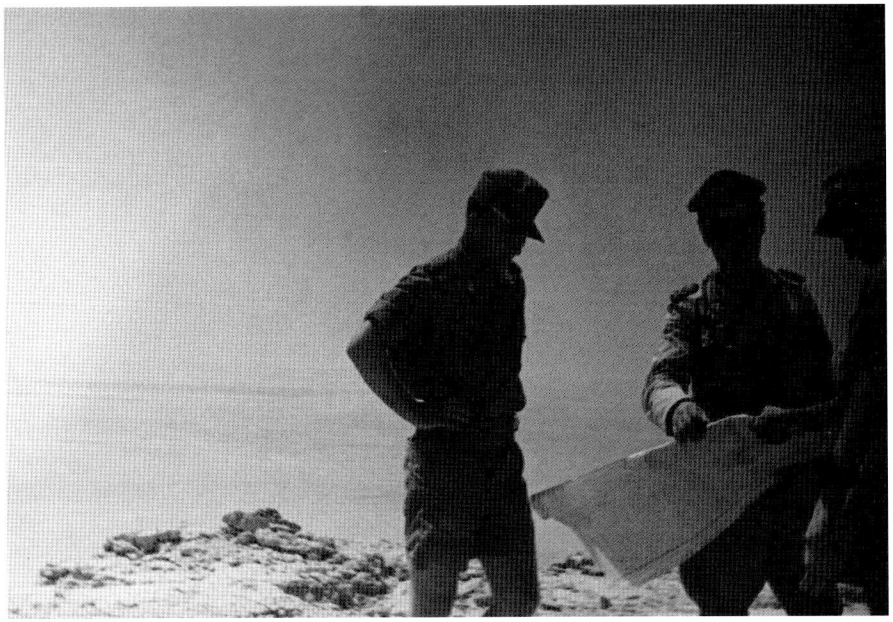

Left
Rommel, Bayerlein and another officer reading one of Bayerlein's ever-present maps.

Opposite
Bayerlein's handwritten note on the photo: "With Rommel in the Western Desert, 10-8-42." Photo appears to be taken from the back seat of Rommel's staff car as Rommel listens to a short briefing. Rommel never appeared to mind his photo being taken.

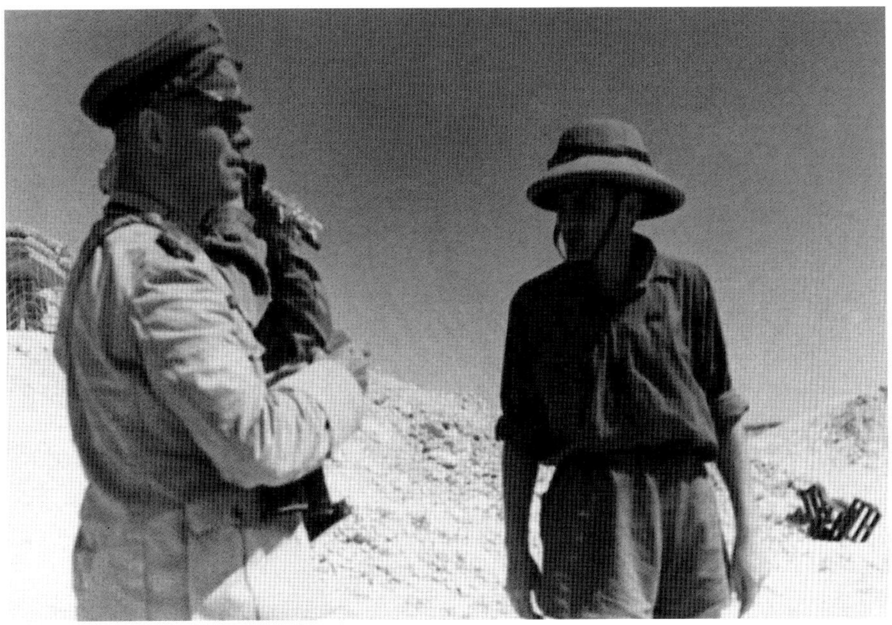

Left
Rommel speaking with one of the same officers from the briefing.

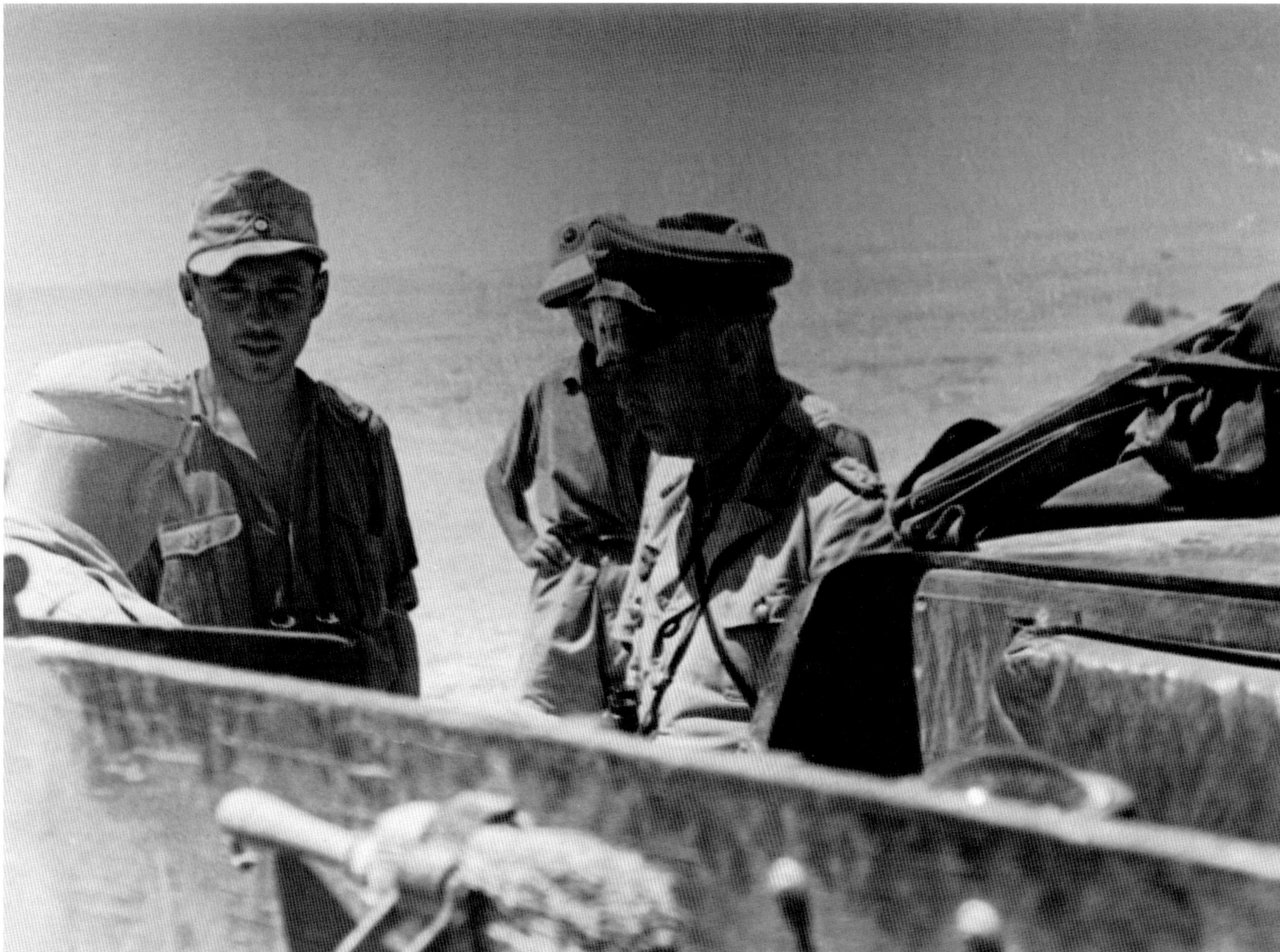

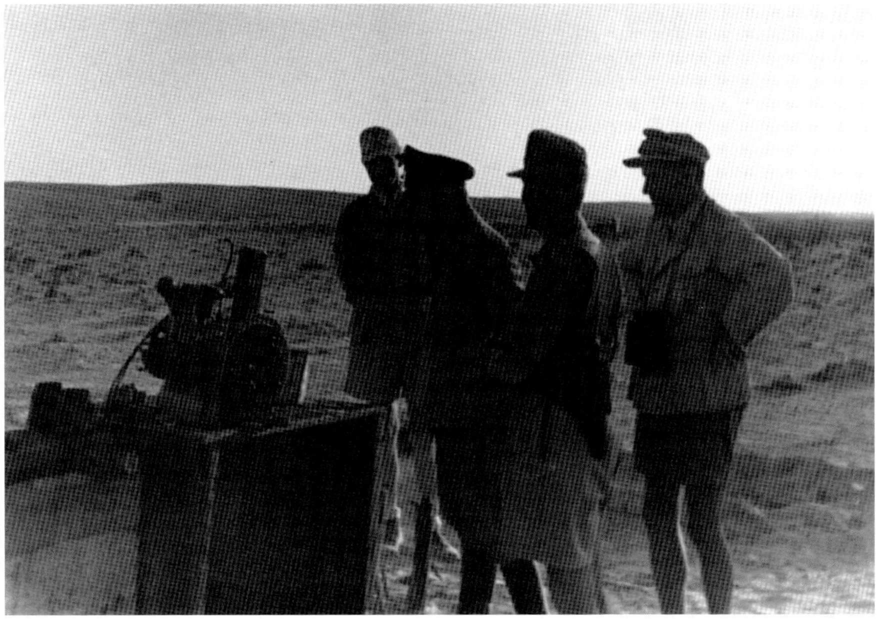

Left
August 1942, Rommel is examining some type of equipment – perhaps a pump – as Bayerlein and others look on. From their mutual interest, it may be of British manufacture.

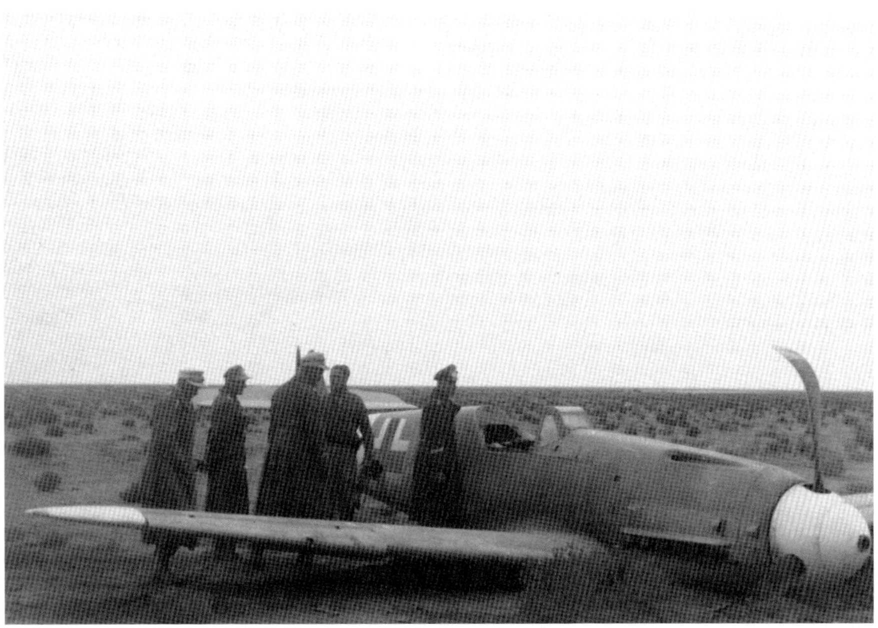

Left
Rommel and his staff examine a downed Messerschmitt Me 109 which has made a crash landing in the desert. One can presume due to the relatively intact condition of the aircraft the pilot survived. It is obvious from Rommel's new uniform that this photo was taken in late 1942 or in early 1943 during the retreat of the DAK from El Alamein to Tunisia.[2]

Opposite
Rommel and his command staff wait for field reports in their desert-worn staff car.

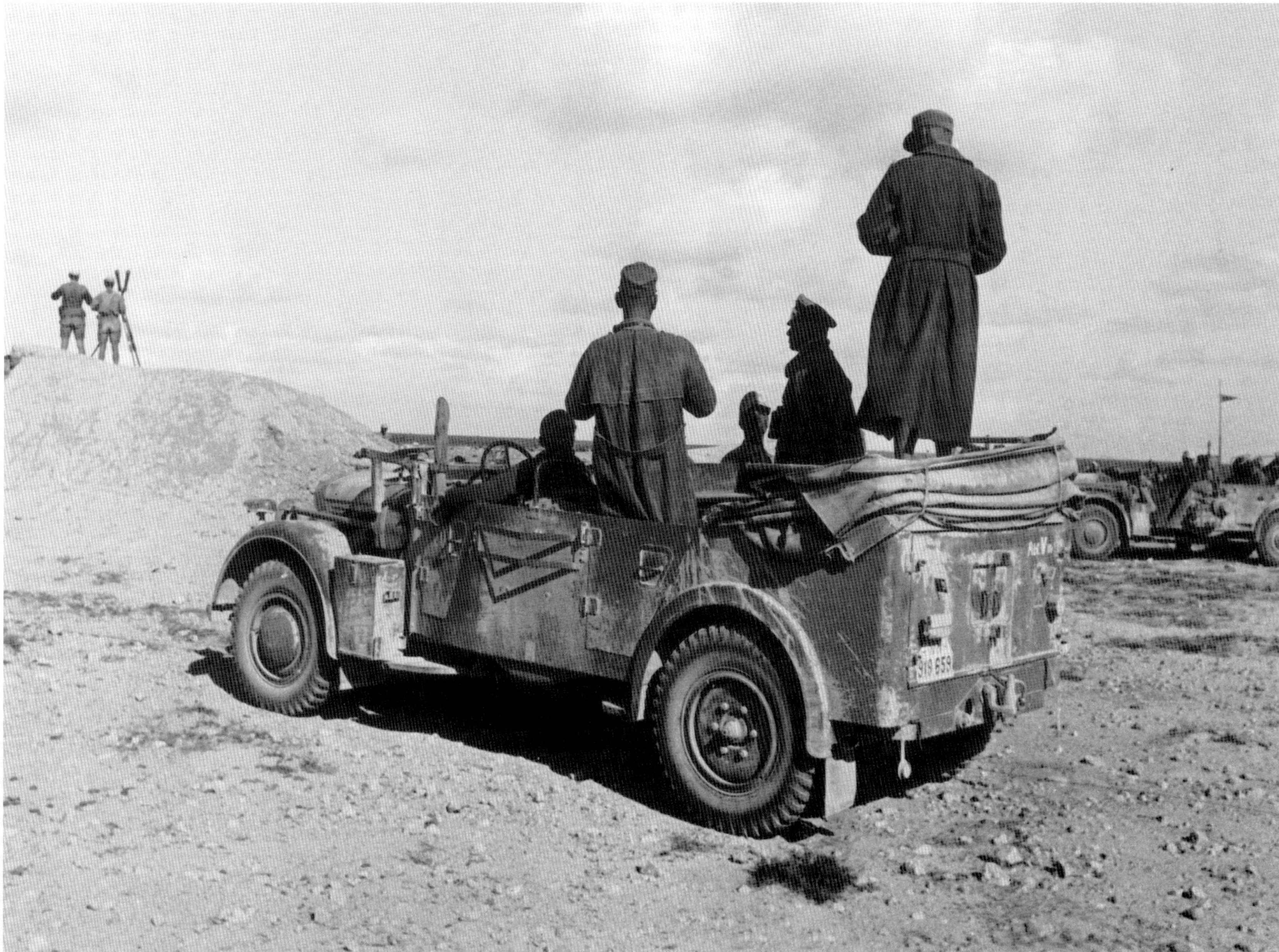

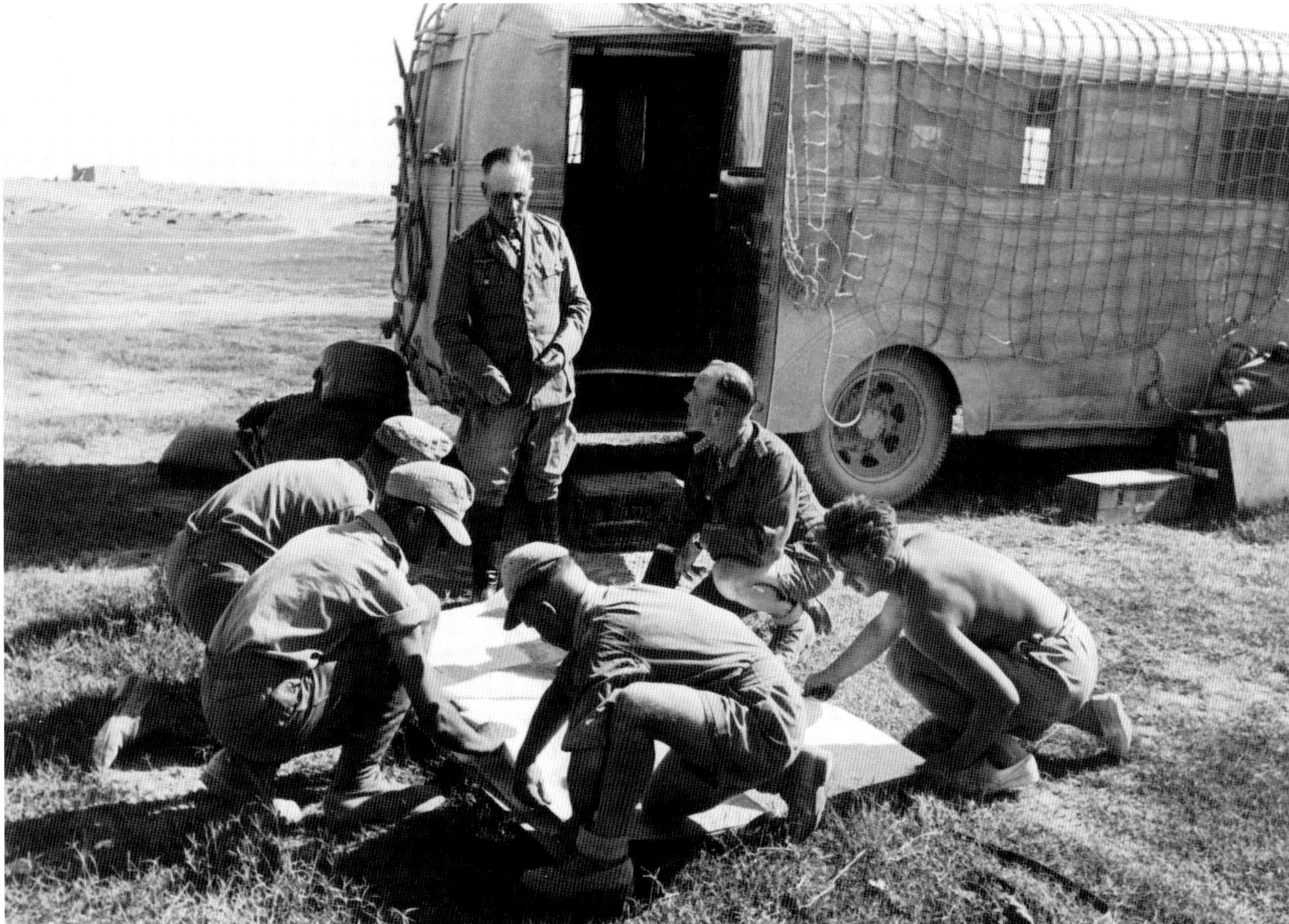

A tired and dusty Field Marshal examines the battle maps. Bayerlein's 'Chefs' bus is the vehicle in the background.

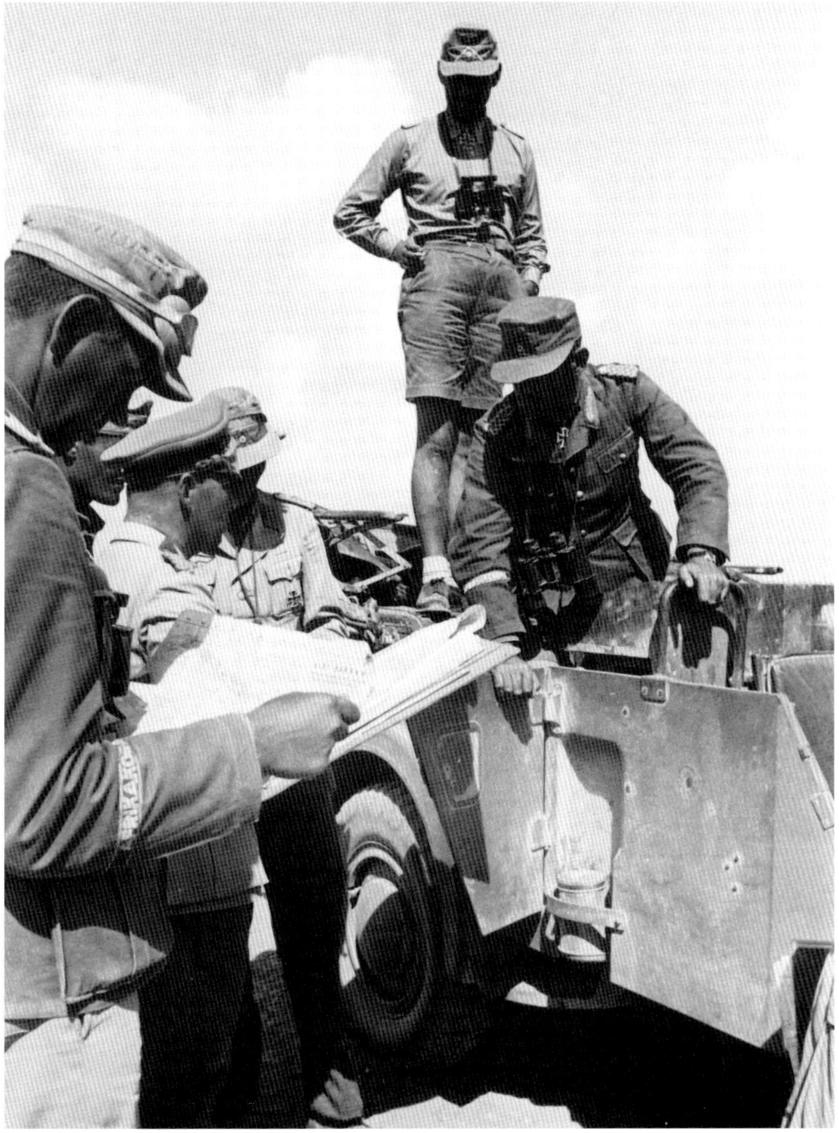

A constant analysis of position of friend and foe – and great attention to enemy positions – are marked on the maps.

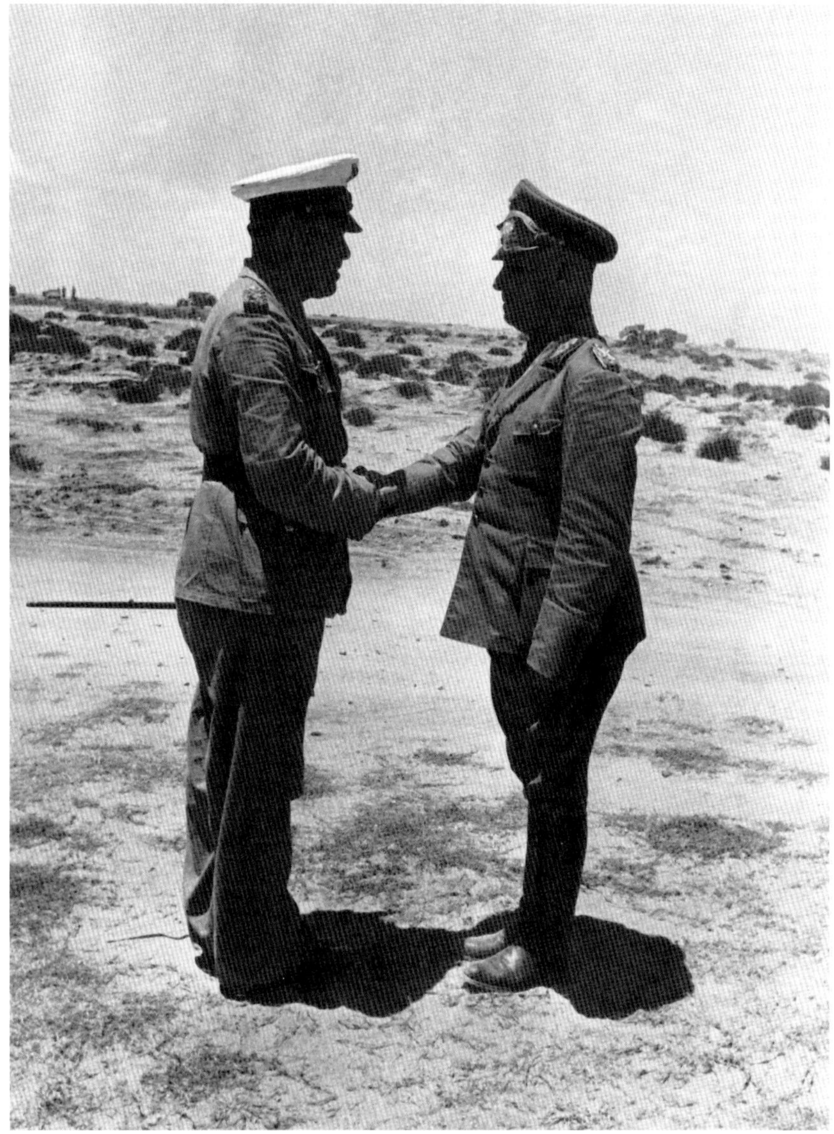

Field Marshal Albert Kesselring on one of his frequent field visits with Rommel. Facing Kesselring's constant over-optimism in the face of supply shortages, Rommel greets his guest.

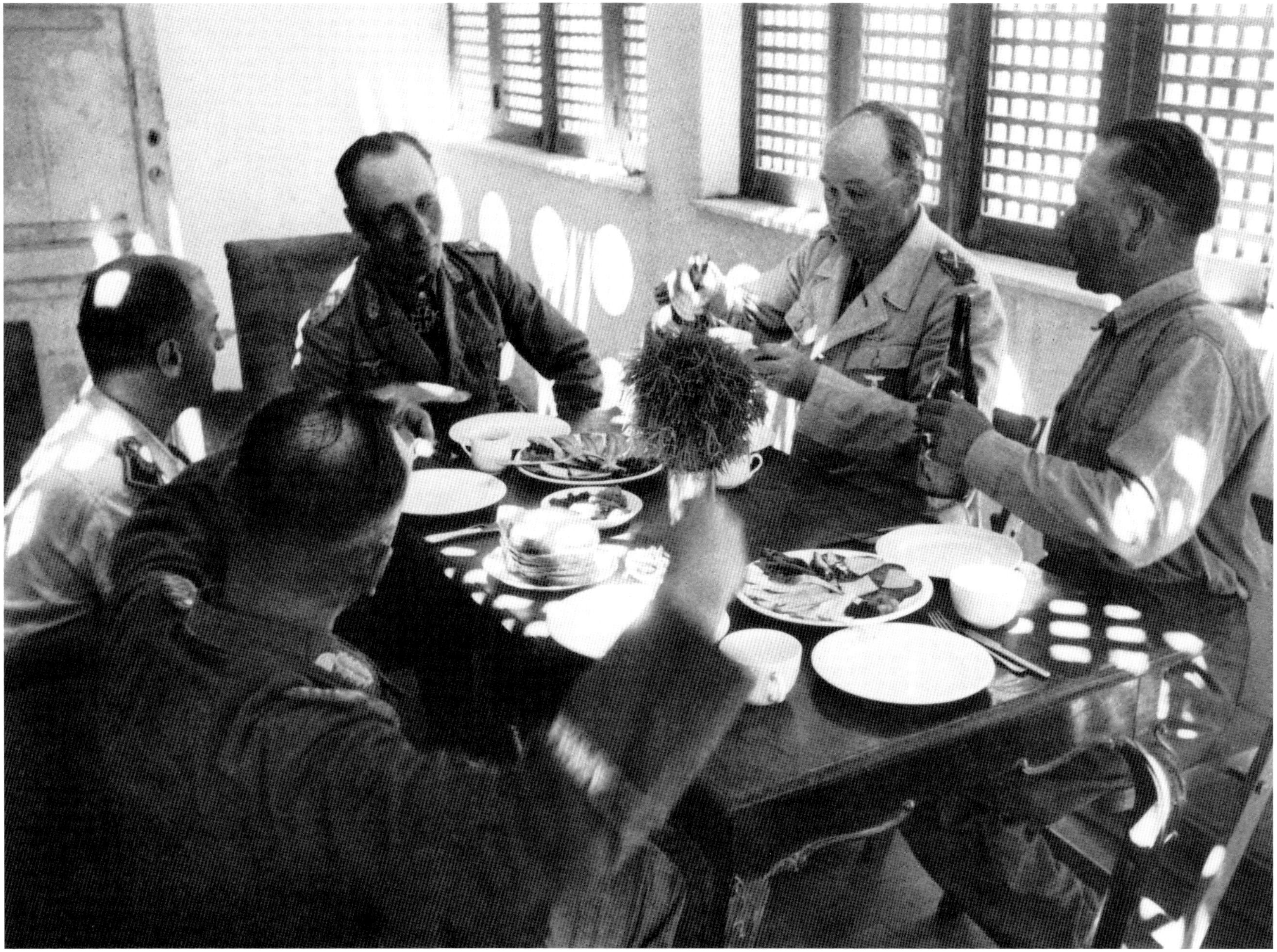

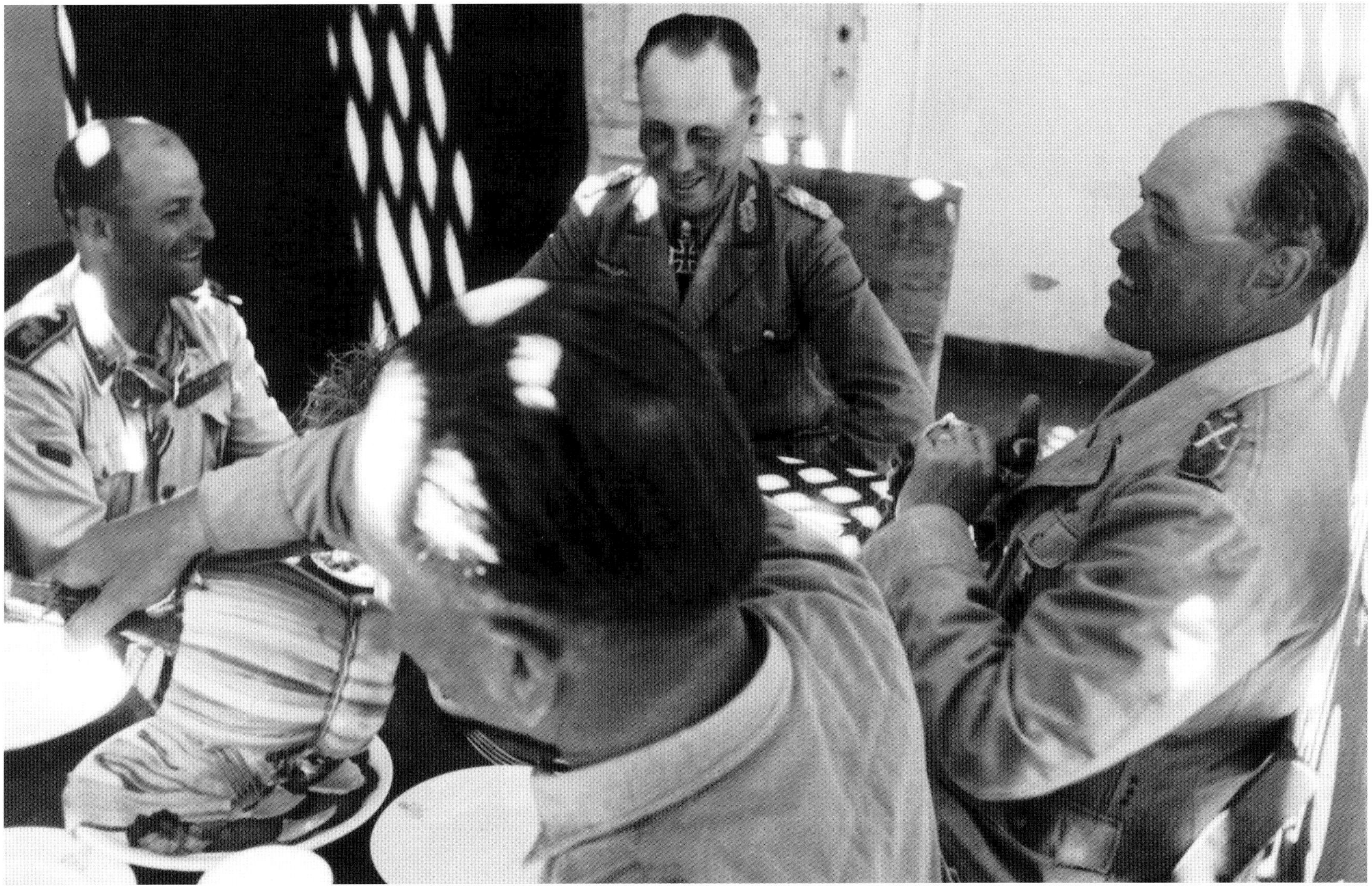

Opposite and above
A notably weary Rommel listens to an Italian officer, as the men enjoy their "Mittagessen" (lunch) of cold cuts and bread, washed down with wine. An equally dusty Kesselring helps himself to more wine. "The officer across the table from Kesselring is a Major of the Bersagalieri, (an elite rifle regiment – sometimes seen in photo's with cockerel plumes in their pith helmets). He has a wound strip on the right arm, and wears the typical tropical dress of an Italian officer in the desert. It appears he has the ribbon for the Iron cross second class in his tunic button."[3]

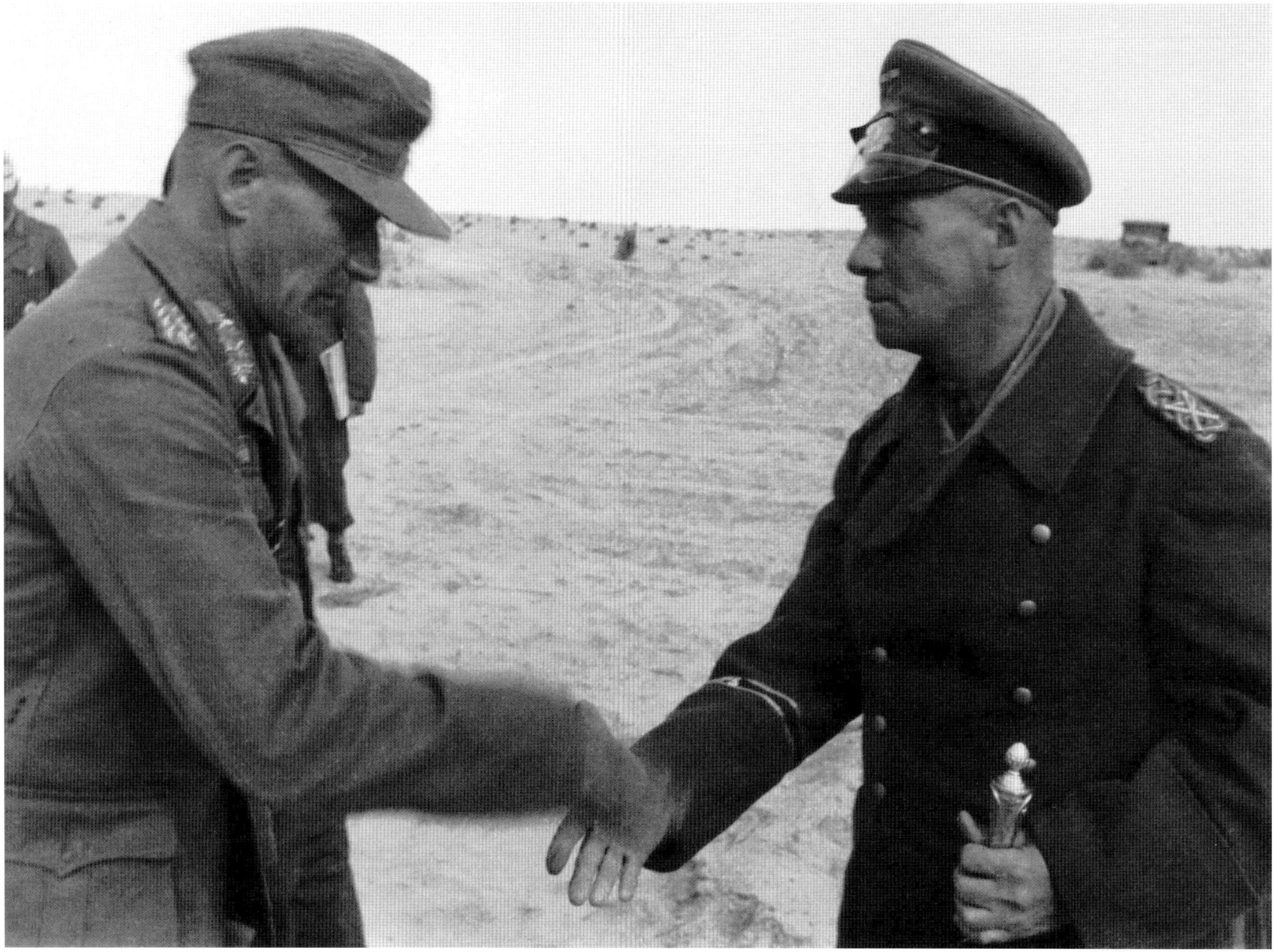

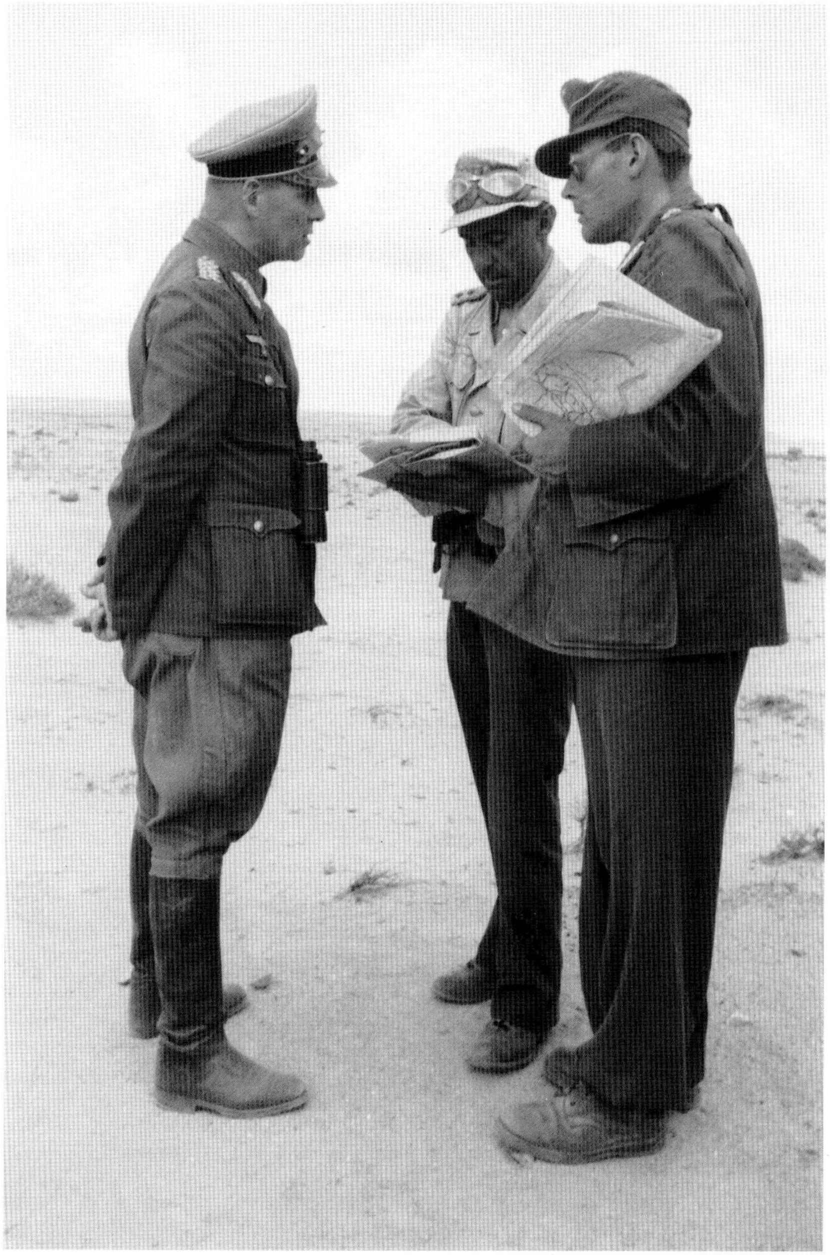

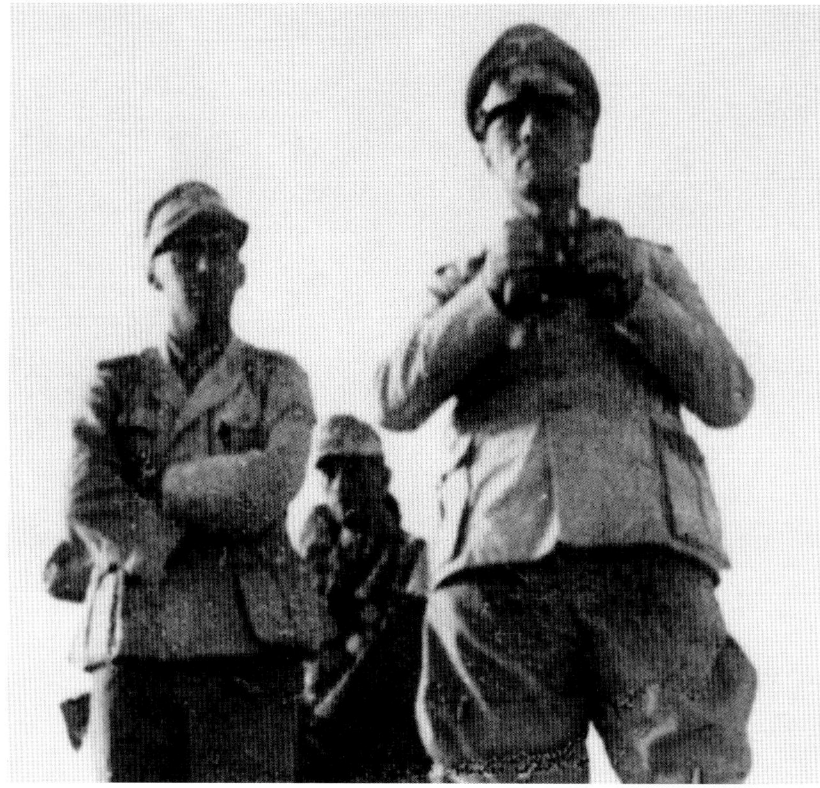

Opposite
Field Marshal Rommel greeting Generalmajor Theodor von Sponeck, commander of the 90th Light Division. It is interesting to note that Sponeck, a General, wears the field cap of an enlisted or other ranks soldier instead of the special version for officers with silver cording along the seams, indicating the general shortage of all uniform items at the time (photo taken at El Alamein, soon after Rommel's return from Germany in late October 1942).[4]

Left
Rommel, just recently returned from sick leave in Germany, arrives in Africa in late October 1942, just before the El Alamein battle. Bayerlein searches his maps to answer the Field Marshal's questions. Rommel awarded his old friend the "Deutsches Kreuz in Gold" in the same sequence of photographs.

Above
Attentive, Bayerlein watches his commander observe the El Alamein fighting in the distance.[5]

CHAPTER FIVE

THE AFRICAN BATTLEFIELD - THE DESERT

"Bayerlein was not an exception in taking so many shots of the desert. Similarly, the Germans who served in North Africa appeared impressed with the landscape and tried to capture something of what they saw on film." — Dal McGuirk, author.

• • •

The desert landscape of Tunisia, Libya, Cyrenaica and Egypt contains oases, a salt marsh, and an enormous escarpment that separates the coast from the high desert interior. The Jebel Achdar (Green Mountains) near the coast west of Tobruk, the Qattara Depression, a salt marsh located southwest of Alexandria, and the Via Balbia, and the ancient coastal road are the major landscape characteristics of the North African theatre. The Jebel el Akhdar or "Green Mountain" is a limestone plateau which rises to a height of over about 500 feet and extends for 150 miles east of Benghazi, following along the coast of Cyrenaica. Wadis bisect the escarpement and provide water run-off and sudden flooding during the winter months.

Opposite
"This view looks across a stony expanse of flat ground to a distant escarpment. The stony surface of the desert evident in this photo is typical of what one would have seen over much of the Libyan Plateau in eastern Cyrenaica where the bitterly fought battles of November and December 1941 were fought. There are indications that the photo was taken near the coast from the appearance of cloud cover over the right hand hemisphere of the sky. In photos that included views of both the coastal strip and inland desert it is often possible to tell the direction of the camera because of the color (or lack of color) of the sky. The atmosphere over the desert was almost devoid of moisture while the air over the coastal region was nowhere near as dry. The absence of moisture in the atmosphere over the desert gave the sky there a very washed out color. If one was looking at a color photo, say taken looking down the coastal road with the sky arcing from the sea on one side to the open desert on the other, one would see a rich blue sky on one side that gradually faded to a steel-gray color sky on the other."[1]

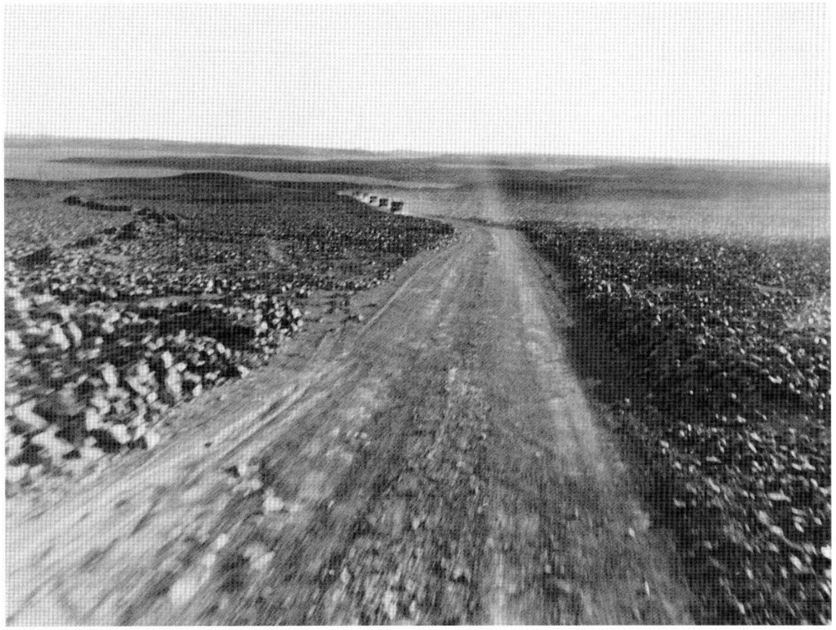

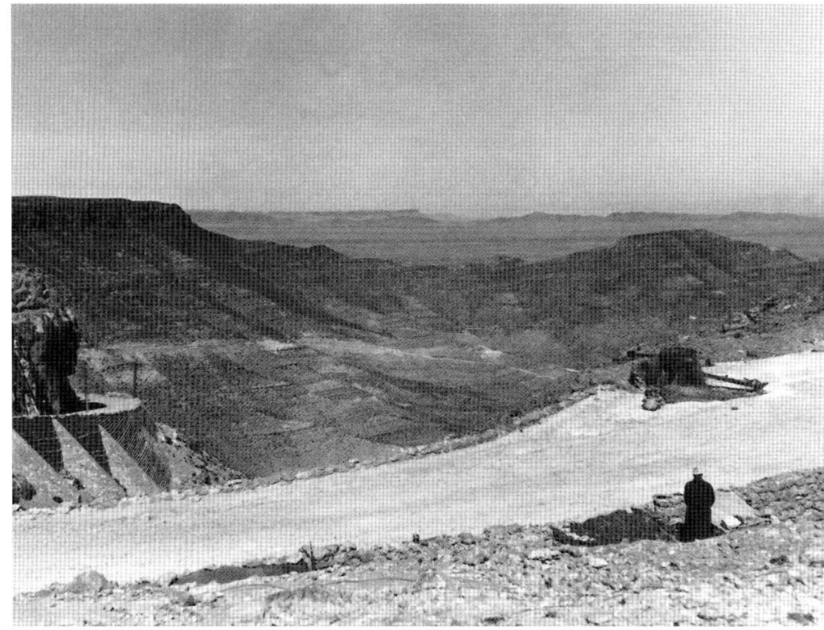

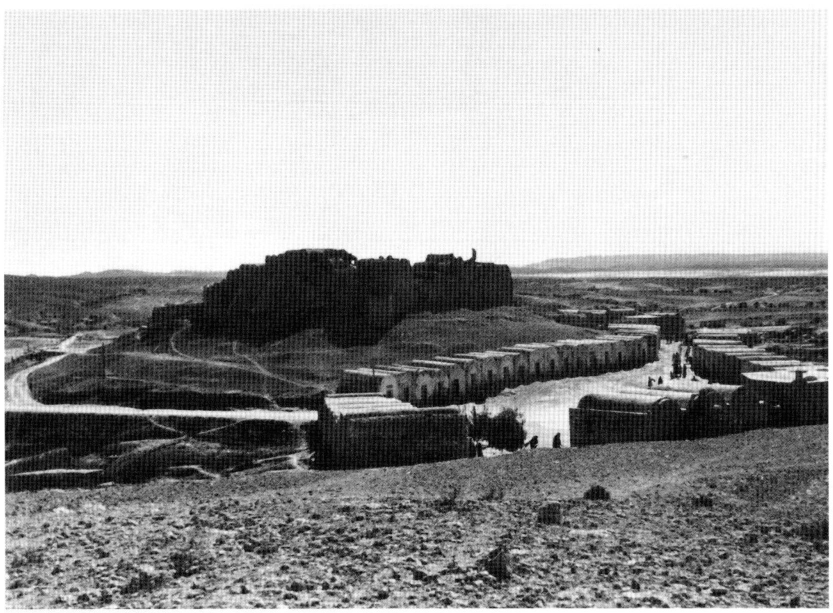

Top left
A long expanse of rock and dust greets Bayerlein along a road linking old desert forts. The vehicles maintain a lengthy following distance to avoid kicking up large dust clouds to draw the attention of any British reconnaissance aircraft – or worse yet – the attention of roving fighter-bombers that would soon relentlessly badger the Afrikakorps and their hapless Italian allies.

Above
A gun-crew member watches over the escarpments on the winding road to the coast. Halfaya as well as Sollum had passes with adequate dirt and gravel roads that wound up the steep escarpments, allowing access from the coastal region to the high Libyan desert.

Left
Newer village huts constructed of available stone surround a larger desert fort.

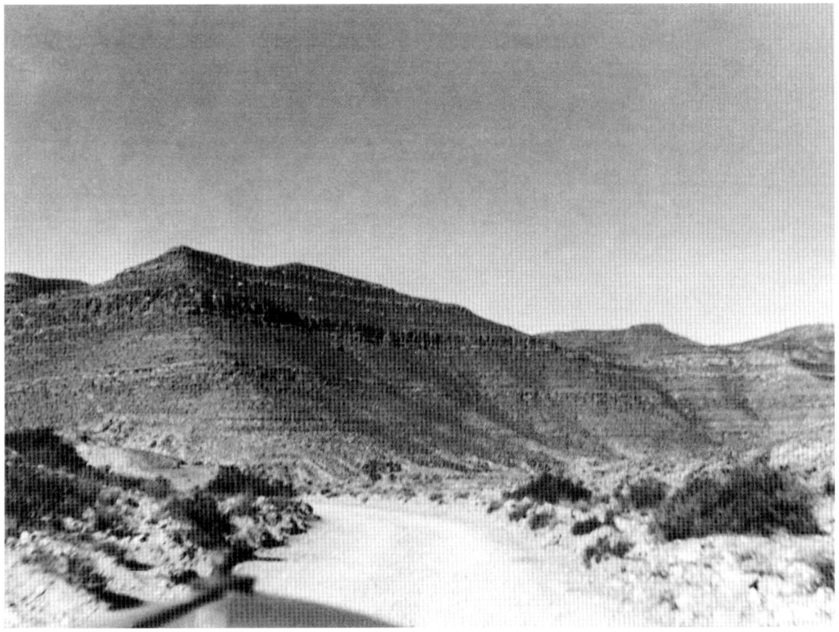

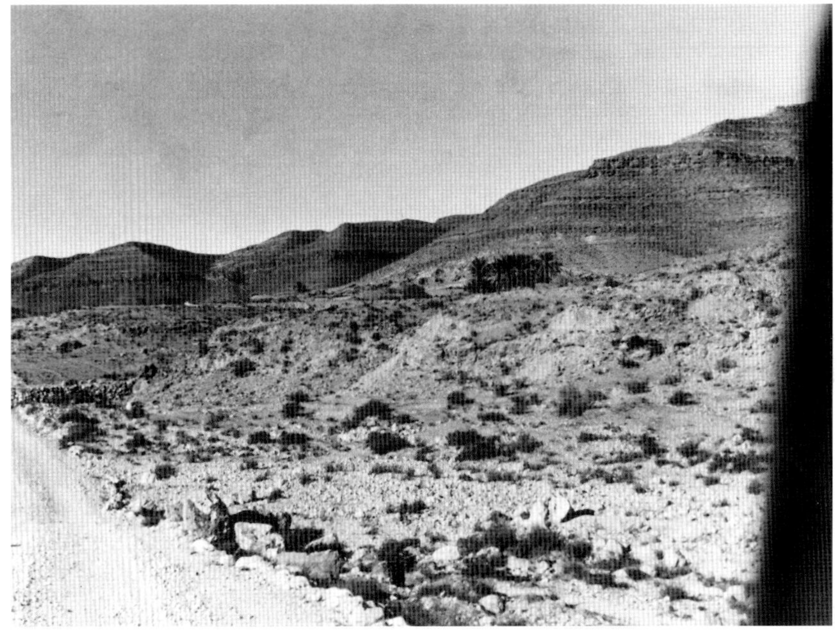

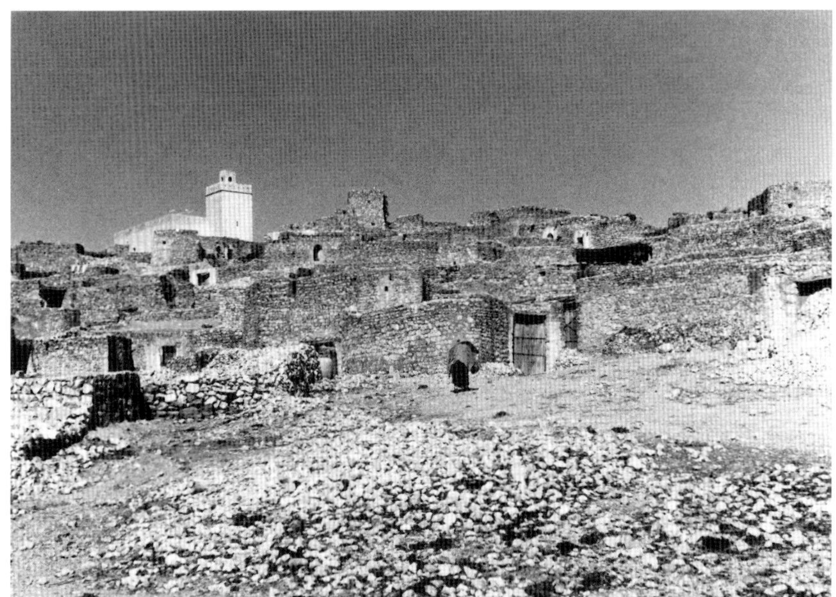

Above
Typical Tunisian landscape of rolling hills and brush.

Top right
Bayerlein's group winds its way amid the indiscernible hills of the endless landscape.

Right
The new amidst the old. A modern building tops the crest of the hill.

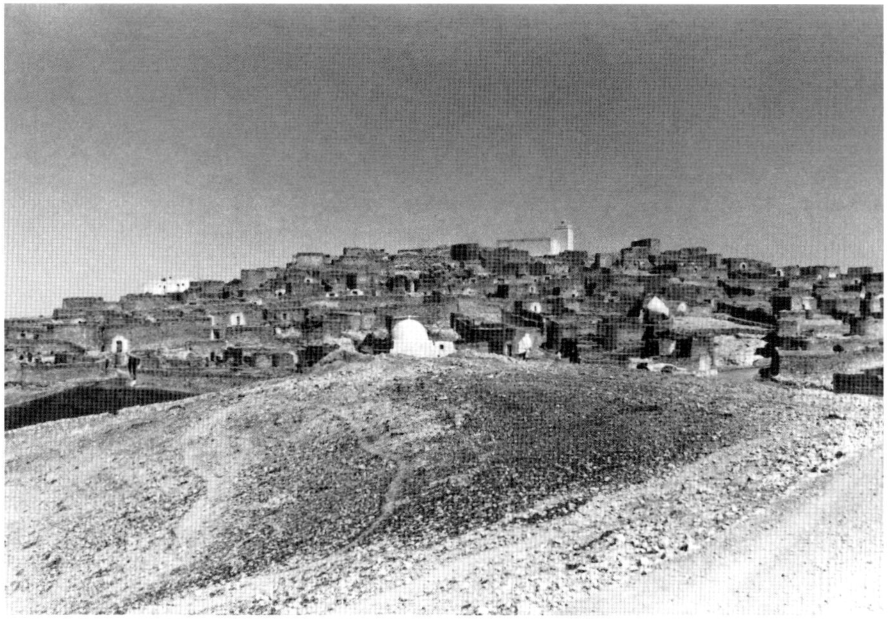

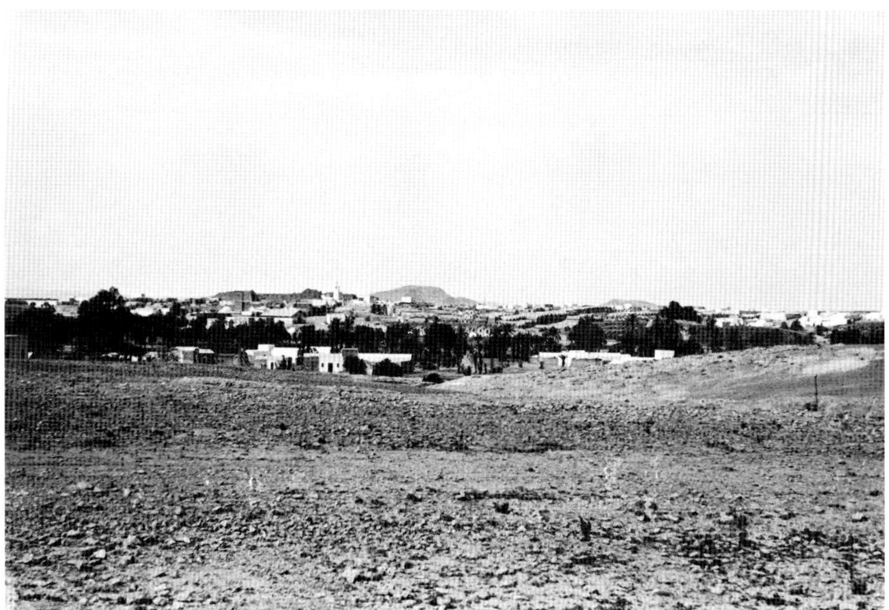

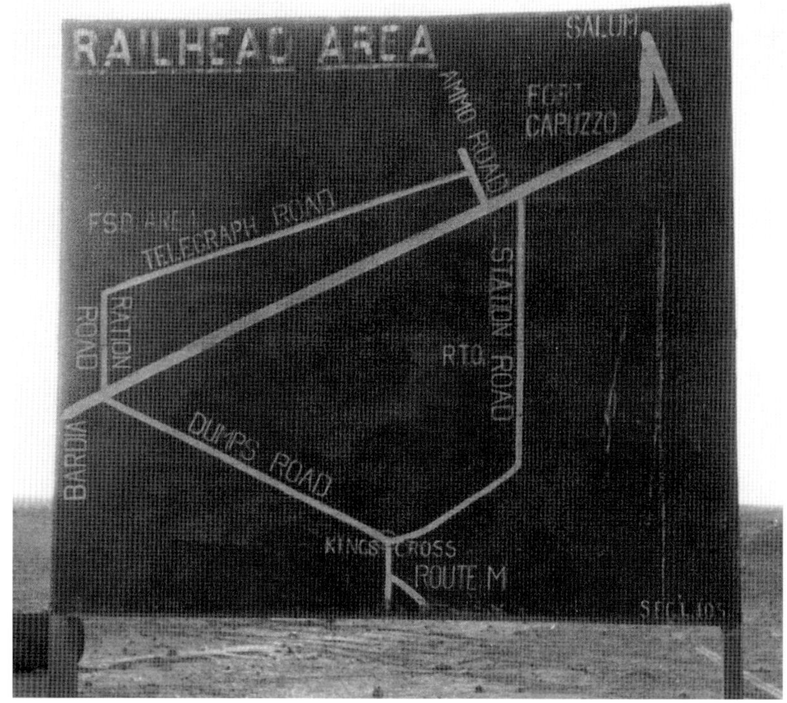

Top left
A different view of the hilltop shows the familiar domed mosque and villagers' stone houses.

Left
Town of El Gazala, Egypt. A respite of greenery breaks up the monotony of desert rocks.

Above
"The signpost is located inside the Egyptian border and marks the point at which the New Zealand Army Railway Construction Companies extended the Egyptian coastal rail line towards the Libyan frontier in 1941 and 1942." (Dal McGuirk.)[2]

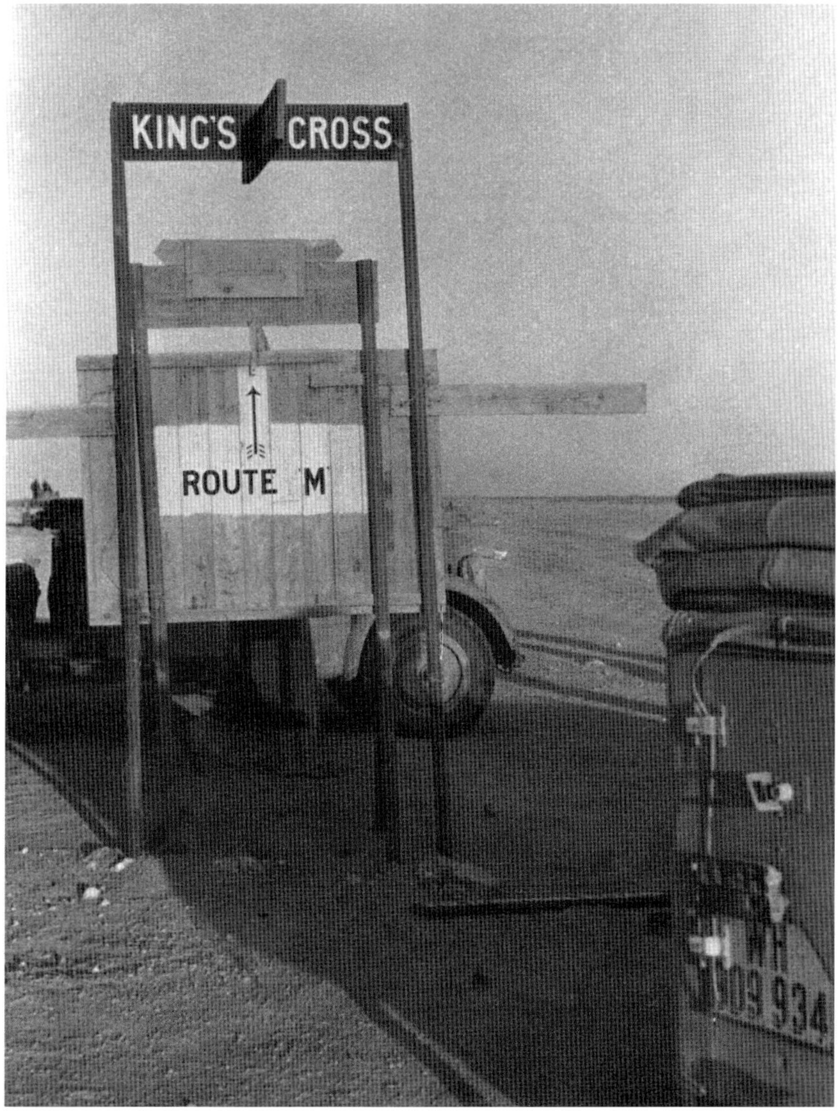

King's Cross is due south of Tobruk. Photo taken in June 1942. King's Cross is also one of the Underground rail stops in London. Bayerlein was impressed enough with the British signpost enough to record it. The marker matches the Fort Cappuzo/Solum/Bardia sign, which provides more detailed directions.

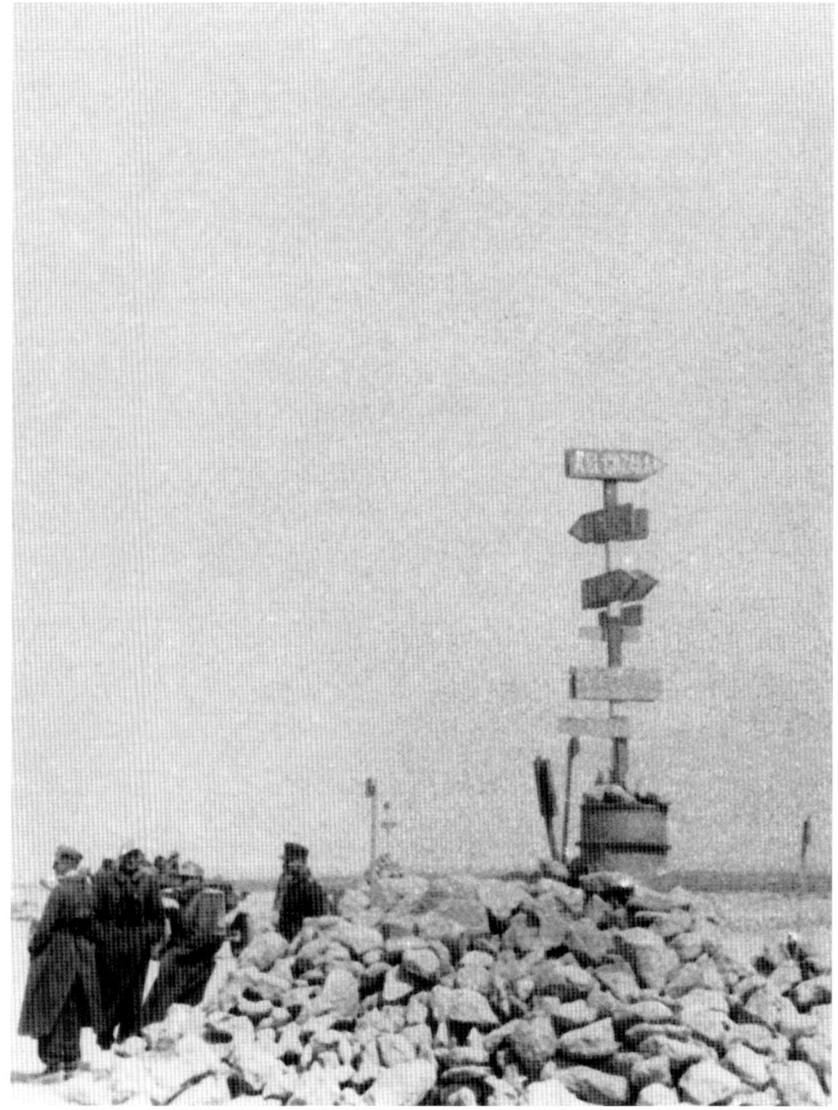

Top sign reads a faded 'Al Gazala' one of the villages on the coastal road on the path to Tobruk.[3] *Staff officers and soldiers meet and wait for further march orders at the British crossroad.*

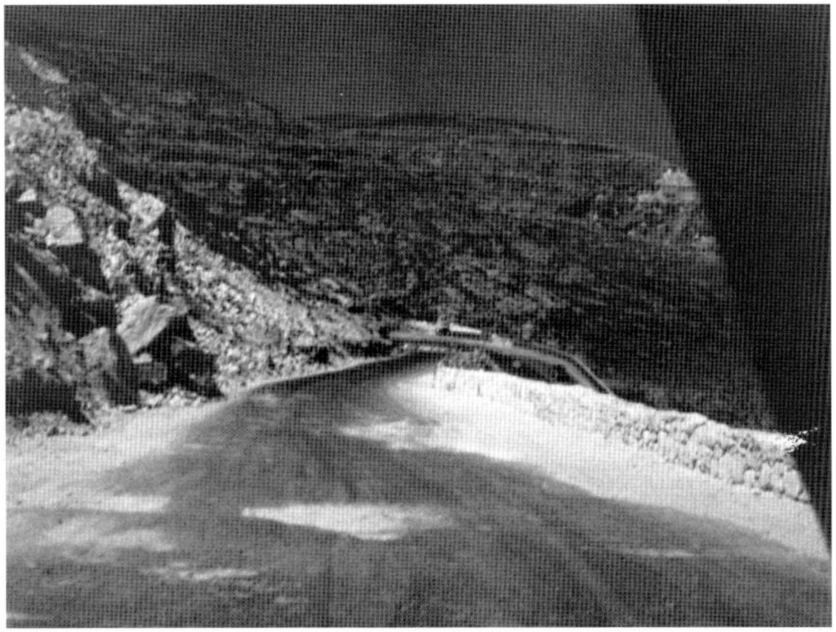

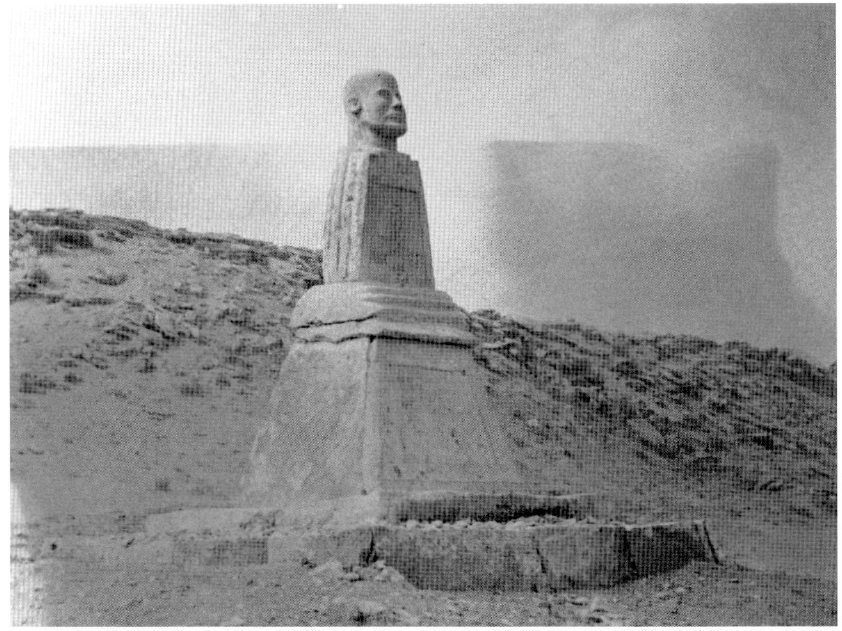

Above
The difference between the high desert plateau and the lower sea level land is evident from the steep slope to the right.

Top right
Bayerlein's handwritten note on back of photo reads: "17.10 [1941], 'Manhz, Mussolini.'"

Right
A rough and rutted dirt road – a path through the desert. The vehicles are spaced at a distance to minimize dust clouds, blending in with the normal desert horizon heat haze.

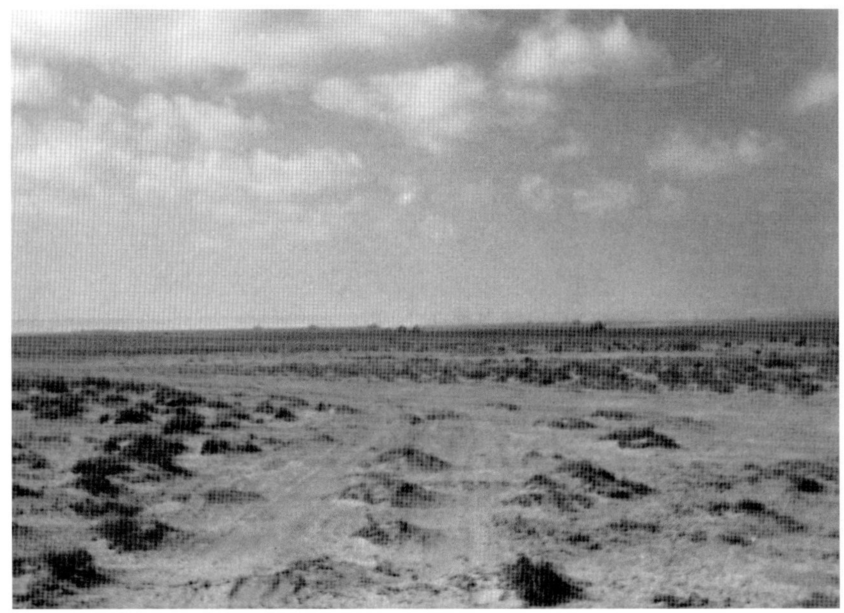

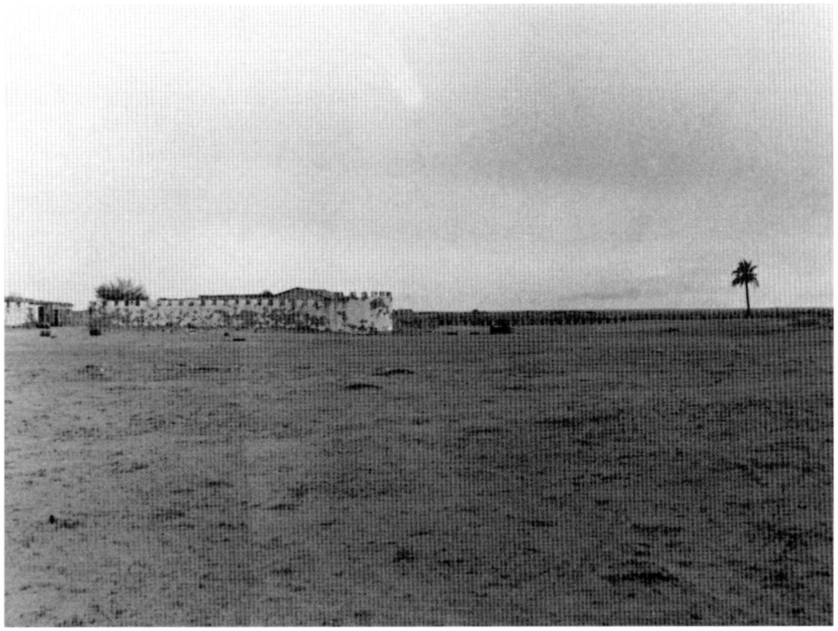

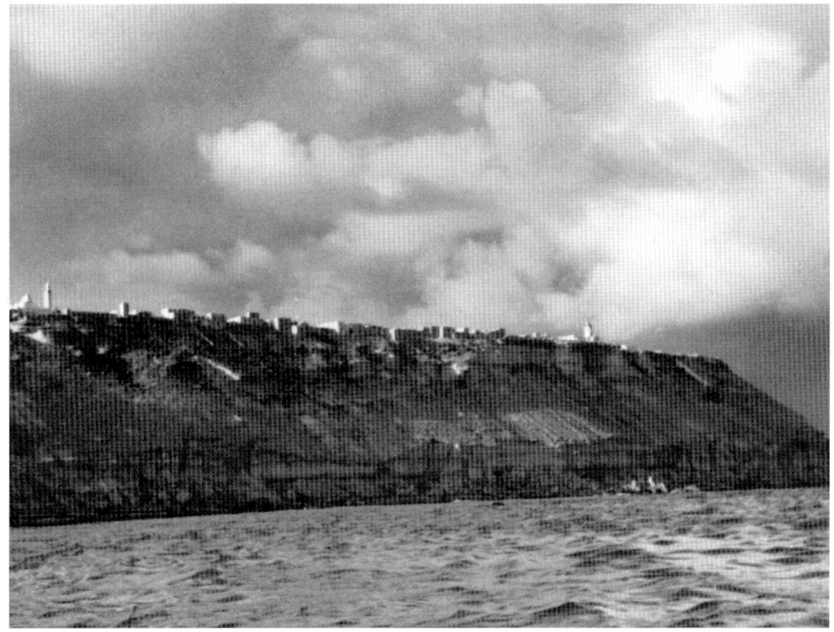

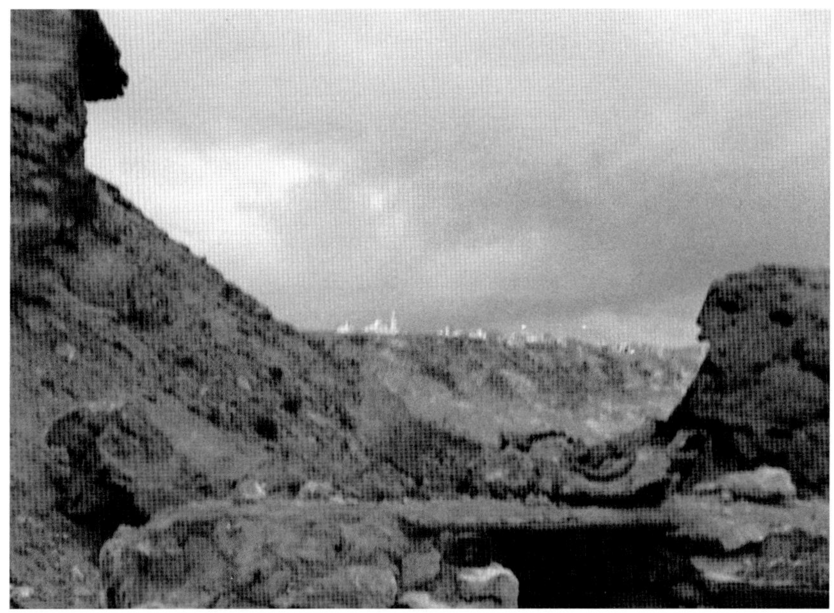

Above
From the round and low turrets, the old desert fort appears to be En-Nofilia. The Italians built many forts throughout Libya. A lone scraggly palm tree ekes out a survival in the sand.

Top right
Bayerlein took a series of photos of Bardia, located on the edge of an escarpment overlooking the Mediterranean Sea.

Right
Bardia from a different angle, as Bayerlein scrambled to frame his subject by the rock outcroppings in the inlet. The town appears to have intrigued him by its dynamic view of the sea.

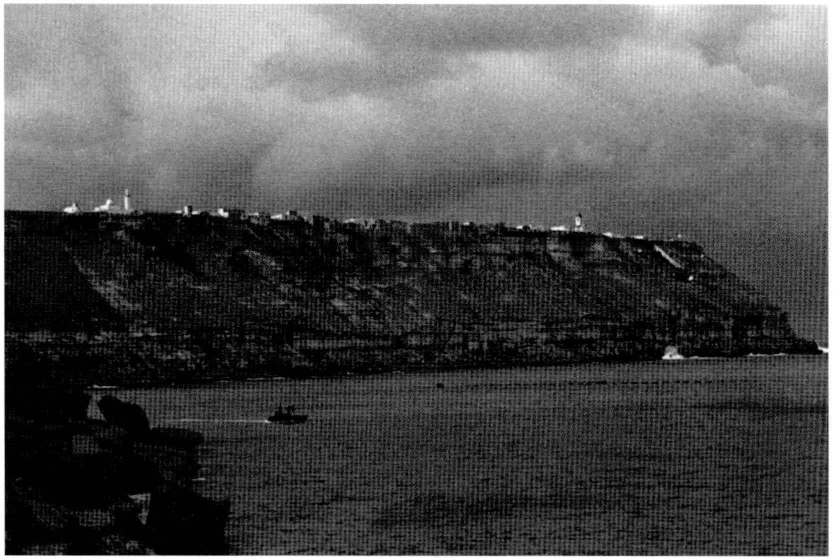

Left
A distant storm brews over Bardia from it's overlook on the Mediterranean – a beautiful location on a cliff top with the distinctive tower of the minaret always visible no matter from what angle the photos were taken.[4]

Opposite
An enormous old Turkish desert fort overlooks a small inlet harbor of Derna in northern Cyrenaica. The two men walking toward the photographer appear to be General Albert Gause, Rommel's Chief-of-Staff (left) and another staff officer. Gause was wounded in the fighting at Tobruk in June 1942, and Bayerlein temporarily replaced him.

Below
Taking a long walk on a hot day, Bayerlein is dwarfed by the immense size of the desert fort in the distance behind him. He's carrying his greatcoat over his shoulder. There were many Italian and old Turkish forts in the desert.

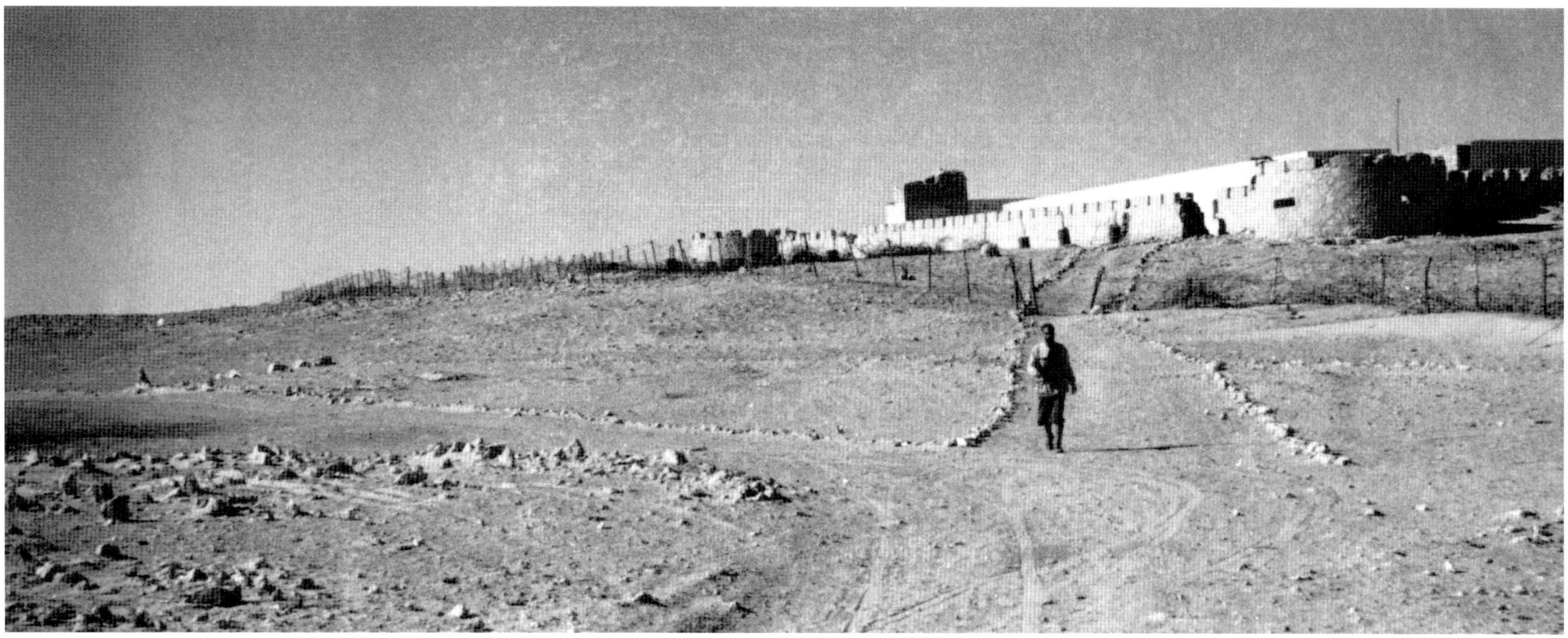

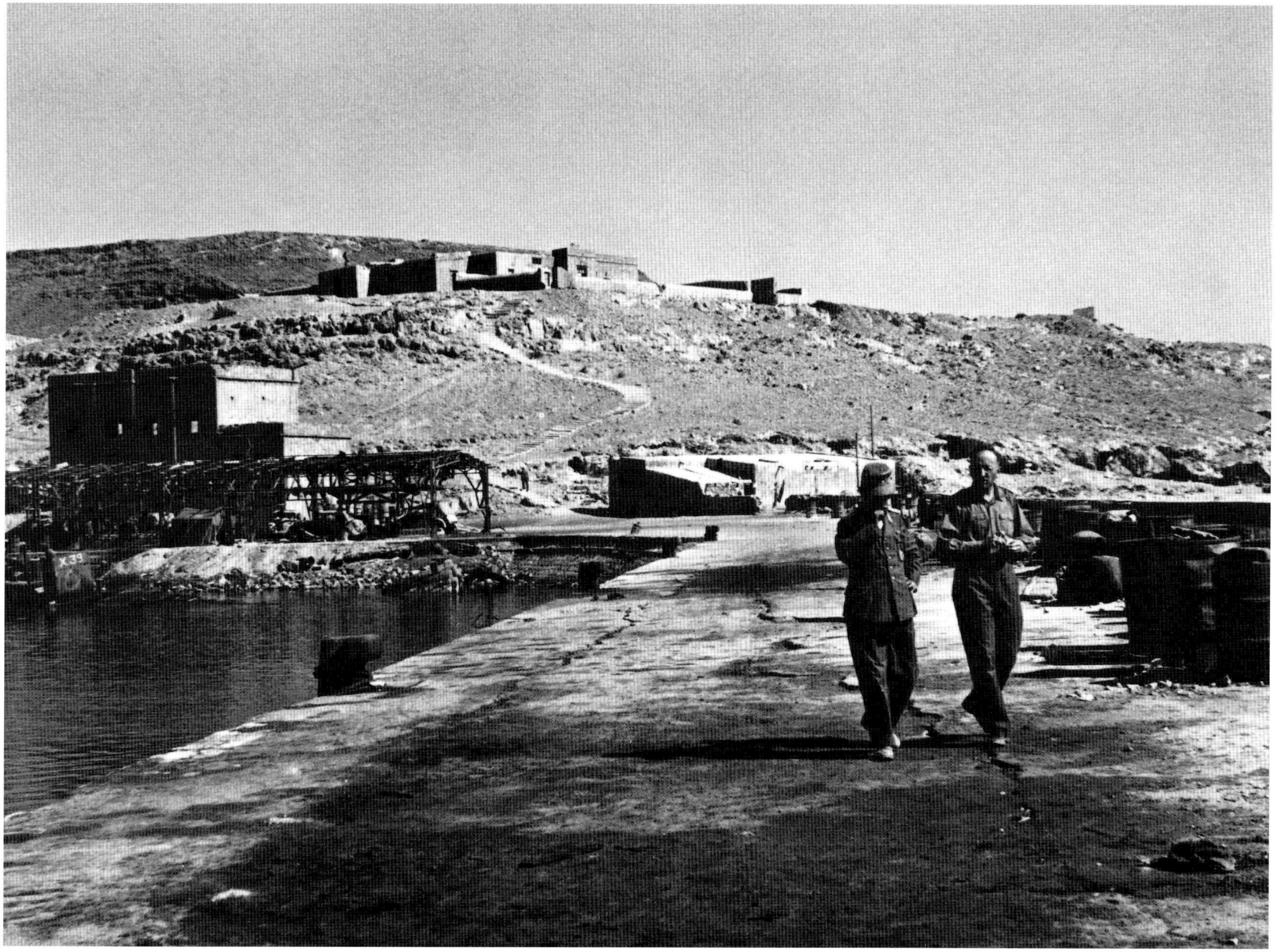
X39

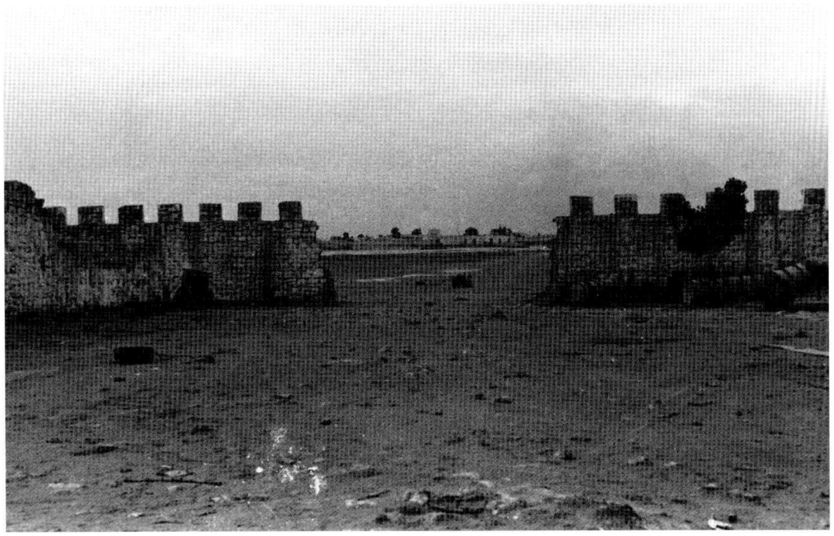

A broken wall with typical desert parapets on a Turkish-era fort. November 1942.

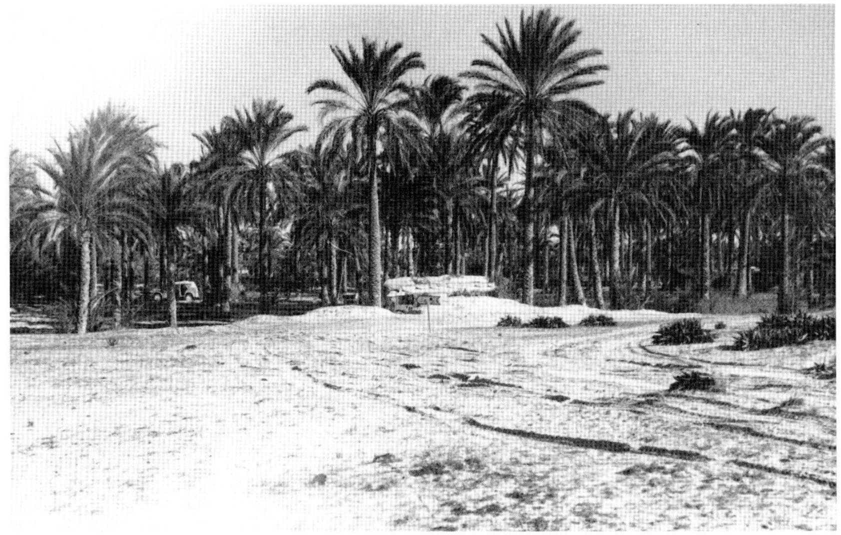

An unknown desert oasis – a respite from the sand and sun.

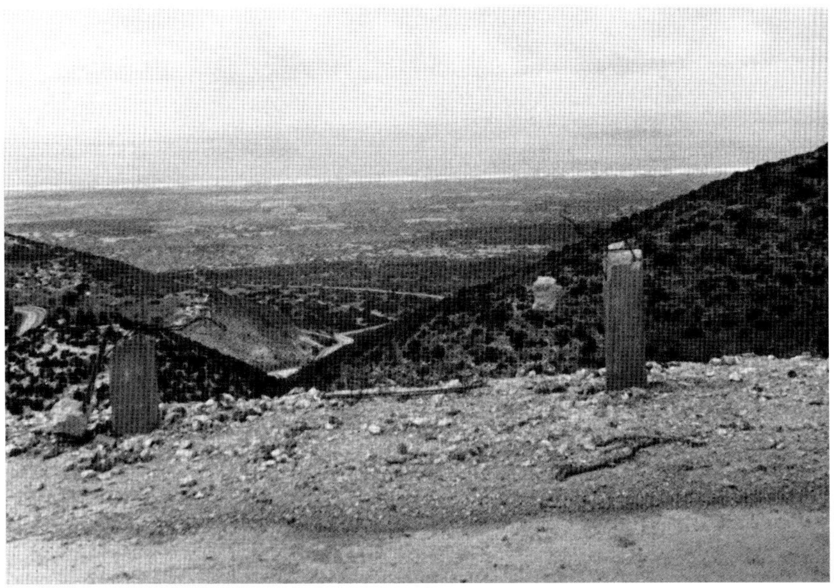

Steep hills and a desert road – an inhospitable battlefield.

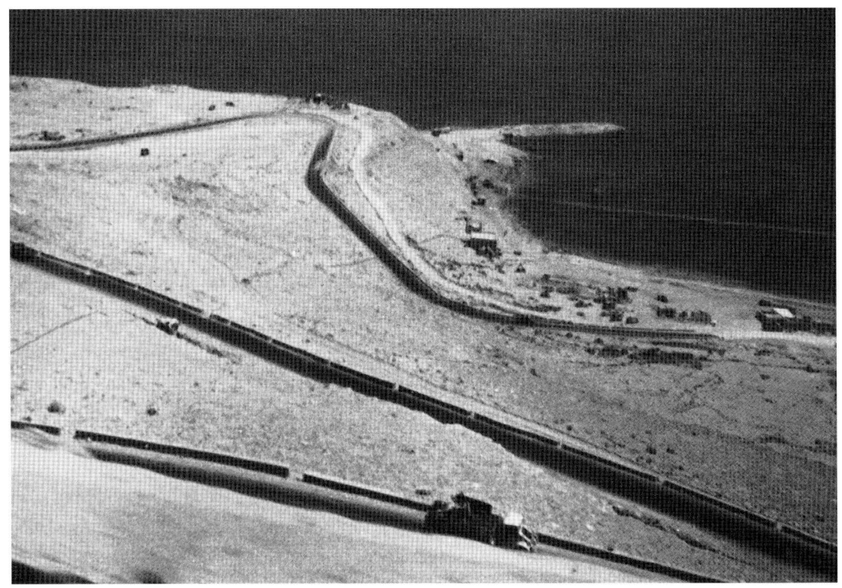

View from the hilltop of Upper-Sollum and the winding coastal road.

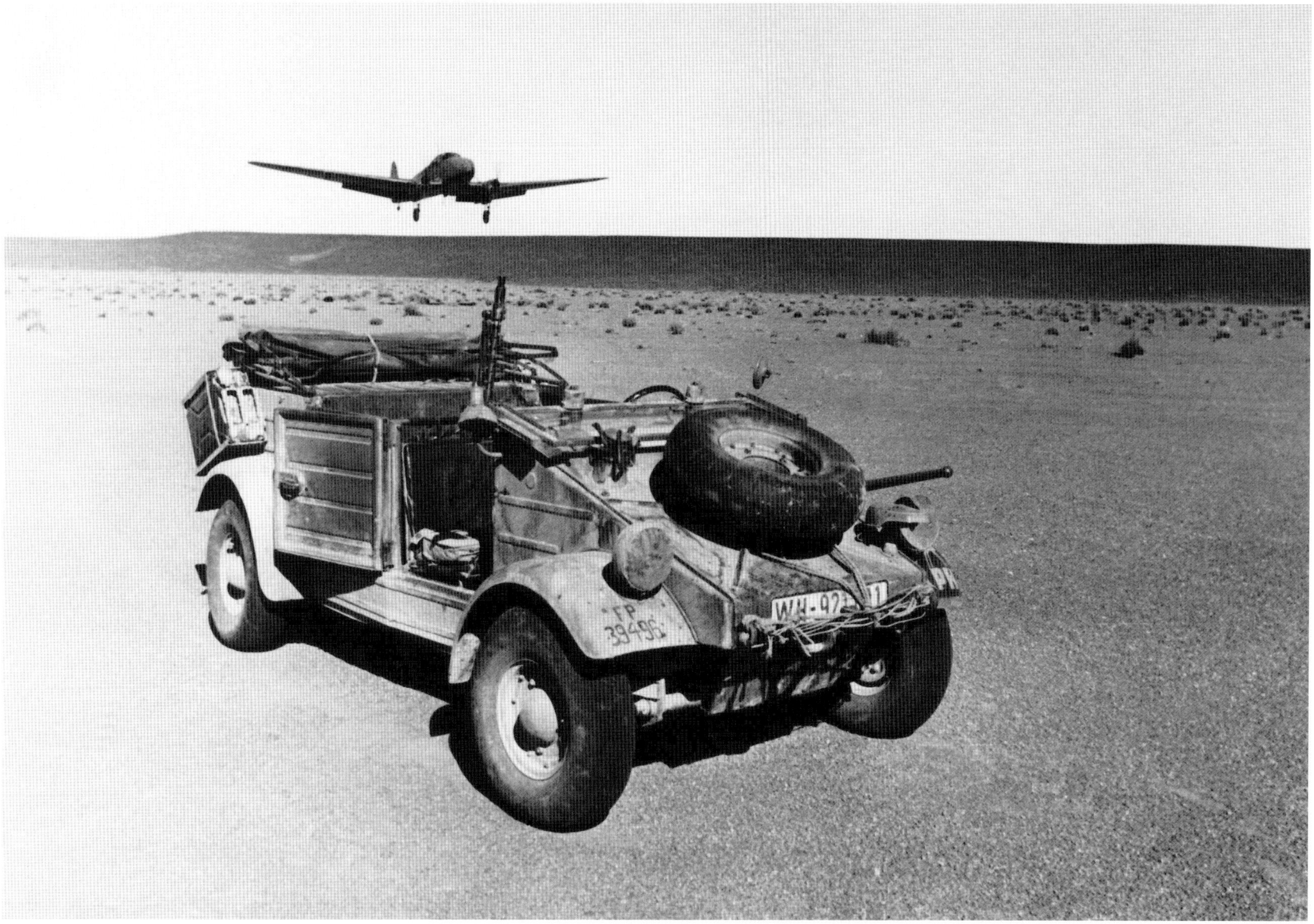

The Chef recognized a good photo opportunity – and his skill as a photographer is demonstrated by this magnificent detail of a Kübelwagen and aircraft.

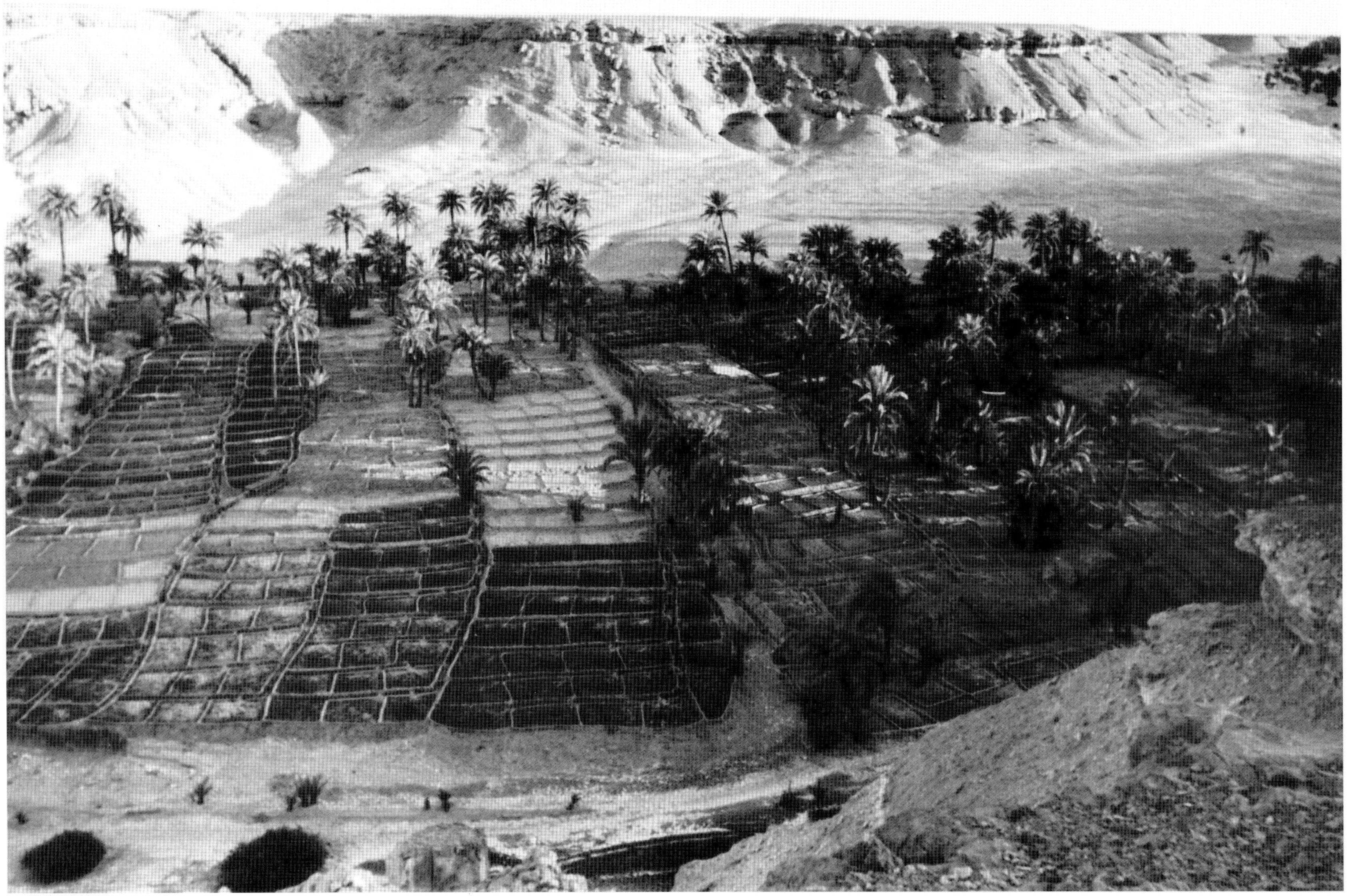

A cultivated oasis in a village perched above a wadi in Tunisia.[5]

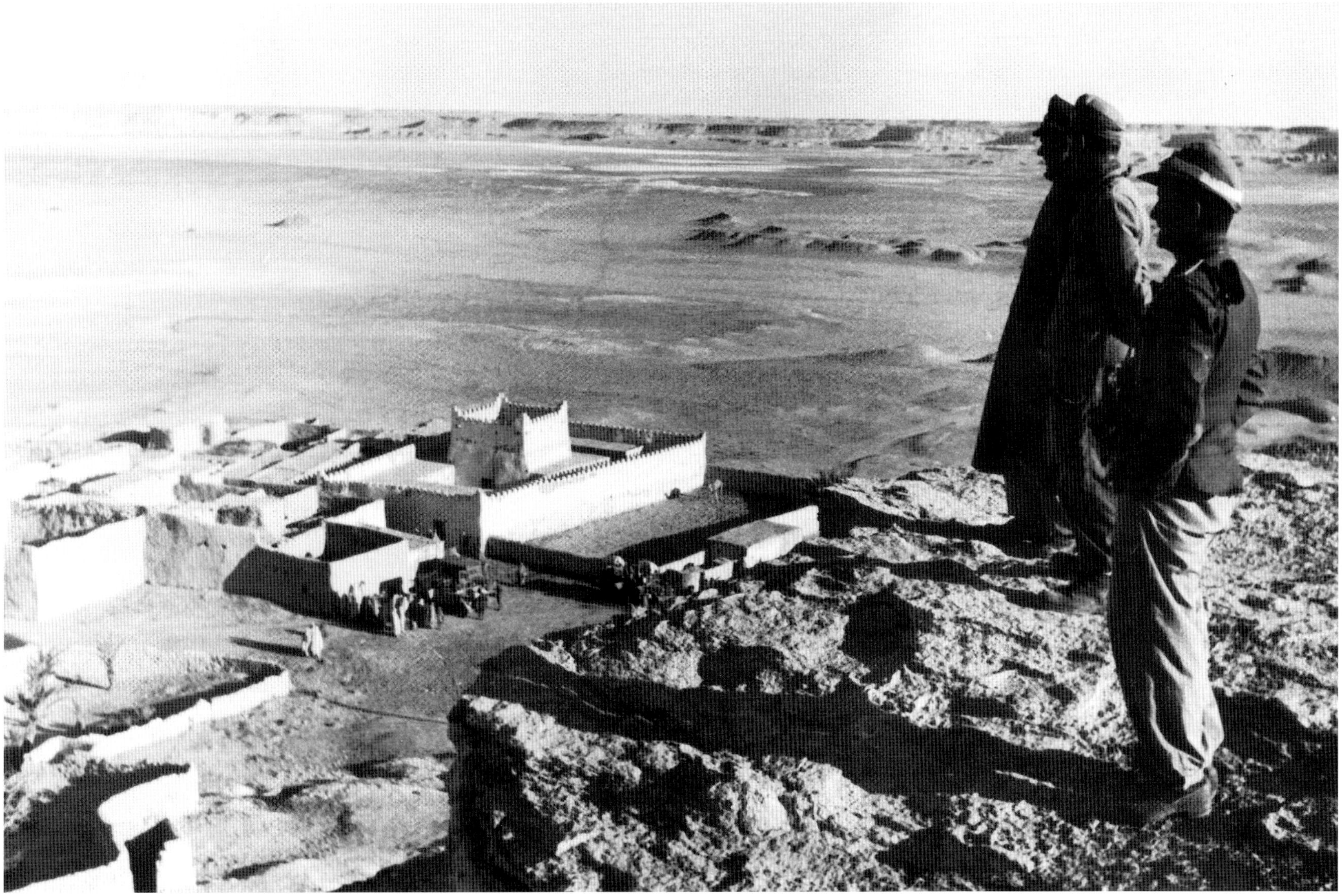

In a panoramic view unparalleled in their native homeland, three of Bayerlein's comrades stand on a vantage point in southern Tunisia and view the distant escarpments beyond a low lying depression and the Arab village at their feet. The two men standing on the left are Rommel's Chief-of-Staff, Generalmajor Alfred Gause and his Ia Operations Officer, Oberstleutnant Siegfried Westphal.[6]

CHAPTER SIX

BATTLES

Bayerlein did not record the battles or the dates on his photographs. He cryptically scribbled on some, as though he were in a hurry, and on others he recorded only the date. Placing his photos in sequence was sometimes difficult, sometimes impossible. On some of the photographs the authors based the location on similar landscapes in Libya and Cyrenaica. A best guess was feasible based on similar battle photos from secondary sources, or asking other Afrikakorps authors and veterans to venture an opinion.

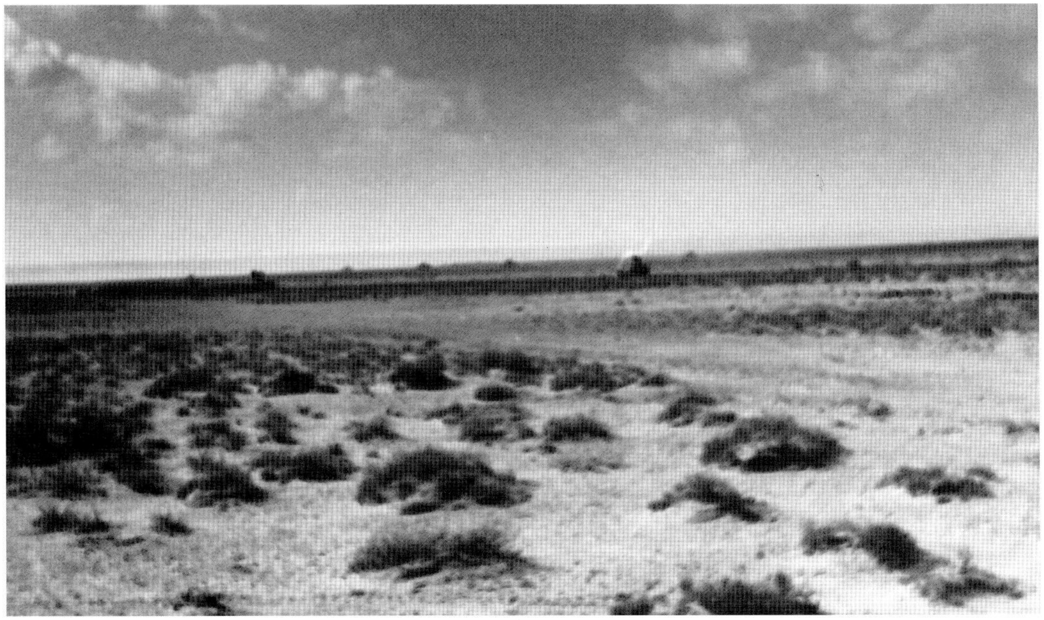

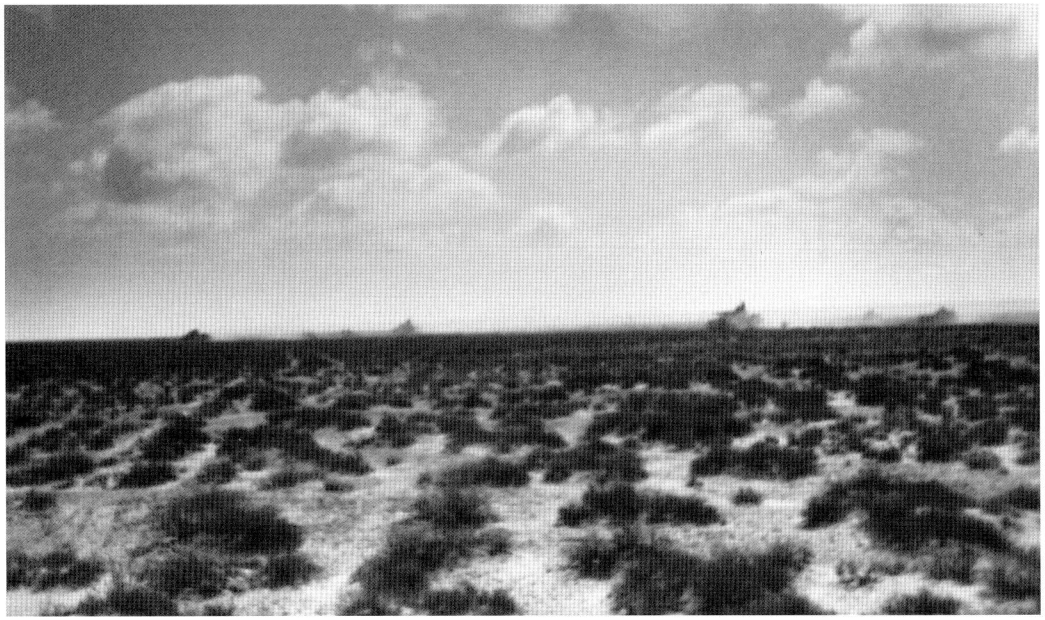

Top
In the distance the panzers begin to move.

Right
Bayerlein moves closer yet to the panzers.

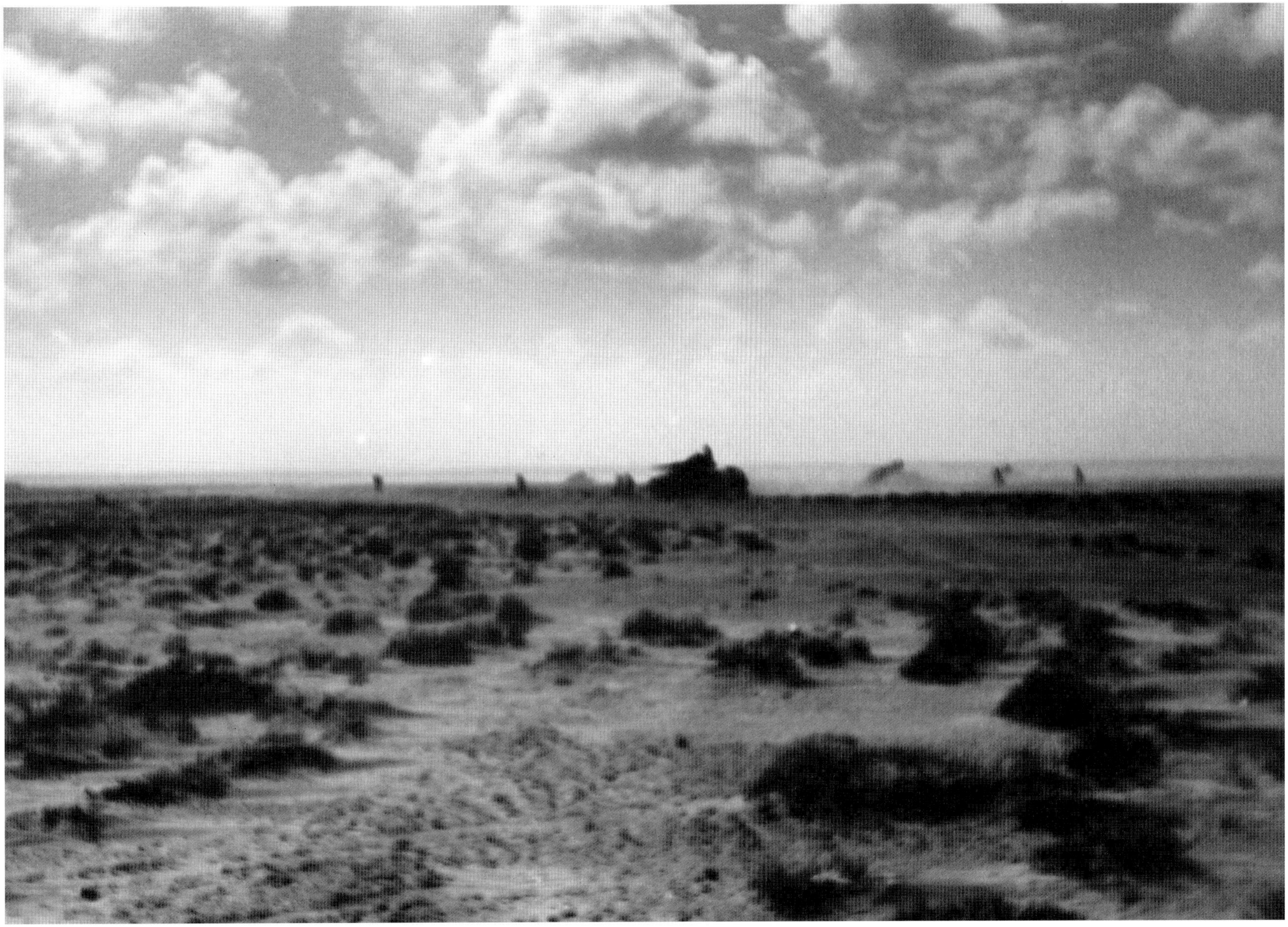

Risking to venture closer, Bayerlein is quite safe on a day without battle action.

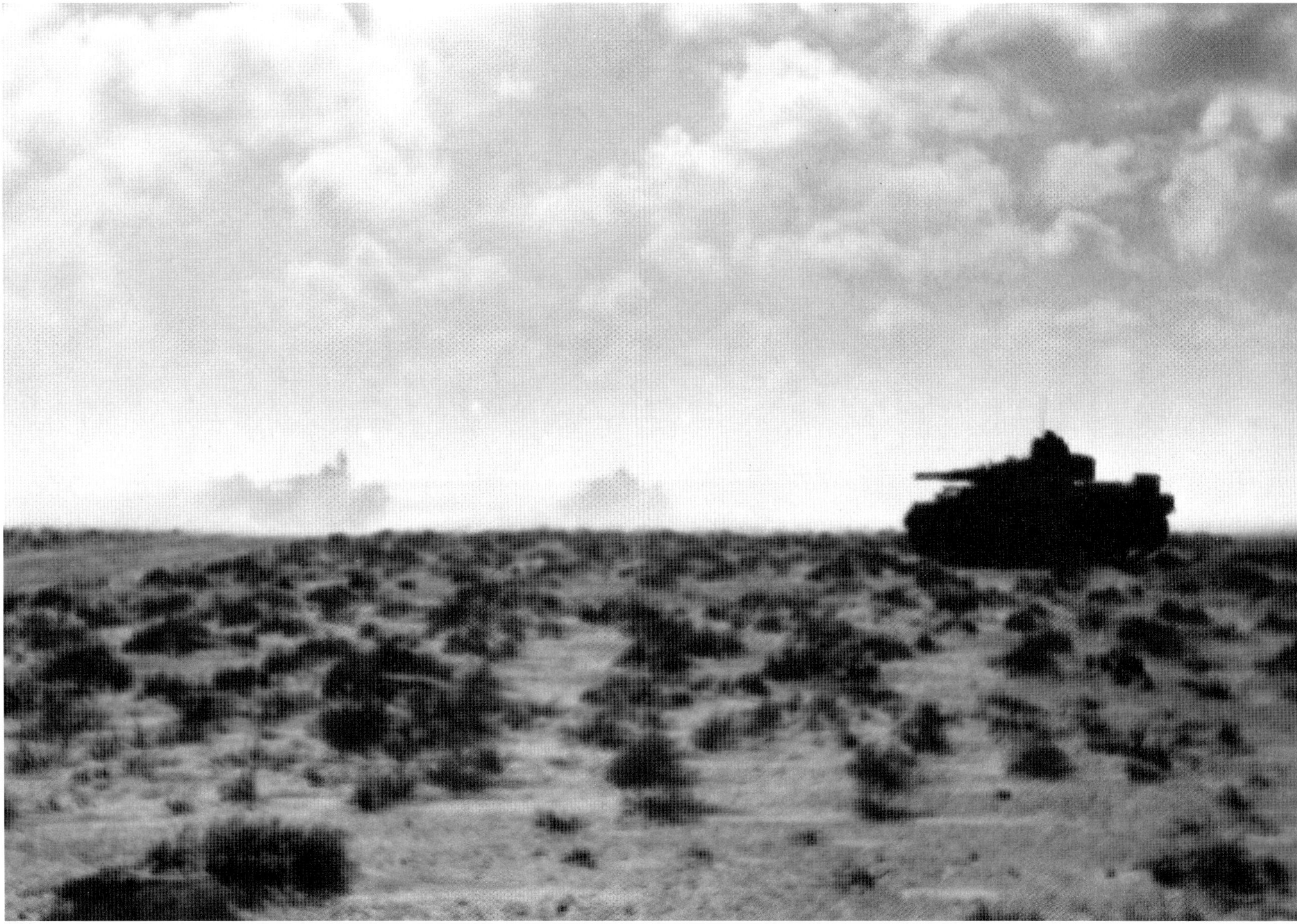

Safe amongst his own panzers, Bayerlein continues his photography. It appears there are no British to fight this day under the picturesque white clouds.

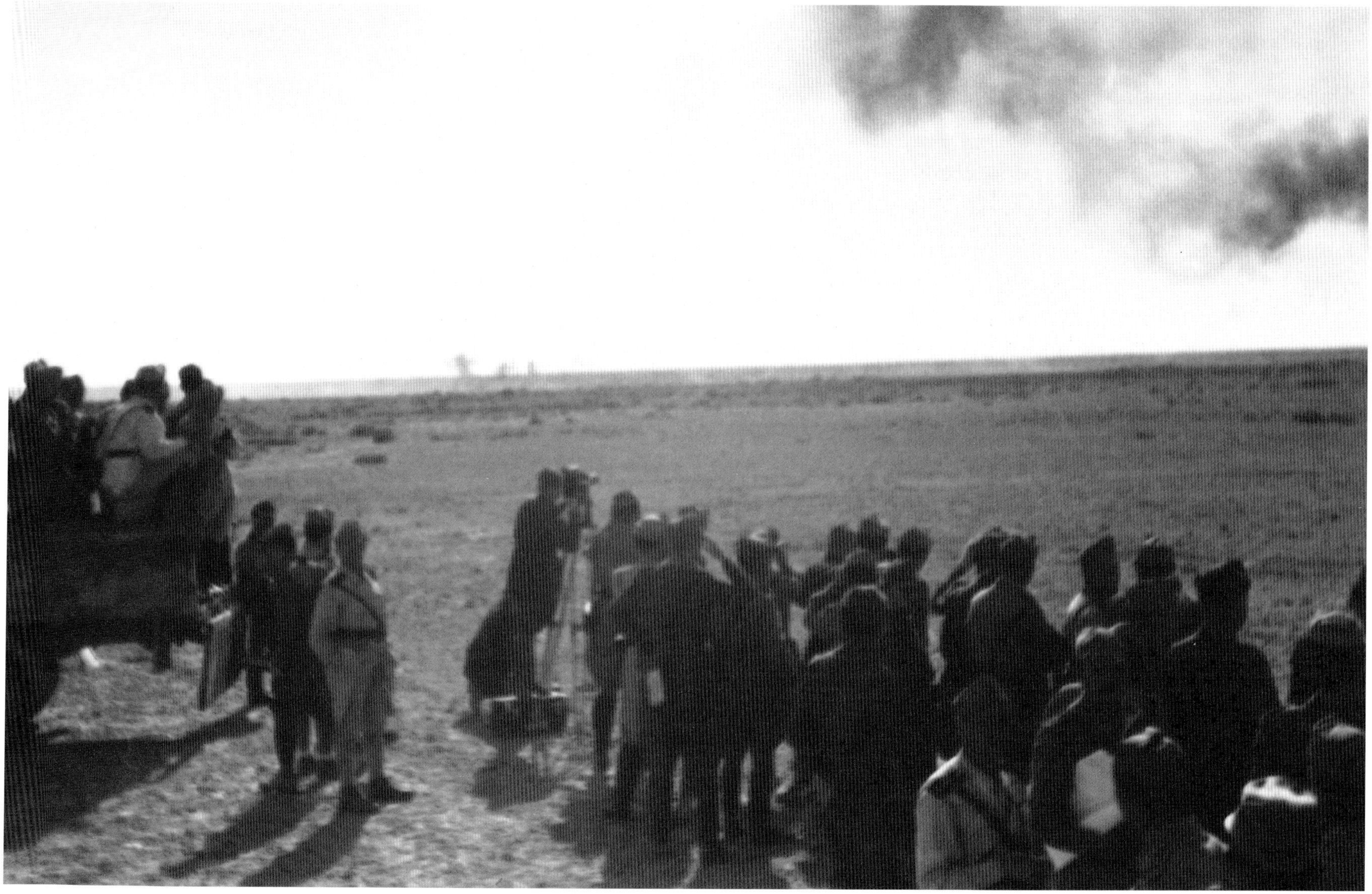

Another day brings a different fortune; the battle begins with smoke from the initial hits burning just out of camera range. The side gallery of officers, both German and Italian, along with a Propaganda Kompanie film crew, observe the distant action from a safe distance.

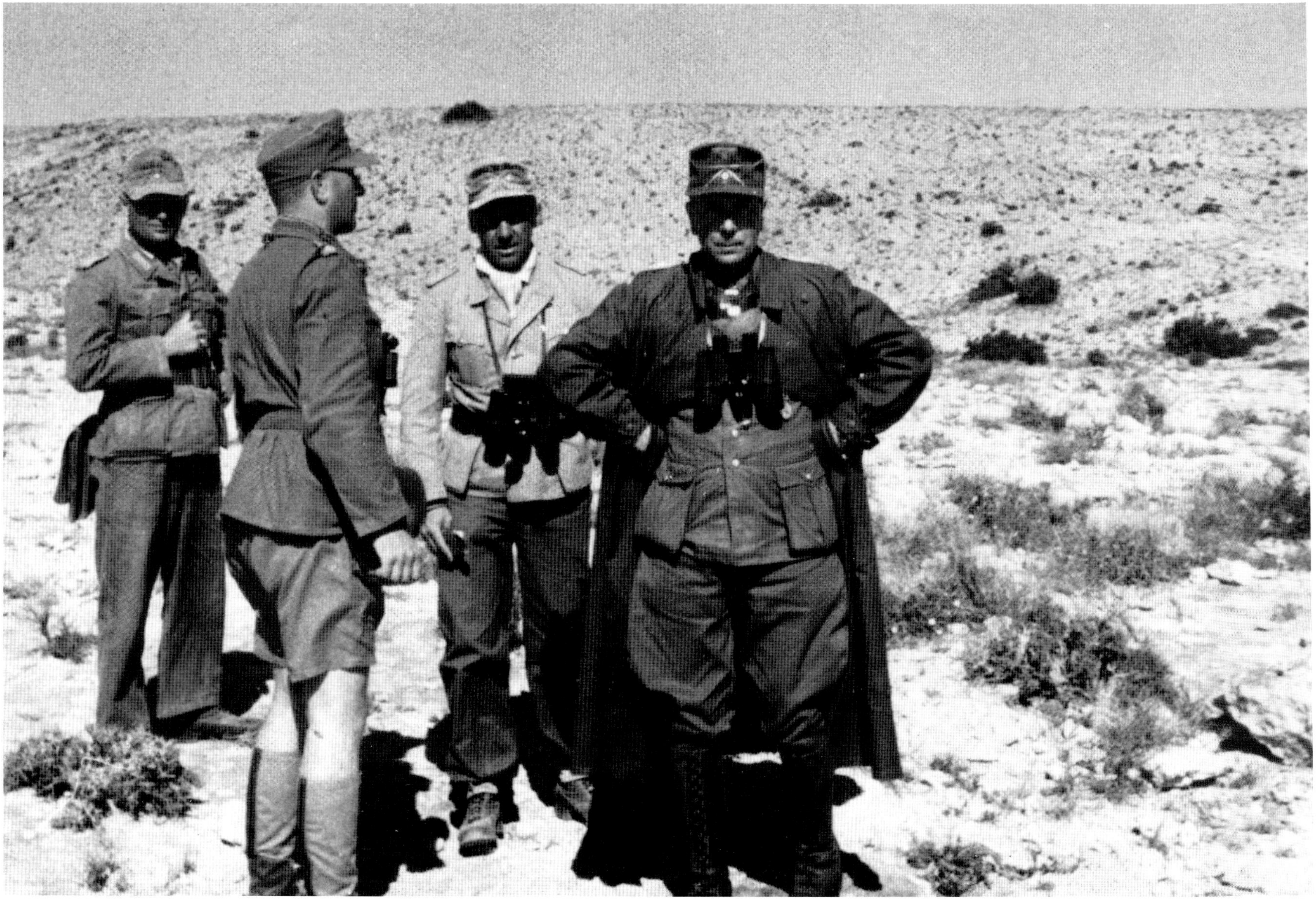

A time and a place for everything – clearly annoyed at the interruption – General Nehring turns to the cameraman, while Bayerlein quickly steps in to retrieve his Leica.

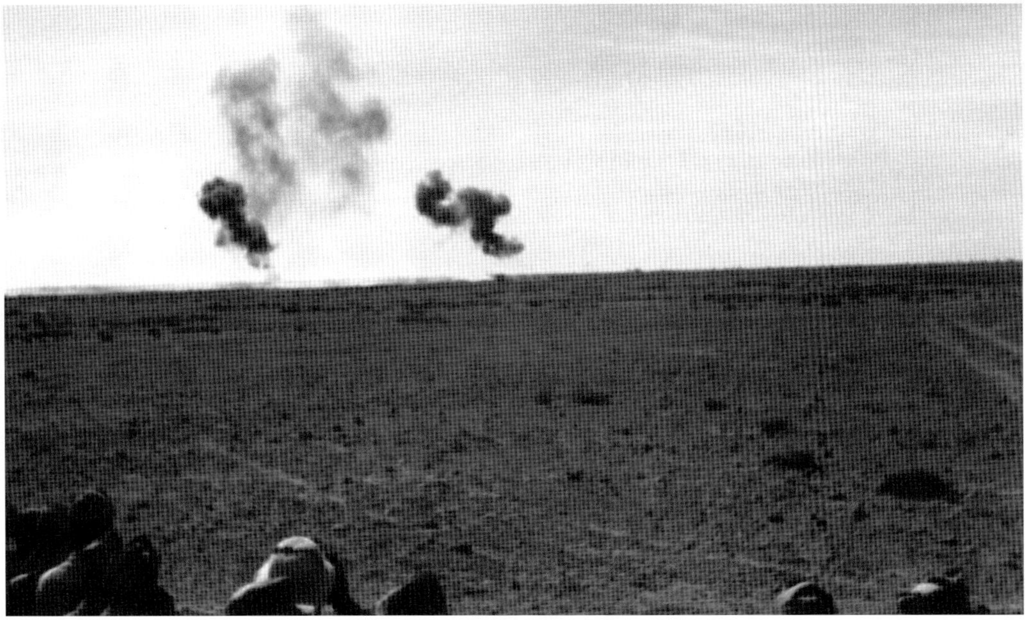

Left
In his command car, Bayerlein captures early hits on the battlefield.

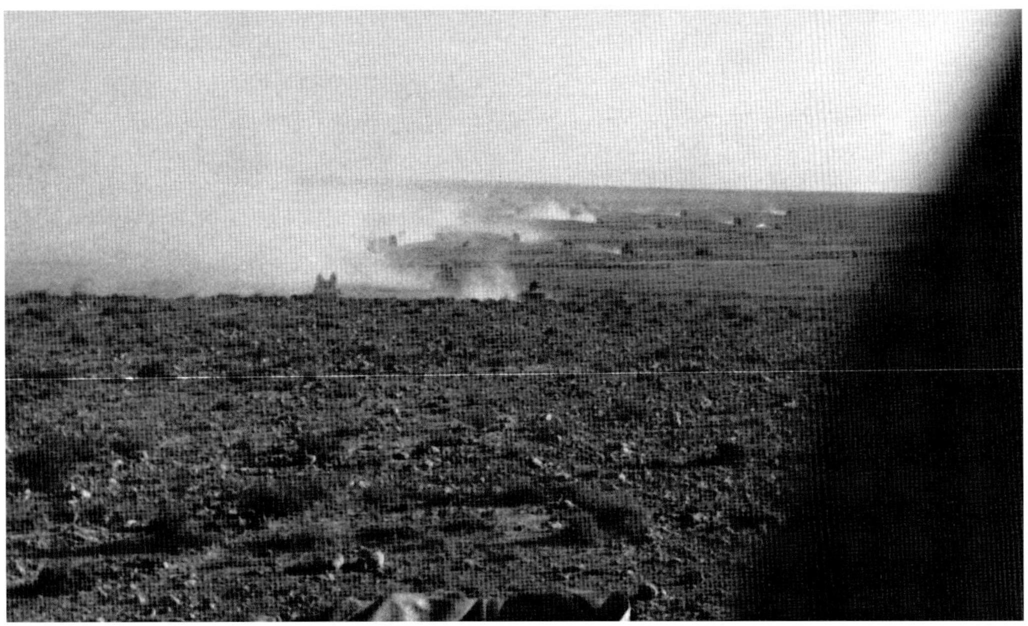

Left
Moving up front with the attacking units, Bayerlein still has time and confidence to use his camera.

Opposite
Bayerlein's handwritten caption reads: "5 November, Fuka" battle action near El Alamein in November 1942.

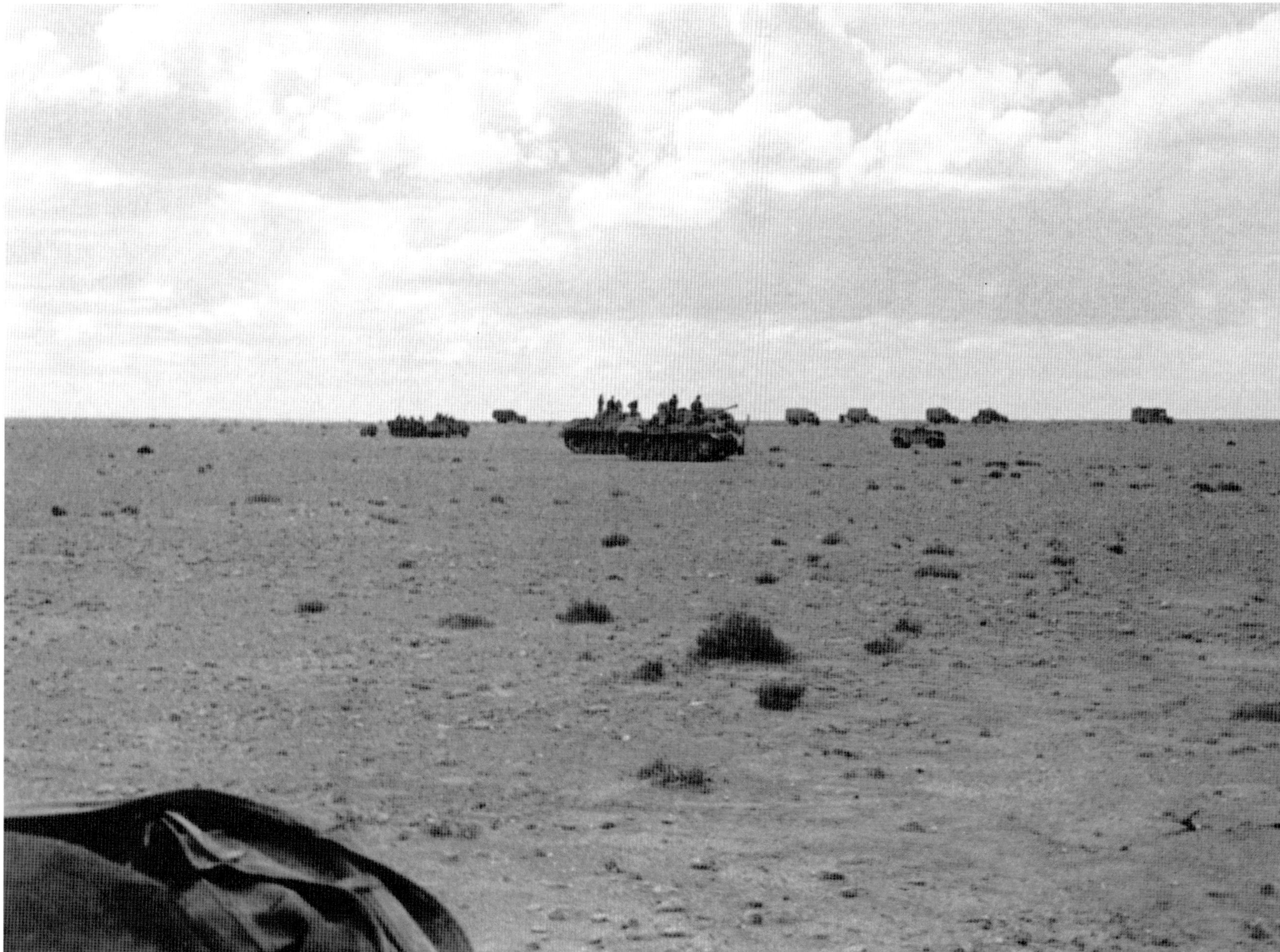

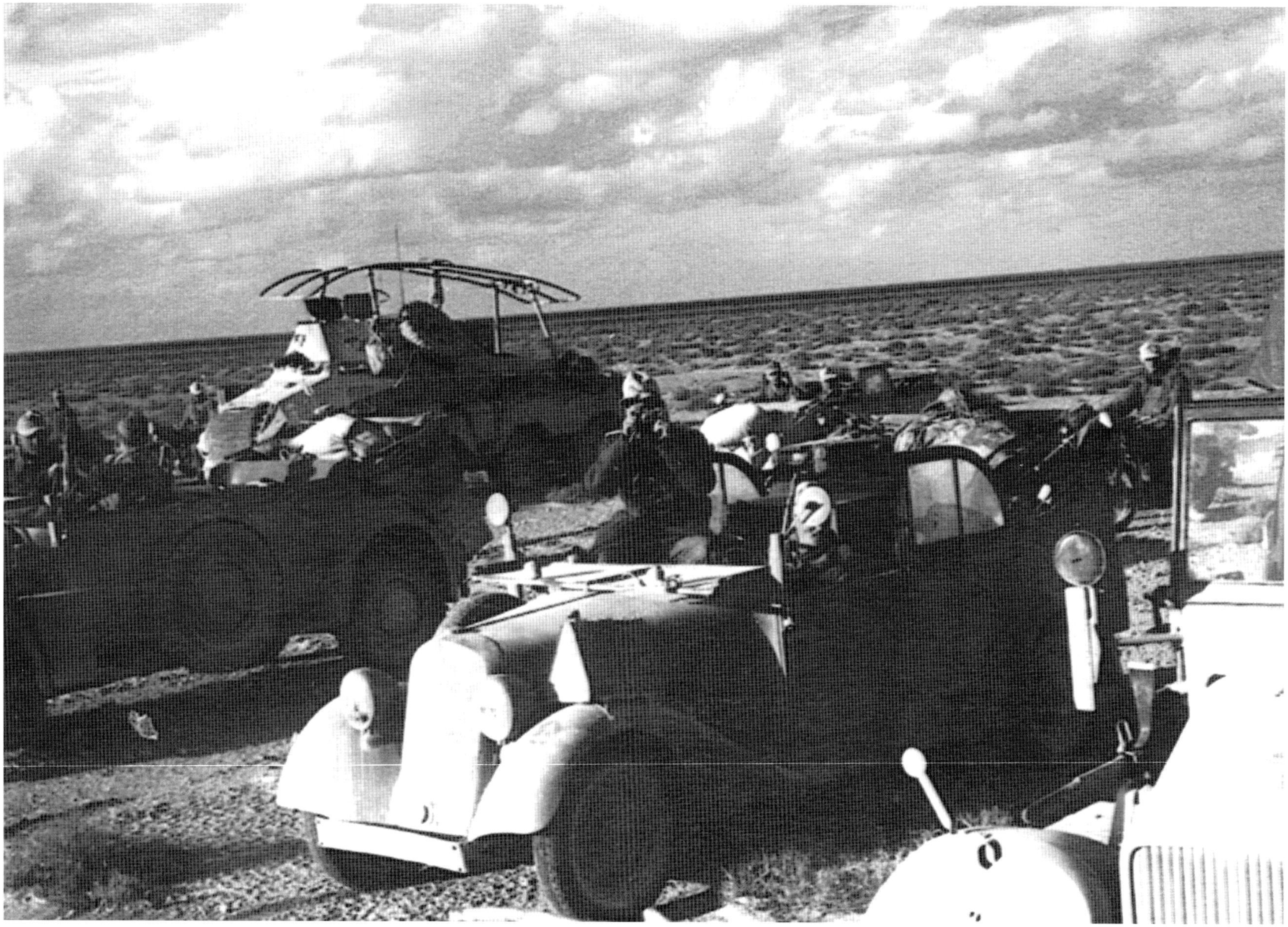

Bayerlein's front row seat during the skirmishes, flanked by a Panzerfunkwagen (SdKfz. 263).

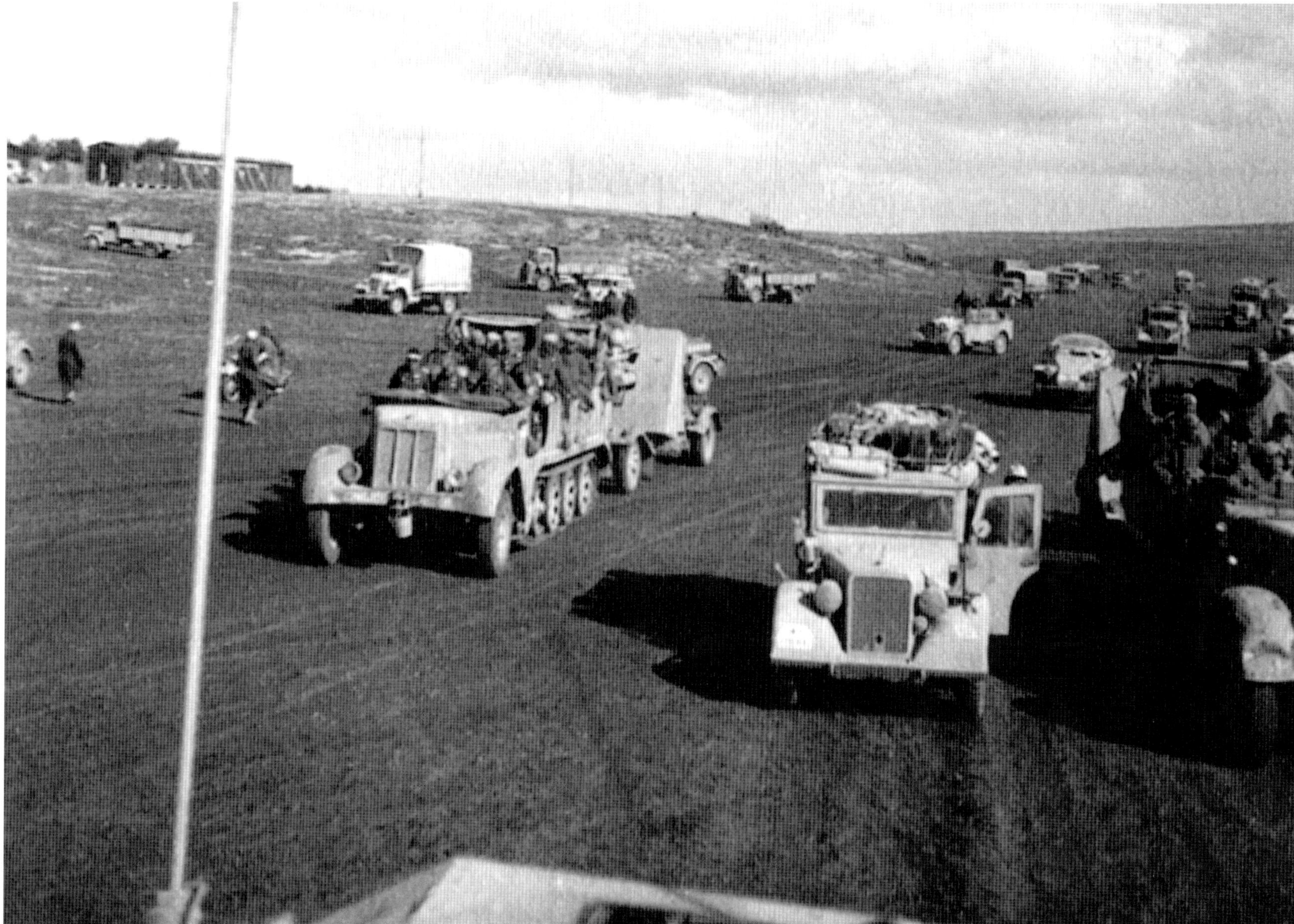

From atop his command vehicle, Bayerlein catches the headquarters group readying for a move.

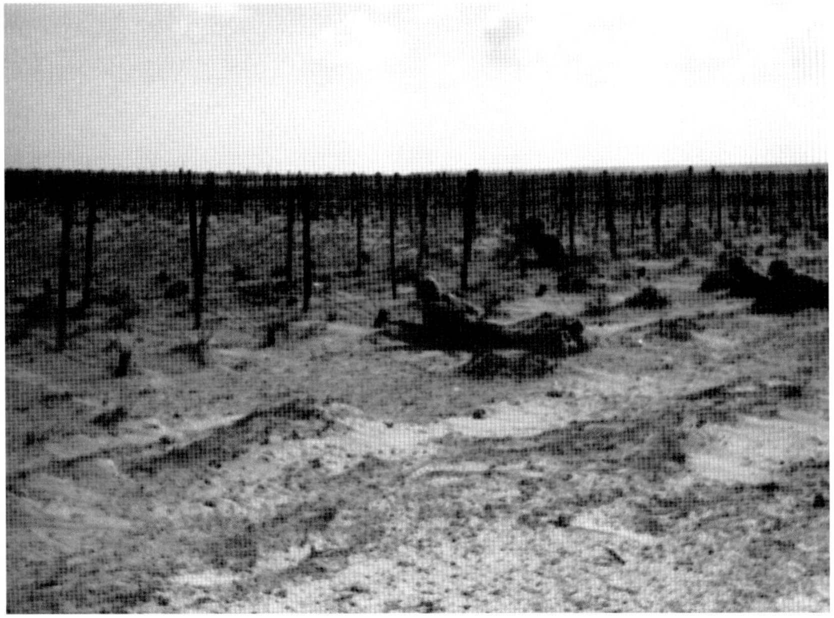

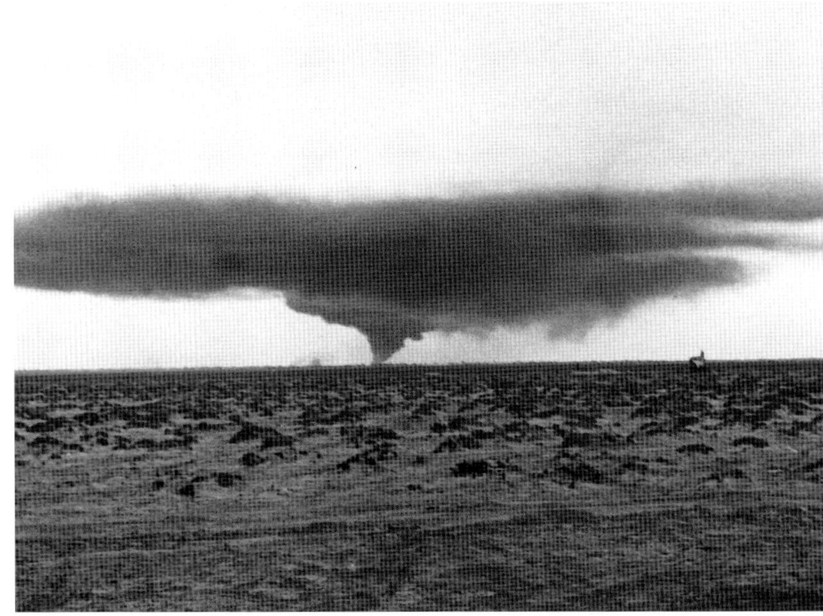

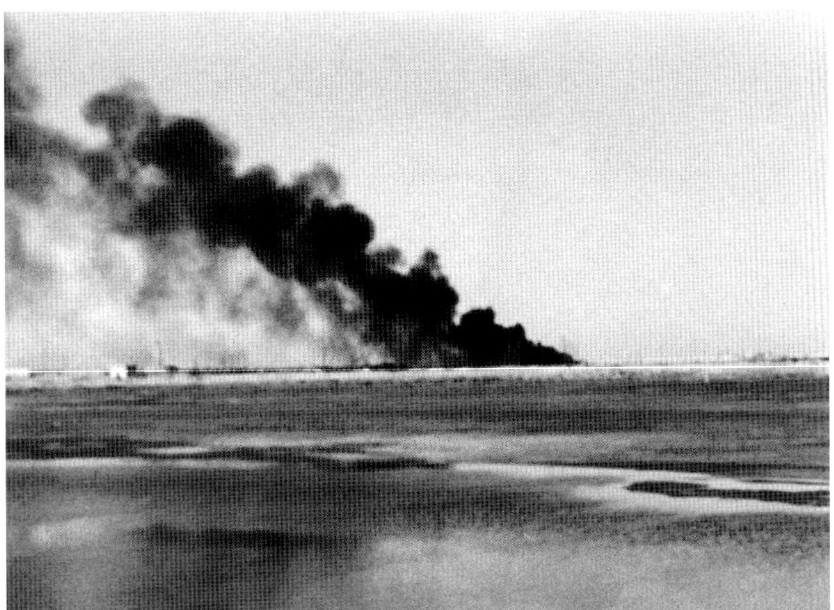

Top left
Troops lie on the ground in front of the lines of barbed wire strung up by the Italians before the war along the Libyan-Egyptian border to try to contain transient Arab tribes (Senussi) crossing uncontrolled from one country to the other.[1]

Above
In the distance a fuel dump burns.

Left
The British destroy fuel supplies rather than fuel their enemies' tanks.

Opposite
Ferocious fuel and ammo dump fires indicate the British aren't handing over their supplies to Rommel.

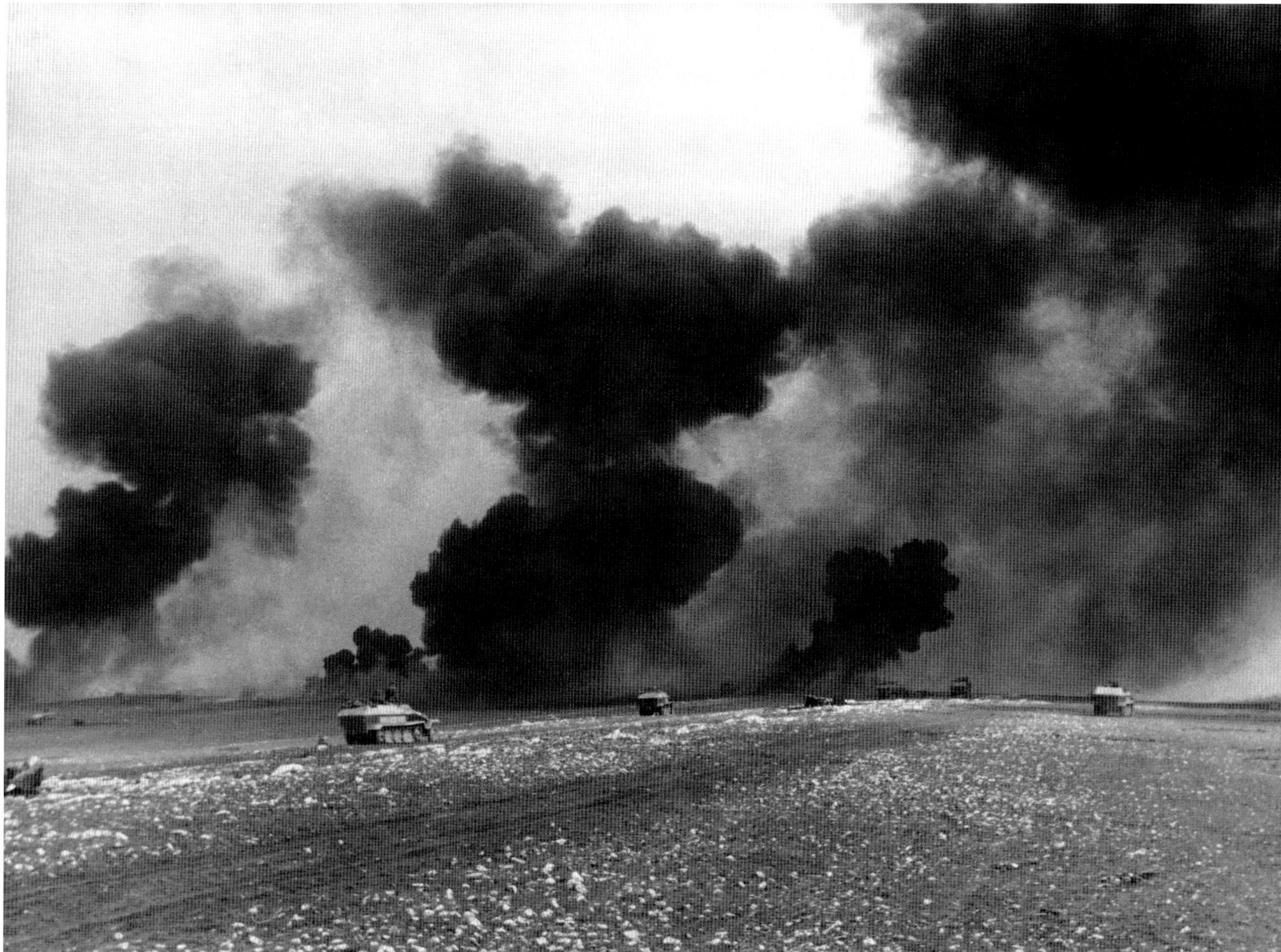

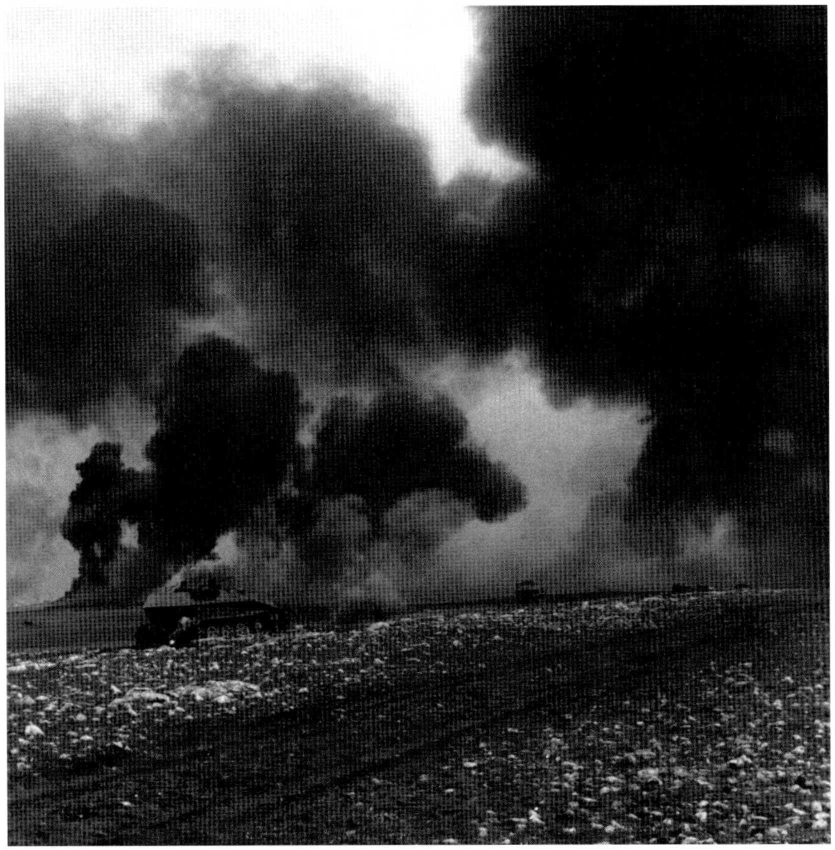

Fires from damaged cargo ships add to the oily, black smoke of a doomed Tobruk in the distance.

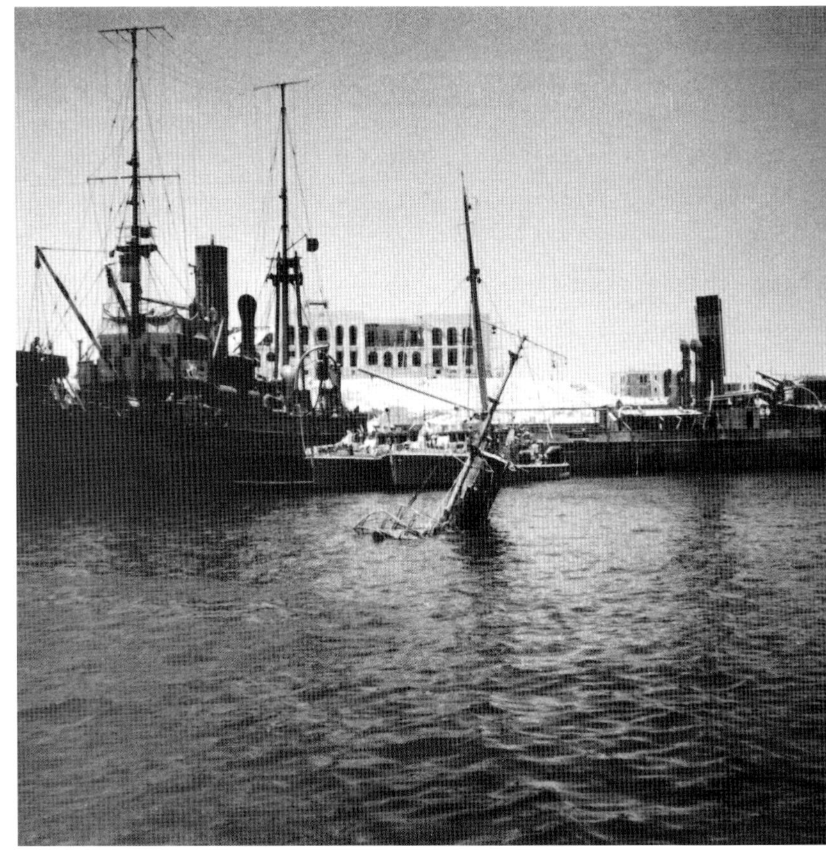

The remnants of a demolished Tobruk harbor.

CHAPTER SEVEN

GENERAL NEHRING'S COMMAND OF THE DAK

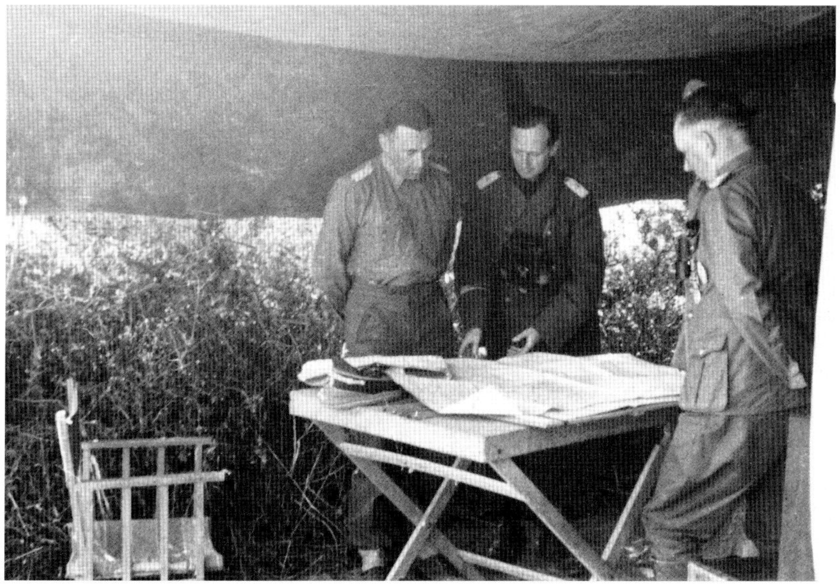

Generalleutnant Walter Nehring (right), Oberstleutnant F.W. von Mellenthin, and Oberstleutnant Fritz Bayerlein confer with Field Marshal Rommel (behind Nehring) at a map table. Both von Mellenthin and Nehring served their last days in Africa during the fall of 1942 – von Mellenthin left in September due to amoebic dysentery. Nehring was wounded in September and was transferred from Africa in December and replaced by General von Arnim.[1]

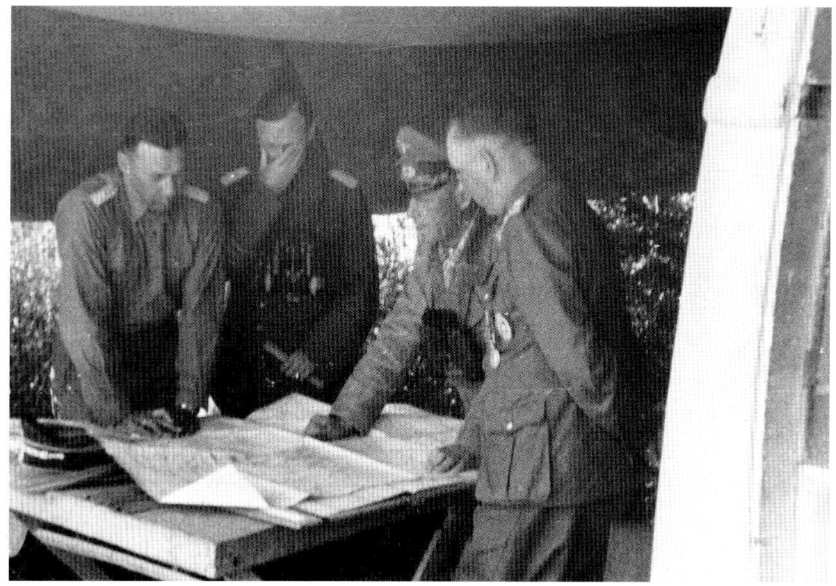

Evidently the Propaganda Kompanie photographer used Bayerlein's camera to photograph the four men, who kept shifting and fidgeting as they looked over the map.

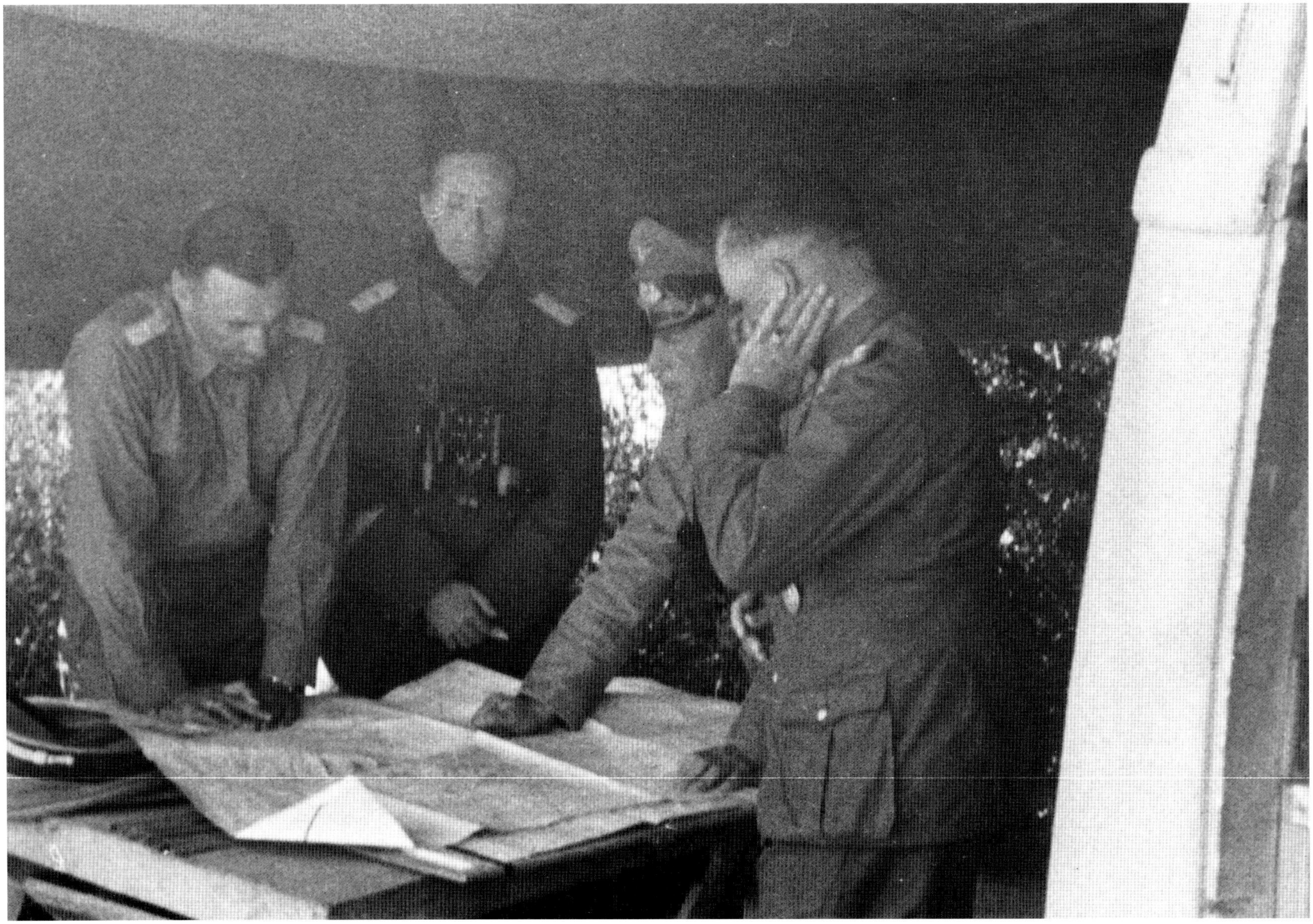

Final attempt to capture all four men at the table using Bayerlein's Leica. The official Propaganda Kompanie photo lined all the men into camera range.

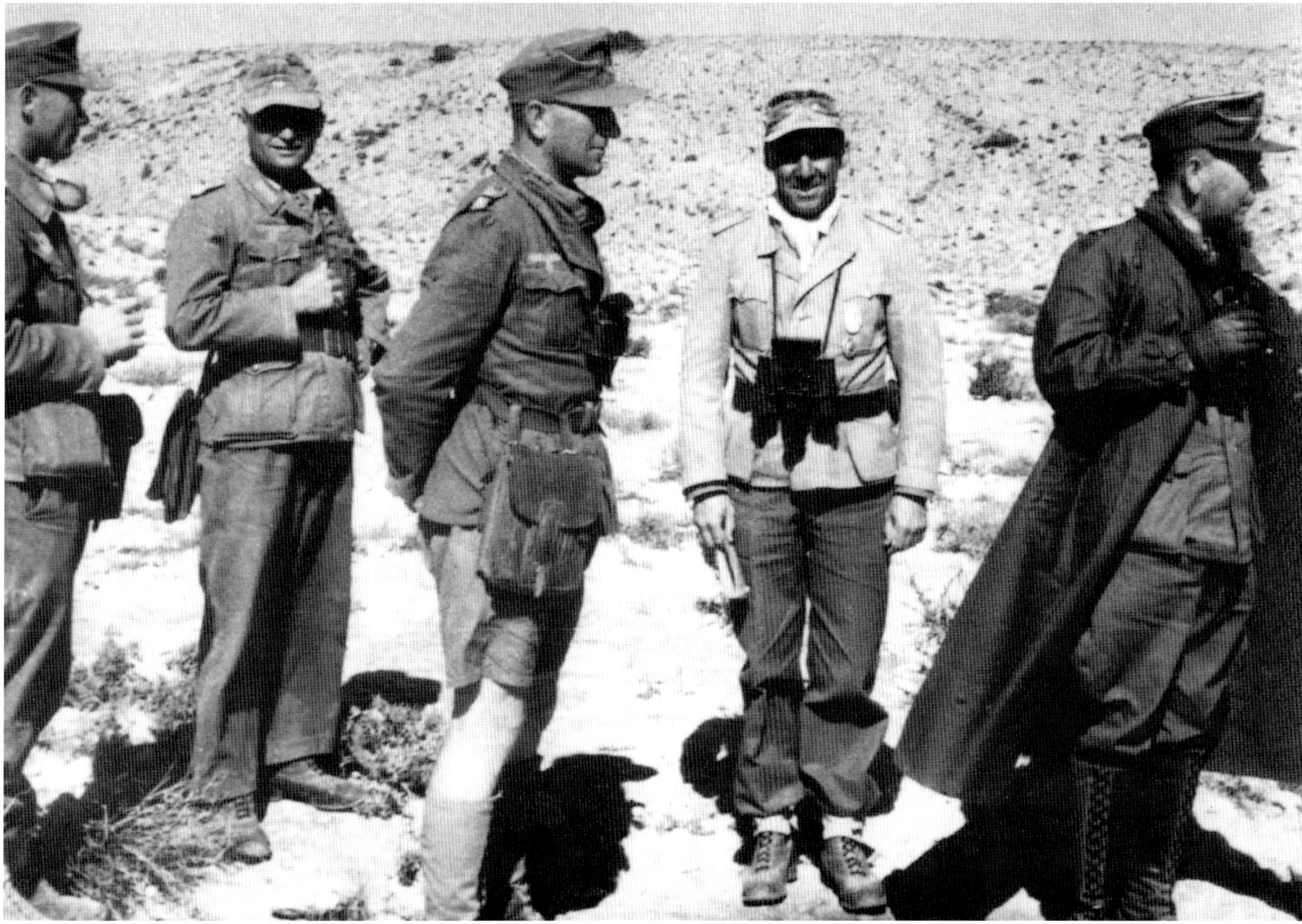

Smiling, Bayerlein stands behind his CO, General Nehring, who is observing British action near the Egyptian border.

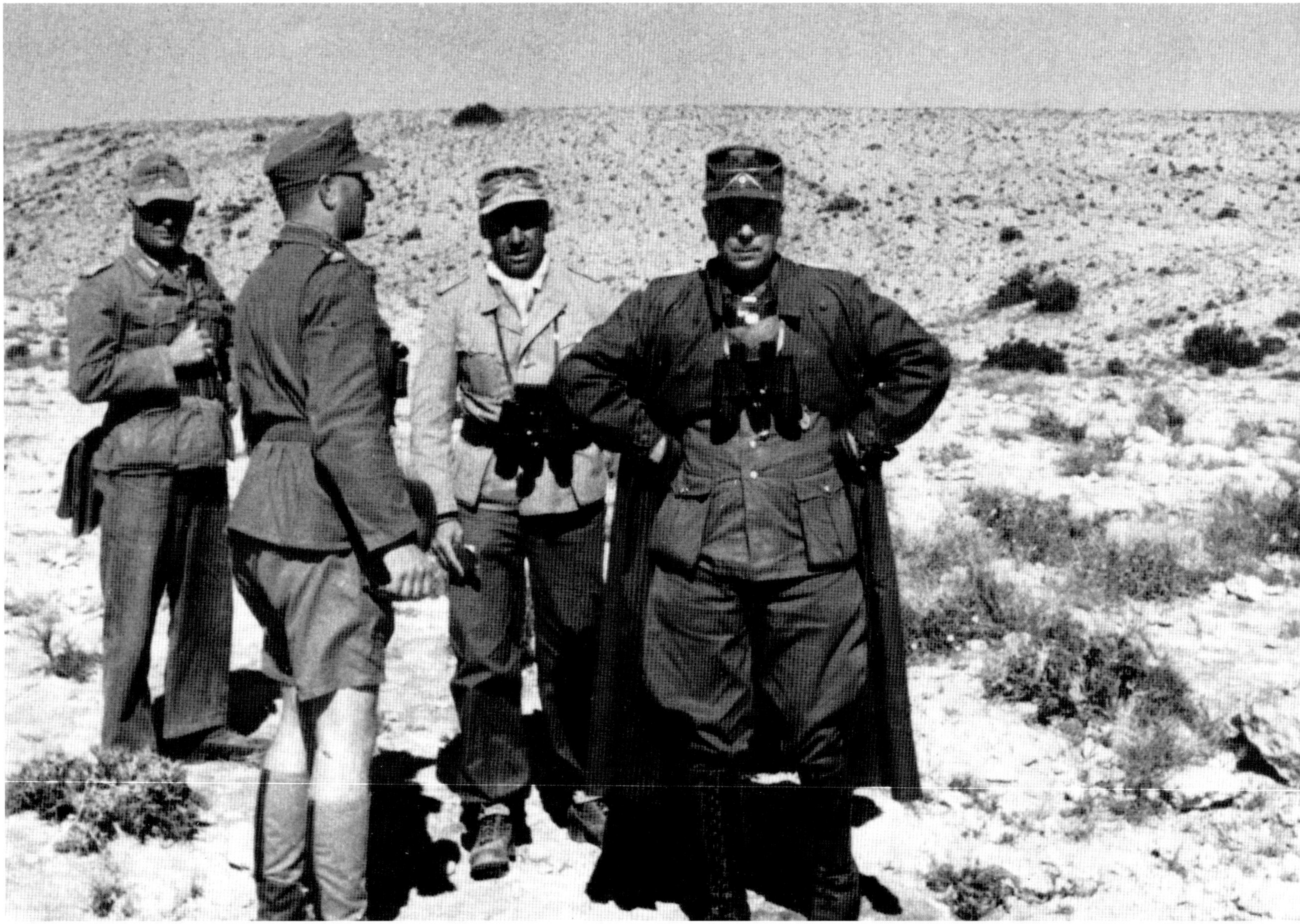

A time and a place for everything – clearly annoyed at the interruption – General Nehring turns to the cameraman, while Bayerlein quickly steps in to retrieve his Leica.

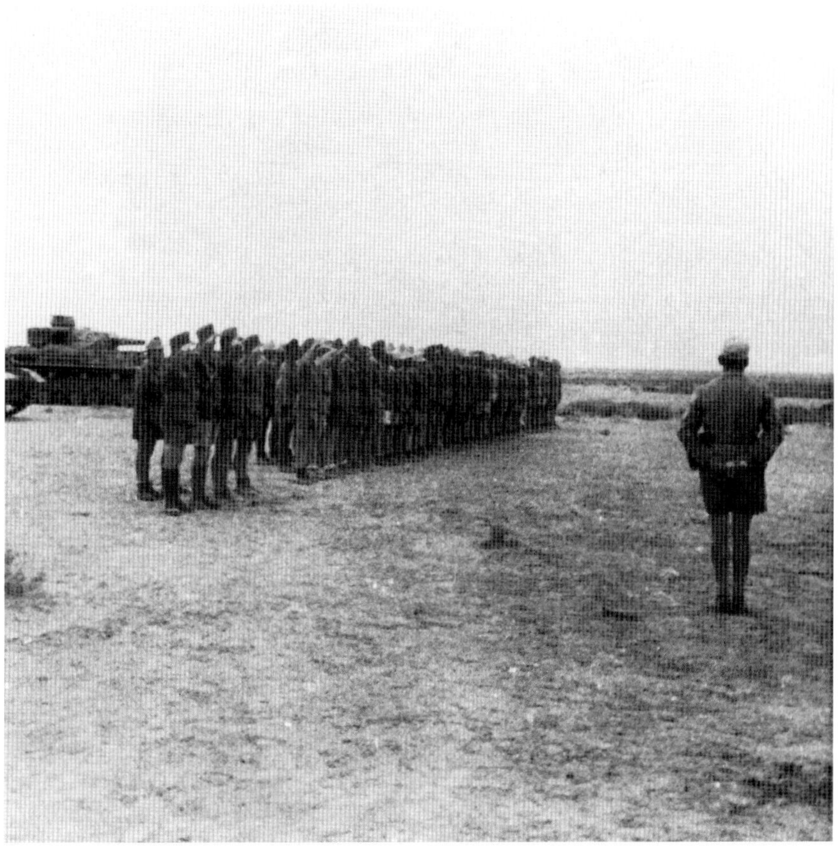

At an award presentation, the soldiers present arms while Bayerlein stands at attention nearby, as General Nehring arrives.

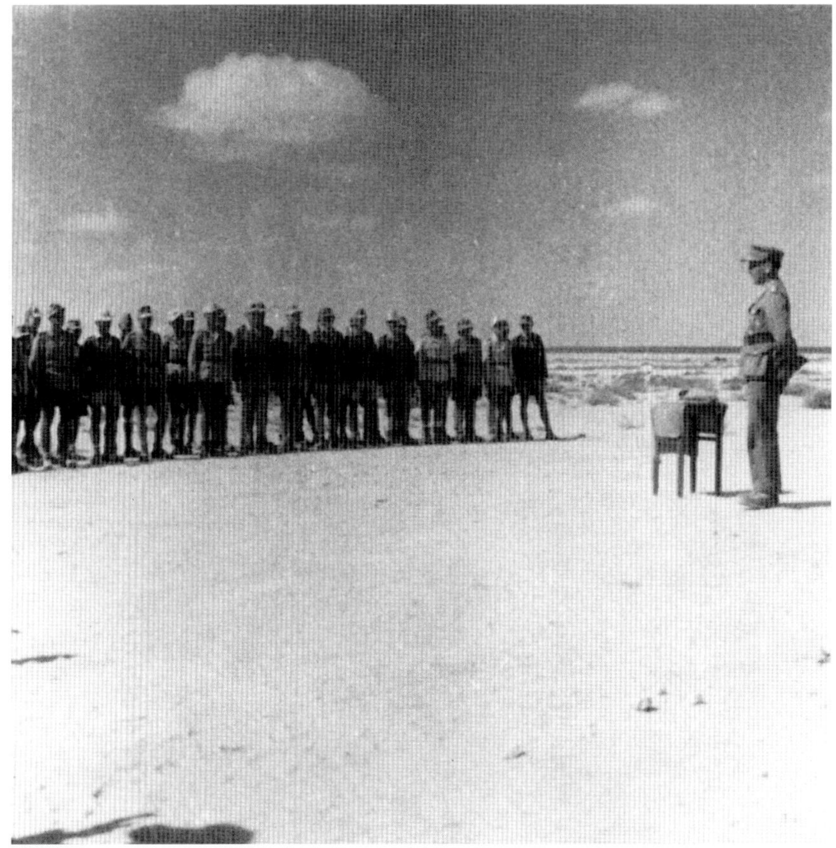

With the soldiers lined up for the presentation, General Nehring gives his short speech of appreciation for the capture of Tobruk in June 1942.

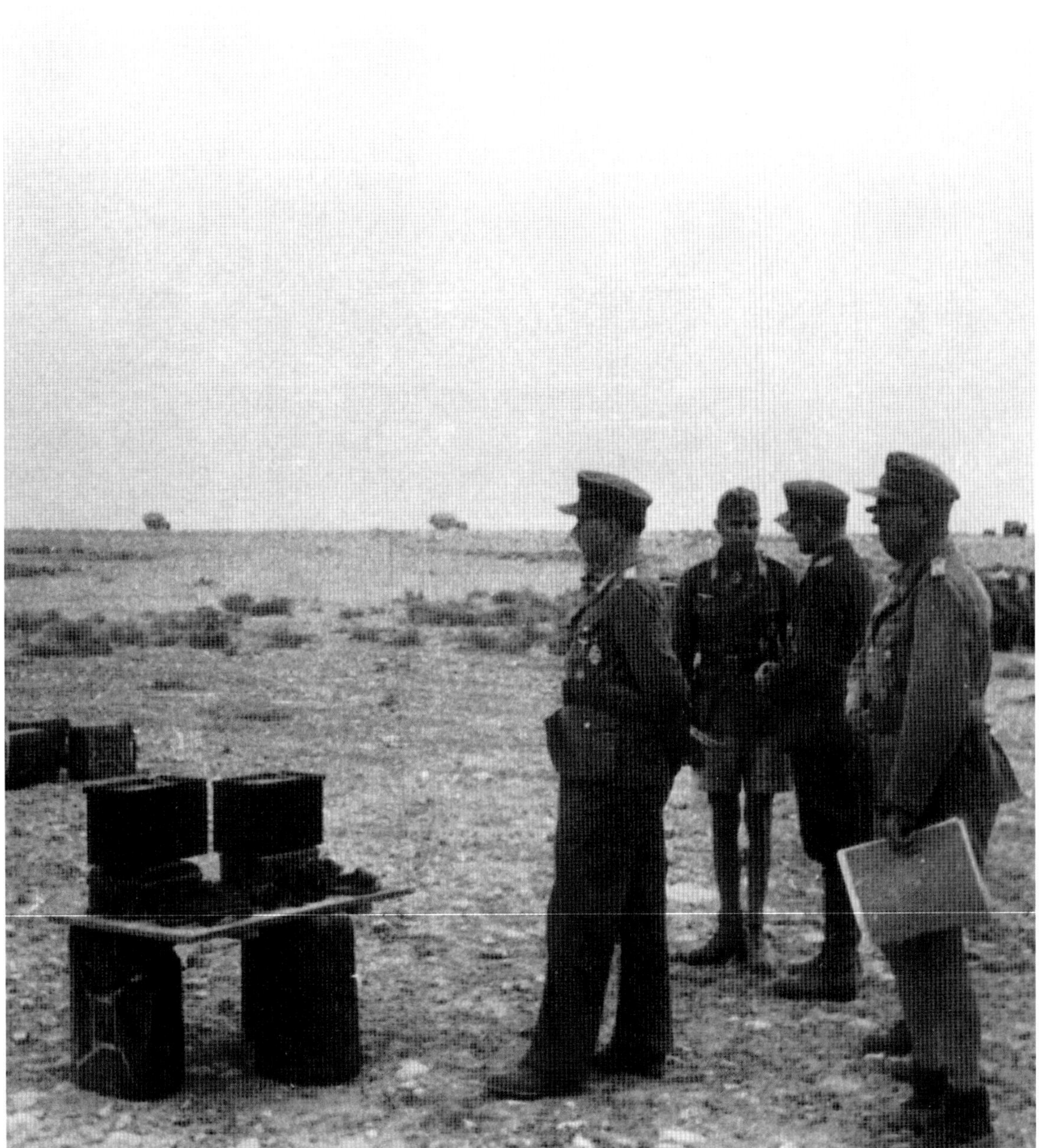

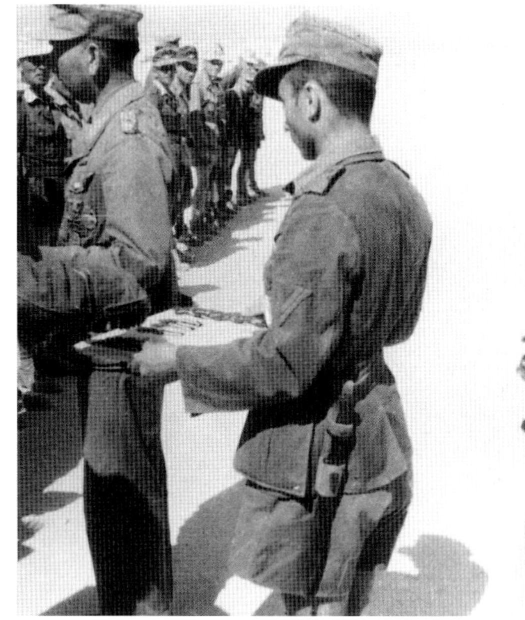

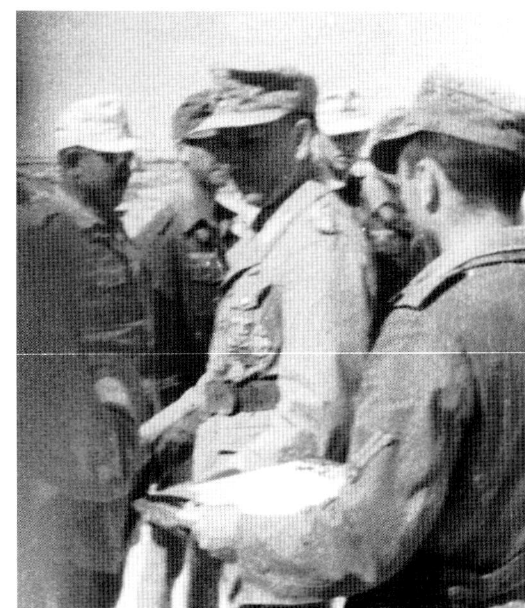

Opposite left
Bayerlein takes another photo of General Nehring's speech to the troops.

Top right
A view of the decorations held by one of the soldiers.

Bottom right
General Nehring moving down the line of soldiers.

Right
A close-up view of Nehring's award presentation.

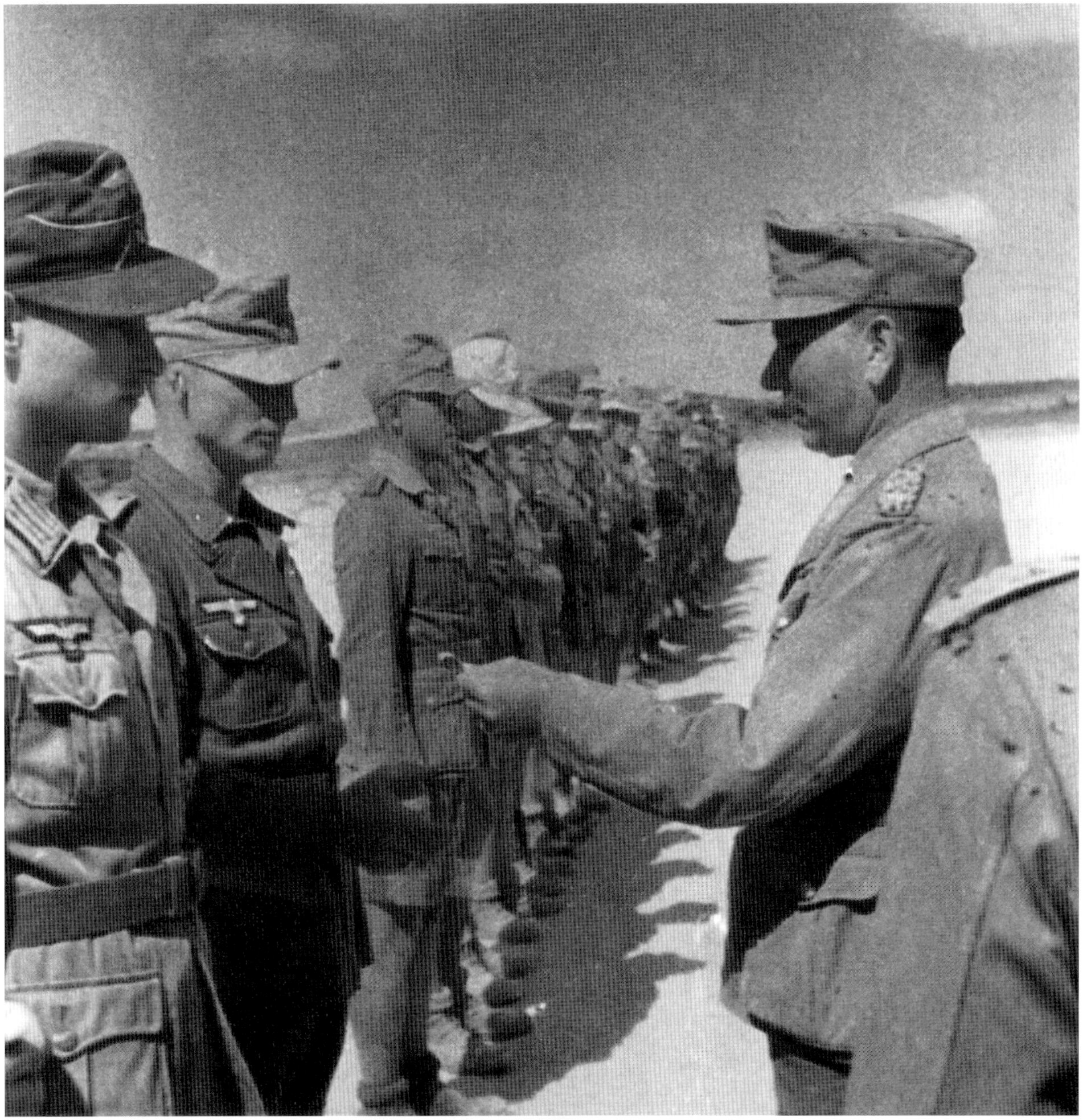

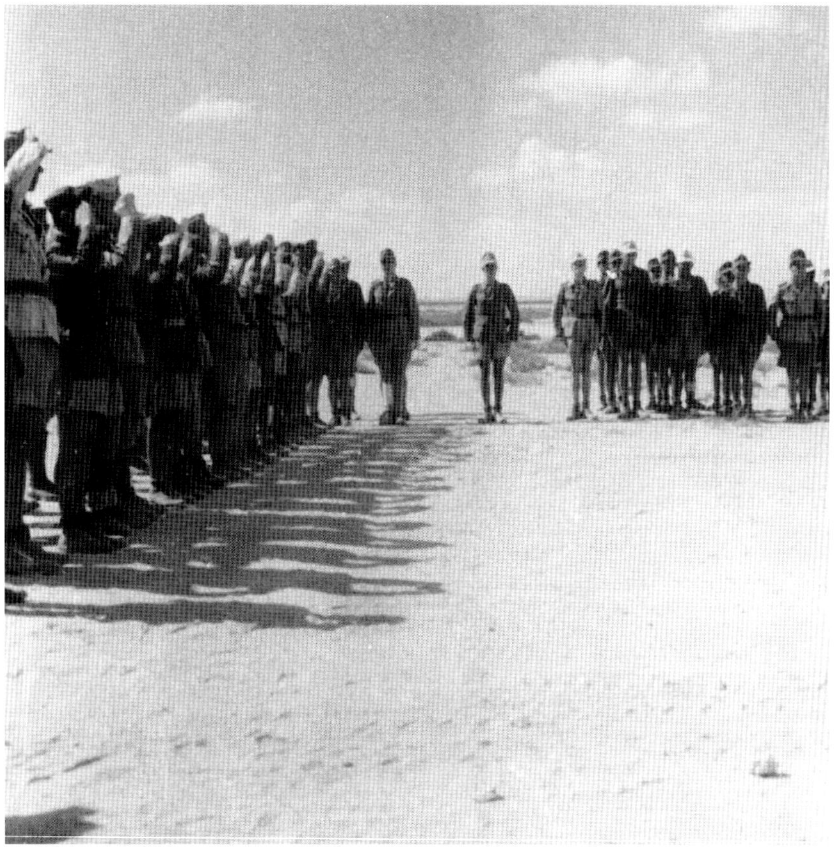

At another unit ceremony, the soldiers present arms for the arrival of the commander, General Nehring.

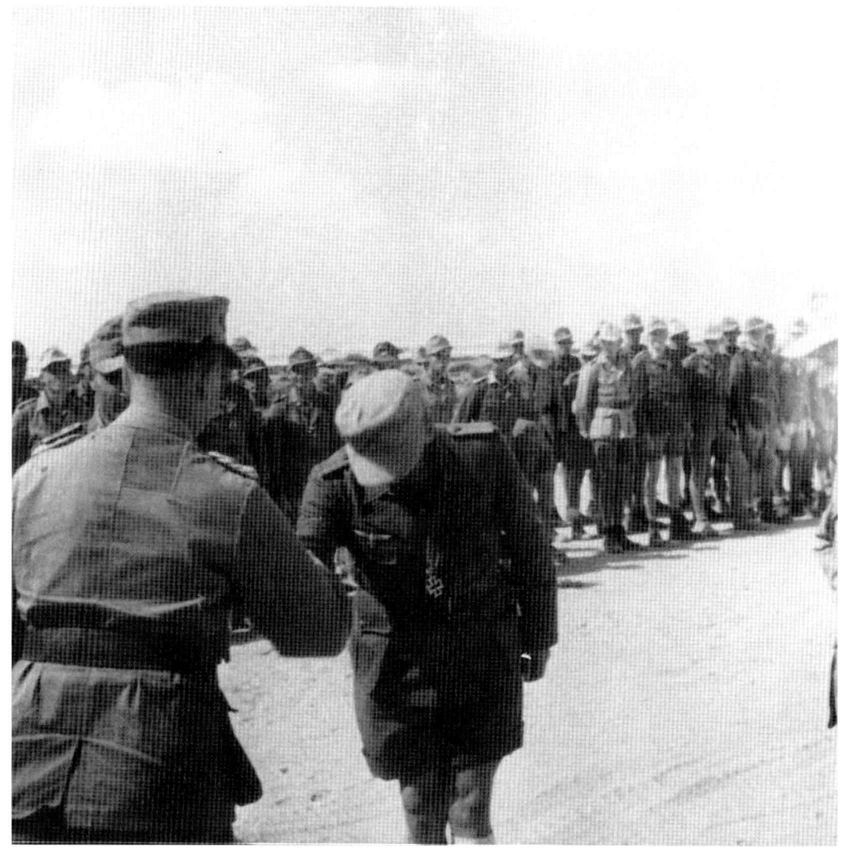

With a great show of respect to his superior, a soldier "macht einen diener." (To make a bow upon shaking someone's hand – done only by men.)

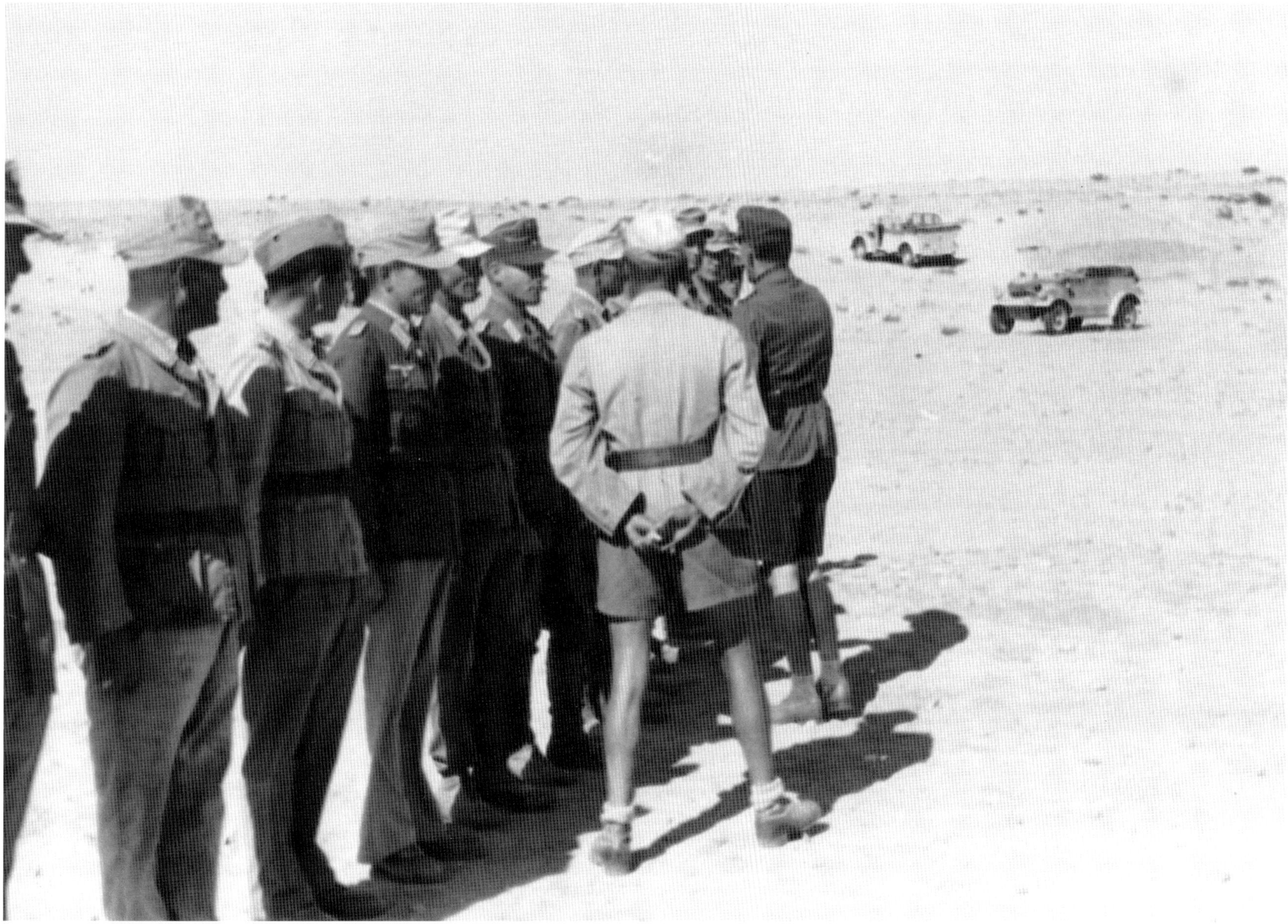

Back to camera, wearing shorts, Bayerlein stands by during the decoration ceremony.

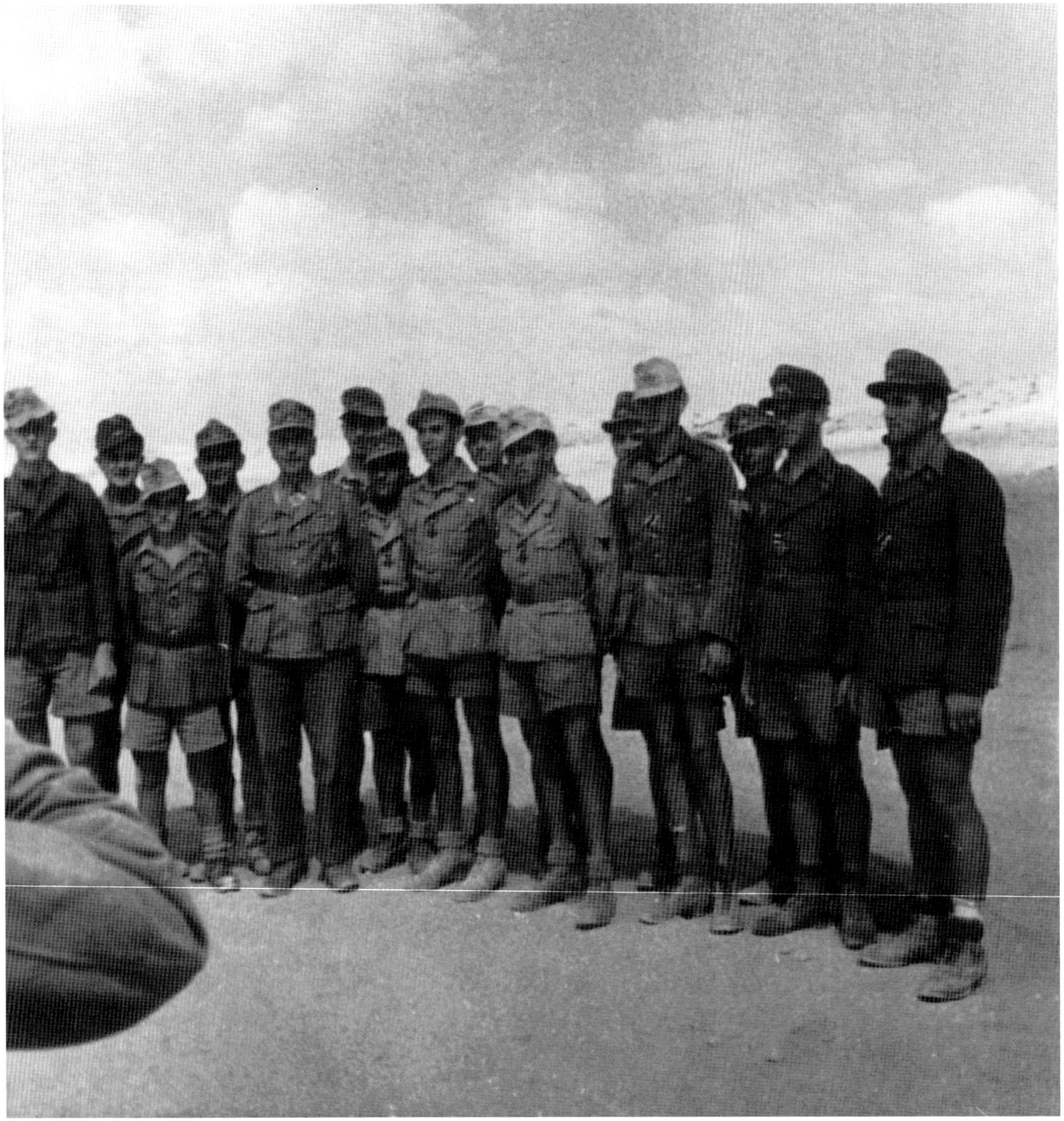

General Nehring posing with the men for their group photo.

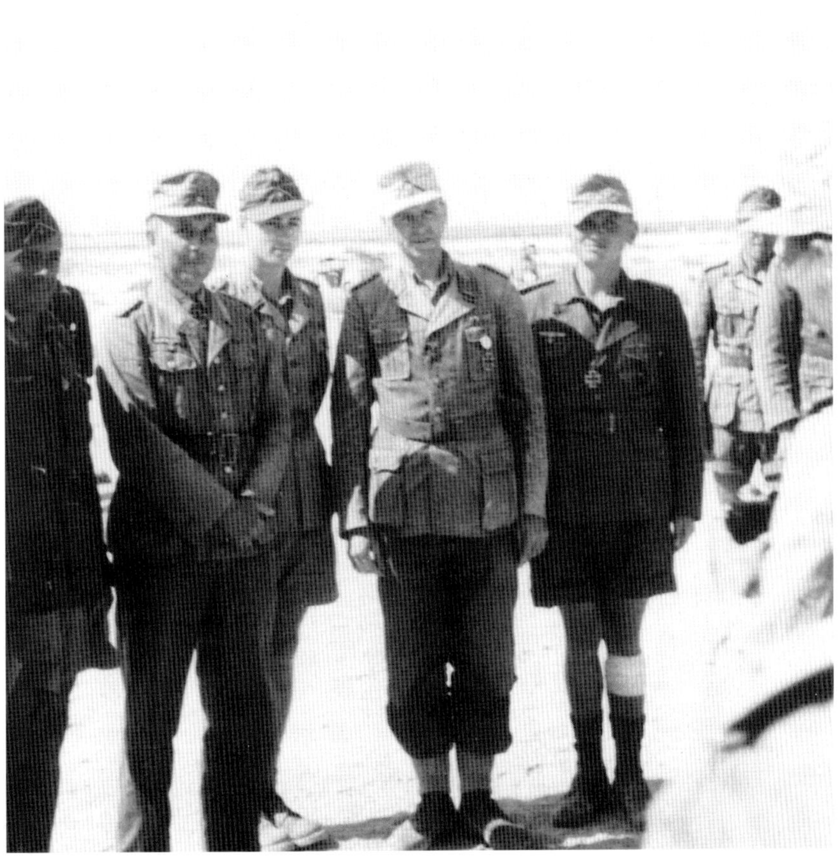

Nehring stands with a smaller group of soldiers.

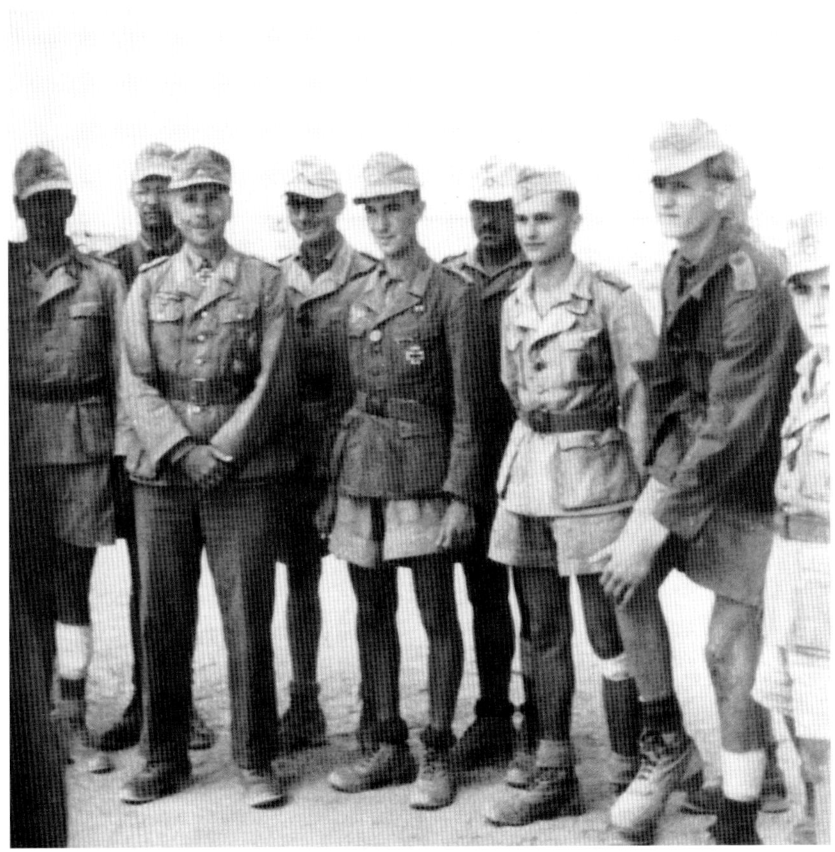

General Nehring stands with his troops as they proudly wear their decorations and gather around their senior commander for a photo.

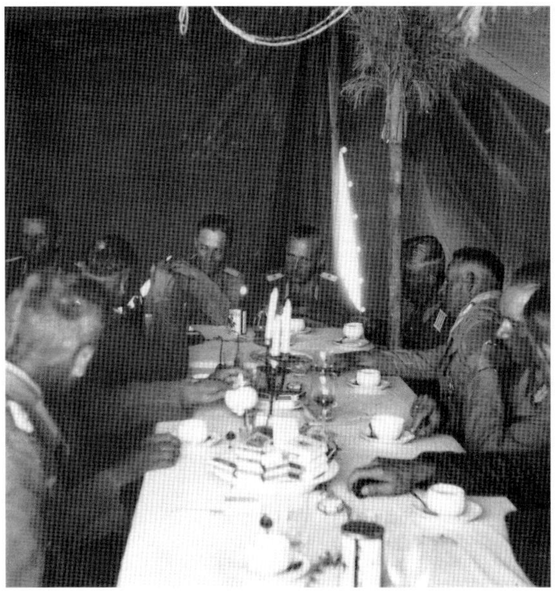

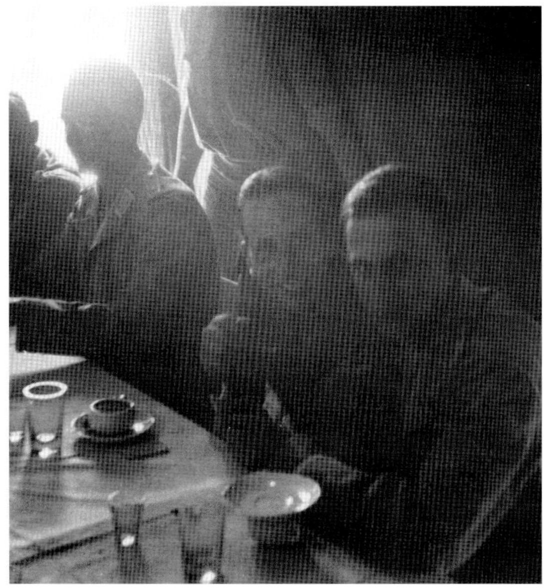

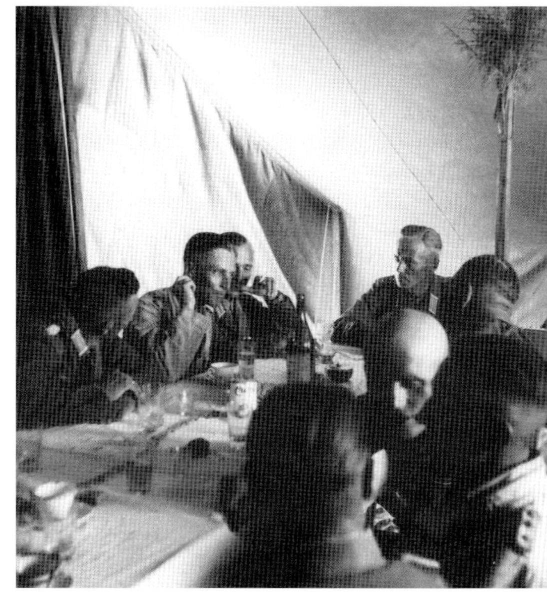

Left: An after-dinner coffee meeting among DAK officers, complete with tablecloths, candles, and a desert brush arrangement hanging on the tent pole. Center: Two of Bayerlein's comrades smile for the Chef. Right: Casual group enjoying drinks.

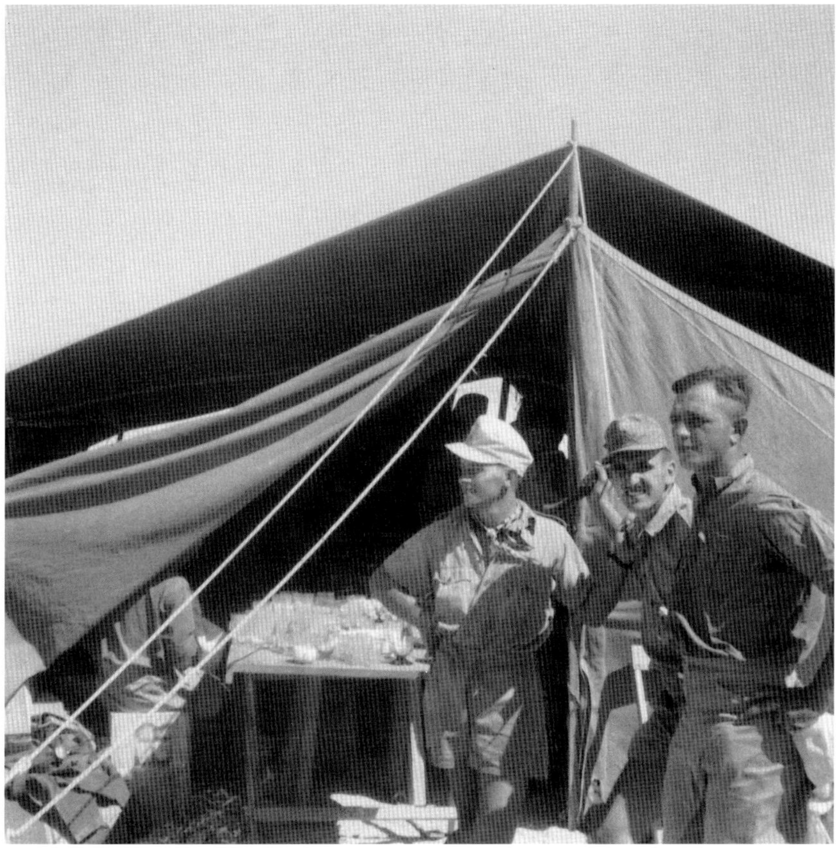

The party moves out of the tent.

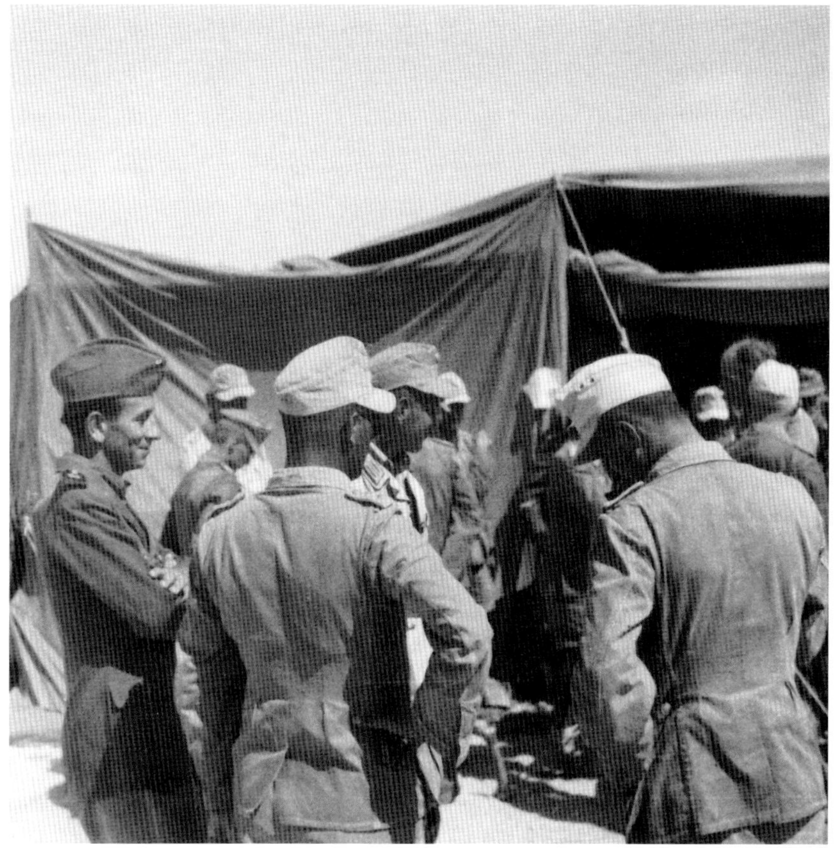

Officers mill around the tent after the award ceremony.

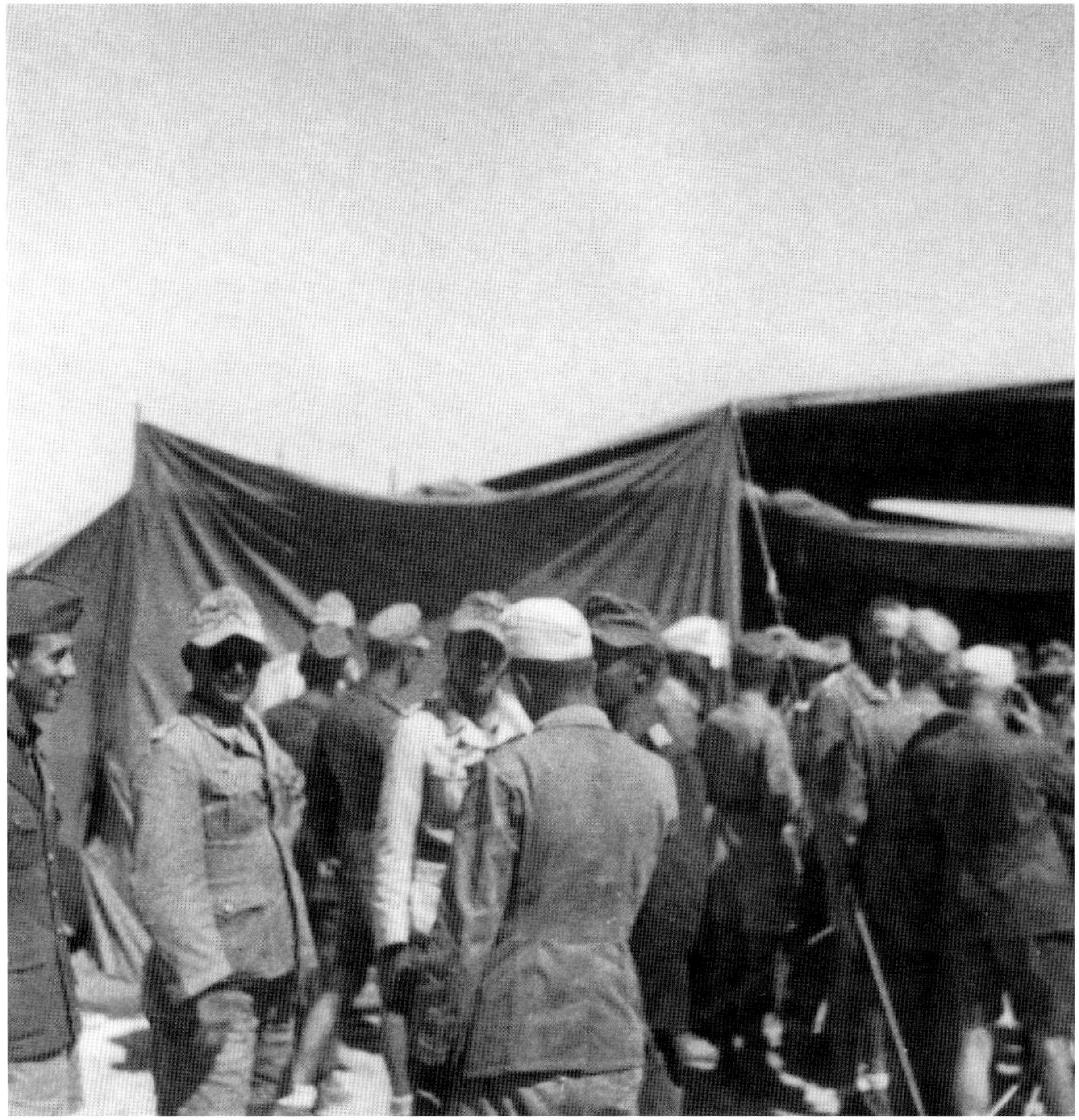

Bayerlein continues photographing his comrades.

Right
A final group photo of the men with their decorations.

Bottom right
General Nehring, (right), Field Marshal Rommel (center) and Oberst Bayerlein.

Below
A Propaganda Kompanie Sonderführer interviews Field Marshal Rommel. Nehring and Bayerlein stand nearby. Photo was taken during the presentation of the Ritterkreuz to Gefreiter Günther Halm, 29 July 1942.

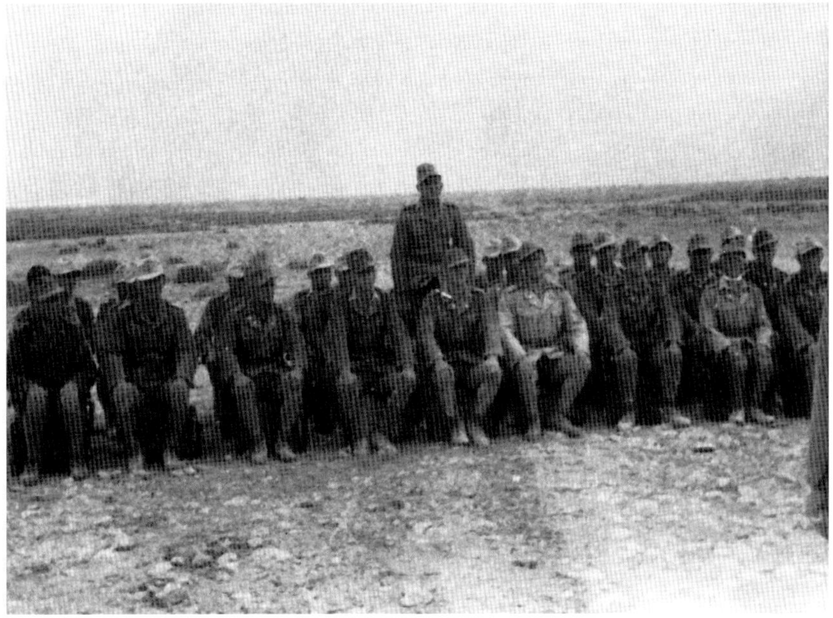

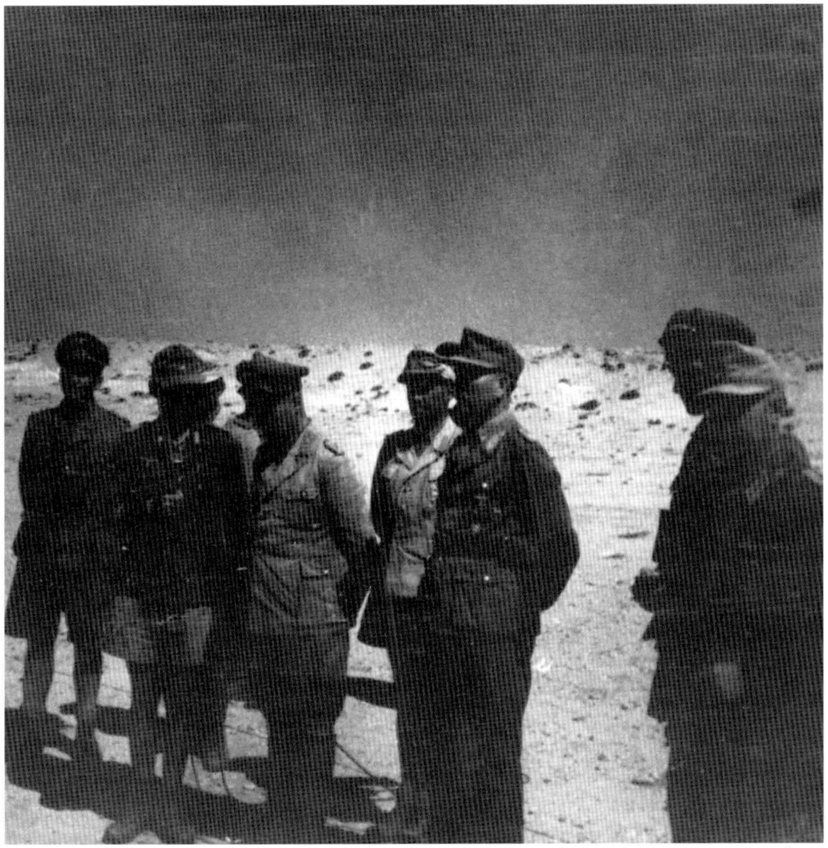

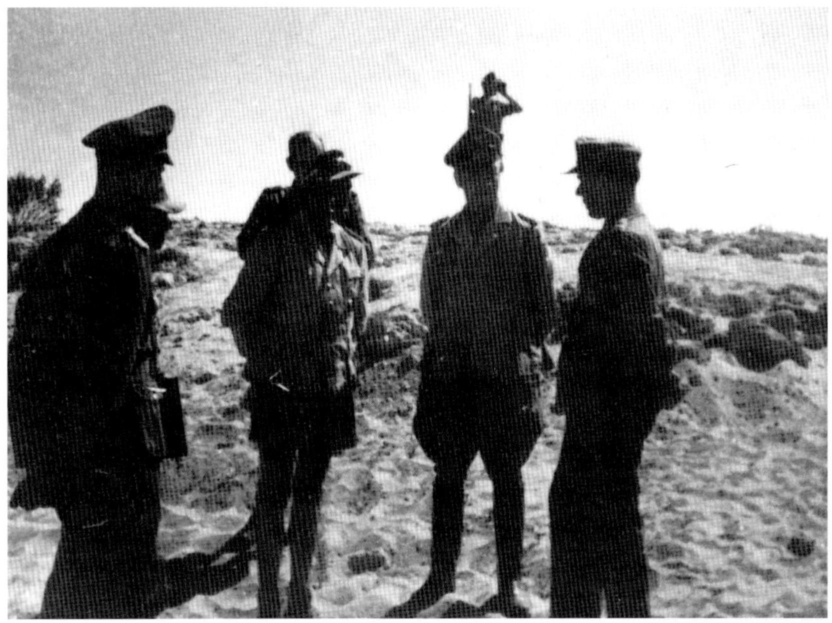

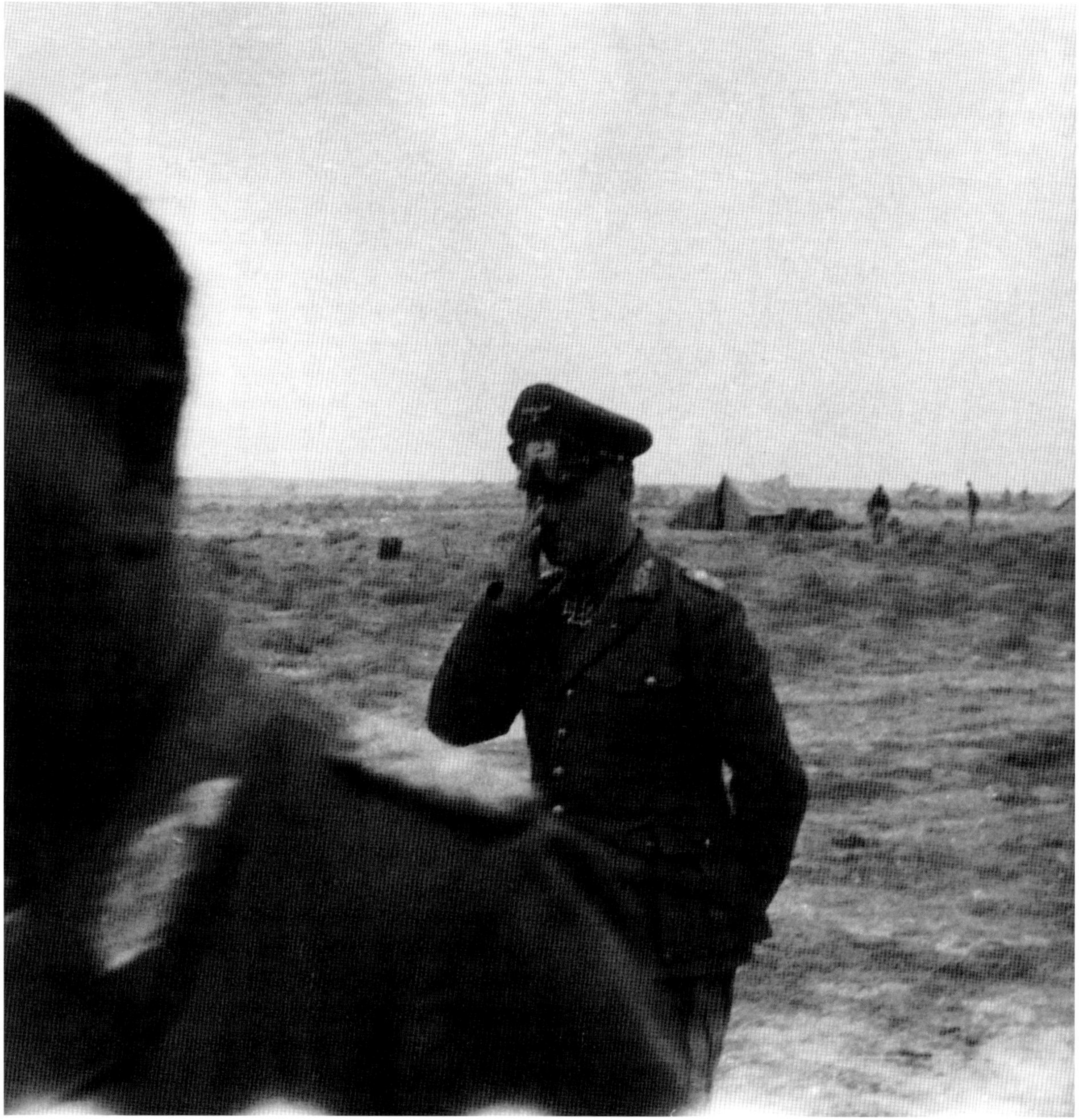

A tired Field Marshal Rommel, summer of 1942.

CHAPTER EIGHT

POWs AND THE DEAD

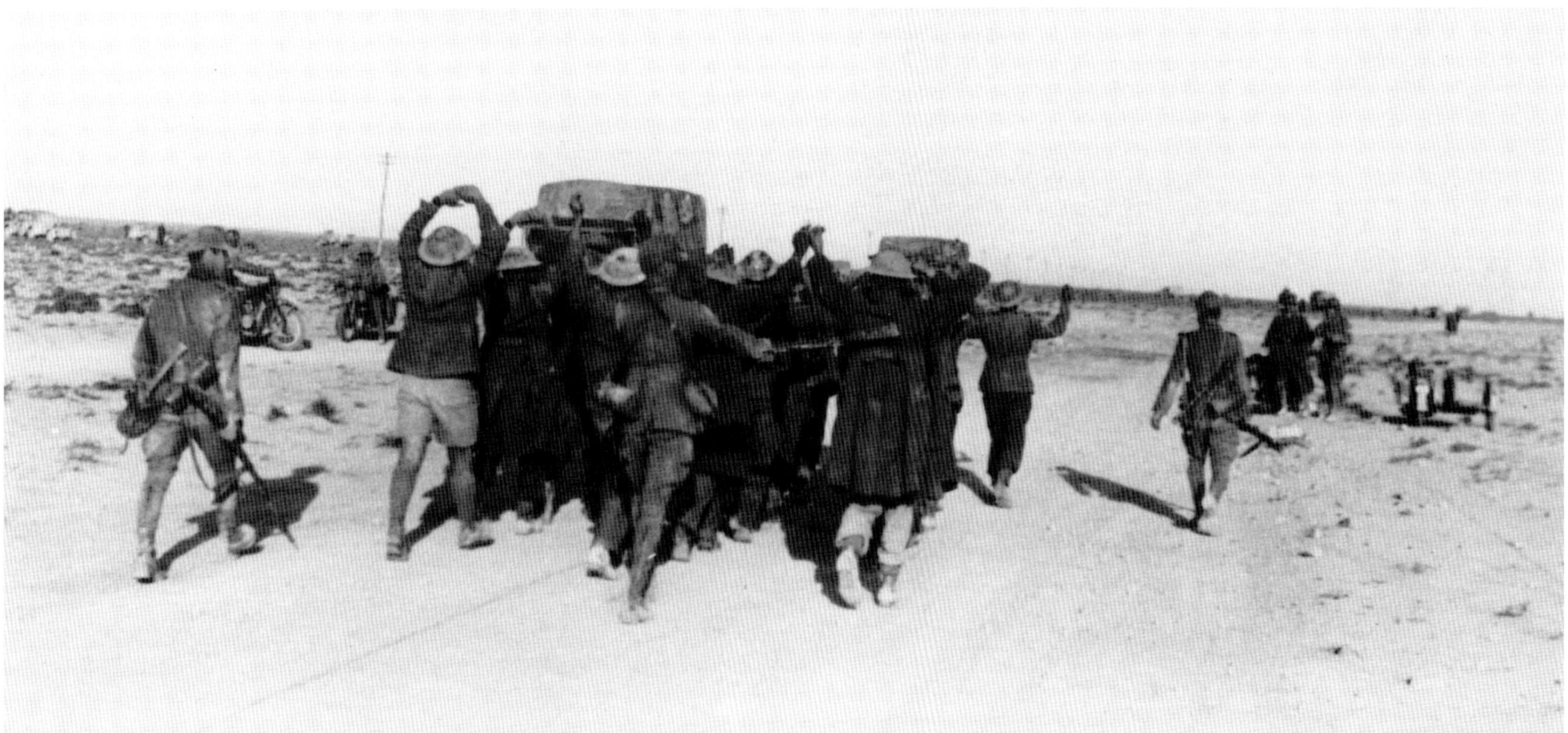

British prisoners are herded along by their guards. Most Allied prisoners would wind up in POW camps in Italy.

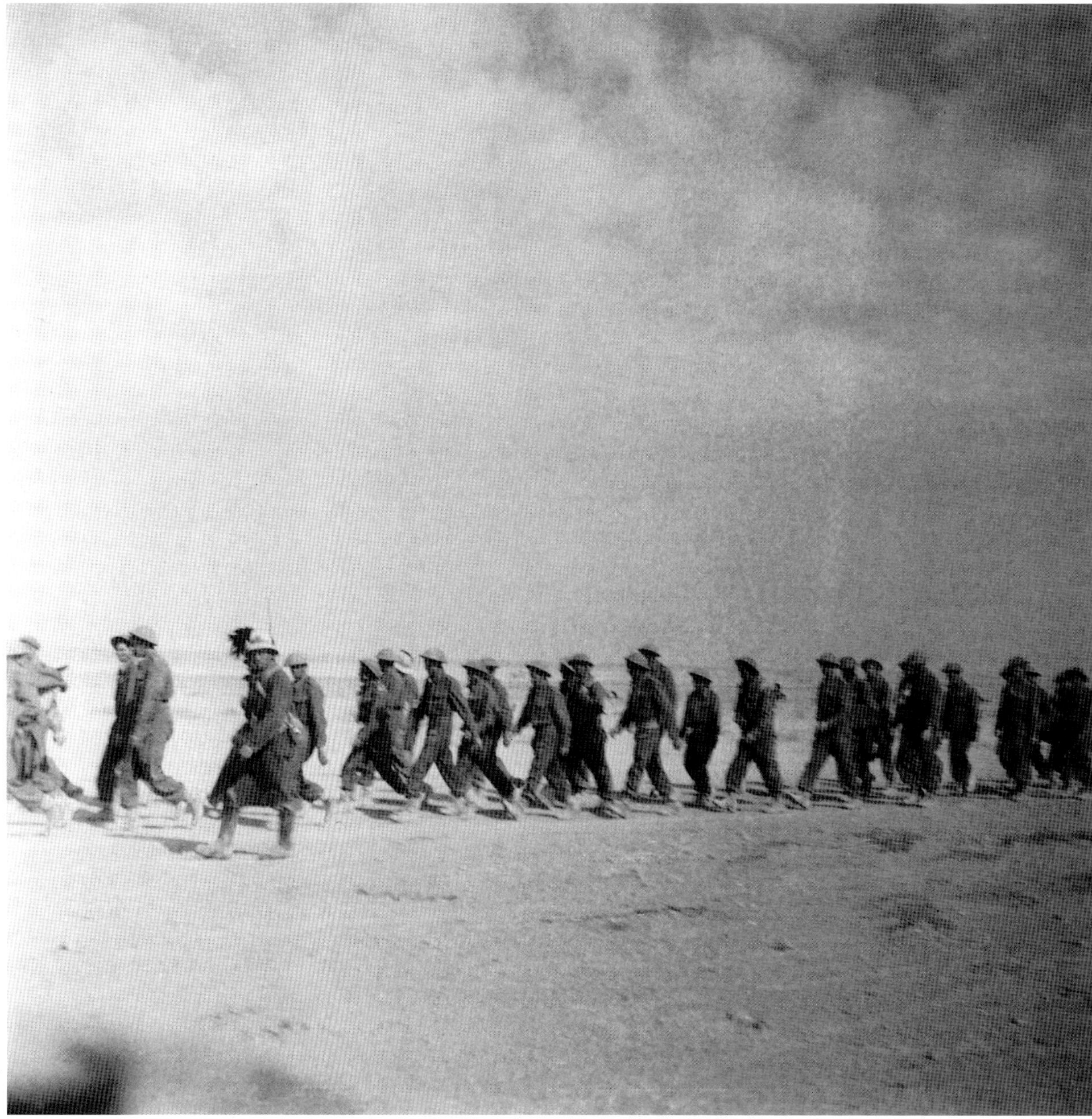

Another group of British prisoners straggles along with an Italian guard.

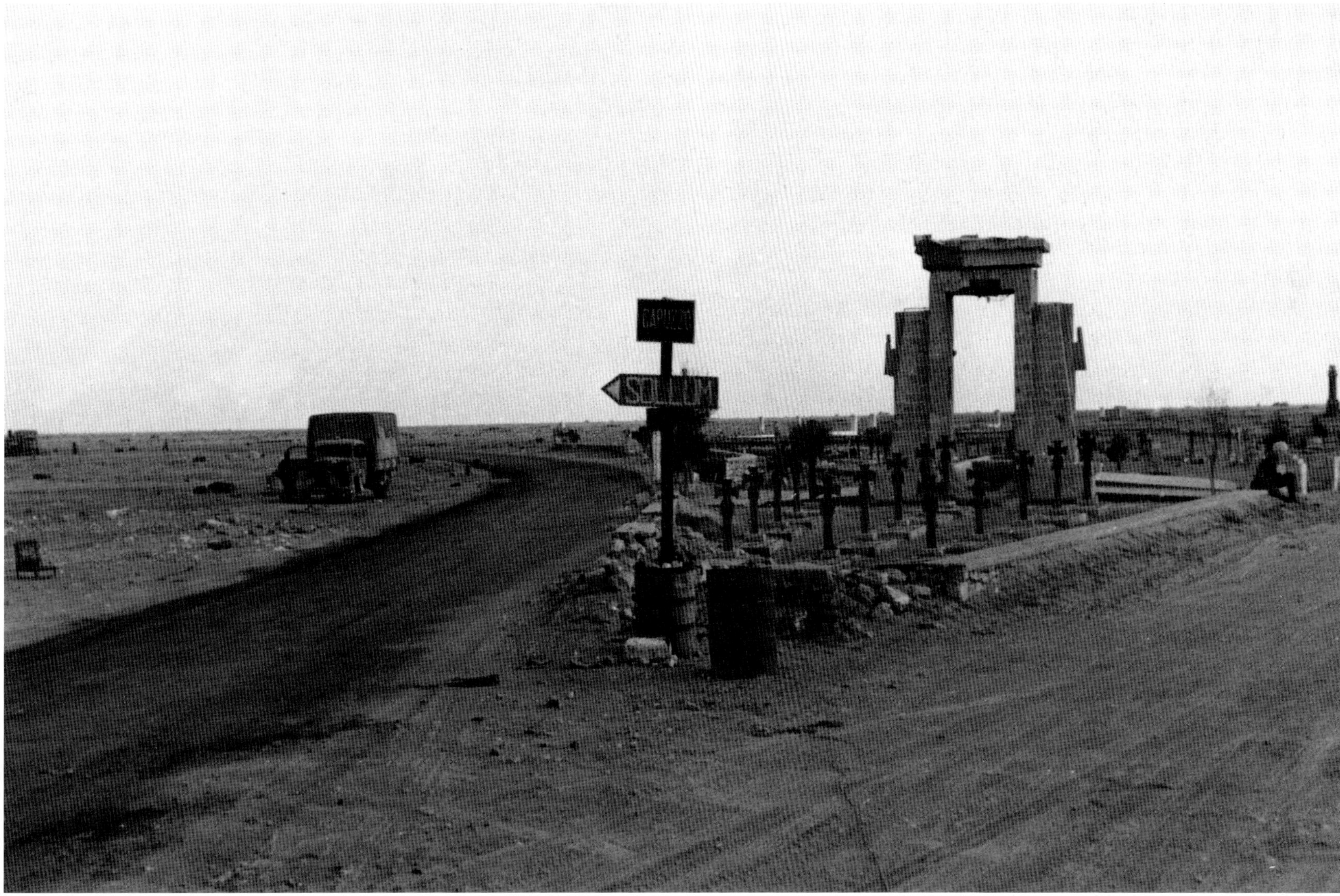

"The military cemetery is near the site of Fort Capuzzo in Cyrenaica; the road on the left leads to Sollum. The brick monument has the Fascio on each side (the rod and axe symbol of Fascist Italy). The tied rod represented the unity of the people, and the axe represented strength. Behind the brick monument are either water or feed troughs for Italian cavalry. The red brick, golden brown desert, blue skies and the monument are still there," — Rex Trye.[1]

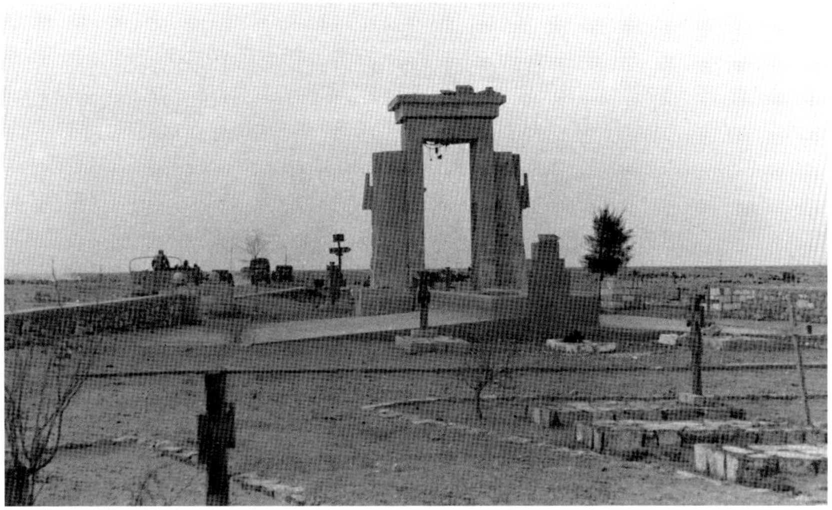

A photo shot taken from the opposite side of the military cemetery.

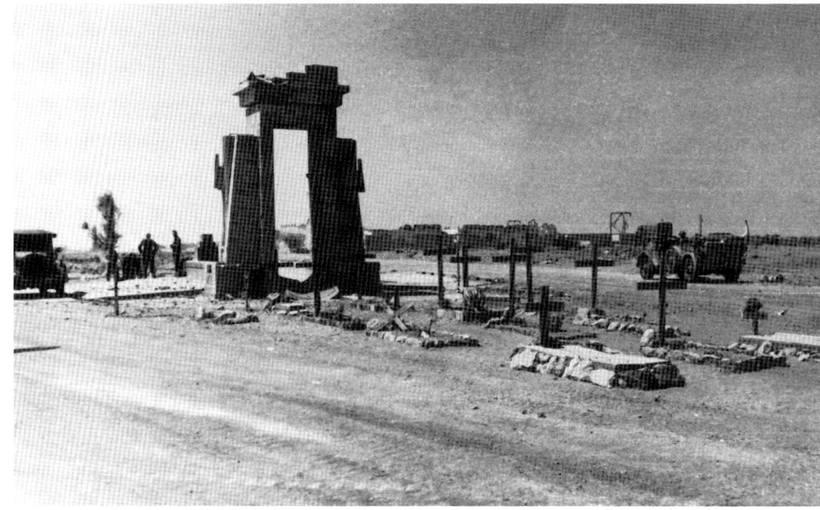

A view of the distant Fort Capuzzo from the military cemetery, along the Sollum road.

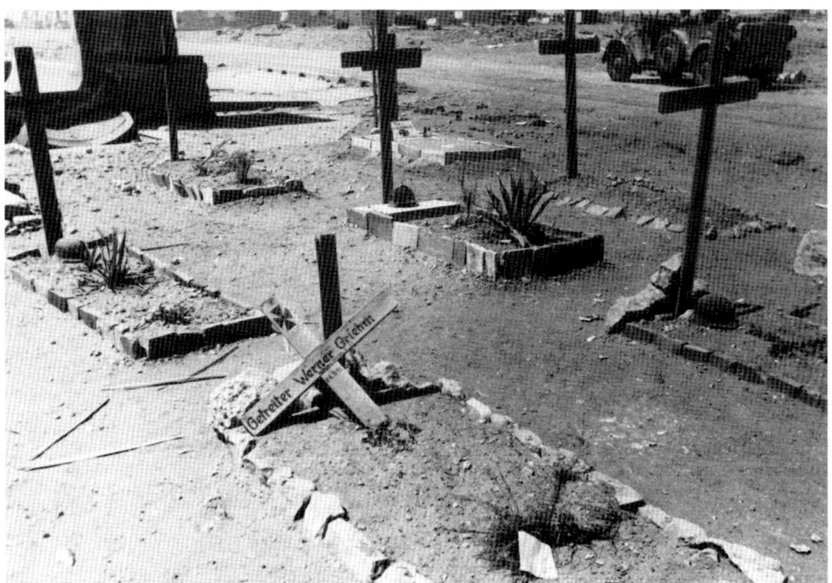

Bayerlein remembers a fallen comrade, perhaps from his Kampfstaffel (Headquarters group combat echelon).

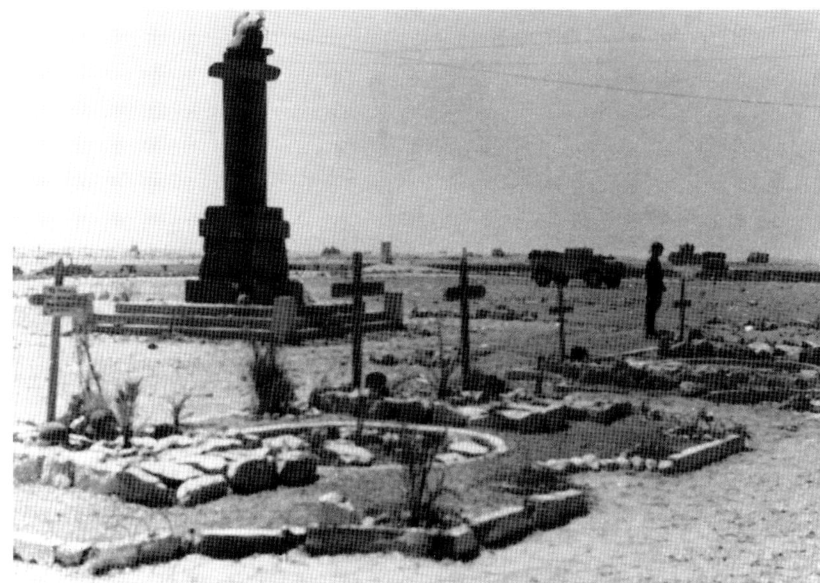

From the number of photographs he took of the small military cemetery, Bayerlein must have several comrades buried here.

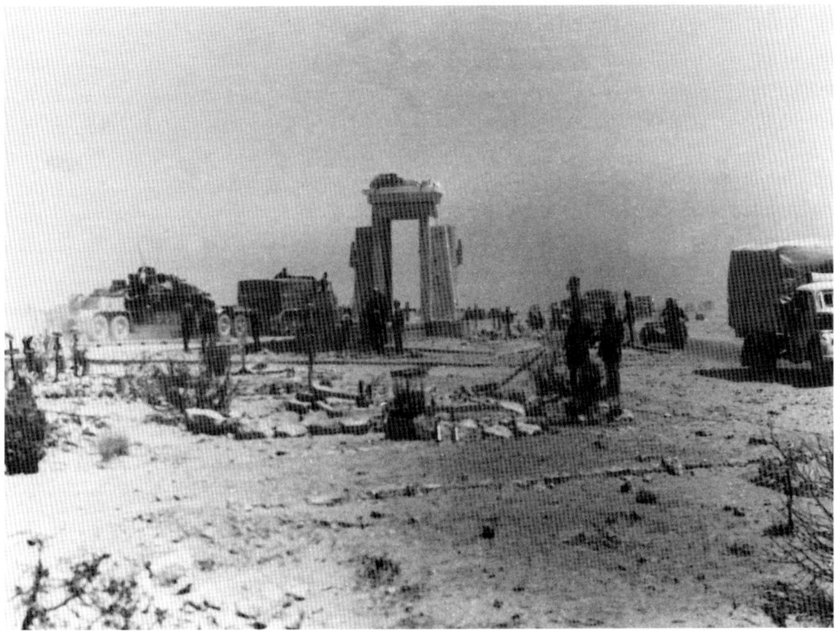

The living rumble on past the graves of the fallen, perhaps trying not to notice the fate that would befall may of them. The prime mover on the left hauls a panzer on a trailer.

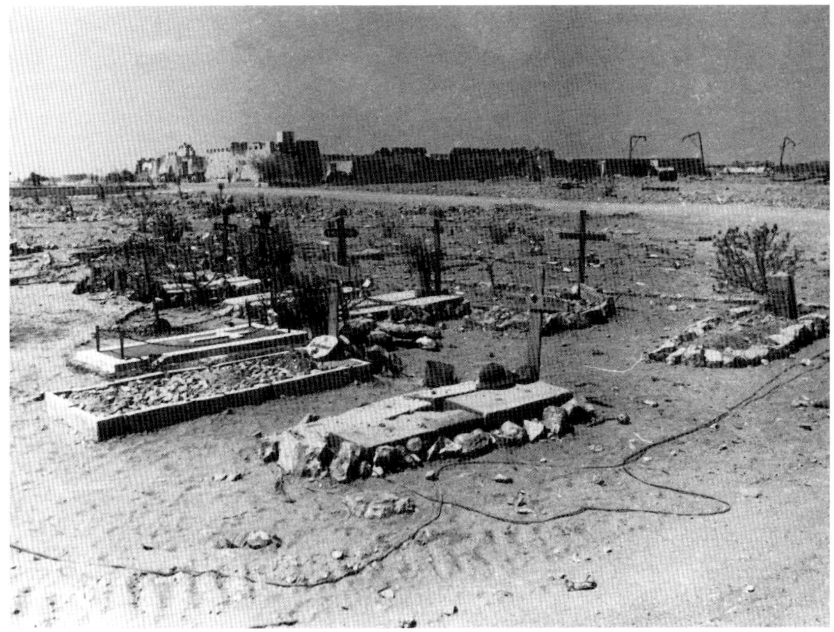

Bayerlein seemed to be affected by the cemetery – and the irony of the life rolling past. It appears he recorded almost 360 degrees in photos of the surrounding countryside.

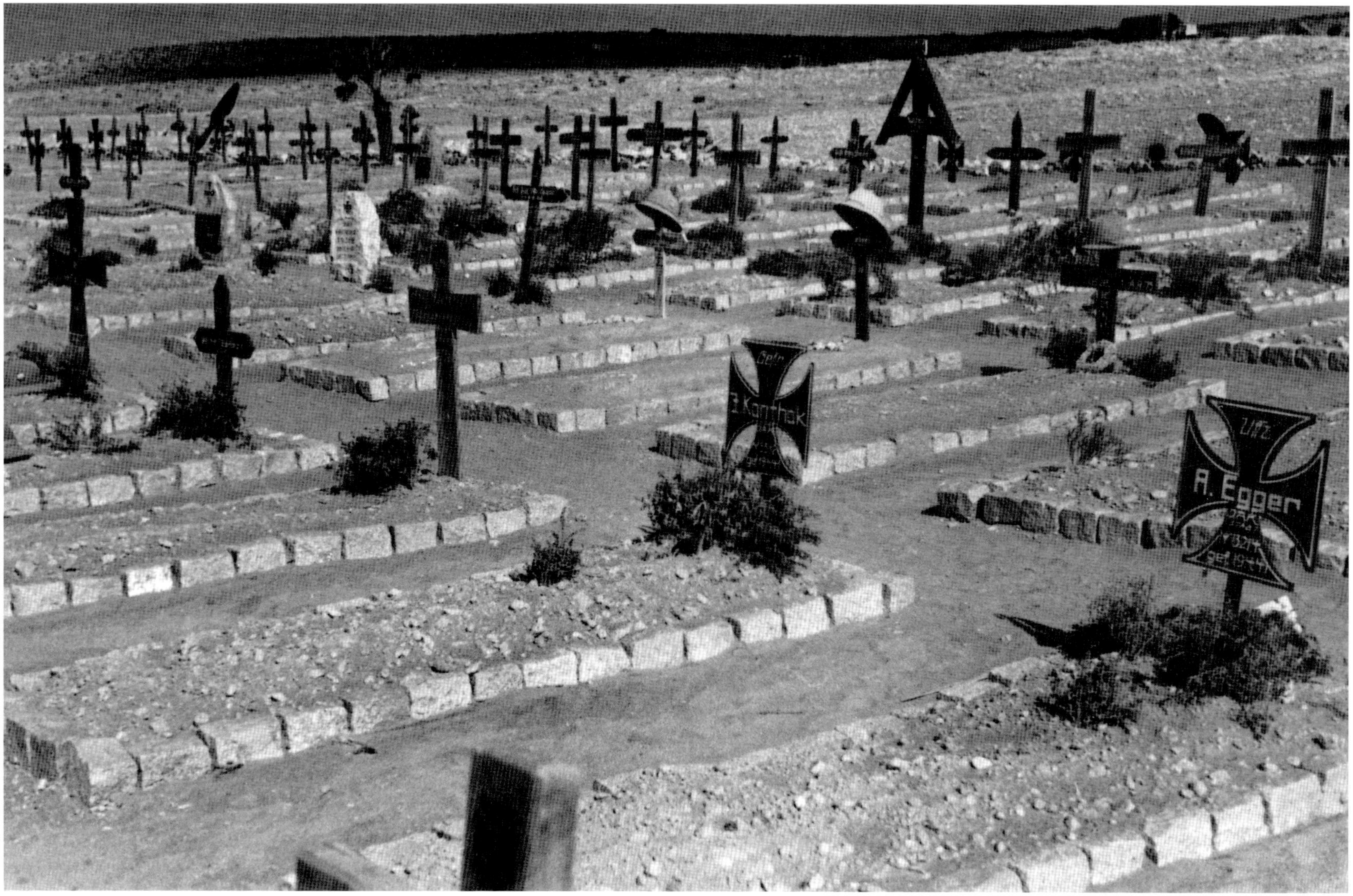

A view of the German and Italian cemetery established at 'Km41' on the Via Balbia west of Tobruk in mid-1941 after the fierce fighting of April and May 1941 after Rommel had launched a number of unsuccessful attacks against Tobruk. The dead of both the German and Italian armies from these battles were gathered and buried in this often visited and photographed cemetery. The grave marker visible in the right hand lower corner dates the death of a German soldier on April 19 1941.[2]

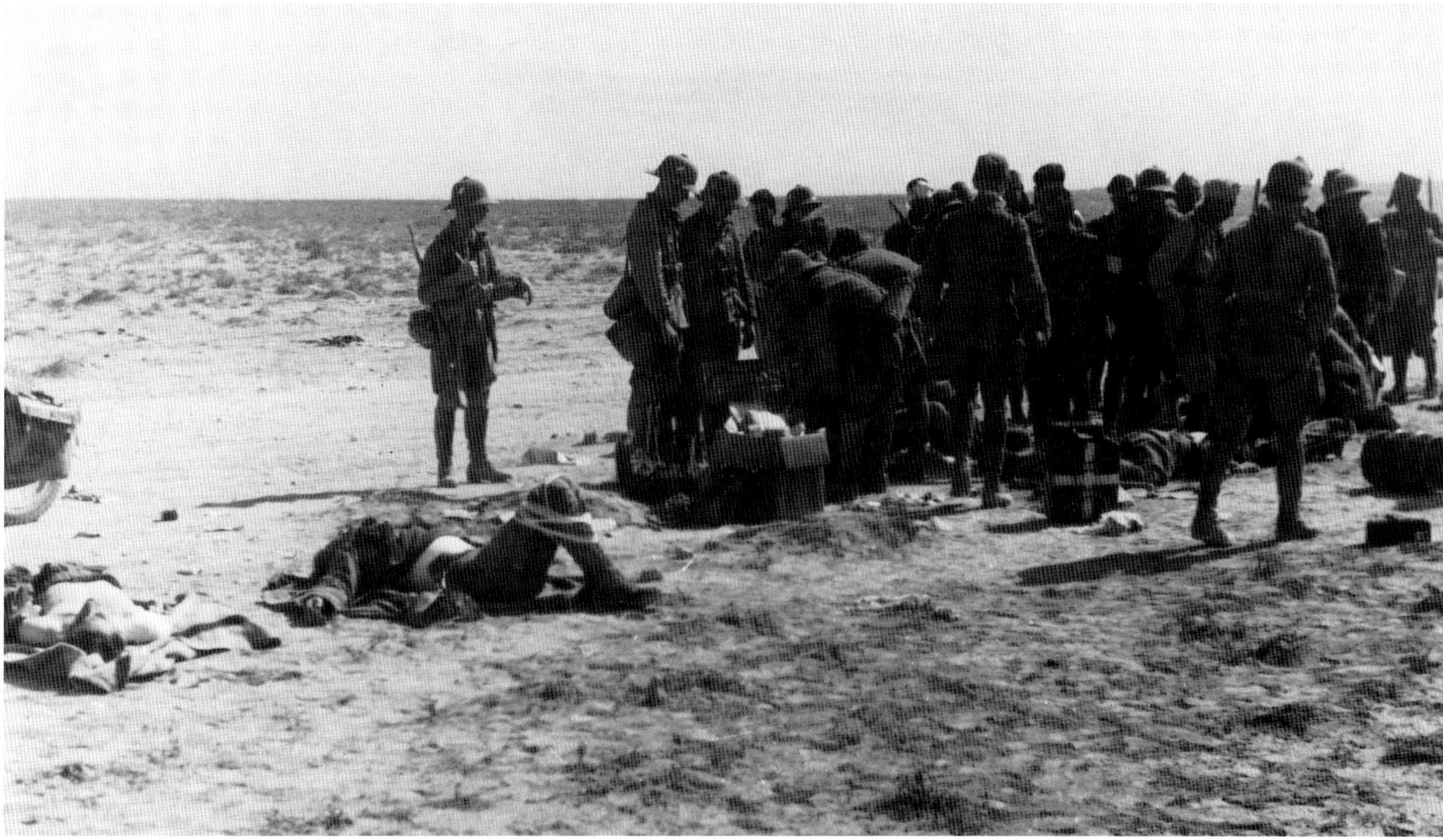

"This photo is a rare one in that it shows the bodies of two dead German soldiers in the foreground. It was a very uncommon act by a German soldier, to take personal snaps of one's own dead. This however would not have been the reason for Bayerlein taking this shot. He was recording the scene where German and Italian soldiers were endeavoring to save the lives of wounded comrades. The state of part undress evident on the two dead bodies indicates attempts had earlier been made to save their lives too. The body with knees drawn up and an exposed abdomen would have received an injection of morphine (which was commonly injected into the abdominal wall) and the bandages draped around his knees indicates an effort was made to dress a wound before he died (not visible in the photo). The other dead soldier, who is bare to the waist, has what looks like one gunshot or shrapnel wound to his right shoulder. It is possible to see more bodies lying on the ground among the group of soldiers standing to the right. It can be assumed that these men were still alive and presumably their condition was being stabilized ready for the arrival of a medical team and an ambulance or a vehicle that could evacuate them to a field dressing station. (The vehicle just visible to the left of the photo appears to be a motorbike and would not be suitable for transporting seriously wounded.) One of those standing around the prostrate bodies was also wounded as is indicated by the bandage around his head. The fact that rifles are slung across the shoulders of some of the onlookers, and that one man is wearing a steel helmet, indicates that they had either recently been in battle or at least close to one." — Dal McGuirk[3]

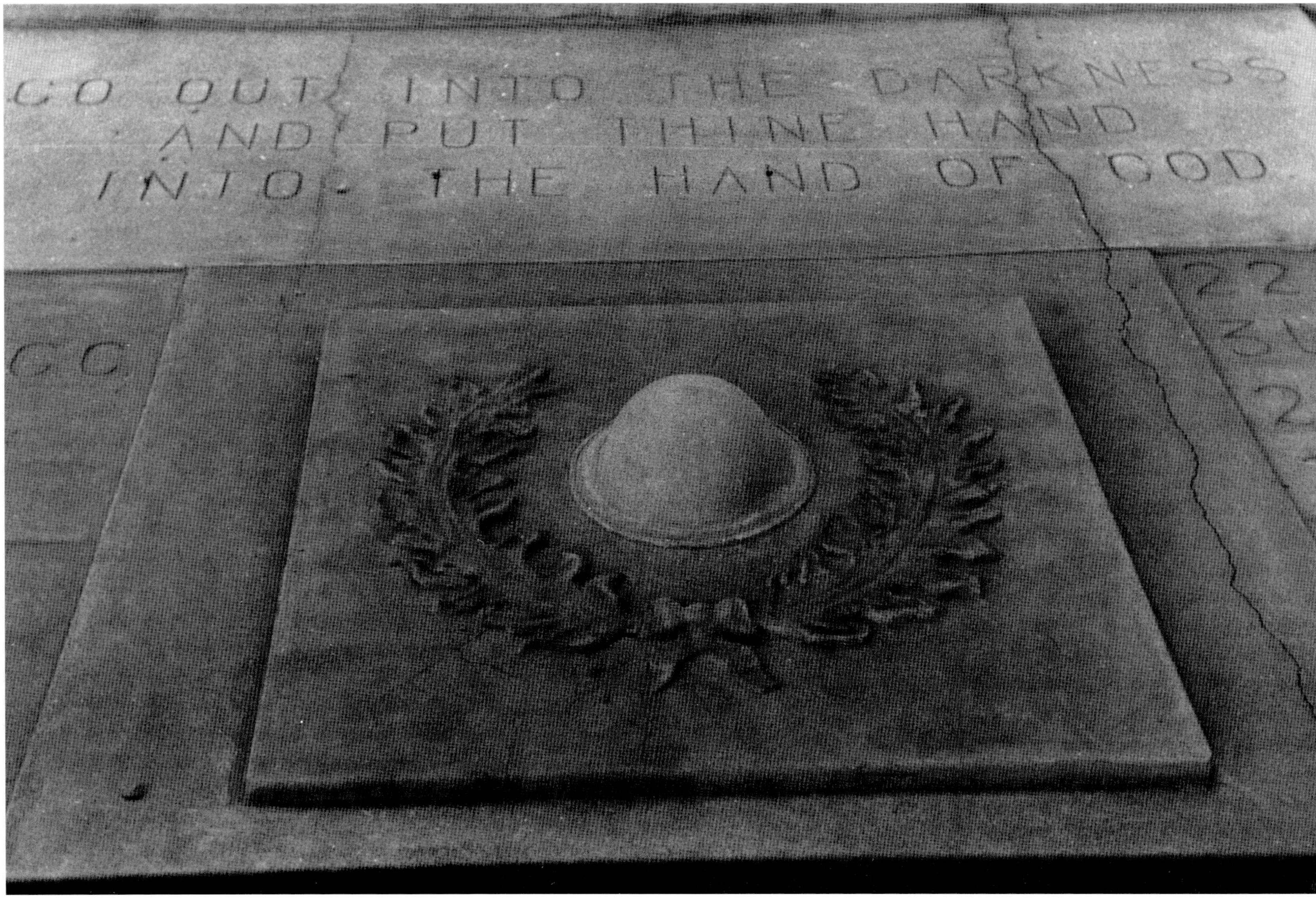

A British memorial fitting for their dead.

CHAPTER NINE

ANCIENT RUINS

In his January 1943 tour of the Tripolitania region of Libya, Field Marshal Rommel was accompanied by his A.D.C., Oberleutnant Alexander Hartdegen, and Chief-of-Staff, Oberst Fritz Bayerlein. The men took a break from the war – and a mental break from the imminent change of command – and visited the ancient ruins of the Roman city of Leptis Magna.[1] Bayerlein also had the opportunity to visit other sites of Roman, Byzantine and Greek ruins. Many Greek settlements were in the areas of Cyrene, Tolomaide and Tocra in Cyrenaica.[2] The Tripolitania-Cyrenaica areas were subjugated by various civilizations, each rising and falling over centuries.

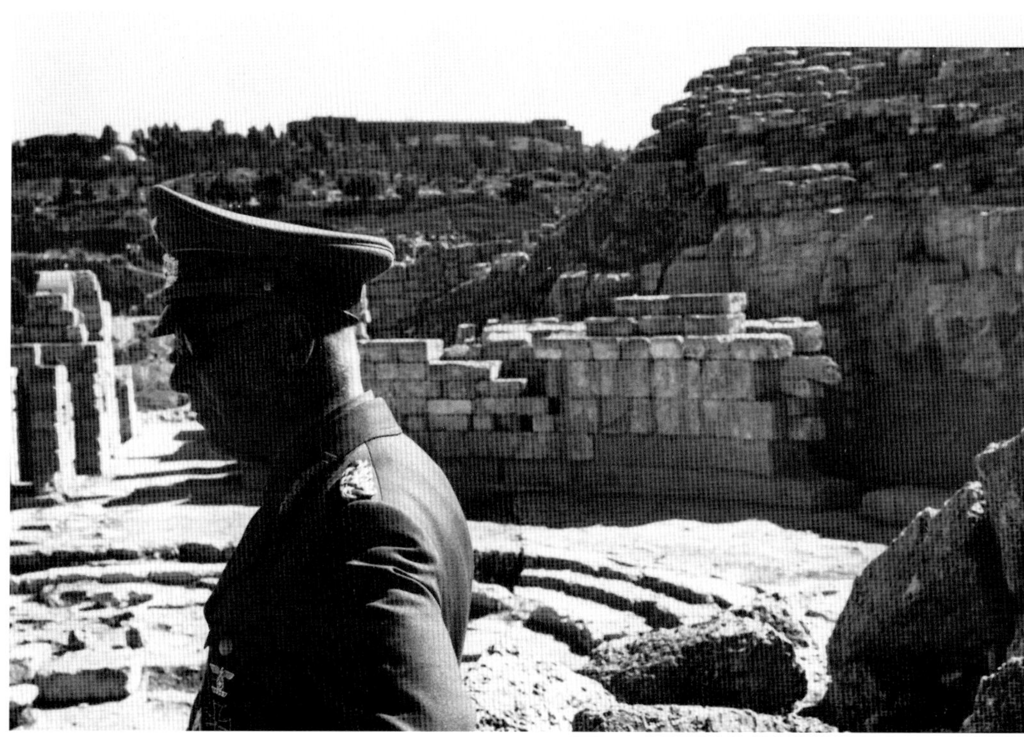

Bayerlein catches a nice profile shot of Field Marshal Rommel wearing sunglasses and studying the ancient ruins on their visit at Leptis Magna. "Our thoughts were more with Montgomery than with ancient ruins. Moreover the strain and lack of sleep of the past few days were beginning to tell", Rommel noted.[3]

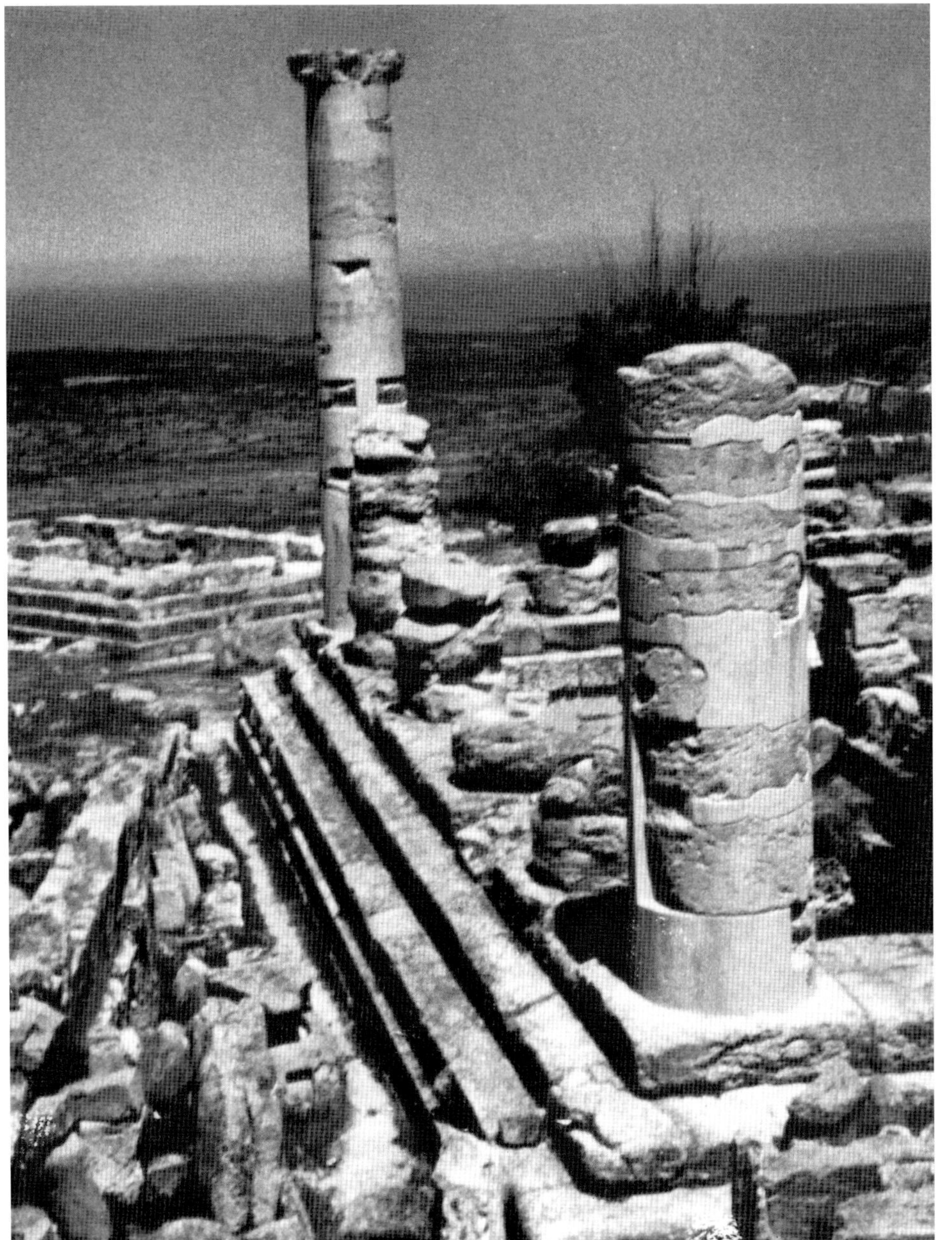

Left
"The city of Leptis Magna, east of Tripoli, was originally a Phoenician port settled in the first millennium B.C. It was later part of the Roman Empire under Emperor Trajan (98-117). It had a large port, warehouses and facilities, some of the best to be found anywhere in the Roman Empire. It later declined, as the port reclaimed from the wadi silted up." — Rex Trye.[4]

Opposite

Top left
Another view on the tour with Rommel. Bayerlein photographs the Hadrianic Baths – some of the largest in Roman North Africa – built in A.D. 126-127 at Leptis Magna.[5]

Top right
View of the Cardo Maximus, close by the market at Leptis Magna.[6]

Bottom left
Close up of the Cardo Maximus.

Bottom right
Bayerlein photographs the ancient columns set against the beauty of the Mediterranean Sea.

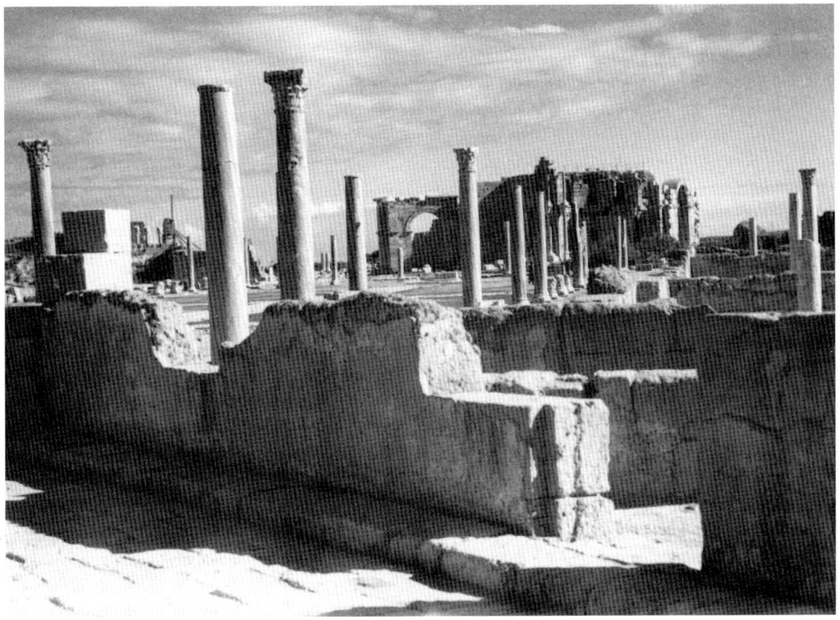

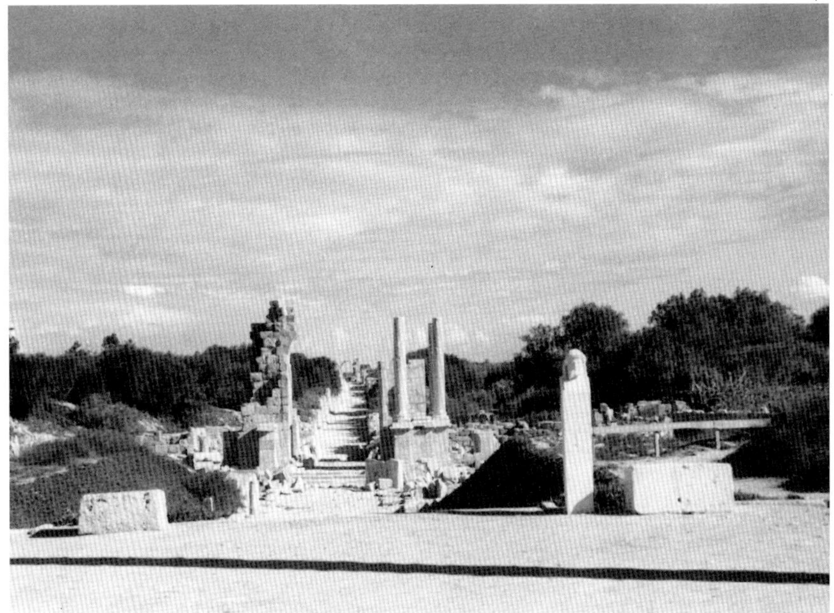

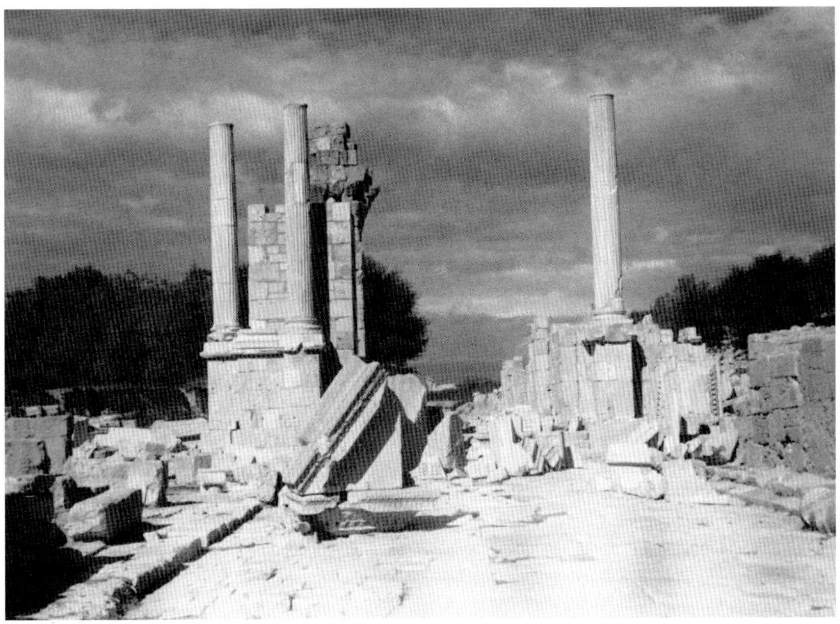

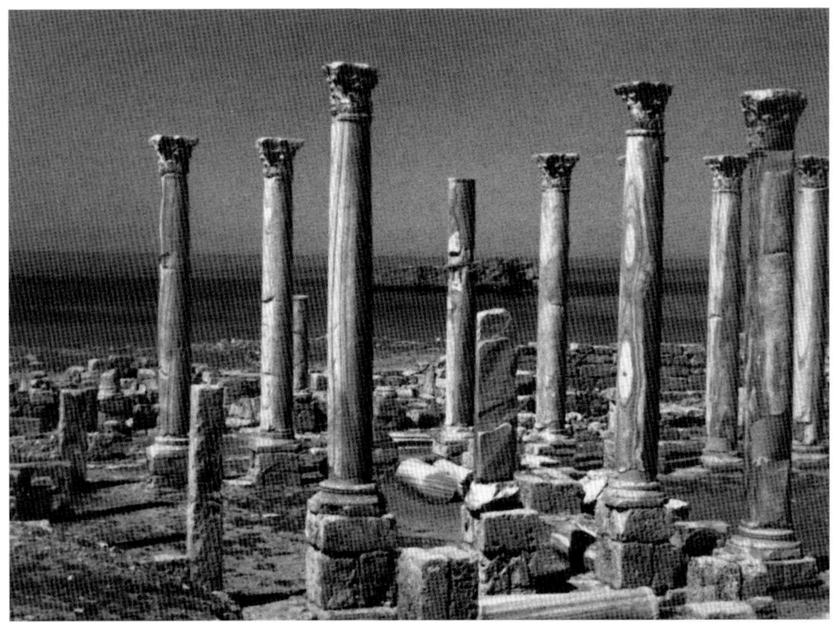

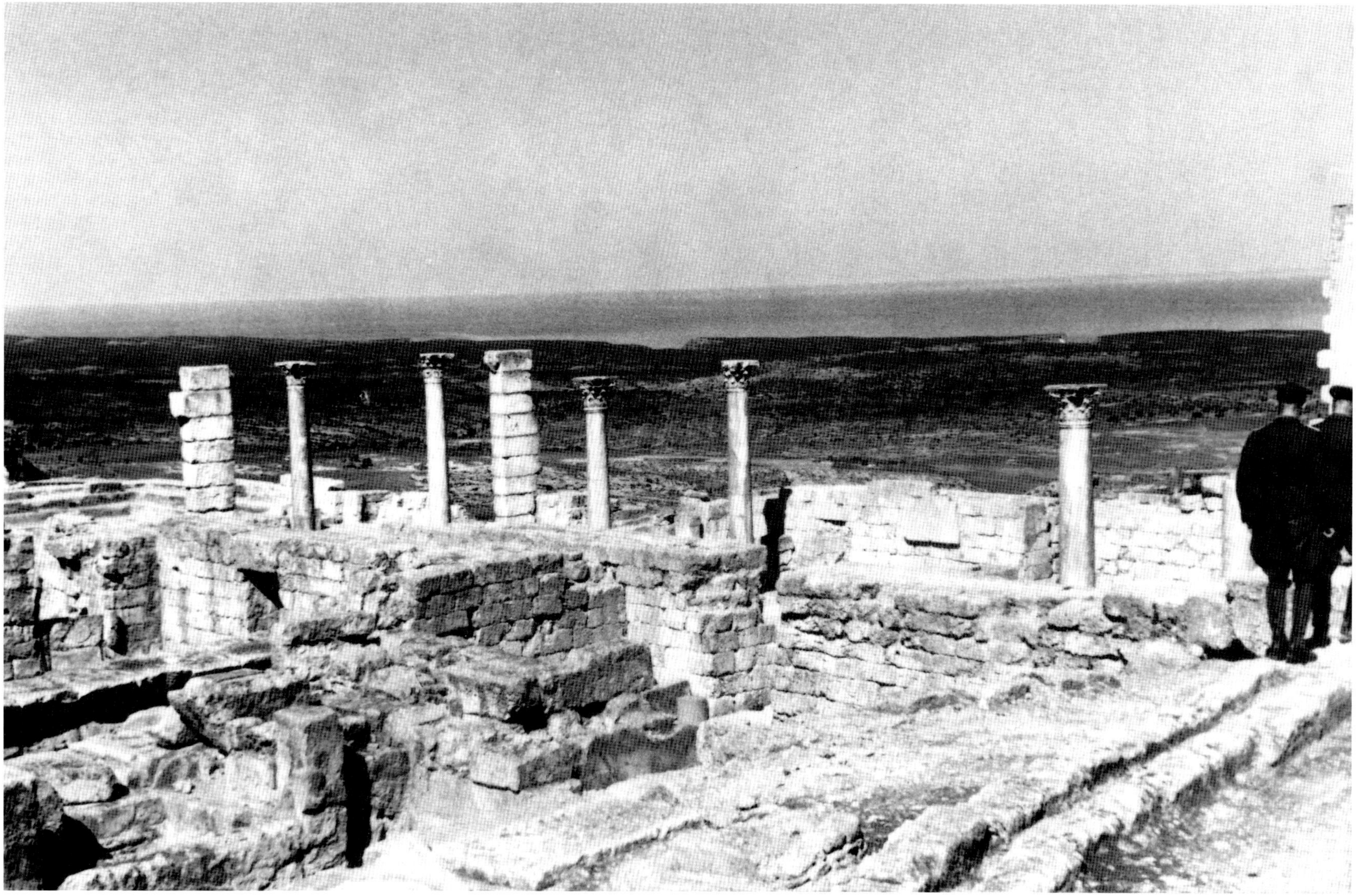

Rommel (on far right) departs this particular sight. This may be an earlier photo. The men's uniforms appear new.

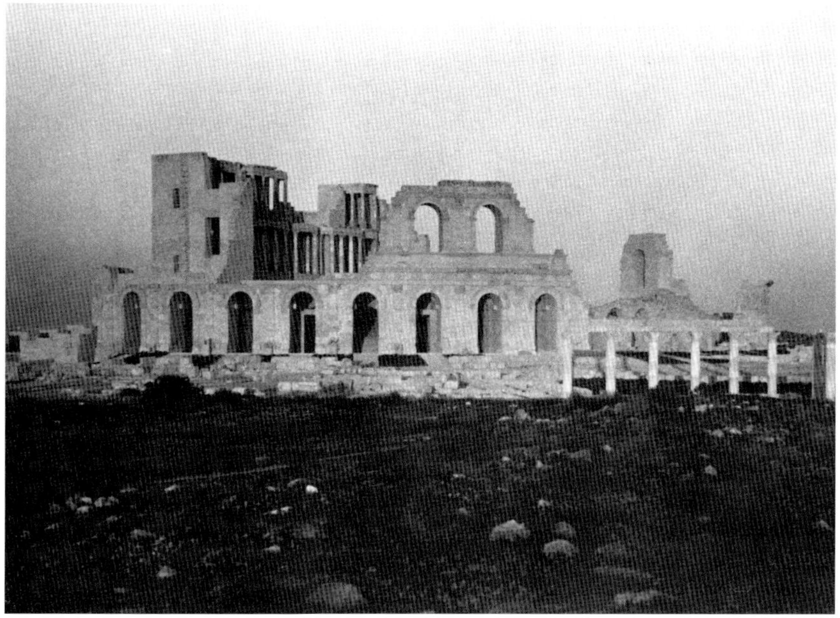

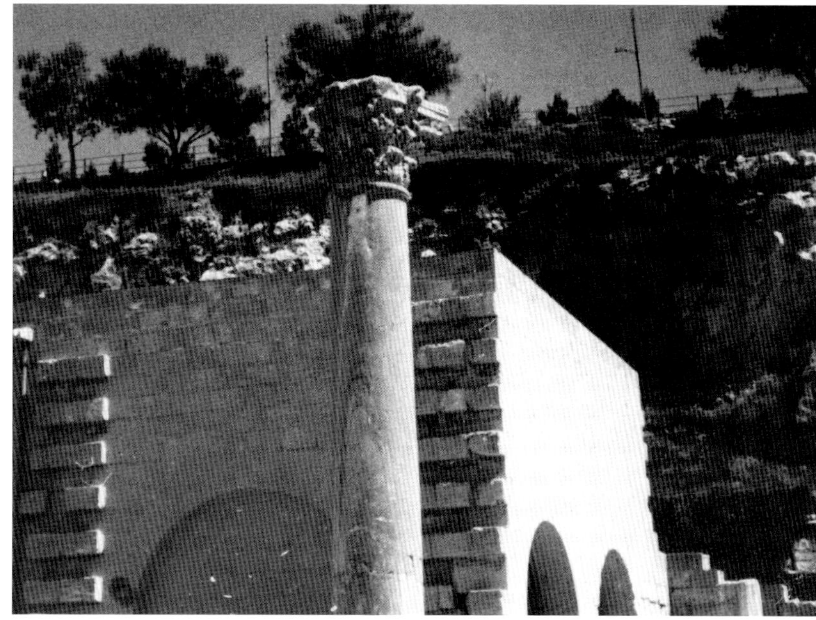

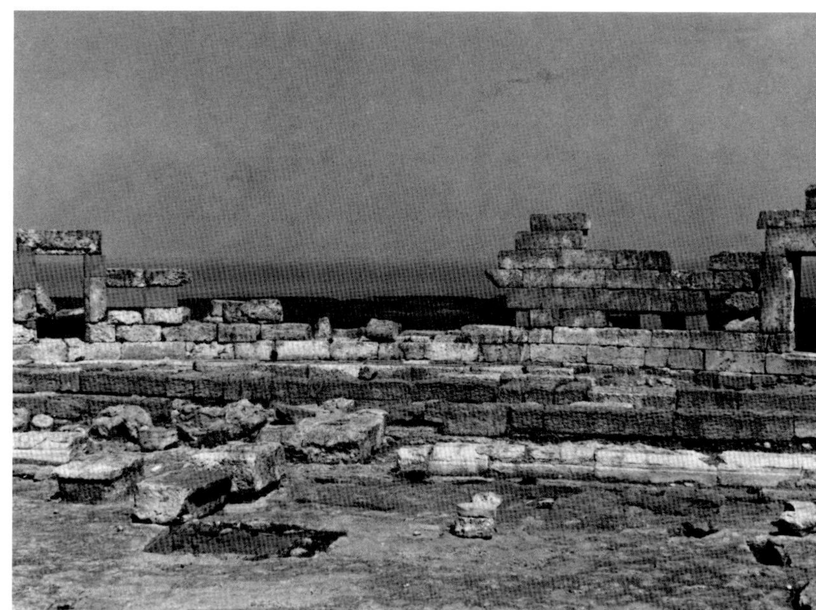

Above
"The Theater at Sabratha in Tripolitania is located 42 miles east of Tripoli. The theater was the most substantial building remaining in this ancient city, built by the Antonines in the second century A.D. It was largely reconstructed by Italian archeologists in the late 1930s. Modern performances were held in the theatre – the first being in 1937 in time for Mussolini's visit: Oedipus the King by Sophocles, with a musical accompaniment by the baroque composer Andrea Gabrieli." — Rex Trye.

Top right
View looking up a steep hill toward the modern development. Italian excavations were quite thorough.

Right
Although in black and white, Bayerlein makes a study with the sky, the sea and the textures from the rubble from civilizations past that demonstrates the fragility of the stone to the elements of time and destruction of long forgotten wars.

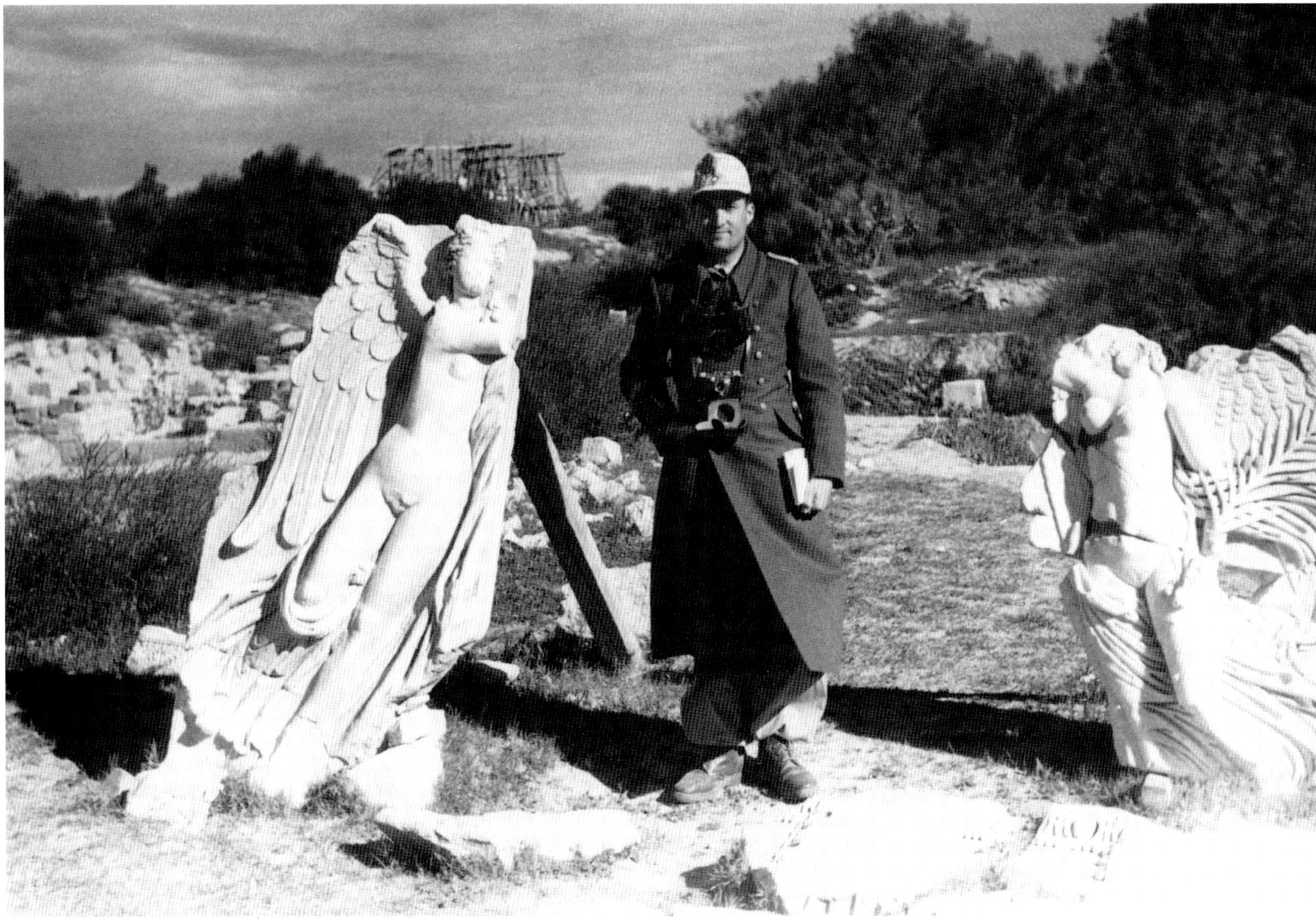

Everyone enjoys the tour – with camera ready: an Oberleutnant in Rommel's entourage poses with the Angels at the Temple of Jove.[7]

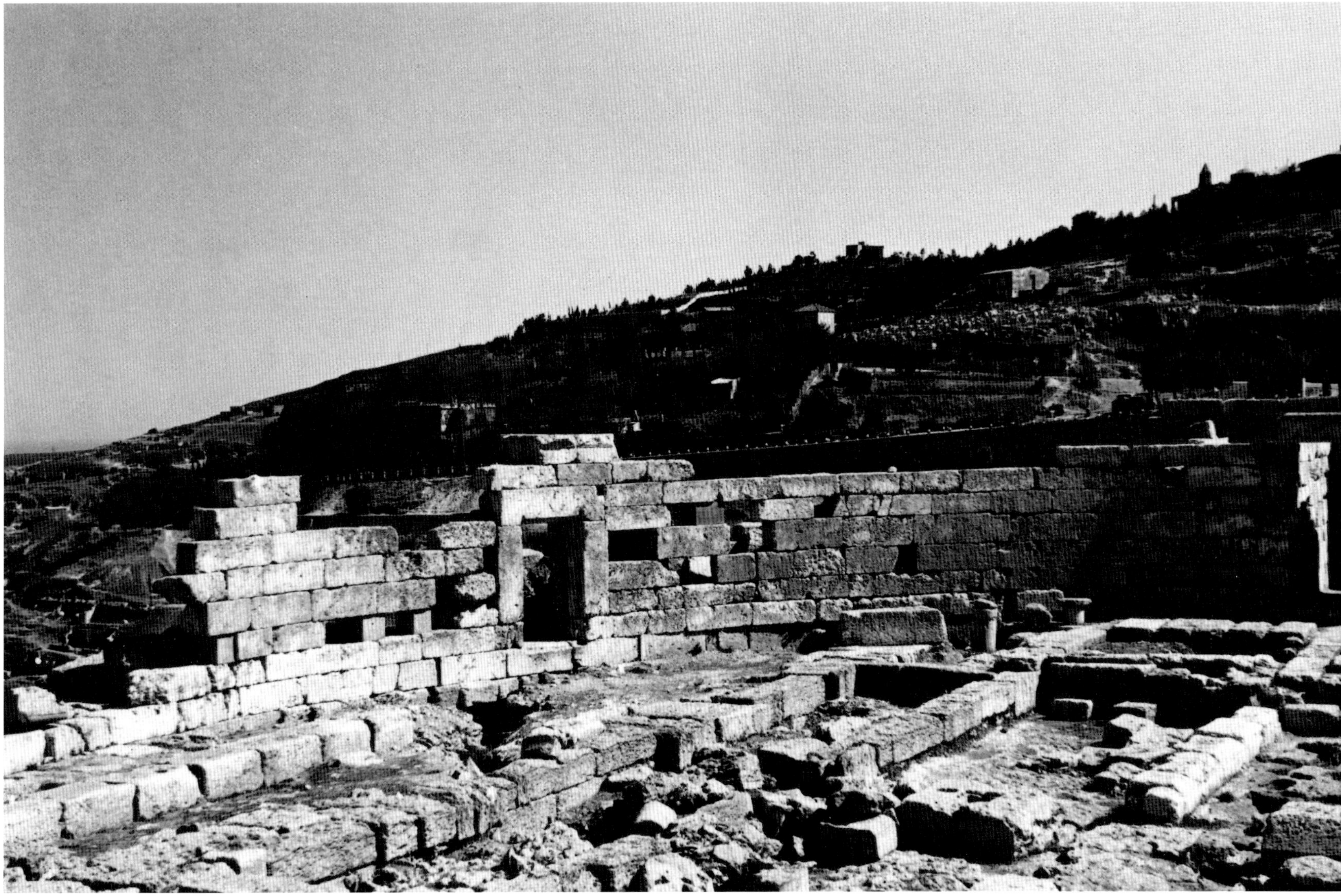

The hillsides rise steeply from the Mediterranean Sea. Building materials from these ruins have been scavenged over the centuries, recycled into new buildings.

CHAPTER TEN

PANZERS

The following selection of Panzerkampfwagen (Pz.Kpfw.) photographs was identified by Thomas Jentz, an author well-known and well-studied in German armor.[1] There were no locations or dates on Bayerlein's panzer photographs. It appears that he deliberately focused on close-ups of the panzers.

A Pz.Kpfw. II stirs up a cloud of dust.

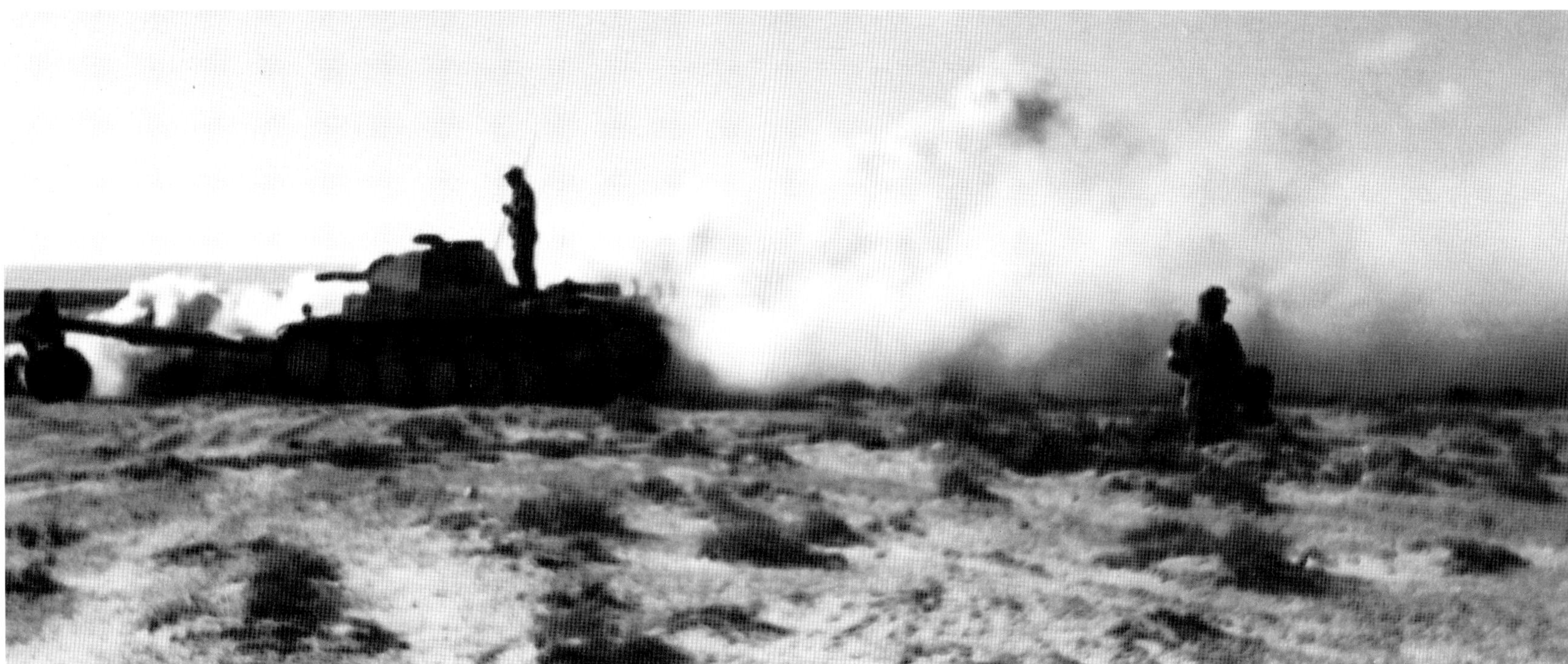

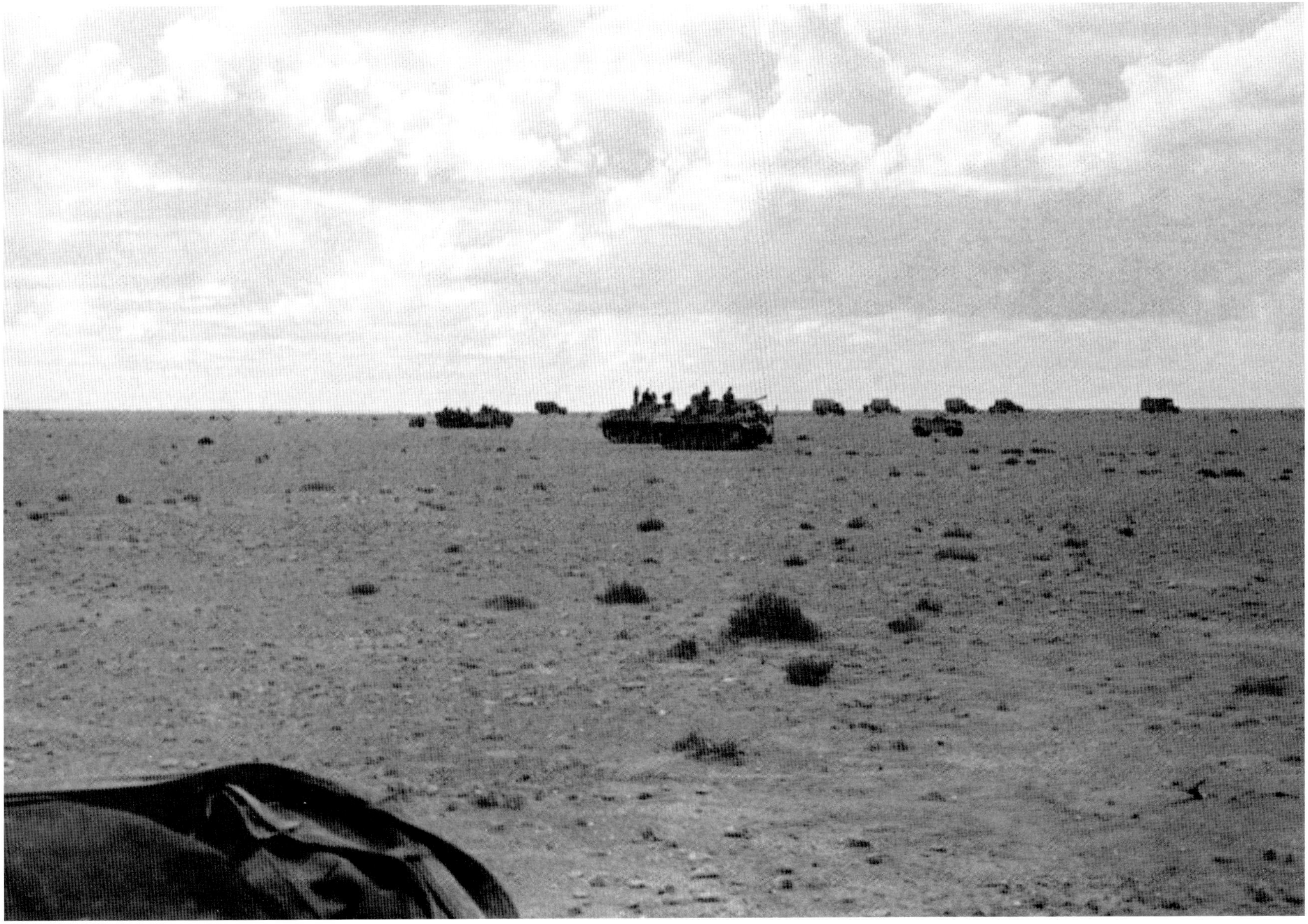

Distant view of panzers and supply vehicles.

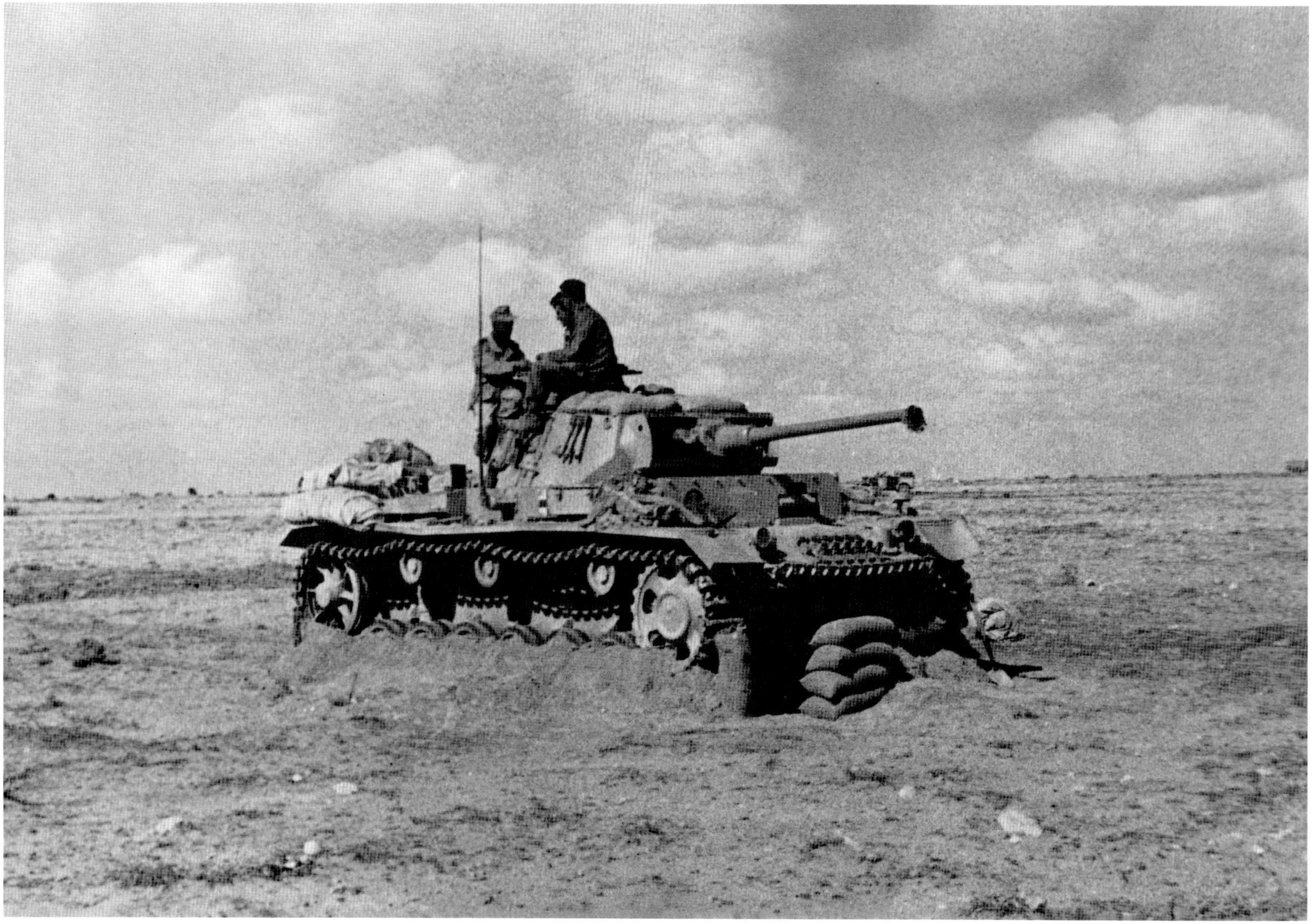

The crew of a Pz.Kpfw.III (Spezial) relax. They have sandbagged around the front and rear, perhaps sleeping under the panzer for protection, as was often done. Bayerlein dated this photo 7 November.

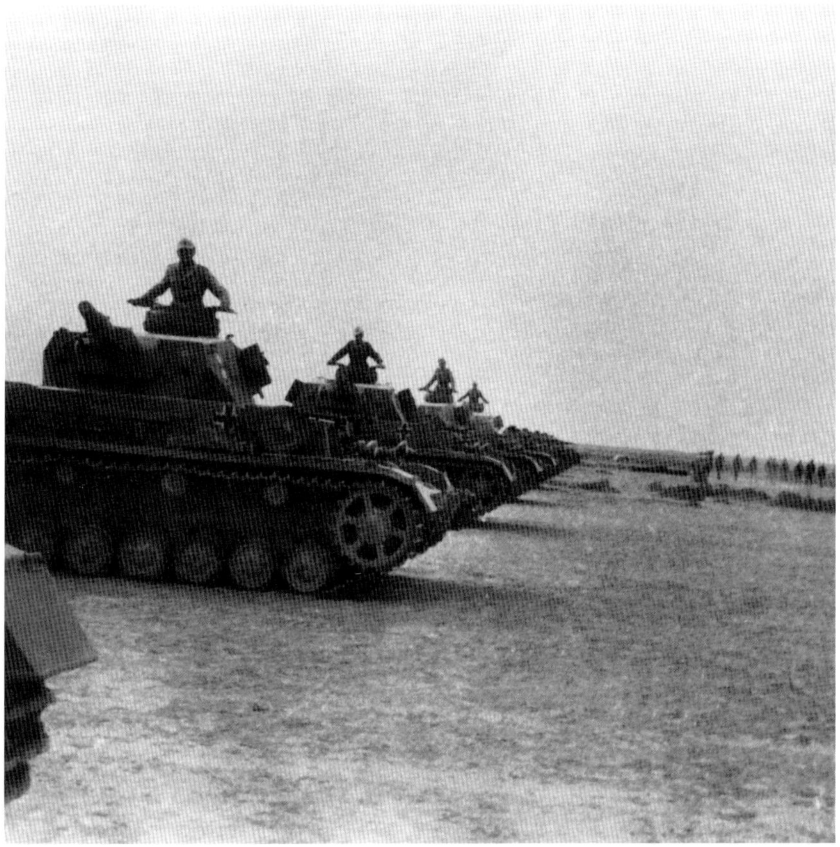

Crews of several Pz.Kpfw.IV line up for an inspection.

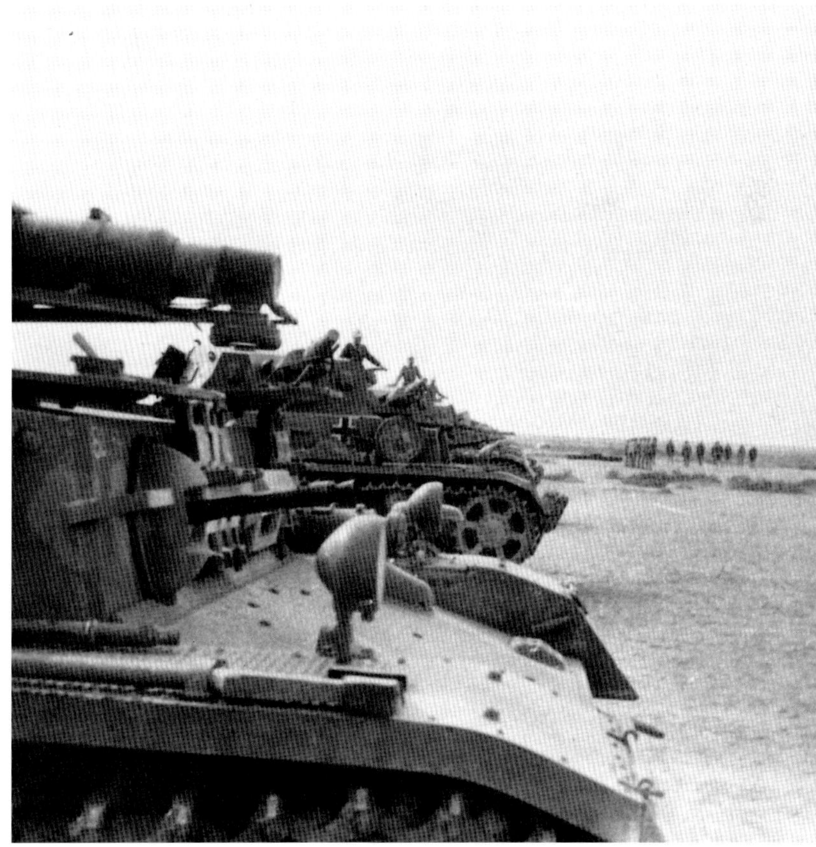

Bayerlein photographs the impressive armor line up of the Pz.Kpfw.IVs.

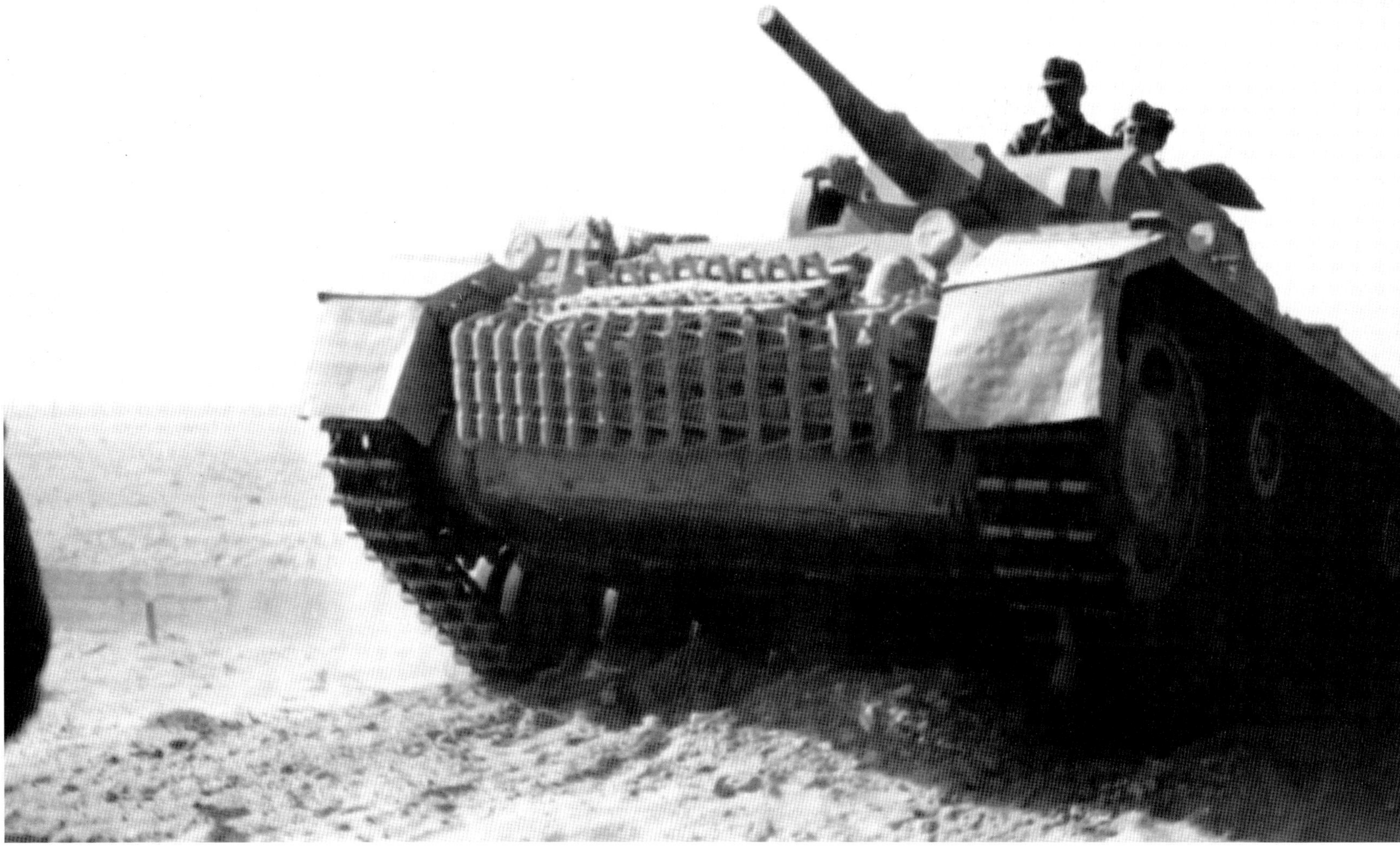

The Chief of Staff stands very close to a Pz.Kpfw.III climbing a small incline.

Opposite: The crew of this Pz.Kpfw.IV (Spezial) have added a camel thorn bush accoutrement to better conceal the beast, although it appears more of an annoyance than any type of benefit.[2]

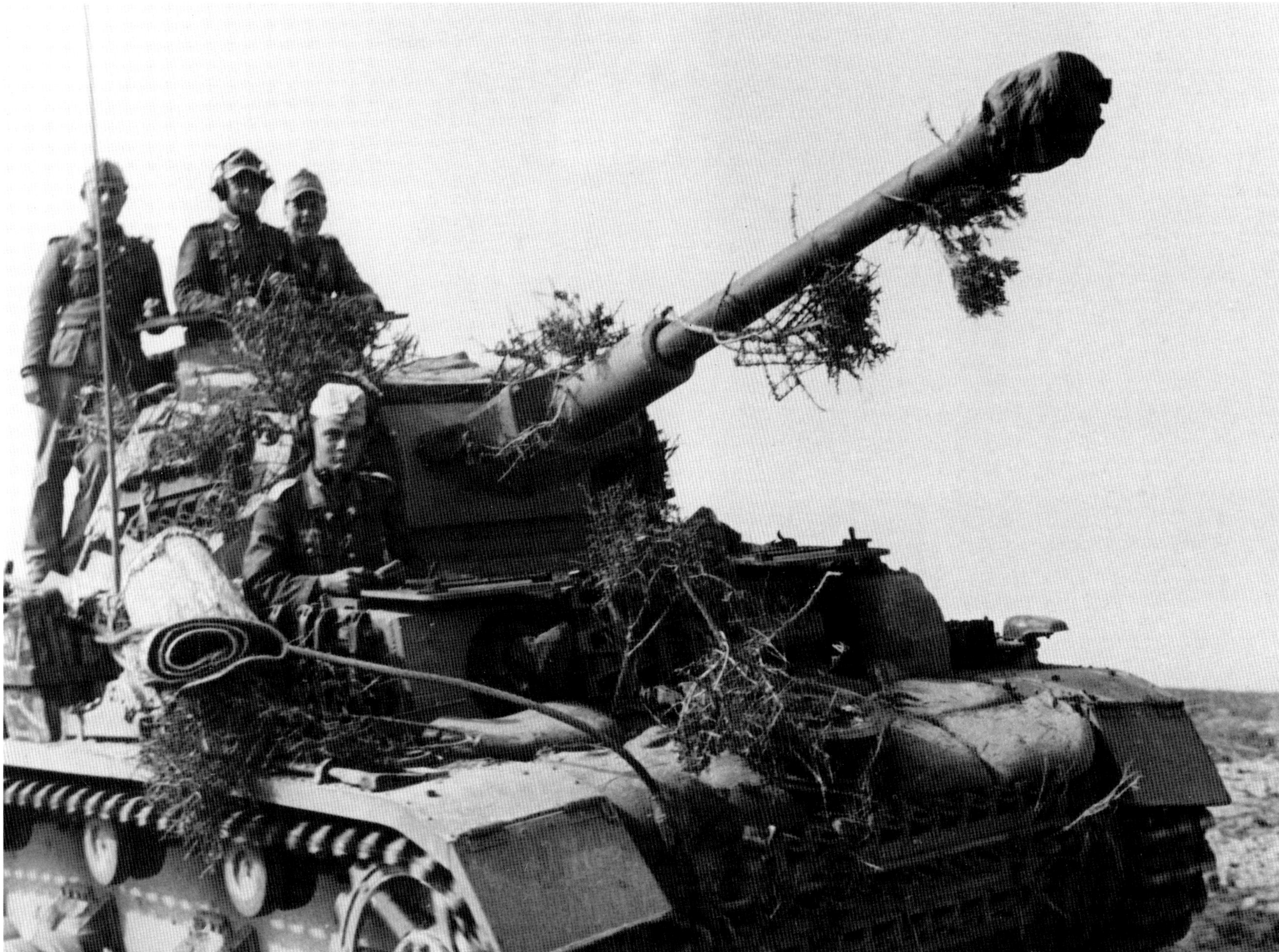

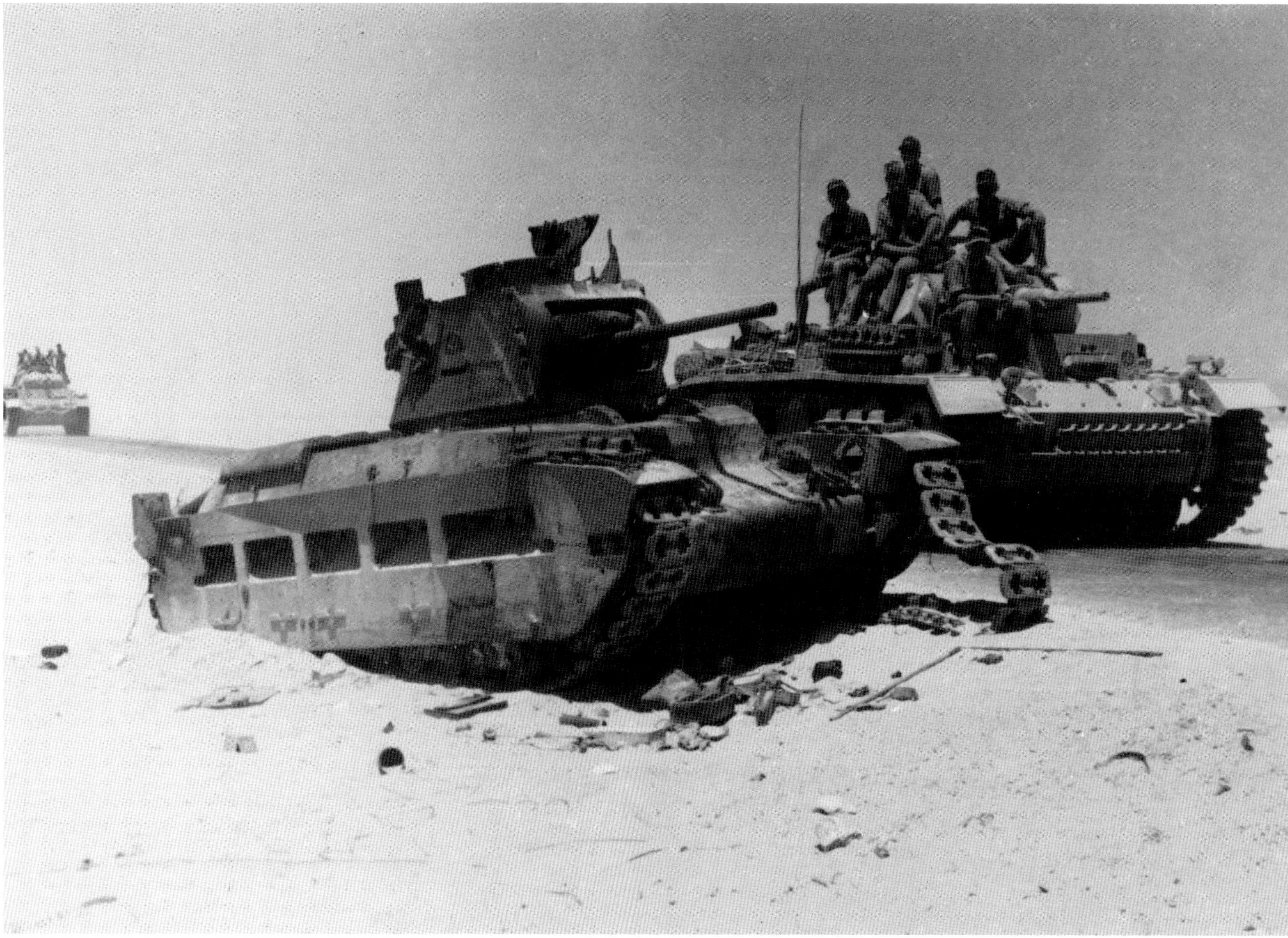

Pz.Kpfw.III, passing a knocked-out British "Matilda" infantry tank.[3]

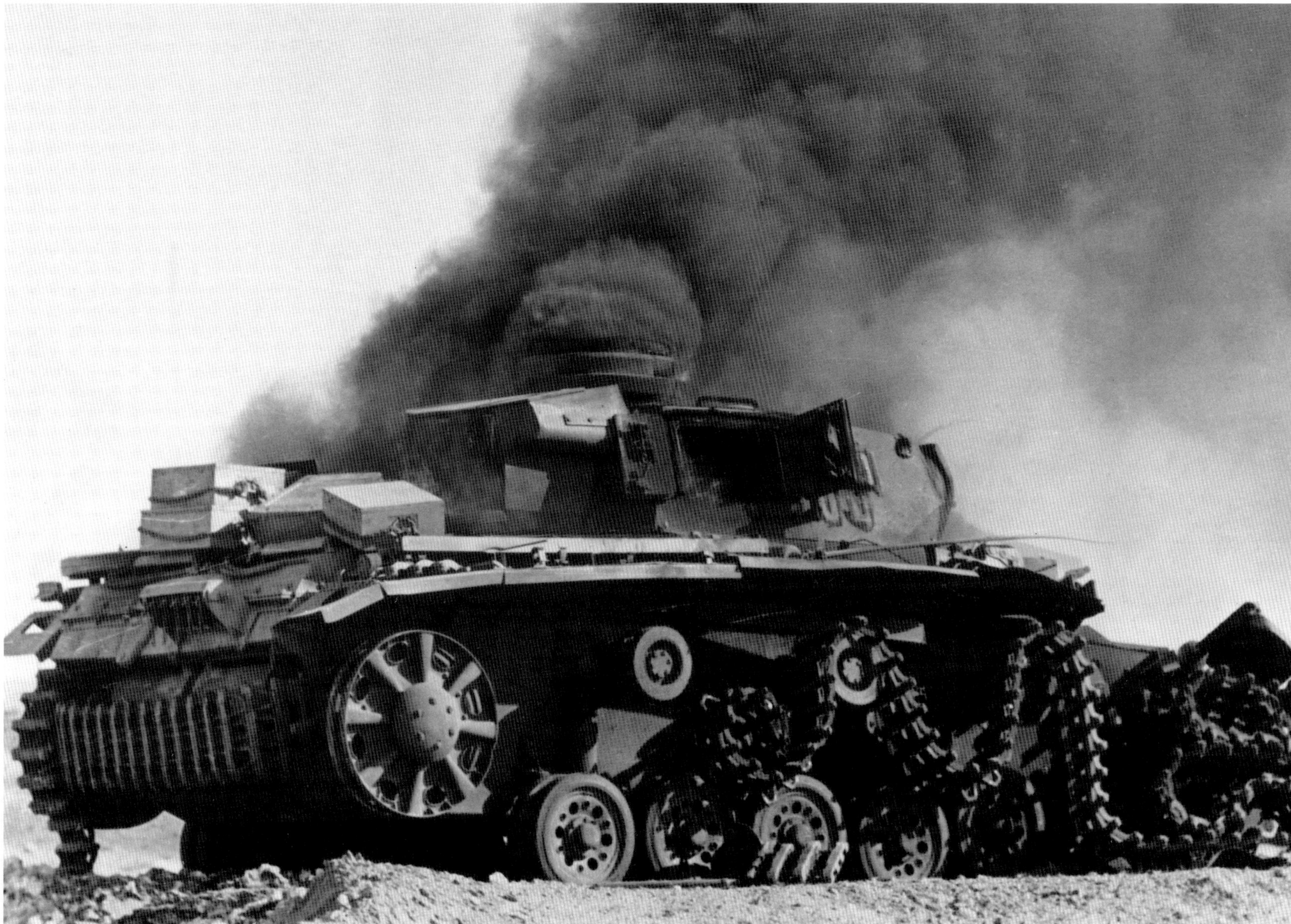

A knocked out Pz.Kpfw.III from Panzer-Regiment 5.[4]

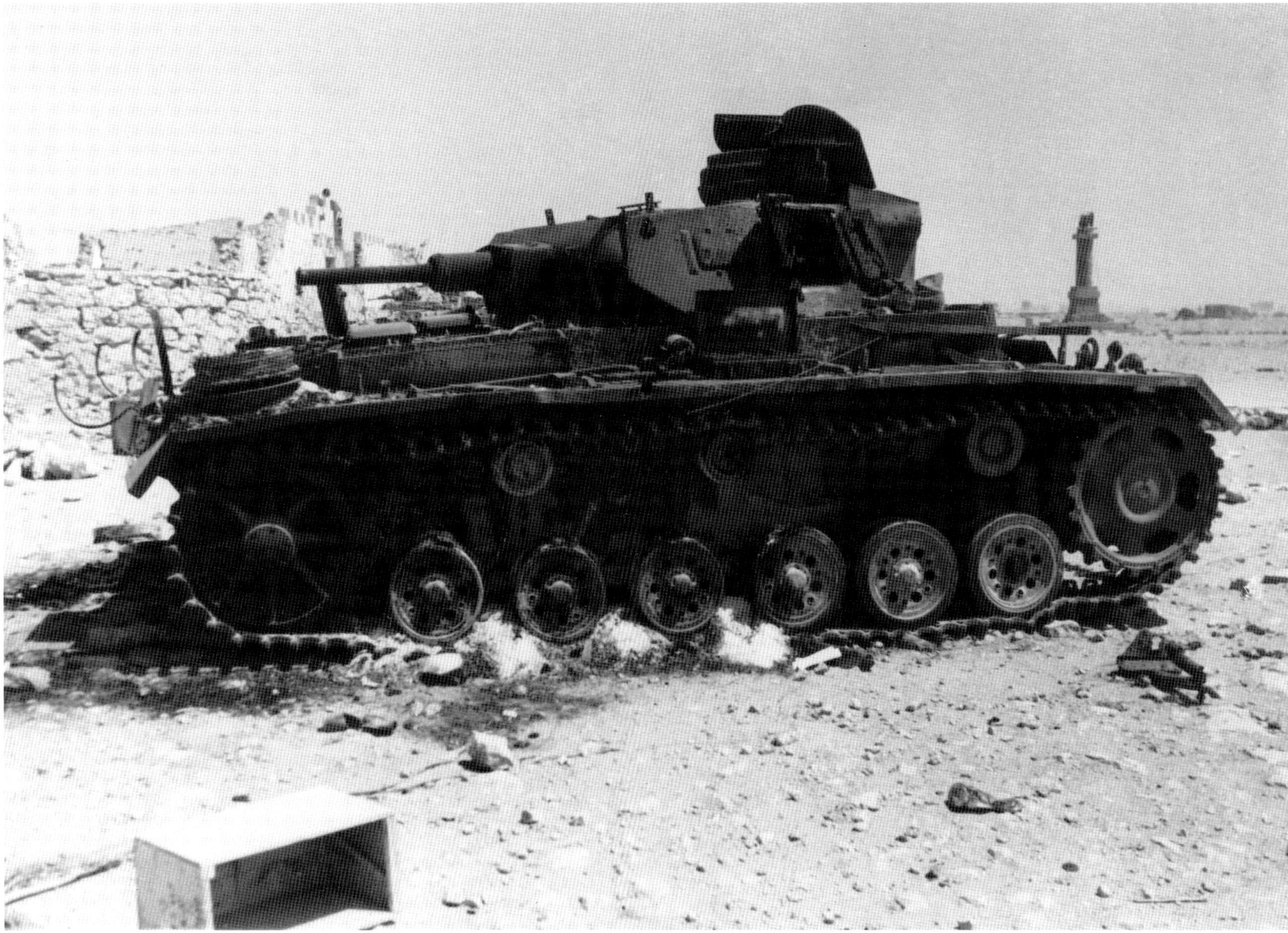

A burned out Pz.Kpfw.III.[5]

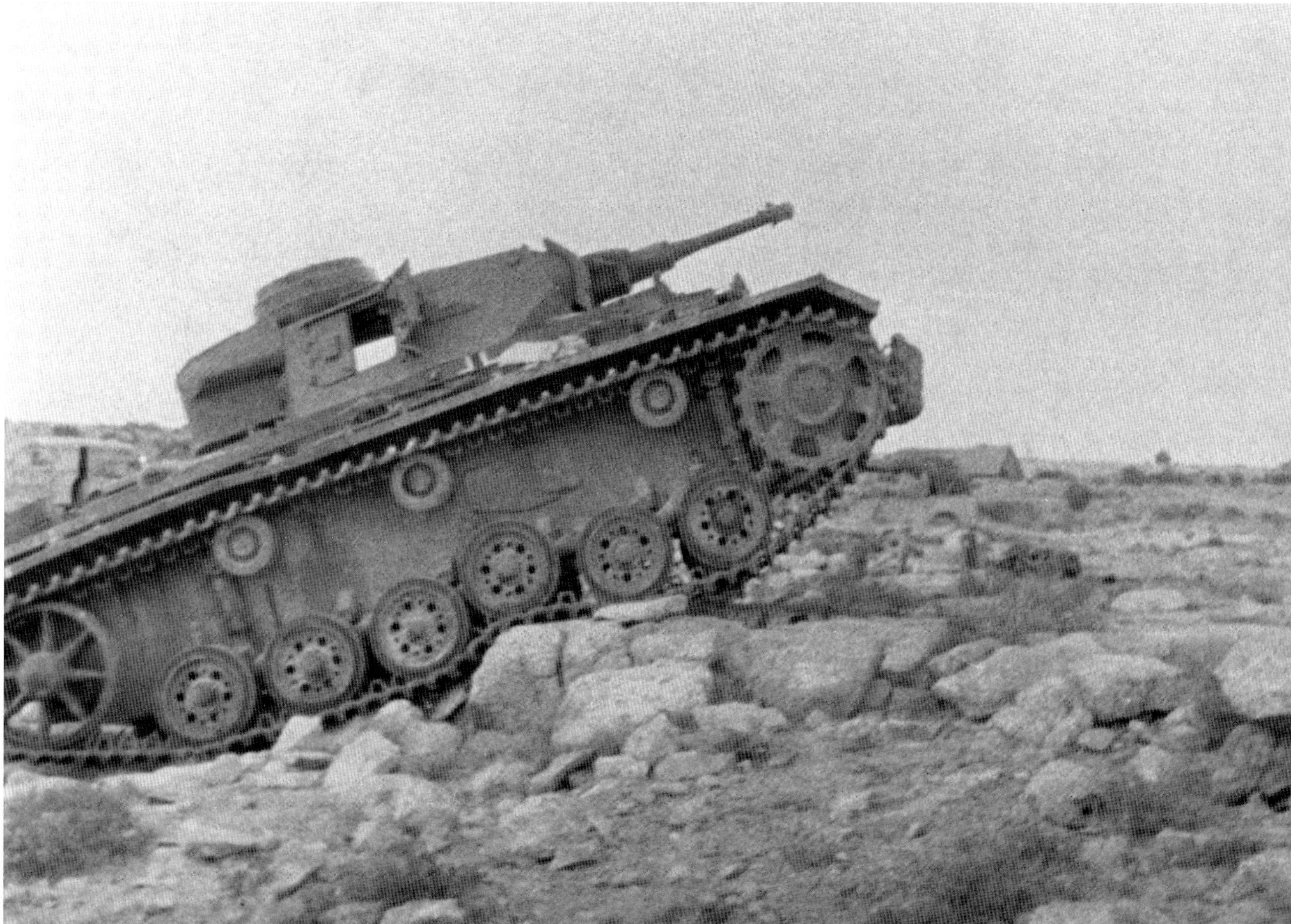

Pz.Kpfw.III

CHAPTER ELEVEN

NATIVES

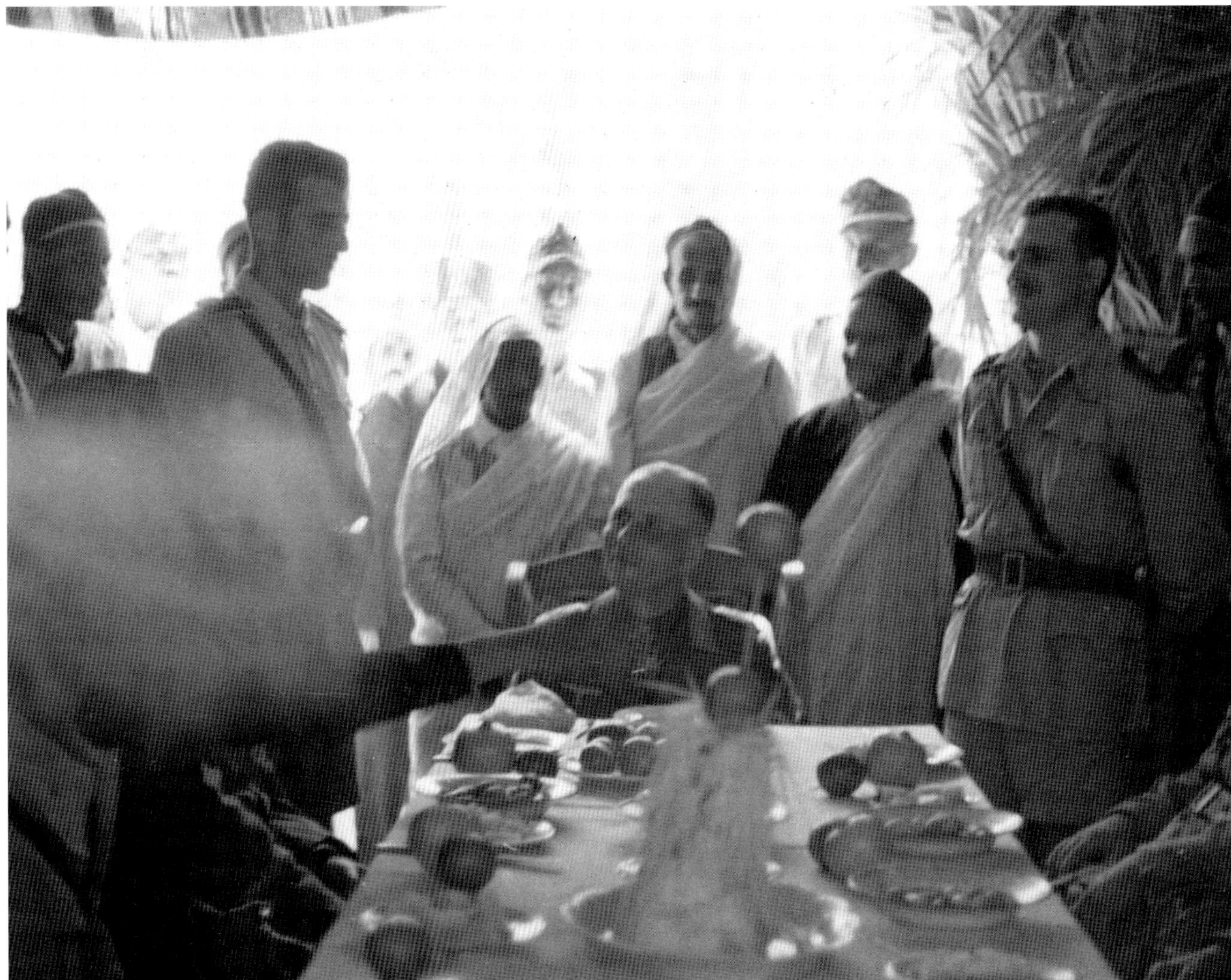

Field Marshal Rommel stated that he, along with Gause and Bayerlein, flew to the Siwa Oasis to meet with local chiefs. Rommel is shown with natives and the staff from the Italian-German garrison at Oasis during an inspection tour with Gause and Bayerlein.[1]

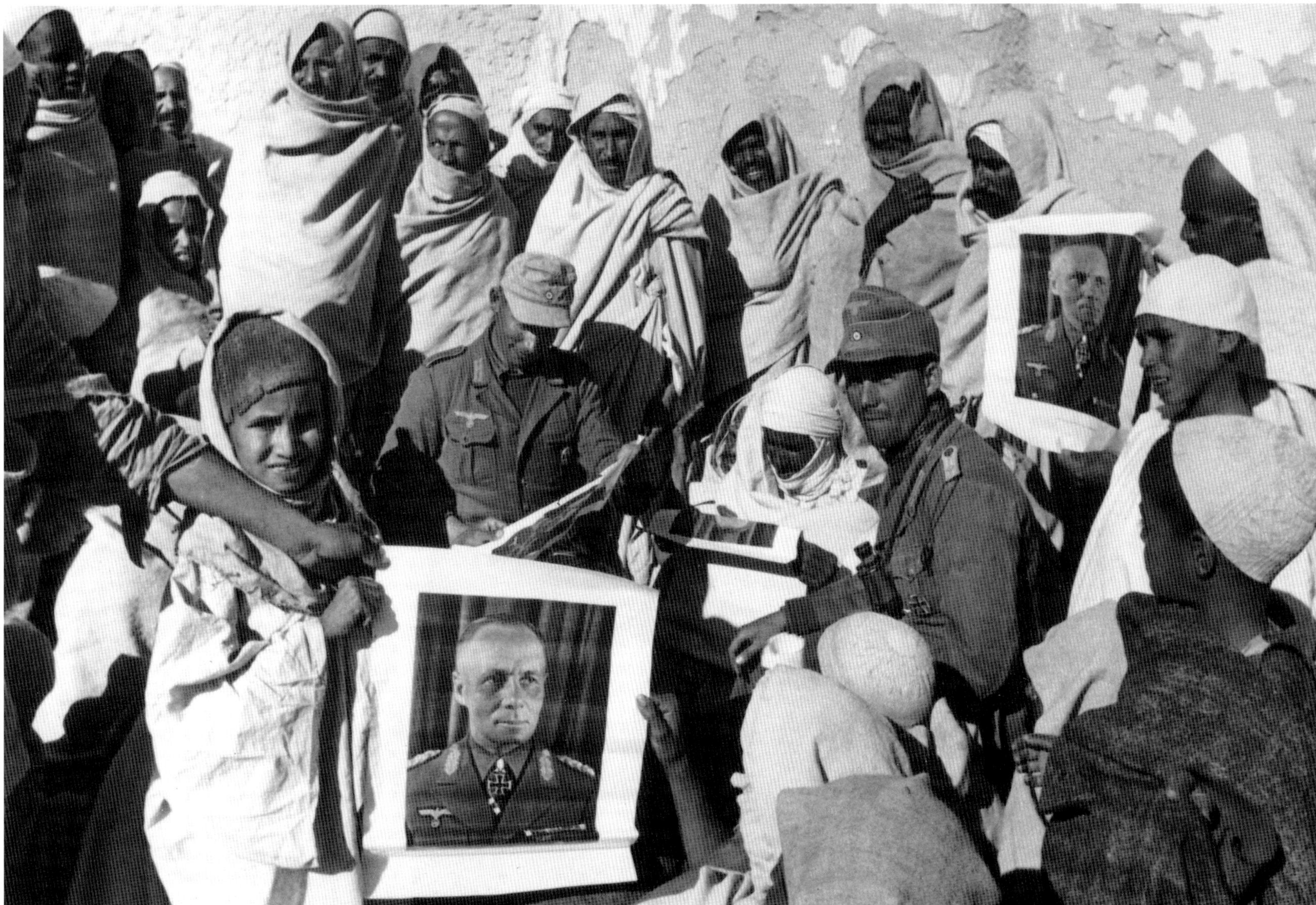

Friendly Arabs smile and hold up portraits of Field Marshal Rommel while Bayerlein records the unusual event. "The German soldier on the left seems to have removed the soutache or Winkel (inverted 'V' of colored braid) over the cockade on his cap, which would definitely date the photo from the latter part of 1942 onwards, again an indication it may be in Tunisia where the Arab population was quite sympathetic to the Germans. The photo of Rommel shows him wearing his swords (awarded January 1942)."[2]

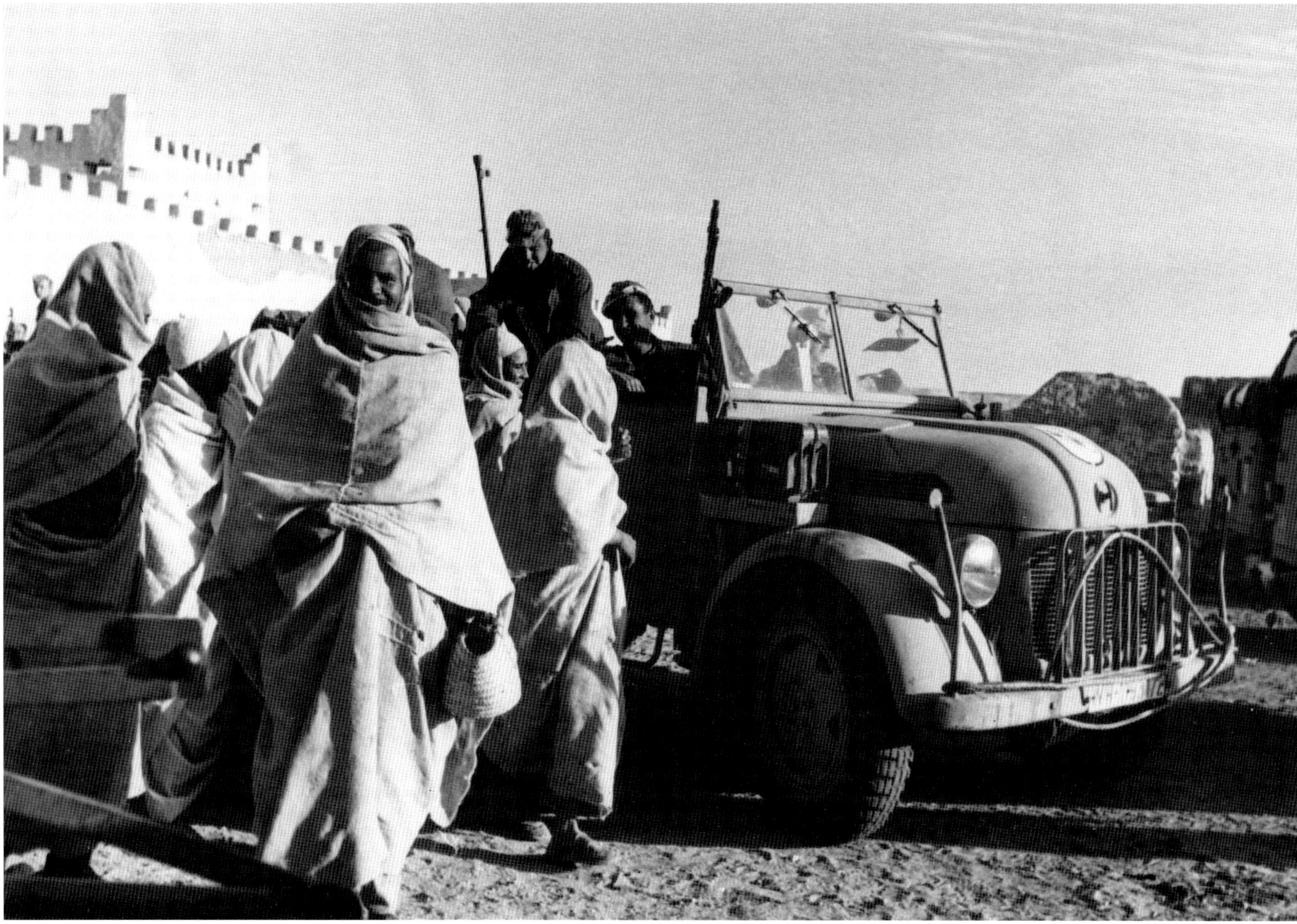

A mix of the nomadic and the modern – natives cooperate with Bayerlein and pose next to vehicles. The locals appear to like the friendly Afrikakorps soldiers, and Bayerlein in particular.

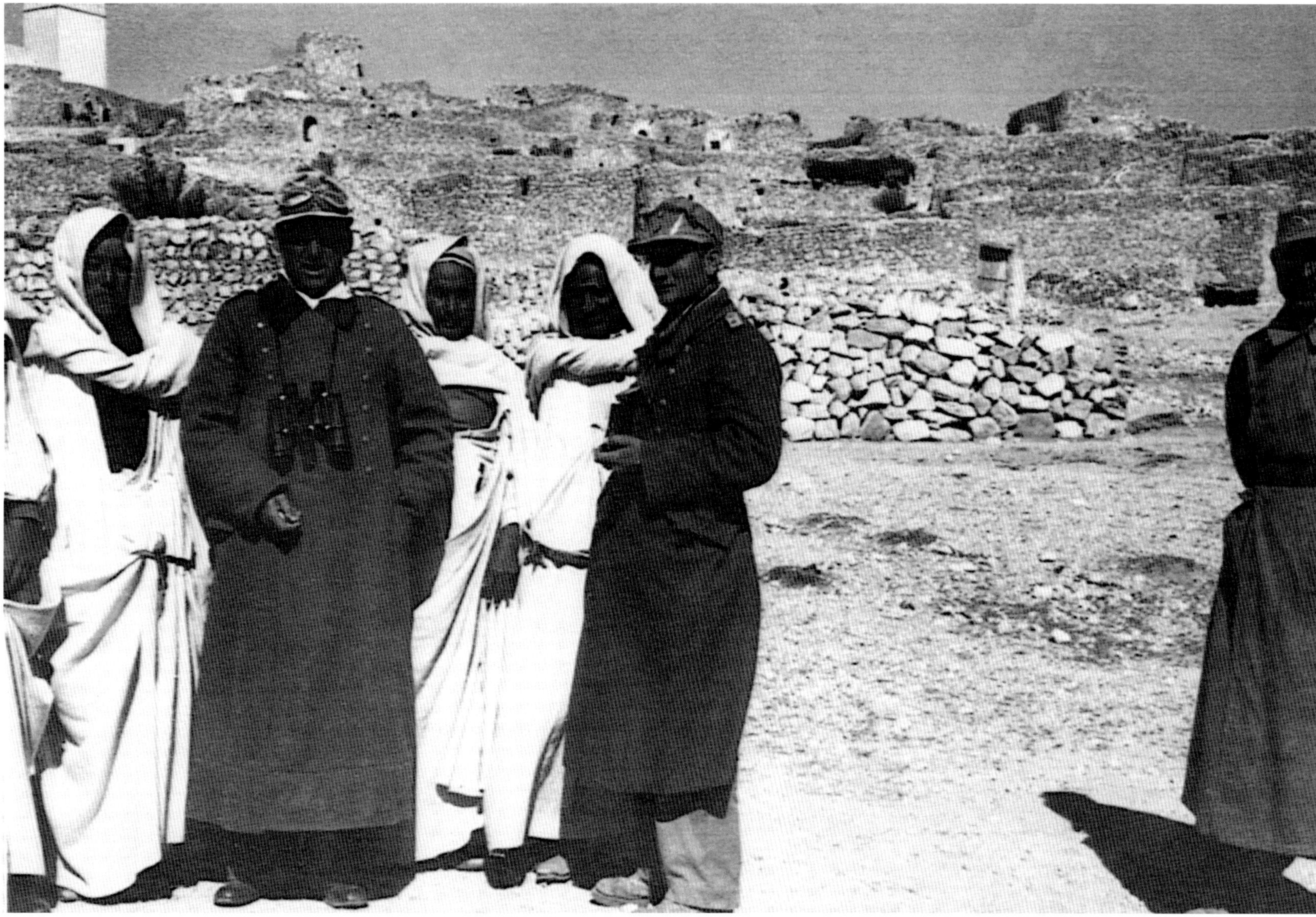

With a suntan as dark as the skin of the locals, Bayerlein stands amid some friendly natives. From their deeply tanned skin, only the uniforms and the natives' clothing separate the men's different worlds.

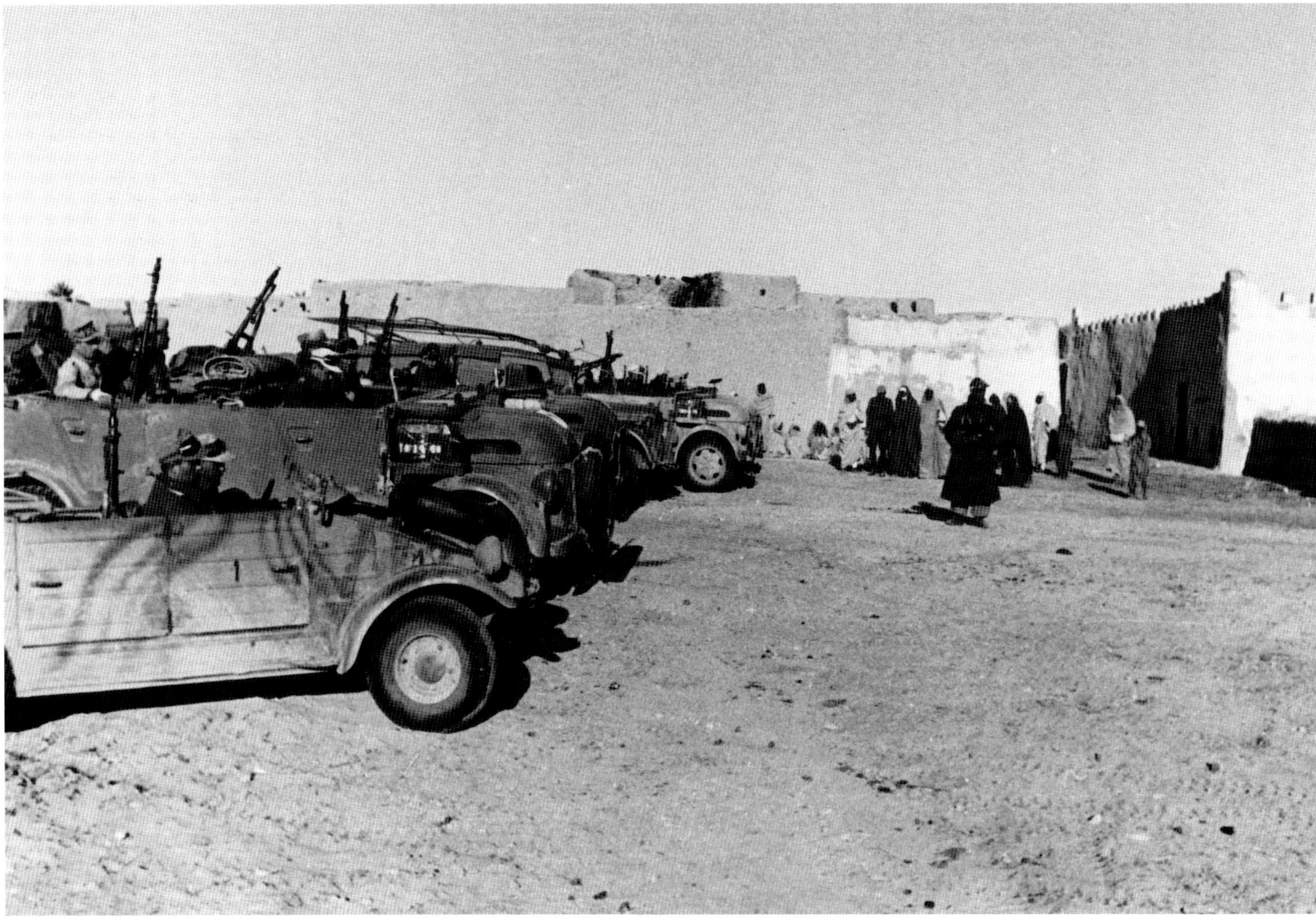

Bayerlein photographs the line-up of a mix of German and Italian vehicles at the Siwa Oasis, September 21, 1942. The natives have moved from examining the line of vehicles and stand with some AK soldiers by one of the buildings.

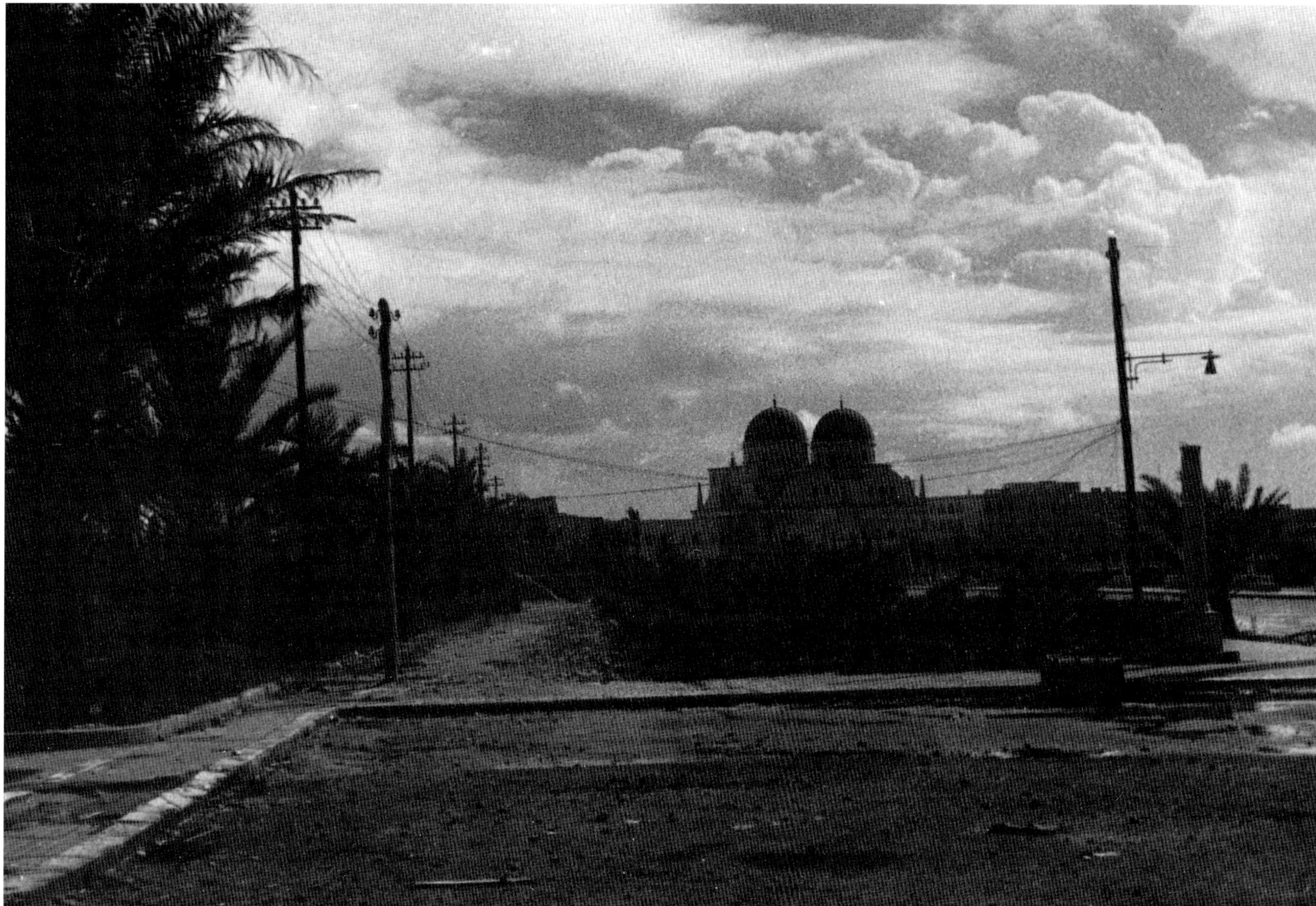

Not all is sand and rock in the African theater. Here Baylerein photographs a more modern reprieve – a modern mosque in a town with electric and telephone lines. The palm trees were a welcome sight from the barren desert.

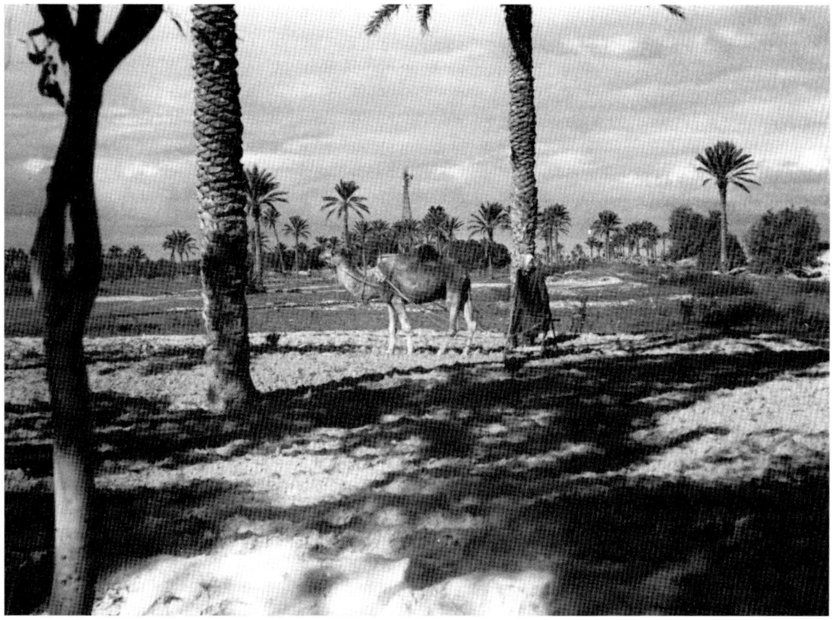

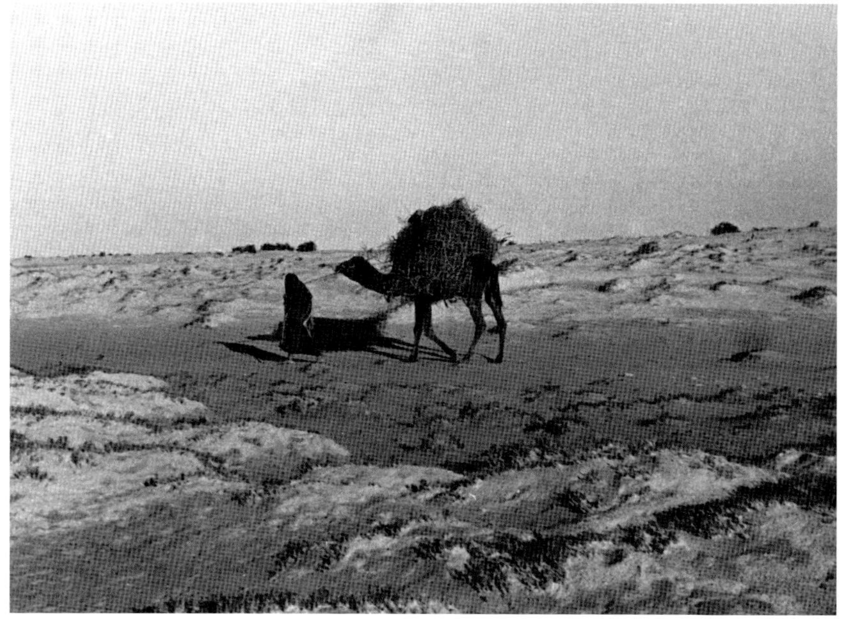

Above
With a good eye for a nice photo shot, Bayerlein carefully focused the camera on the best angle of a camel.

Top right
Selecting a sole native with a burdened camel going about his daily business, Bayerlein captures the exotic image.

Right
Bayerlein's garnering of a close-up of the odd-looking desert animals; the air of the camels is patient and timeless.

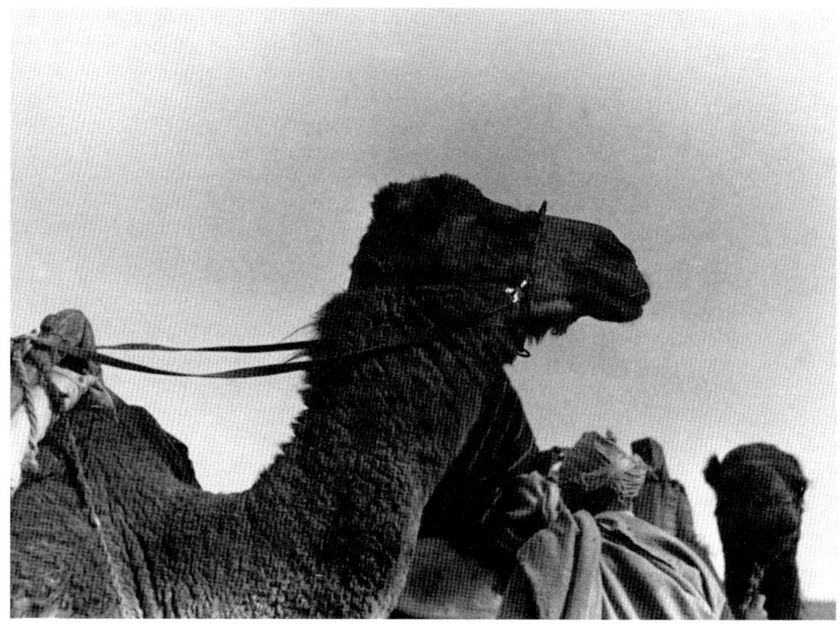

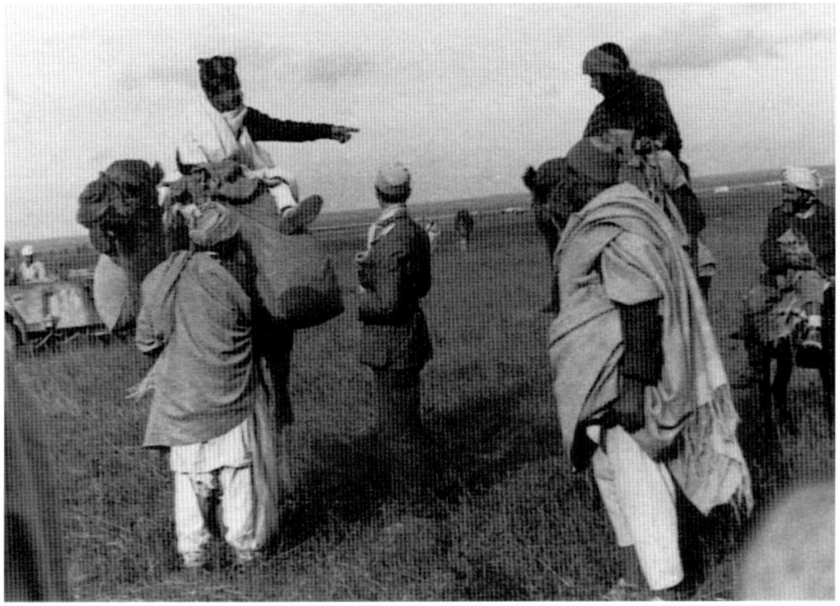

Above
Even the Afrikakorps needs directions. Bayerlein photographs another officer asking directions of the locals.

Right
An old native relaxes on his heels eating bread as Bayerlein records his interesting subject.

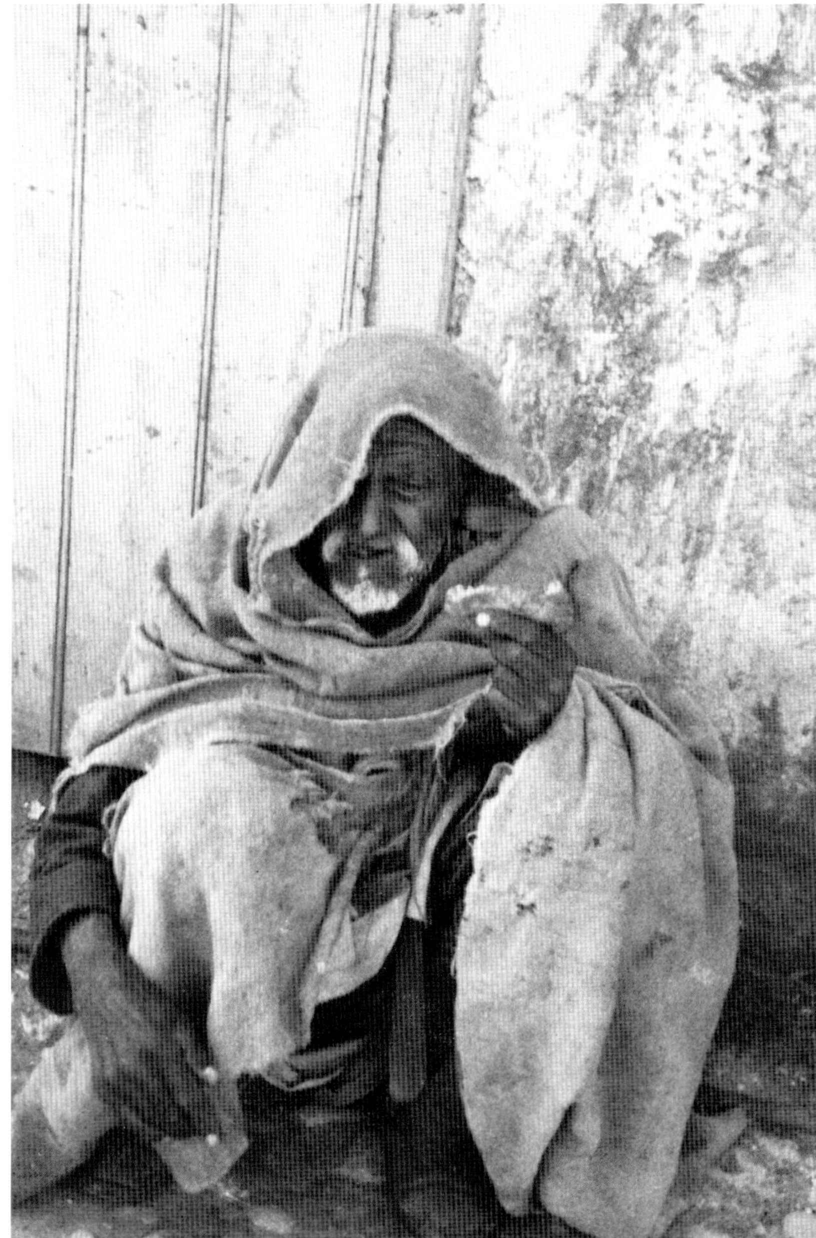

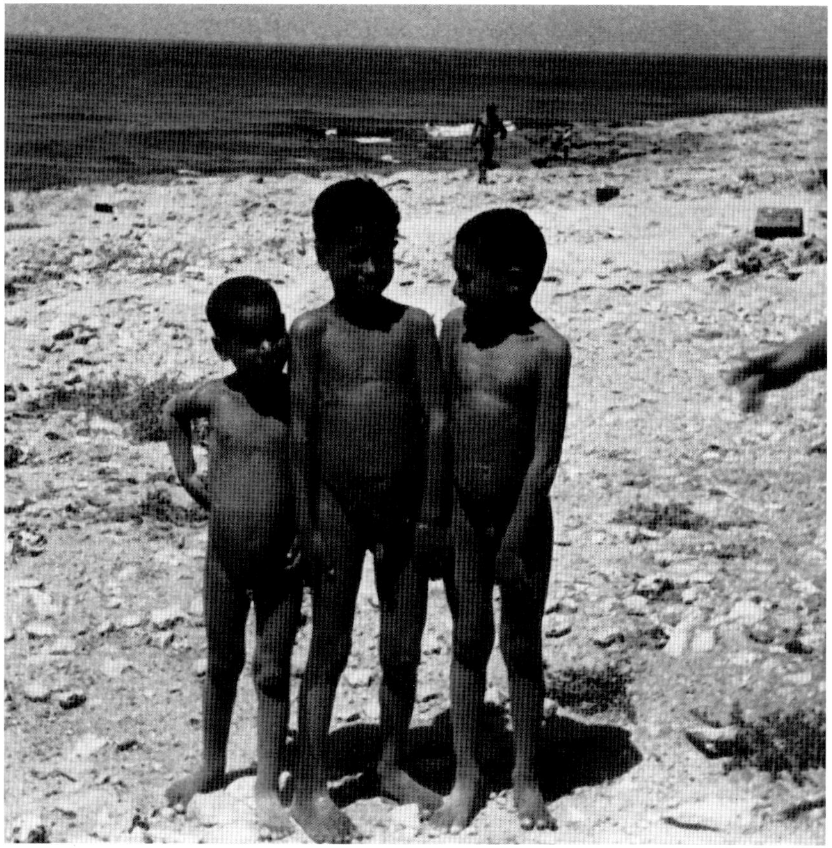

Three smiling Arab children enjoy a cool playground in the Mediterranean. The locals enjoyed the same pastimes as the soldiers.[3]

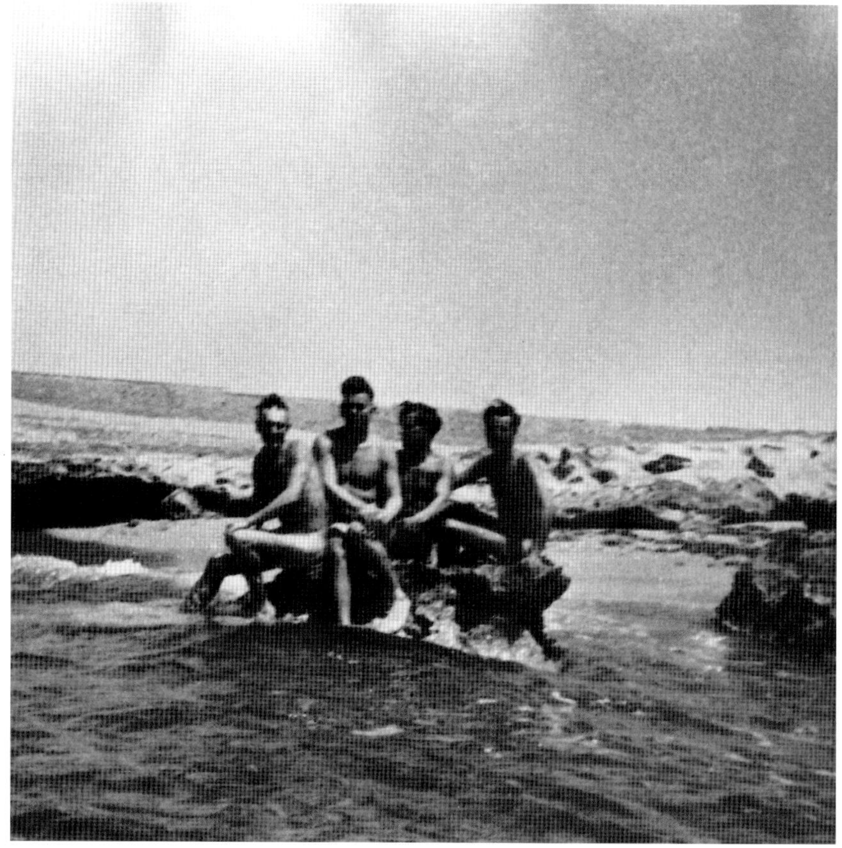

Following the children's example, Bayerlein and the Headquarters group join in the swim. Who needs clothing on a hot day? Swimming in the sea was one of the most popular leisure activities for the troops – followed by sunbathing – although not always in the nude.[4]

CHAPTER TWELVE

OVERFLIGHTS AND VIEWS

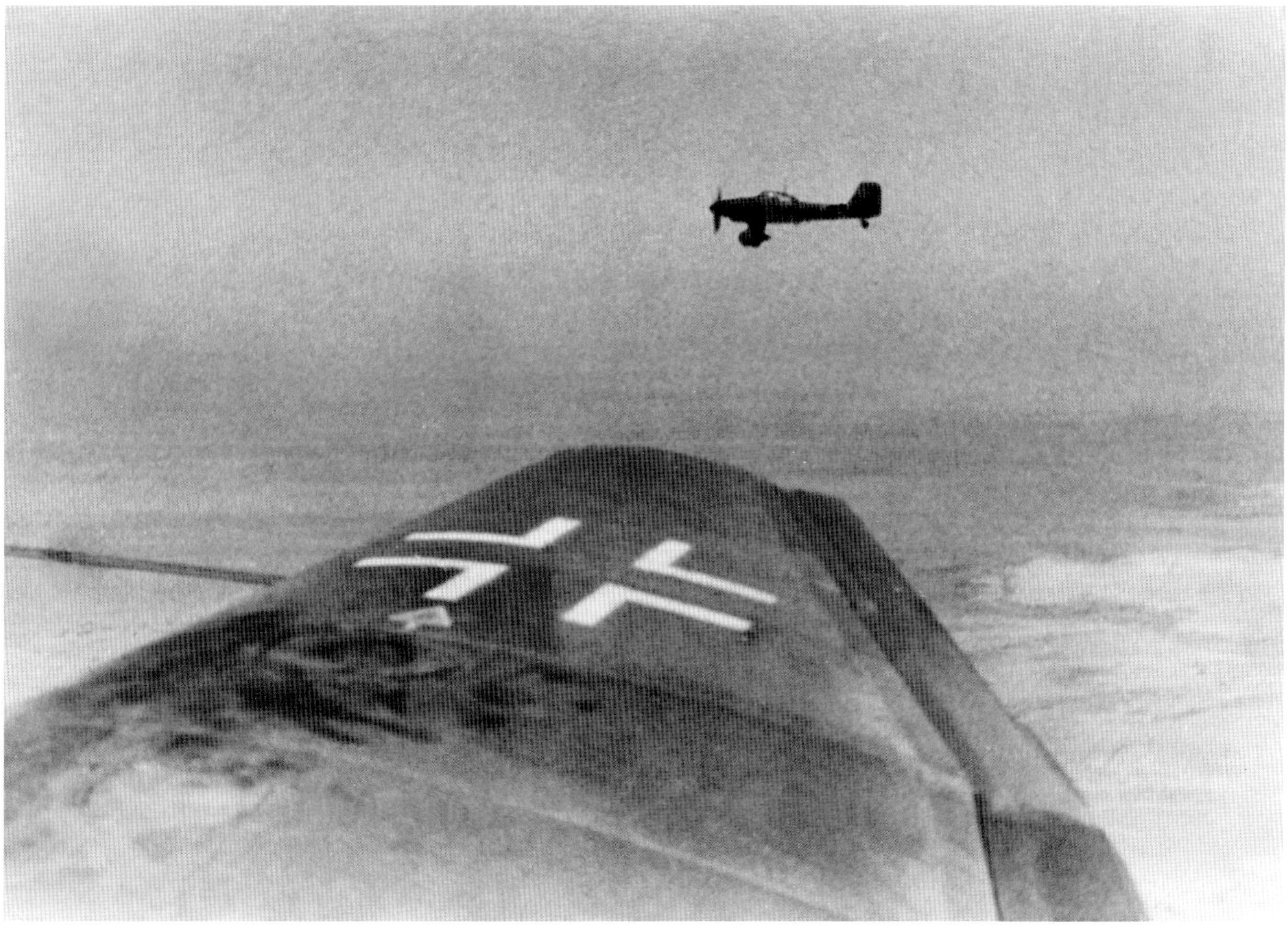

Bayerlein was given a ride in a Stuka from which he took this photo showing another Stuka flying in formation beside it. The wing structure and trailing edge of the wing is unique to Stuka dive brakes.[1]

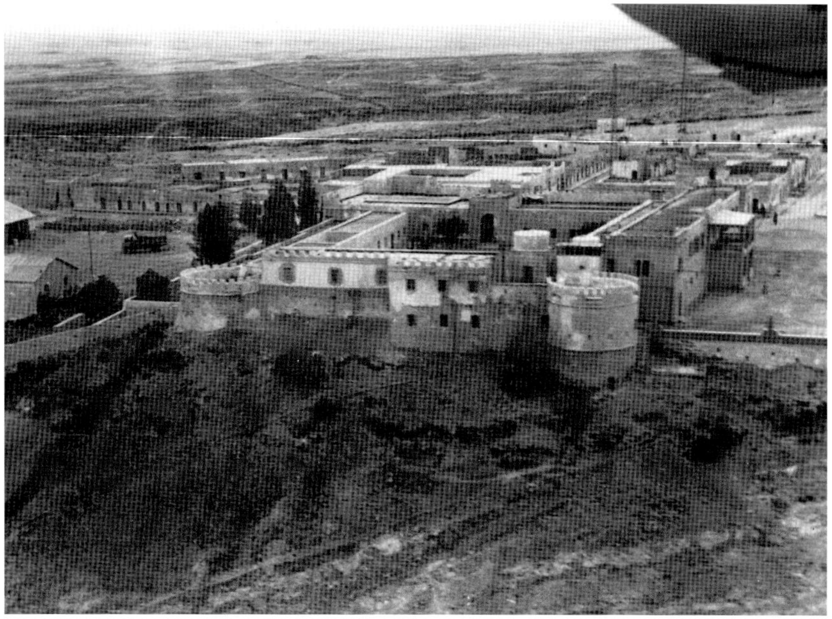

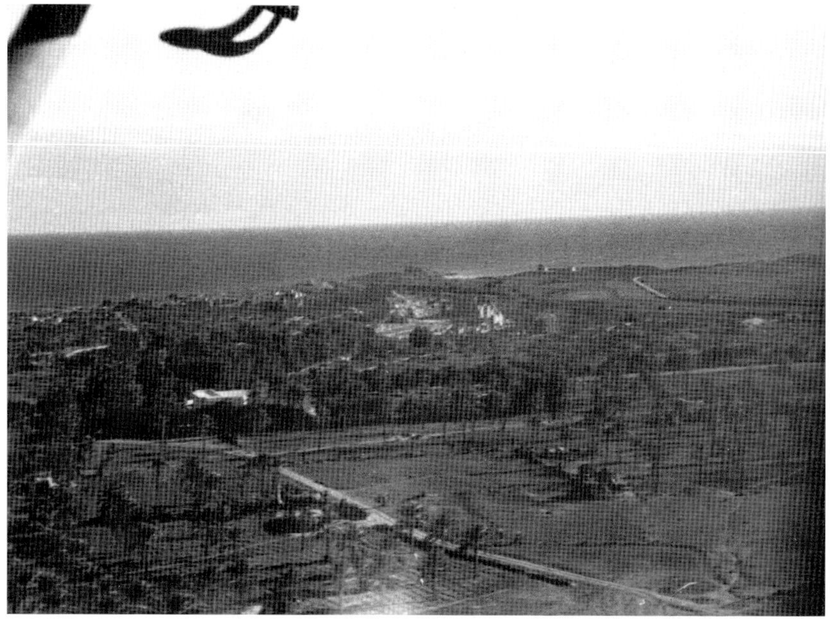

Above
Overflight of an oasis located somewhere in the region of eastern Tunisia, presumably taken in early 1943 when the Afrikakorps were pulling back into southern Tunisia from Libya.[2]

Top right
A view of a settlement somewhere on the southern coast of Tunisia, presumably also snapped in early 1943 around the time the Afrikakorps were taking up positions in southern Tunisia.[3]

Right
Amid the ruin of a desert fort, supply vehicles are parked and hidden from ground view. Nearby, cultivated crops show up clearly on the view. Possibly Tobruk.[4]

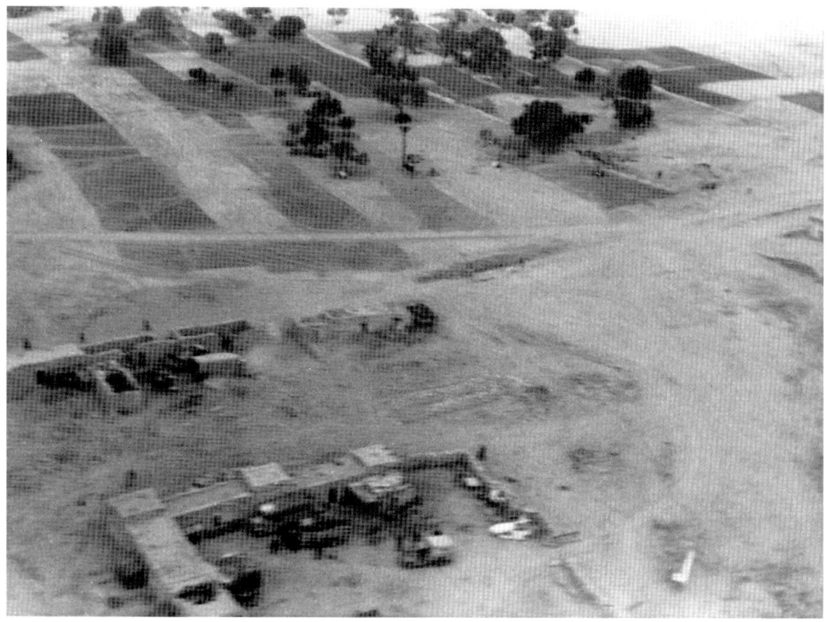

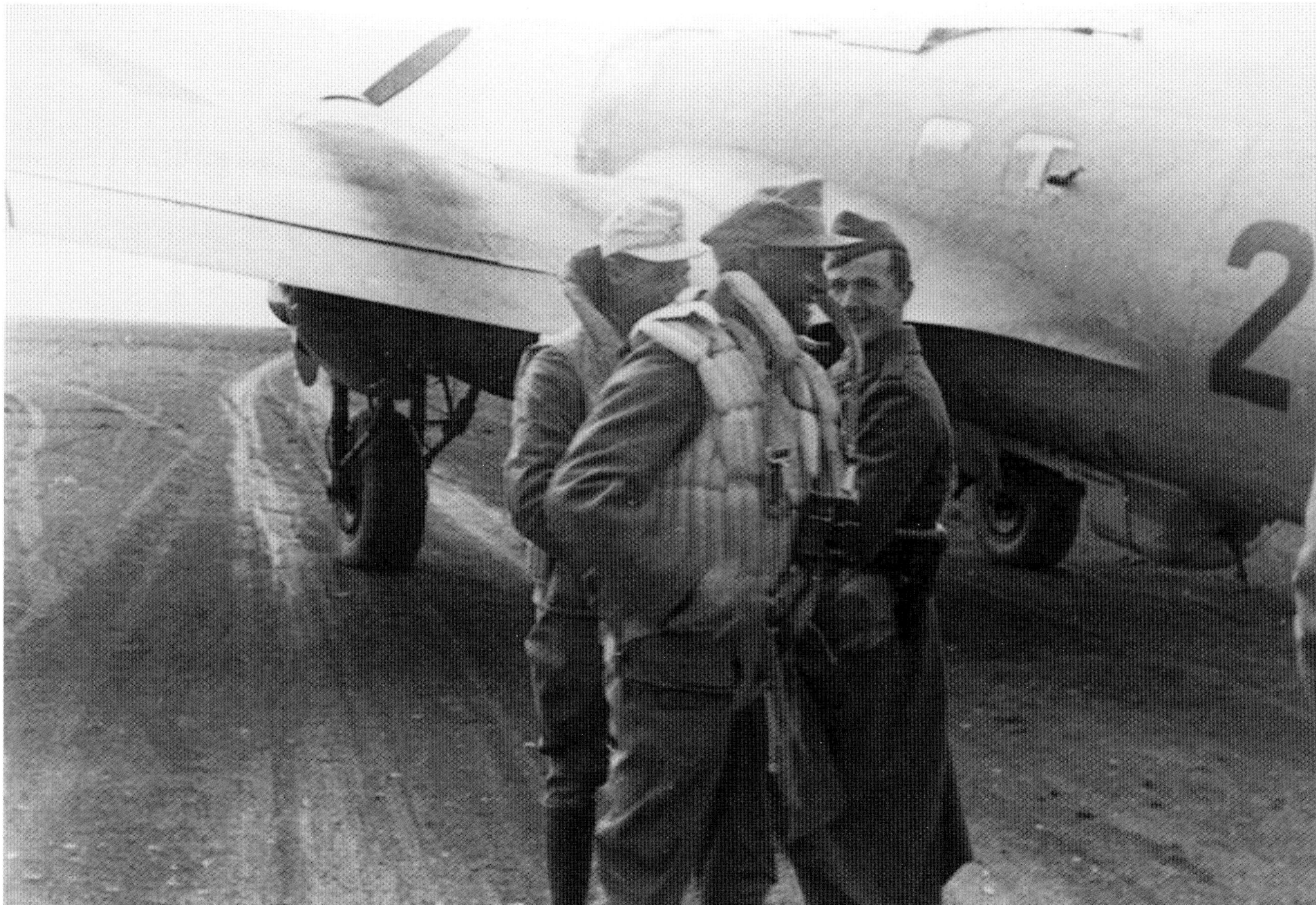

Preparing to depart on the waiting aircraft, Bayerlein jokes with a Luftwaffe officer as he hitches up the straps of his life jacket between his legs. No doubt the logistics of the straps location are the cause of the men's laughter.

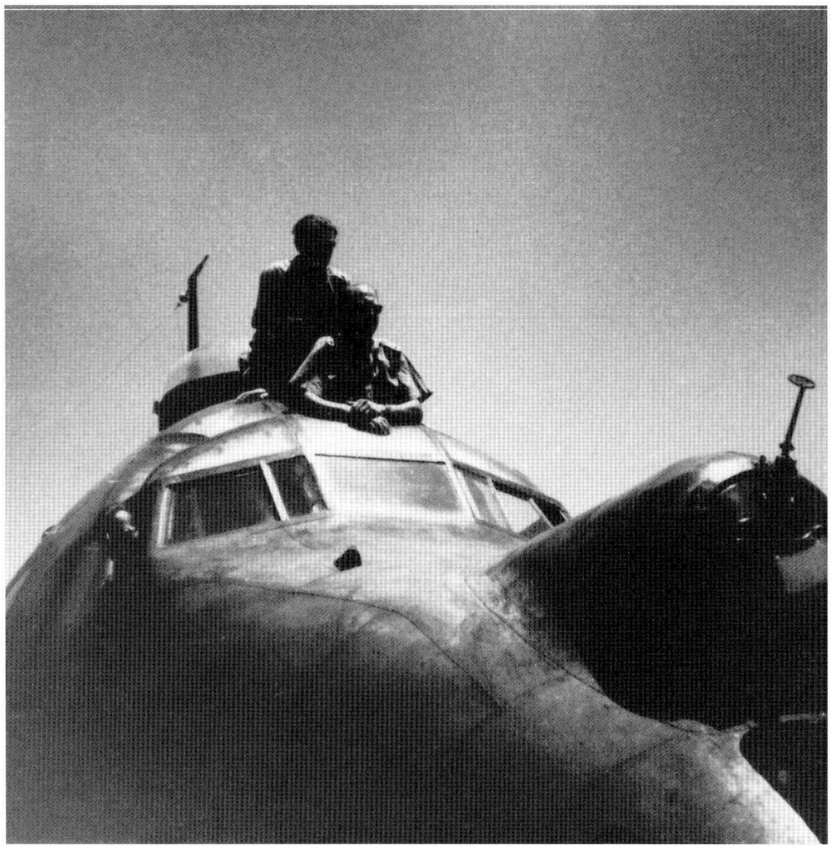

A flight crew readies a large Blohm und Voss Bv 222 "Viking" used to ferry supplies and equipment from Italy to Derna in 1942 for takeoff.[5]

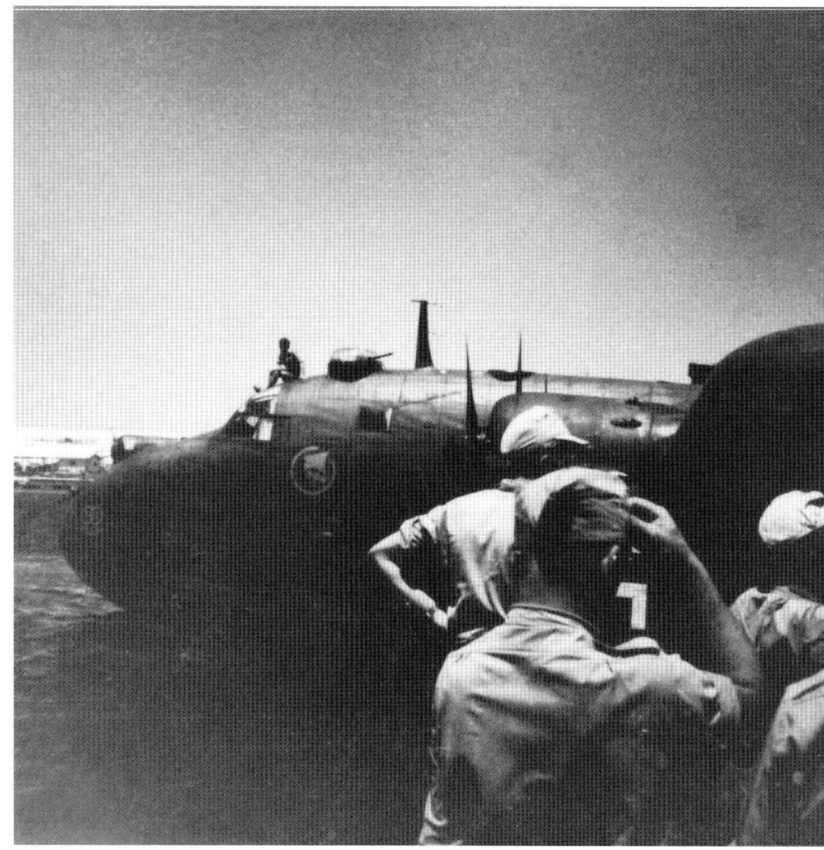

Preparing to depart on the waiting seaplane (the giant six-engined Bv 222) Bayerlein photographs the aircraft from another angle. Using these giant aircraft were one of the ways Kesselring tried to honor his promise to Rommel that he would ensure adequate supplies of the vital fuel and ammunition reached the Afrikakorps.[6]

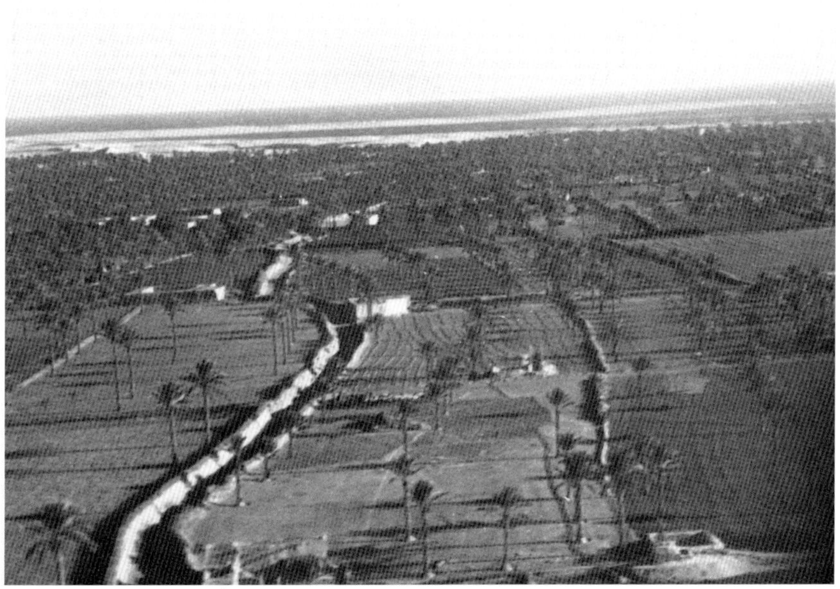

As the Chief-of-Staff to Excellency Meese of the 1st Italian Army, Bayerlein takes a recon flight over a large village off the coastal road.

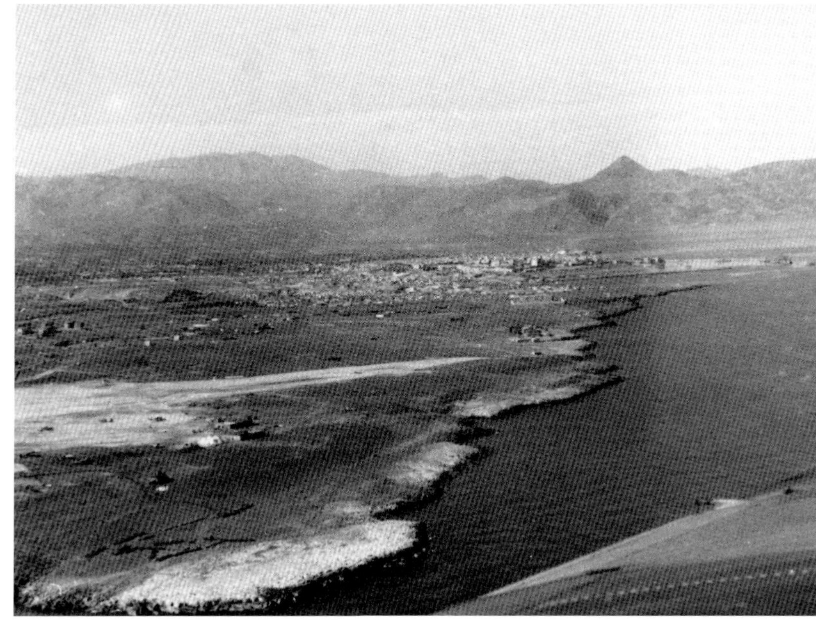

With the aircraft wing in view, Bayerlein captures a magnificent view of the town and hills of Tunisia.

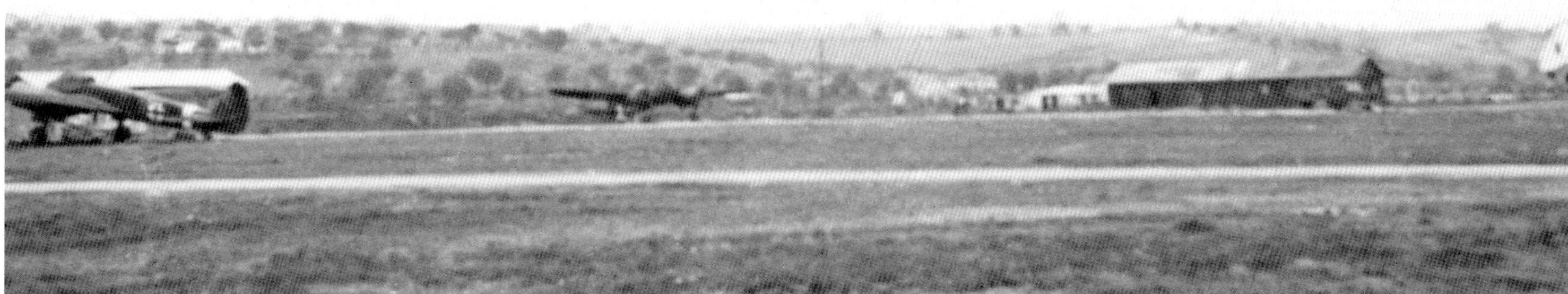

View of an airfield in the desert.

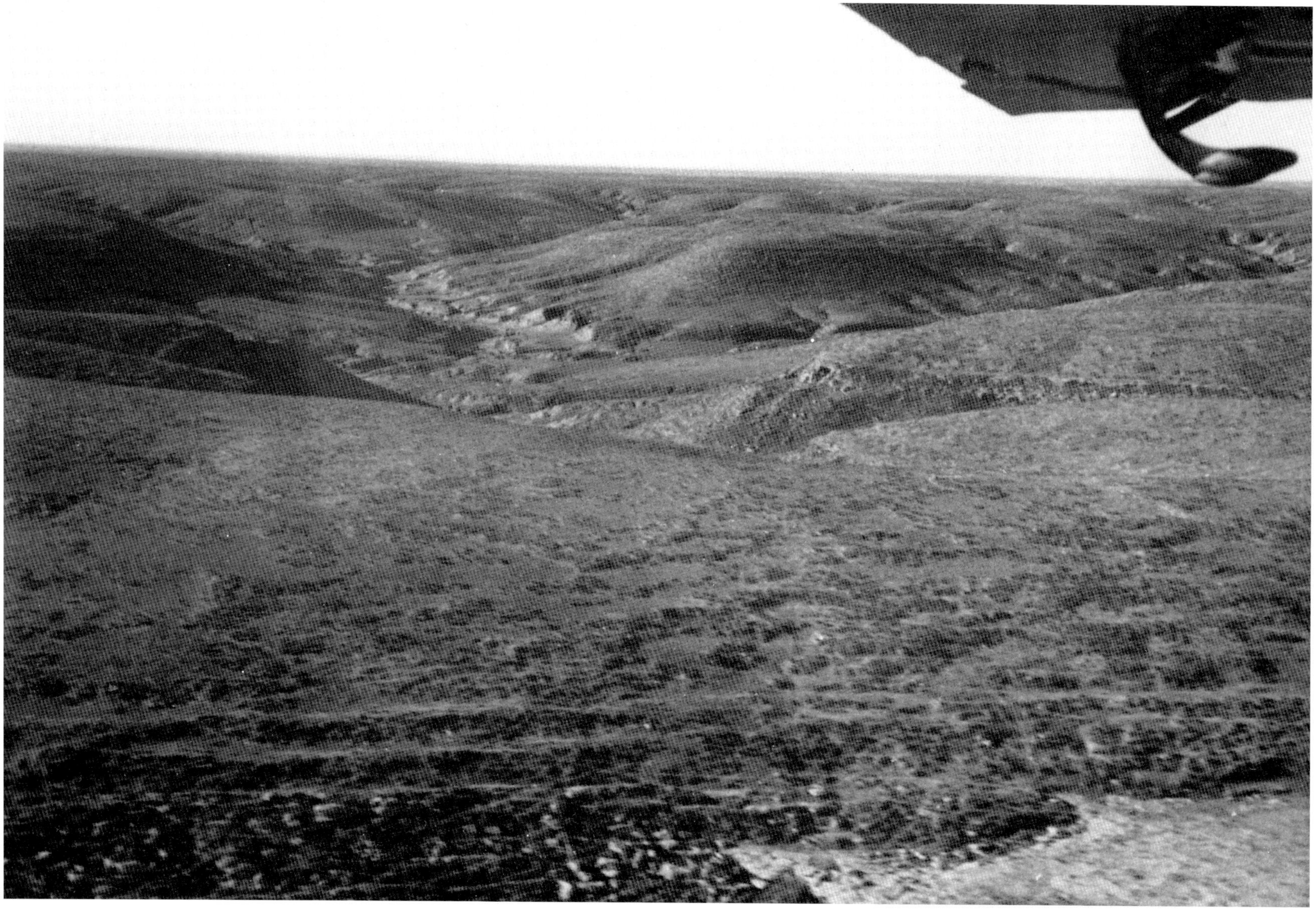

The facets of the war in Africa – from the transition of the Tripoli coastal plain to the high plateaus of Libya.

CHAPTER THIRTEEN

GENERAL VON THOMA

Bayerlein returned from furlough in late October 1942 and reported to his new commander, *General der Panzertruppen* Wilhelm *Ritter* von Thoma. *General* von Thoma assumed temporary command of the Afrikakorps in early November, and Bayerlein was assigned as his Chief-of-Staff. However, he did not report to von Thoma for long because the General surrendered himself to the British shortly after Hitler's "Victory or Death" order days later. Speaking to Bayerlein, he called Hitler's order to hold to the death "a piece of unparalleled madness." Von Thoma gave himself up after fighting until his *Kampfstaffel*[1] was destroyed. Bayerlein returned to the battlefield to search for von Thoma, only to find the British approaching him. Bayerlein beat a hasty retreat and reported to Rommel.[2] From the notes written on the back of his personal photographs and the men's casual manner with each other, it was apparent that Bayerlein knew von Thoma quite well.

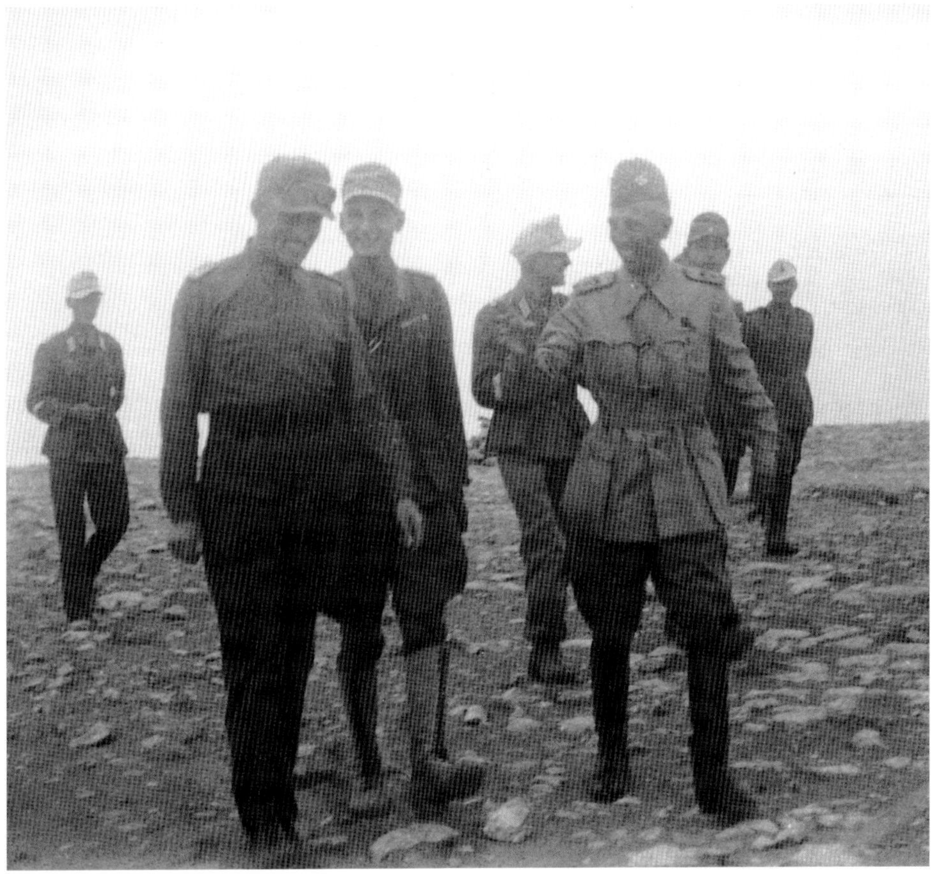

General von Thoma with a group of Italian and German officers. The General appears to be in a particularly good mood, considering the circumstances in November 1942.

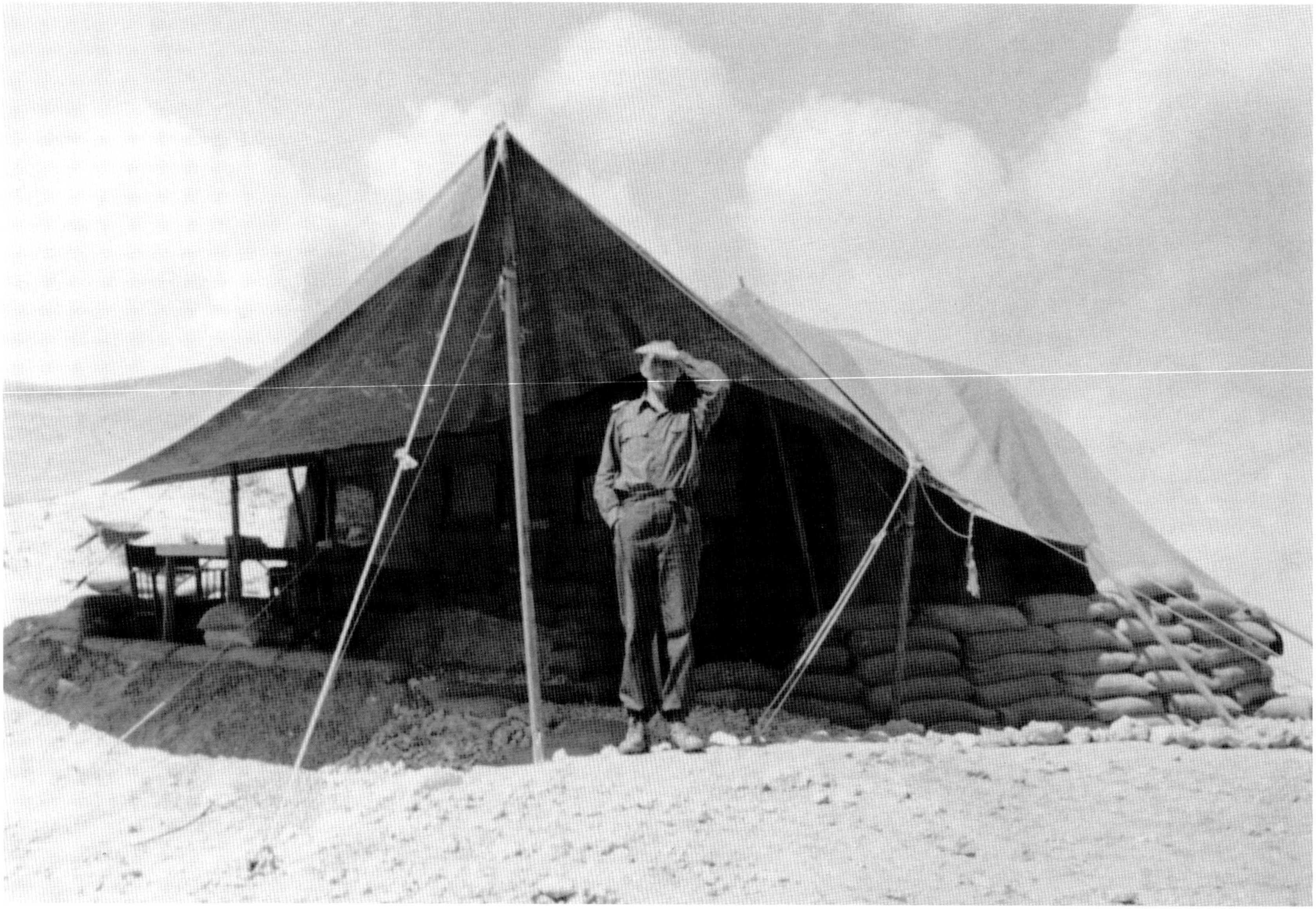

Bayerlein's caption reads: "14 October, Manhz. General von Thoma. Thomas-Bus." Note the bus under the large tent. The General was known for his casual attire, rarely wearing his tunic and decorations.

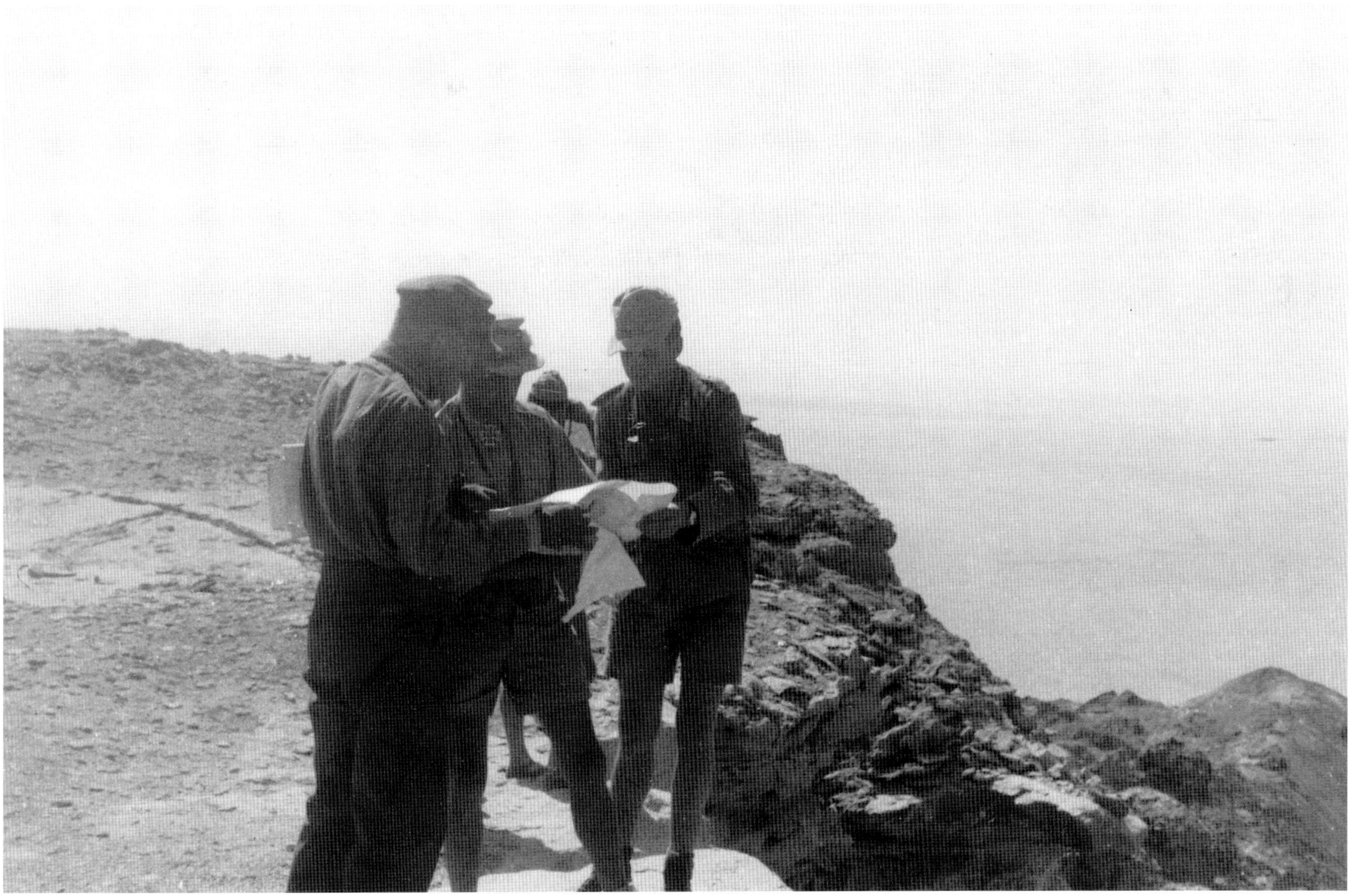

Bayerlein (center, wearing shorts) talks with his CO, General von Thoma. Bayerlein is wearing his Ritterkreuz, awarded to him by Generalleutnant Crüwell. The man with the binoculars and wearing sandals is an Italian.[3] *No one had to worry about the military dress code when out of the front line, as this shot obviously was. The photo looks like it was taken from the high bluff next to the township of Bardia.*[4]

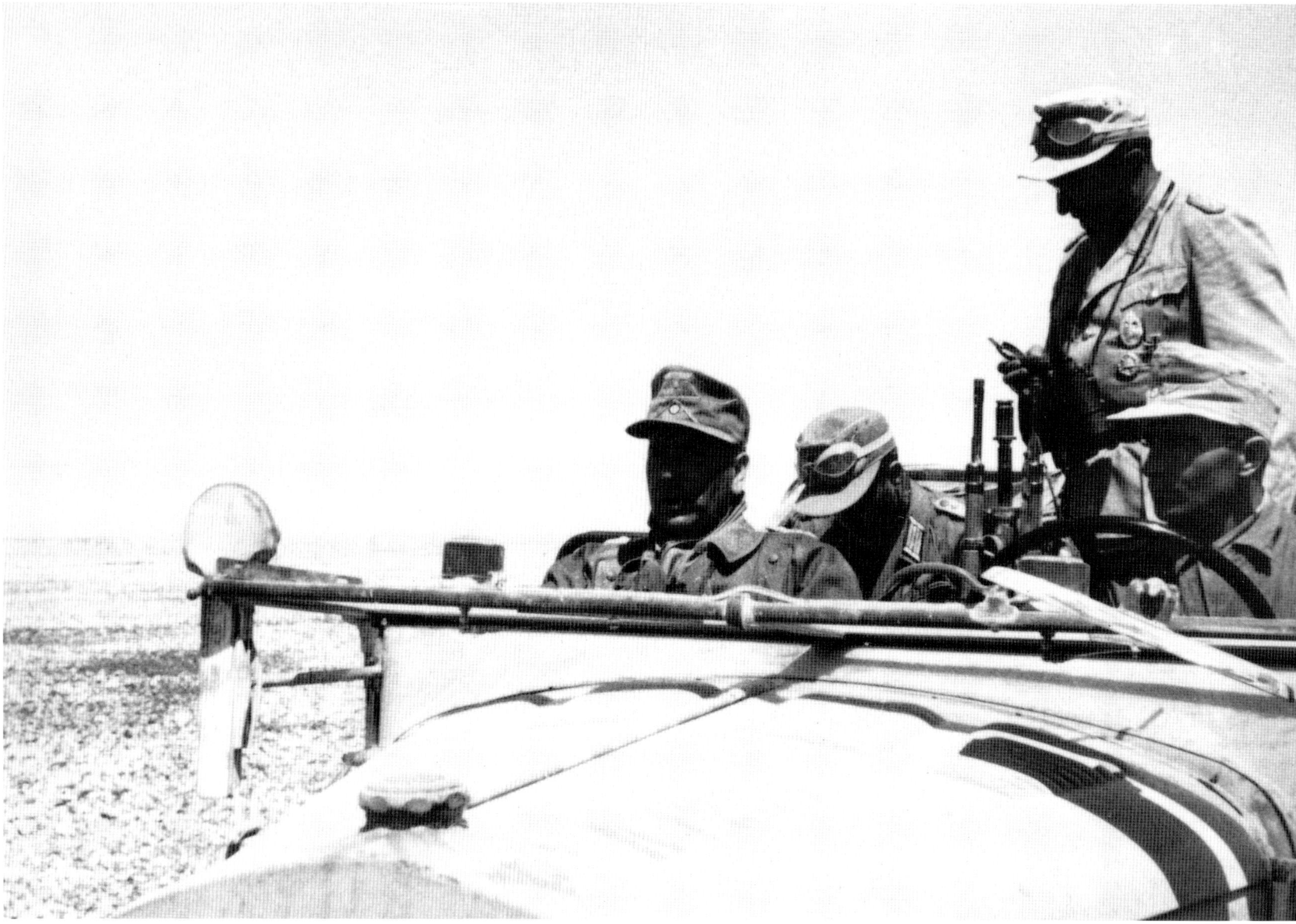

General von Thoma, (front seat passenger) in a more pensive mood, sits in his staff car with Bayerlein standing for the better view while his ADC sitting next to him rummages through a case of maps.

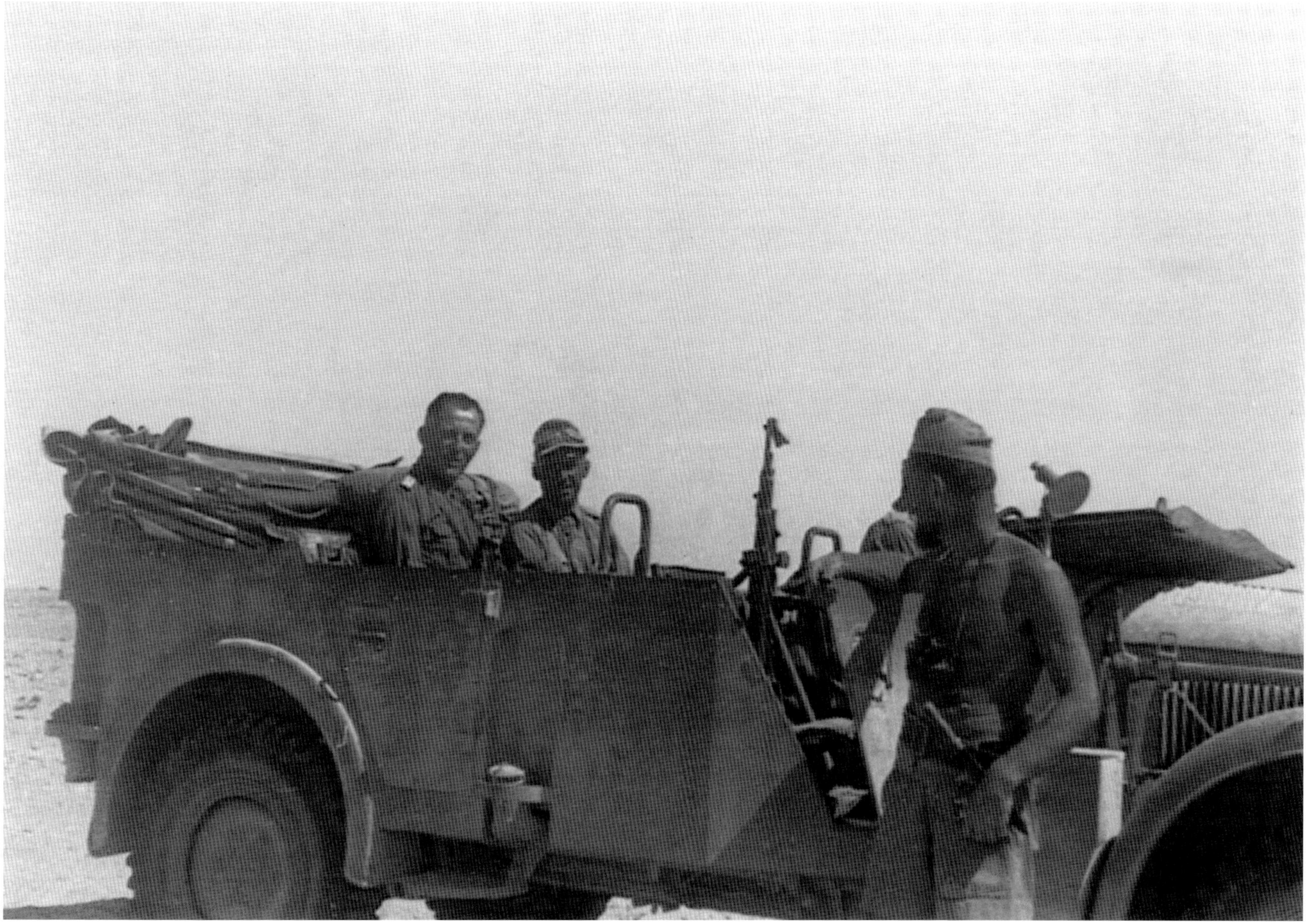

Commander and Chief sit together in their vehicle. Smiling, von Thoma (left) appears in a good mood.

CHAPTER FOURTEEN

GENERALMAJOR BAYERLEIN AND THE END IN AFRICA

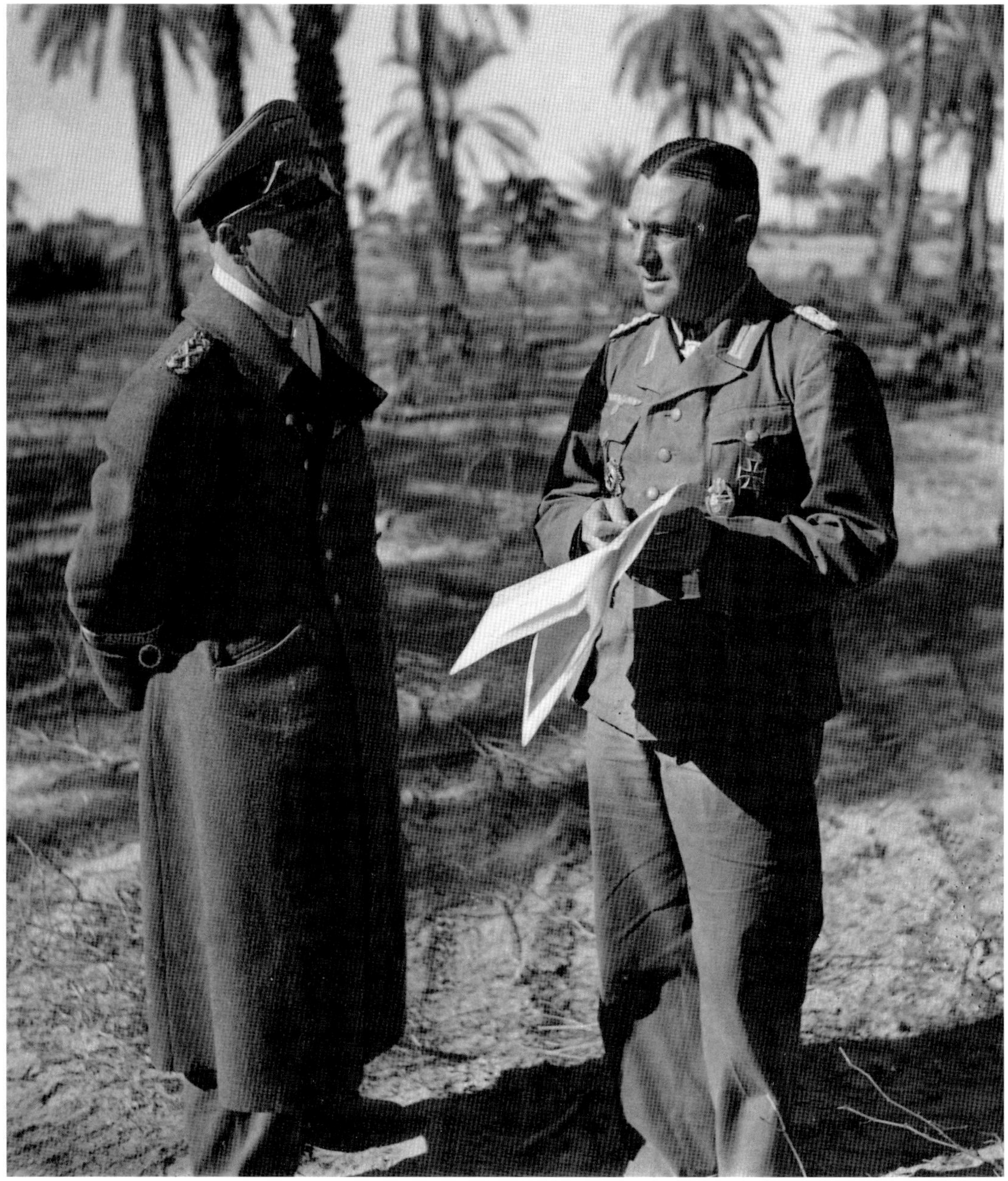

Field Marshal Rommel and Oberst Bayerlein in Tunisia talking shortly before Bayerlein's promotion to Generalmajor. Photograph could be dated in a range from late January to February 1943. Bayerlein has his map ready, although Rommel doesn't appear to be interested in looking at it. He always seems to be in possession of a map, a habit Bayerlein seemed to keep throughout the war. Rommel watched over his friend's African career, promoting him from his arrival as an Oberstleutnant in October 1941 to Generalmajor in March 1943 – a brief span of seventeen months. The men's friendship dated back to the Lehrgang Infantry School days in Dresden in 1928-1929, when Oberleutnant Bayerlein served as Hauptmann Rommel's assistant instructor.[1]

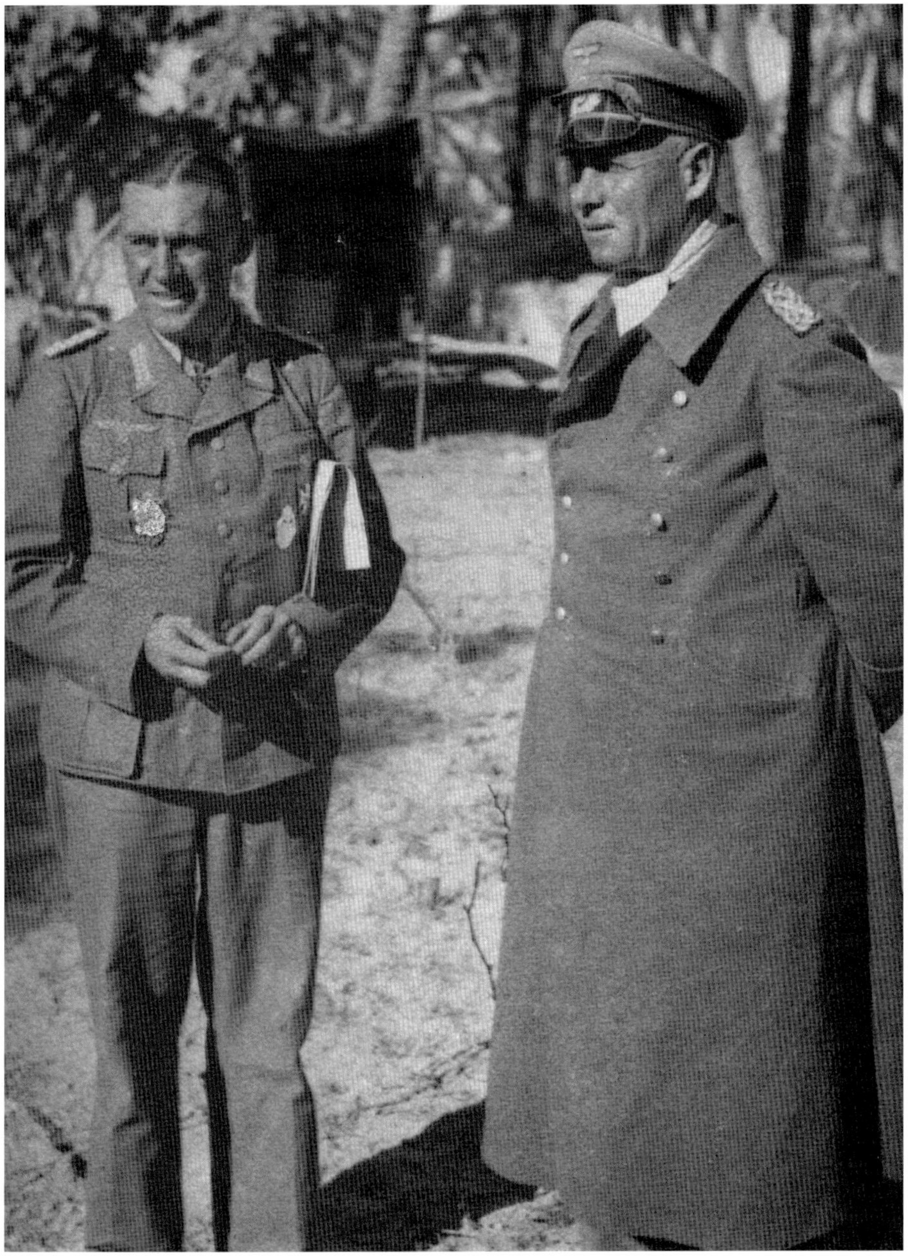

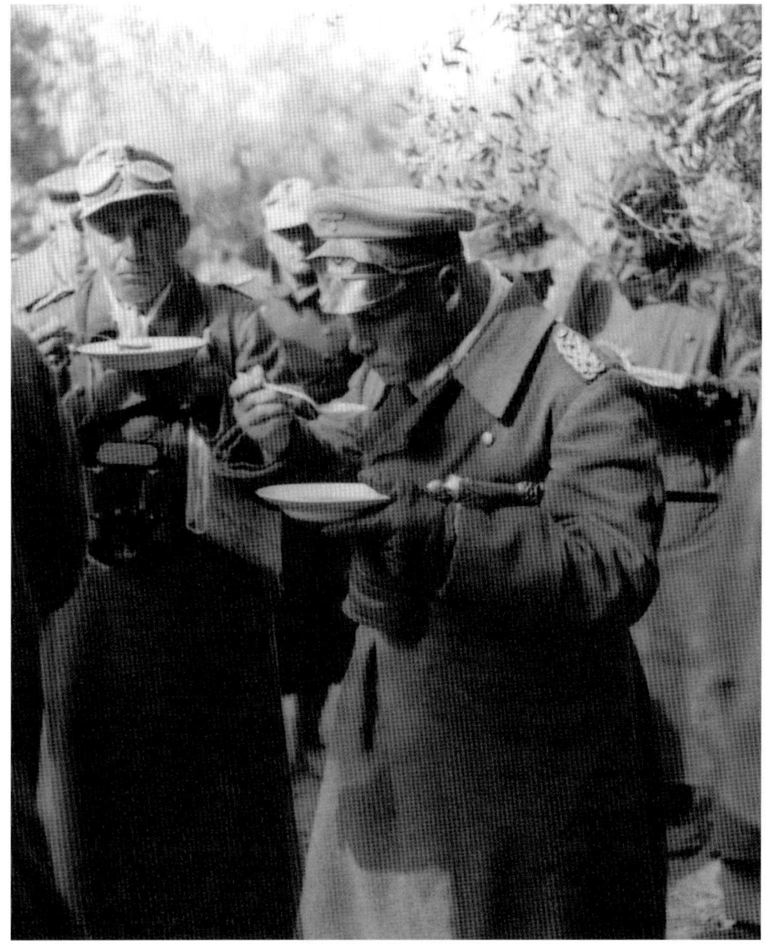

Left
The two men stand together talking, while awaiting the arrival of Field Marshal Kesselring. Bayerlein nervously picks at his fingers, the ever-present map now tucked under his arm. Evidently this photograph was used post-war because the Deutsche Kreuz in Gold swastika is blotted out, as required by German law. Many, including Bayerlein, disliked the Kreuz decoration because the swastika appeared more like a large Nazi brand than a distinguished award.[2]

Above
A rare photo: Rommel and Bayerlein dine on a quick meal of soup. (Photograph provided by courtesy of Mr. Manfred Rommel.)

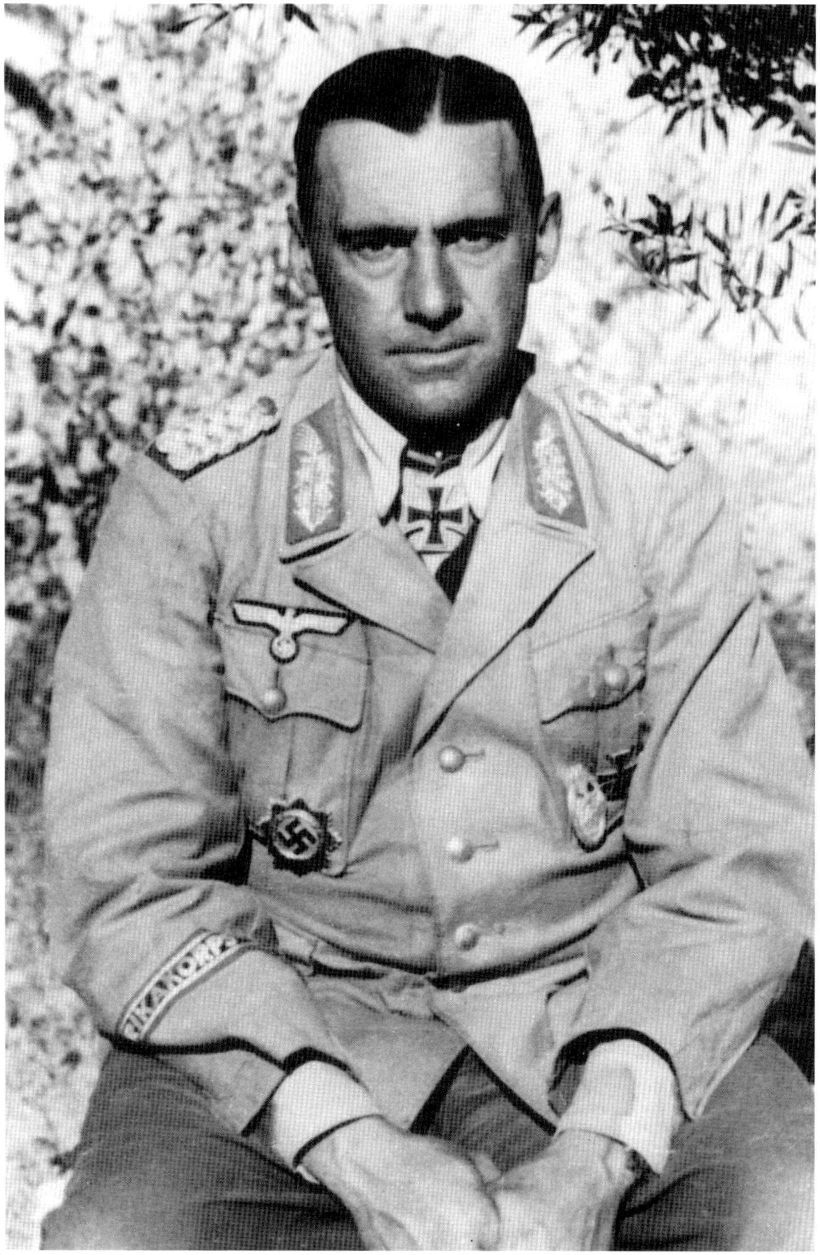

Left
Field portrait of newly-promoted Generalmajor Fritz Bayerlein. Appearing a bit somber from the daunting task awaiting him – his new assignment as Chief-of-Staff for the 1st Italian Army. His new CO was Italian General Meese, a man he neither liked nor respected. Rommel promoted Bayerlein to the rank of Generalmajor effective on March 3rd, 1943, thus giving him the prestige of a higher rank in dealing with the Italian commander. Meese replaced Rommel as theater commander in March when Hitler recalled Rommel back to Germany.

Opposite
Bayerlein, as the newly-promoted Generalmajor and the Deutsche Chef des Generalstabes bei 1. italienischen Armee, awards the Ritterkreuz to Hauptmann Günther Strähler-Pohl, leader of the Luftwaffe Jäger Battalion in late April 1943.[3] Contending that Meese disregarded the sacrifices of the German soldiers, Bayerlein ensured his troops were rewarded for their bravery in the last days.[4] Bayerlein wrote an account of the final battle, severely critical of Meese and his bad leadership. "So I decided not to be 'der Deutsche Chef' for General Meese any longer. From the first day on, I considered myself as the 'Befehlshaber' of the German troops."[5]

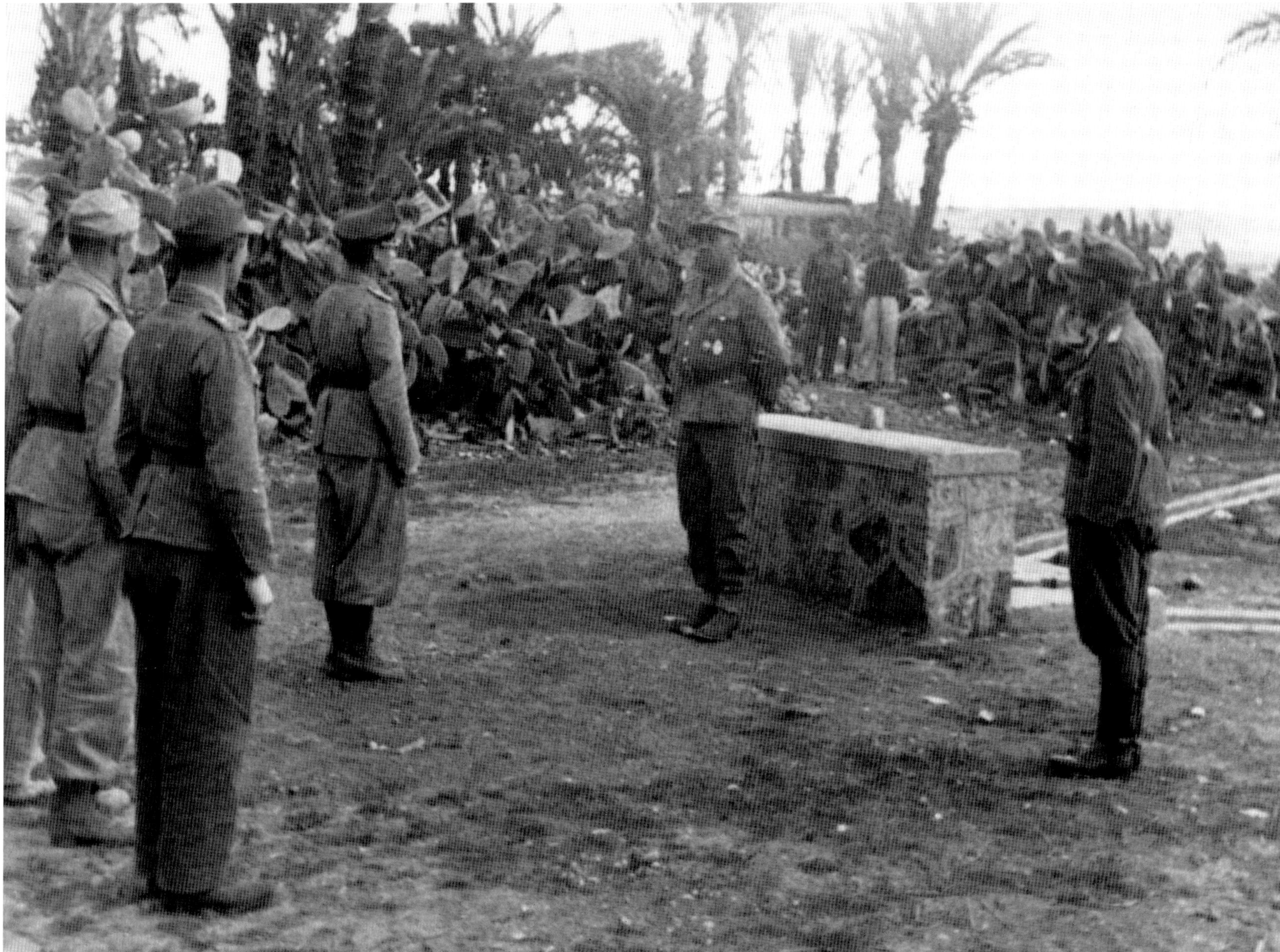

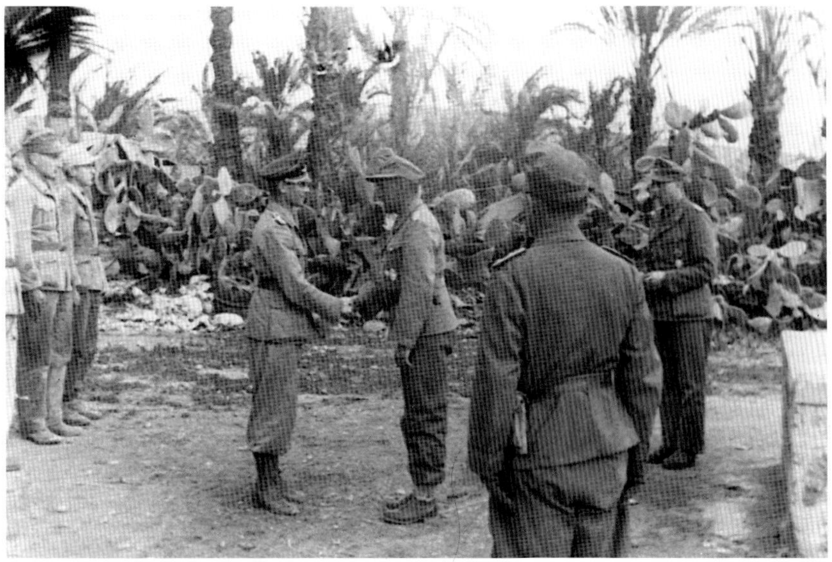

Hauptmann Strähler-Pohl and Generalmajor shake hands as the Deutscher Chef congratulates the younger man.

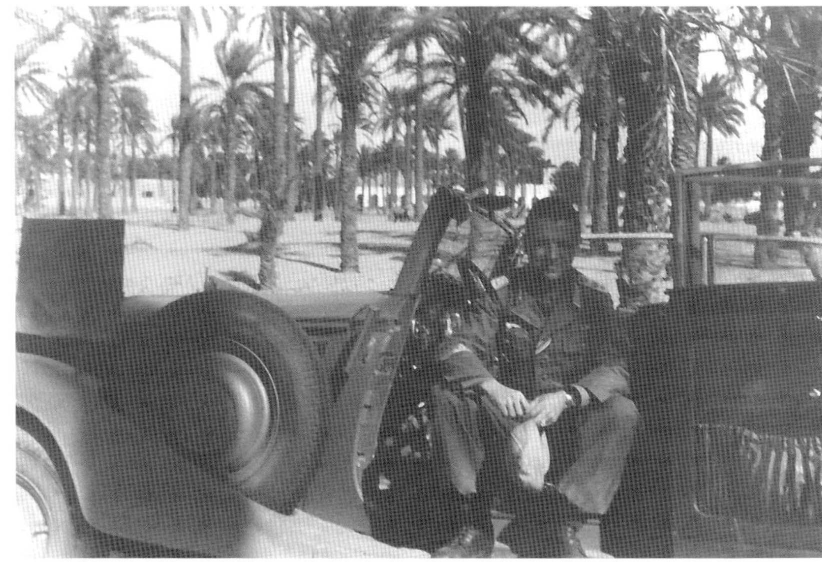

Oberleutnant Alexander Hartdegen, Ordonnanzoffizier for Generalmajor Bayerlein. The Ordonnanzoffizier at the general or brigade level was a staff orderly/aide-de-camp who handled requirements missions too delicate or critical or otherwise important to be delegated to an individual less capable, skilled or trustworthy.[6] *Hartdegen was a staff officer generally not favored by other commanders in the European theater; he was anti-Nazi, caring little whether he was promoted or not. His wife, of German parentage, was born in Brazil, also a factor that was viewed as negative at the time. His officer personnel file contained many concerned references to her Brazilian origins. For his independence and intelligence, Bayerlein found a loyal friend for his entire life.*[7]

CHAPTER FIFTEEN

AWARDS AND HOMECOMING

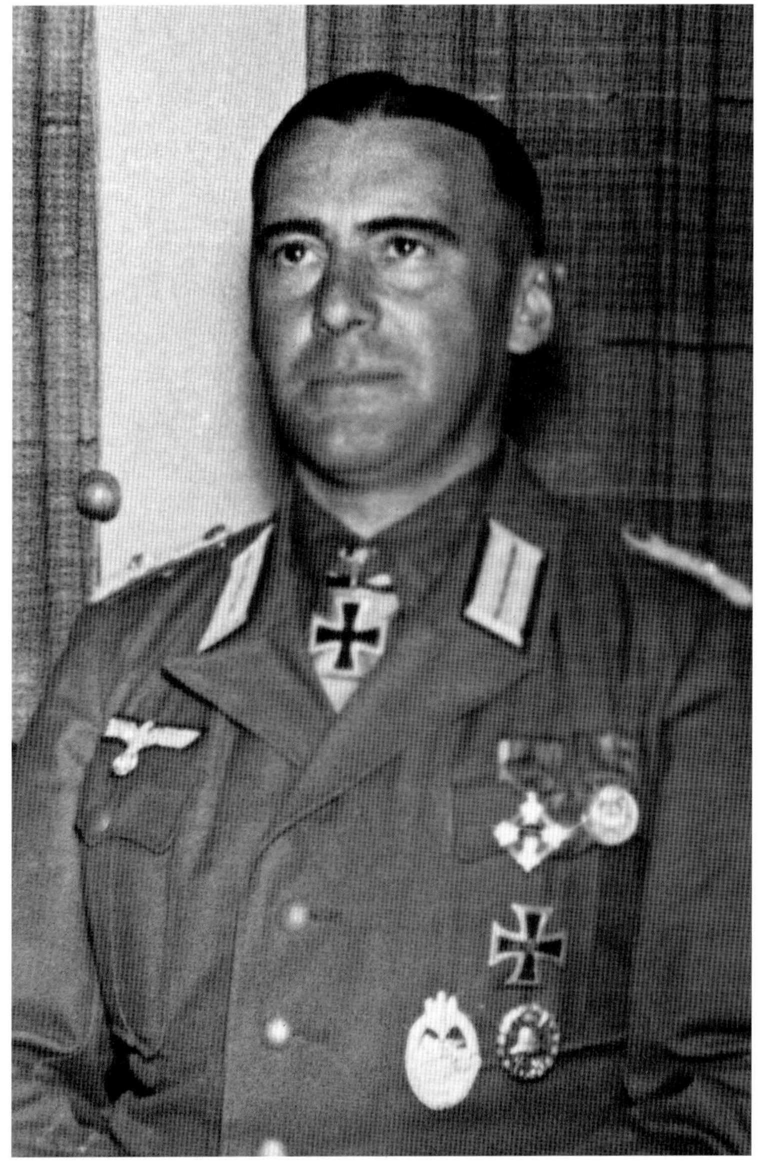

On a home furlough – a rare occasion – Bayerlein models the Italian decorations awarded to him by Mussolini: the Cavaliere des Militärordens von Savoyen awarded for his actions in Cyrenaica in December 1941, and the Italiensche Tapferkeitsmedaille in Silber, awarded on 7 May 1942 in Rome.

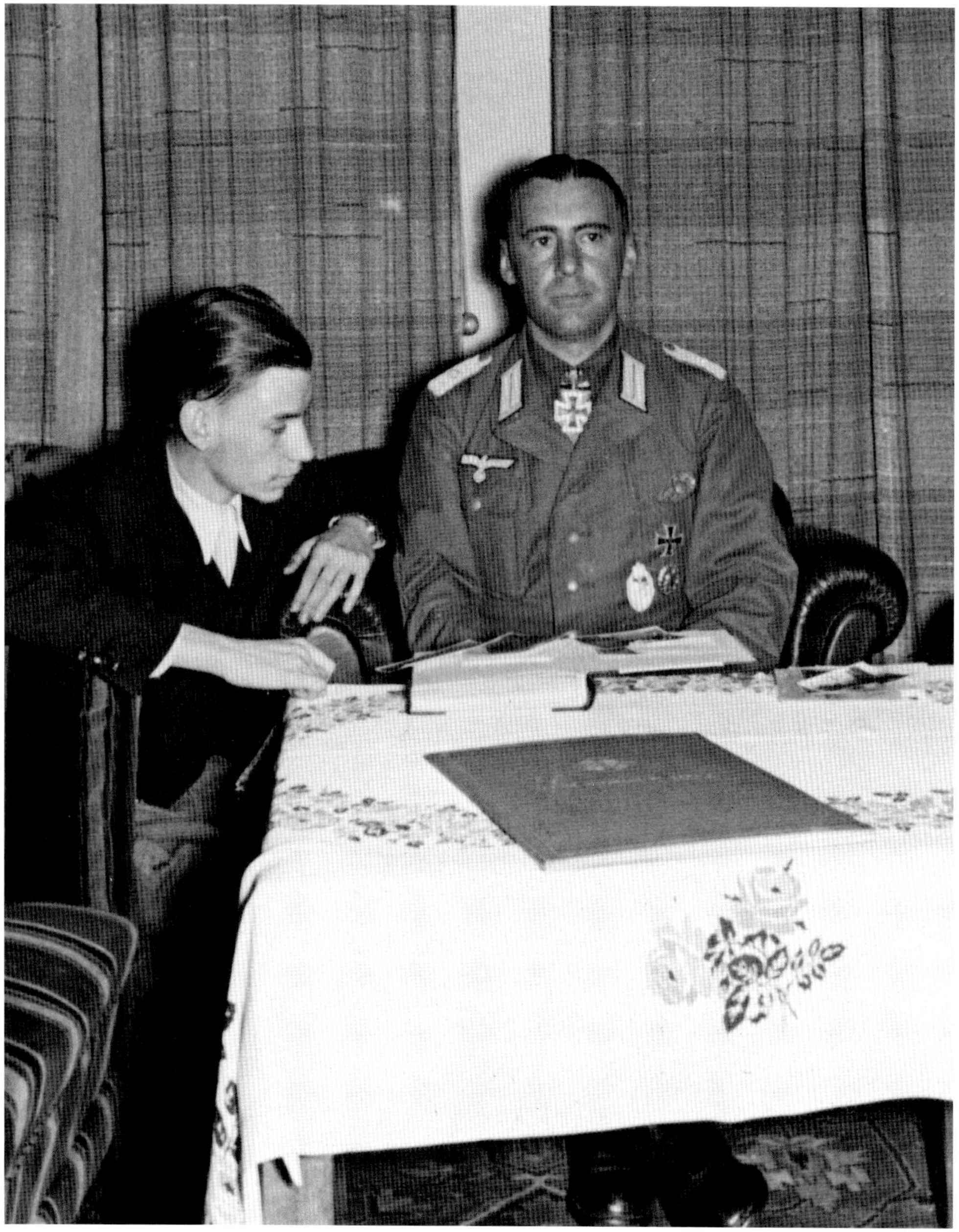

Left
As nephew Friedrich Dittmar watches, Bayerlein dutifully poses for his sister as she interrupts his reading to record a family event – his Ritterkreuz, to include the gold-stamped eagle emblazoned on a red leather folder, which includes Hitler's signed award document protected inside.

Opposite
July 7th 1943. A smiling Adolf Hitler awards Bayerlein the Knight's Cross with Oakleaves (Eichenlaub zum Ritterkreuz). Field Marshal Rommel closely watches his subordinate's somber expression, knowing the man's opinion of the Führer – one that Rommel also shared. Field Marshal Keitel watches from the sideline on the right.

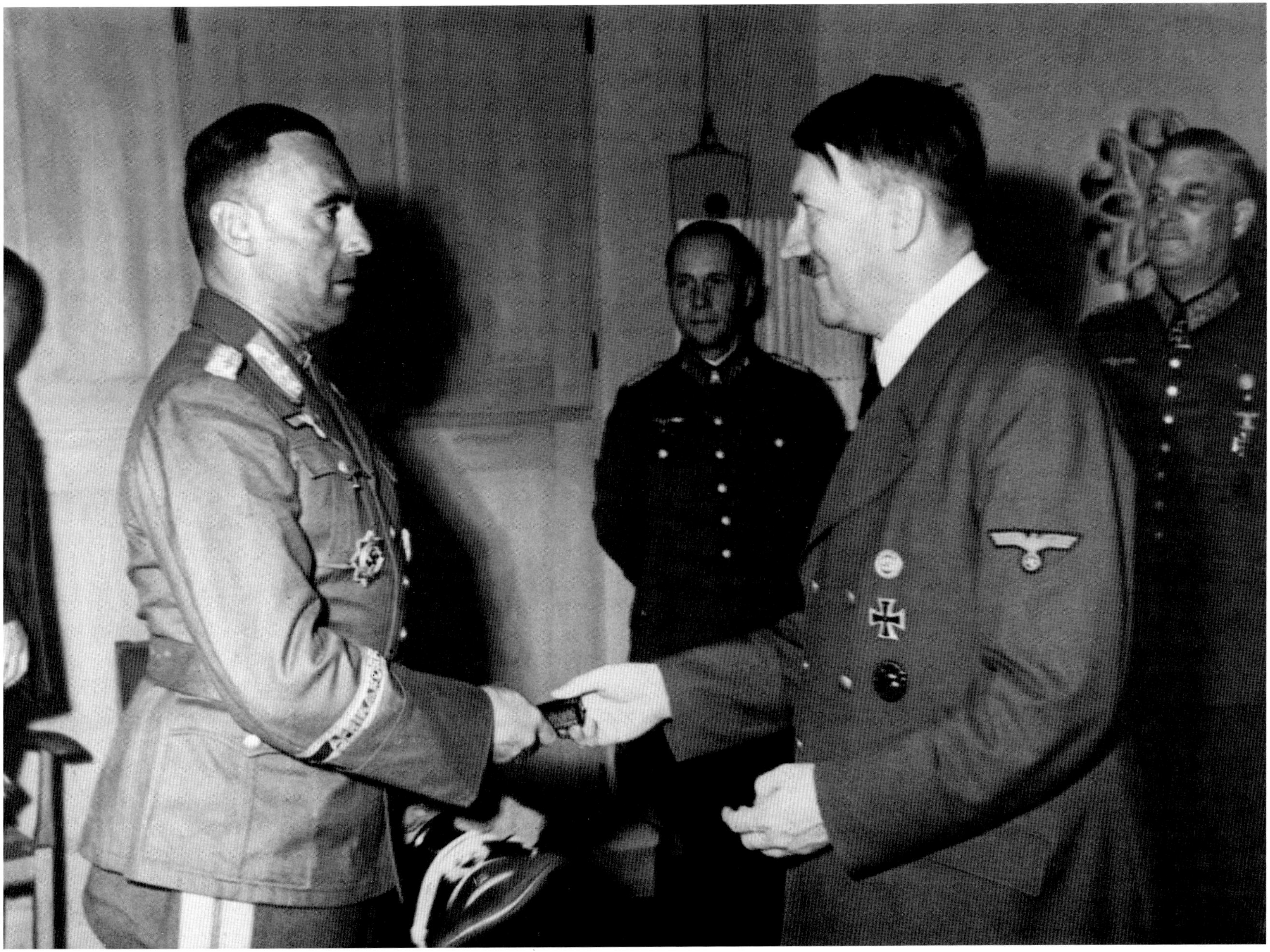

Bayerlein and his brother-in-law, Hauptmann Matthäus Dittmar, enjoy the sun and conversation – a quiet time a few weeks before the storm of D-Day. The photograph was taken after Bayerlein's promotion to Generalleutnant in May 1944. In this photograph Bayerlein's Afrikakorps armband is visible on his left sleeve. He was proud of his service with the Deutsches Afrikakorps in the Western Desert and wore the armband throughout the entire war.

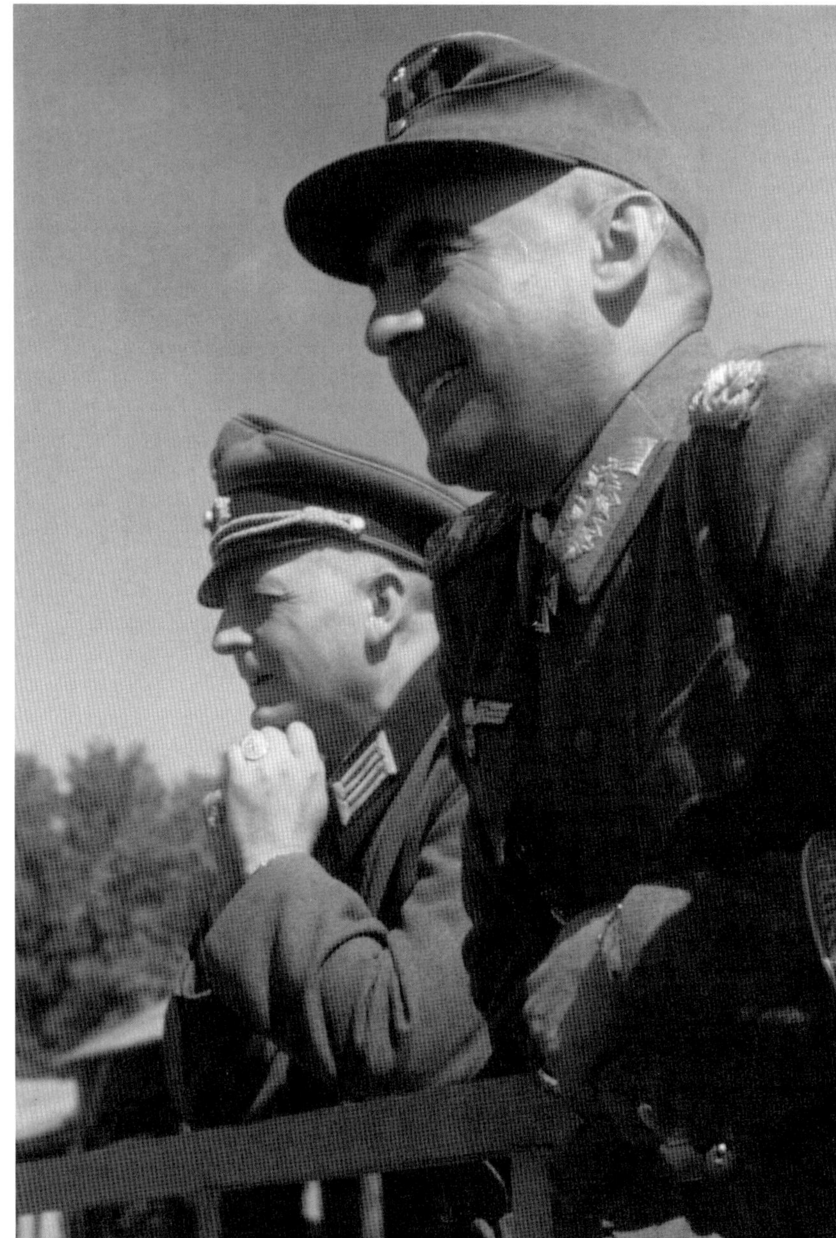

• • •

In his experience of desert fighting with Field Marshal Erwin Rommel as his commander, mentor, and friend, Bayerlein matured from an ambitious officer, to a commander who oversaw the care and lives of his soldiers as paramount to a battle's success. From the D-Day invasion through the failed Ardennes Offensive to the last weeks of fighting at the edge of his homeland on the Rhine River, Generalleutnant Fritz Bayerlein recognized the ultimate end and seized the initiative to stop further battles of "useless bloodshed." He was the only Corps commander to surrender with his entire command in the Ruhr Pocket – to General Robert W. Hasbrouck and his 7th Armored Division on April 16, 1945. His surrender was largely responsible for the total collapse of the Ruhr Pocket – a tally of over 300,000 German soldiers. The opinion of his superiors and contemporaries varied as to whether his surrender was a traitorous act to the Third Reich and his oath as an officer, or the actions of a courageous man.[1] Ultimately, Bayerlein would defend one and would be called to account for the other.

BAYERLEIN'S PERSONALAKTE AND NACHWEISS: PERSONNEL FILE FROM WORLD WAR I AND LISTING OF HIS MILITARY RECORD THROUGH WORLD WAR II

Fritz H. Bayerlein
Generalleutnant

Personal *Nachweiss* and *Personalakte*

Source documents from Bundesarchiv Freiburg, Bayerisches Hauptstaatsarchiv-Kriegsarchiv and Wirsberg Gymnasium Würzburg. Translated from the German old script by Ms. Helga Woods and Mr. Niels Cordes.[1]

Promotions, Awards, Decorations and Unit Assignments

* January 14, 1899, Würzburg
† January 30, 1970, Würzburg

Drafted as the 55th student from Gymnasium Class for School Year 1899 (*Eintritt i. Heer*): June 5, 1917
Surrendered to 7th Armored Division, First U.S. Army: April 16, 1945
Released from captivity, MISC# 4, Oberursel, Germany: April 2, 1947

Awards and Decorations

Wound Badge, World War I, (*Verwundetenabzeichen*), August 31, 1918
Iron Cross Second Class (*Eisernes Kreuz [EK] II. Klasse*), August 30, 1918
Iron Cross Second Class, 1939 Clasp, *(Eiserne Kreuz [EK]II. Klasse [Spange])*, September 13, 1939.
Iron Cross First Class, *(Eiserne Kreuz [EK]I. Klasse)*, September 27, 1939
Knight's Cross (*Ritterkreuz*), December 26, 1941 (#764)
German Cross in Gold, (*Deutsches Kreuz in Gold*), October 23, 1942
Knight's Cross with Oakleaves (*Eichenlaub zum Ritterkreuz*), July 7, 1943 (# 258)
Knight's Cross with Swords, Oakleaves (*Eichenlaub mit Schwertern zum Ritterkreuz*), July 20, 1944 (# 81)
Wound Badge in Silver – wounded over three times (*Verwundetenabzeichen in Silber*)
Panzer Assault Badge (*Panzerkampfabzeichen in Silber*): December 16, 1944

Italian Decorations awarded in North Africa
Cavaliere des Militärordens von Savoyen
Italienische Tapferkeitsmedaille in Silber
Italian German medal

Promotions

September 13, 1918	Non-commissioned officer's rank (*Fahnenjunker-Unteroffizier)*
July 5, 1919	Officer cadet (*Fähnrich*)
Jan. 1, 1921	Officer candidate (enlisted rank of master sergeant) (*Oberfähnrich*)
January 1, 1922	*Leutnant*
January 1, 1927	*Oberleutnant*
March 1,1934	*Hauptmann*
June 1, 1938	*Major*
September 1, 1940	*Oberstleutnant*
April 1, 1942	*Oberst*
March 1, 1943	*Generalmajor*
May 1, 1944	*Generalleutnant*

Note: RDA (Rang-Dienst-Alter), service time in grade, not provided.

Units

June 5, 1918	Enlisted as a private in the 9th Bavarian Infantry Regiment, registered as a *Fahnenjunker*
June 24, 1917	Sworn in; 4th Bavarian Infantry Division
January 12, 1918	Field Recruiting Depot of the 4th Bavarian Infantry Division
May 28, 1918	7th Company, (a Machine Gun Company), II Battalion, 9th Bavarian Infantry Regiment
April 15, 1919	Transferred to the 5th Company of the Volunteer Battalion "Dittmar"
May 28, 1919	Transferred to the 3rd Company of the 3rd Bavarian Reserve Infantry Regiment 45
October 16, 1919	Sworn in
January 1, 1921	*Oberfähnrich*, 3rd Company of the 21st Bavarian Infantry Regiment
March 1, 1930	4th Machine Gun Company, of the 21st Bavarian Infantry Regiment
October 1, 1930	Adjutant for the 1st Battalion of the 21st Infantry Regiment
August 3, 1934	Sworn in. (Hitler Oath)
April 15, 1935	Assigned to the General Staff of the Artillery Leader V
October 15, 1935	General Staff officer of the 15th Division, Infantry Regiment 21. Frankfurt am Main
Apr. 8, 1936	General Staff 15th Division
December 21, 1936	*Landwehr* Company in Hanau
October 12, 1937	Company Chief, 2nd Company, Machine Gun Battalion 6
November 12, 1938	Ib (Logistics) Officer, General Staff of the XV. Armeekorps
April 1, 1939	Ia (Operations)of the 10. Panzer Division
February 25, 1940	Ia (Operations) General Staff of the XIX Armee Korps
June 1, 1940	Ia (Operations) General Staff of *Panzergruppe* Guderian
November 16, 1940	Ia (Operations) General Staff, 2. Panzerarmee
August 30, 1941	*Führerreserve Oberkommando der Heeres* (OKH)

October 5, 1941	Chief of the General Staff of the *Afrikakorps*
December 7, 1942	Chief of the General Staff of the German-Italian *Panzerarmee Afrika*
March 1, 1943	Chief of the General Staff of the 1st Italian Army (North Africa under Italian General Meese)
May 7, 1943	Evacuation from Africa
May 31, 1943	*Führerreserve* OKH
October 20, 1943	Commander 3rd Panzer Division
January X, 1944	*Führerreserve* OKH
January 10, 1944	Commander Panzer Lehr Division
January 20, 1945	*Führerreserve* OKH
March 29, 1945	Commander, LIII Army Corps
April 16, 1945	Surrender – Prisoner of War Camp through 2 April 1947

Schools

September 14, 1918:	12th Bavarian *Fahnenjunker* Course in Freising
May 27, 1920	Infantry School II, Wünsdorf. (through November 30, 1920)
July 7 - Dec. 13, 1922:	Wünsdorf, training to become a Physical Training Instructor and Lifeguard/lifesaving swim test
June 20 - Nov. 24, 1924	Pionier Training/Physical Training for the 7th Pionier Battalion (Engineer)
October 1 - Nov. 25, 1925	Training for *Pionier* Duty at the 7th *Pionier* Battalion
April 21, 1927	Transferred to the Infantry School – recalled back to the Company. Received the Honor Sword for accurate shooting
September 12, 1930	Attended Infantry School
March 8-11, 1932	Military district exams
November 25, 1932	School and exam for English
1932-1935	*Kriegsakademie* (War College)

Note

[1] Bayerlein's complete *Personalakte* from the *Heerespersonalamt* (German Army Personnel Office) could not be located. The only existing file contains his Nachweiss, a chronology listing of his service; however all supporting documents have been purged from these files. The Microfilm Branch Records on General Officers of the National Archives and Records Administration (NARA II) in College Park Maryland also does not contain a complete file on Bayerlein. From post-war conversations, Bayerlein confessed to his American captors that he was to be discharged from the Army in 1934 based upon "non-Aryan" descent, but was retained due to his capabilities. It is known that Field Marshal Rommel knew the personnel office of the Army, and may have been instrumental in removing this information.

NOTES

CHAPTER ONE

[1] Liddell-Hart, Sir Basil, editor, *The Rommel Papers*, Harcourt Brace, London, New York, 1953. 161.

[2] Heckmann, Wolf, *Rommel's War in Africa*, Doubleday and Company, New York, 1981. 212, 213.

[3] *Ibid., 219-220.*

CHAPTER TWO

[1] Information in this caption is provided and written by New Zealand, author Rex Trye.

[2] Kurowski, Franz, *Knight's Cross Holders of the Afrikakorps*, Schiffer Publishing, Ltd., Atglen, PA, 1996. 284-285.

[3] Per Dal McGuirk.

[4] Kurowski, *Knight's Cross*, 209, 303.

[5] Heckmann, *Rommel's War*, 213-214.

[6] Bayerlein's handwritten note translated by Gary Wilkins and pilot identified. Caption written by Wilkins, author of *The Collector's Guide to Third Reich Military Headgear.*

CHAPTER THREE

[1] Telephone conversation and correspondence with Hartdegen's daughters by author P. Spayd, July 2003.

[2] Staatsarchiv, Würzburg Germany: Akten der *Geheimen Staatspolizeit,* Würzburg, über Langguth, Michael, Signature 5640 (Gestapo file).

[3] U.S. Army War College, General Robert W. Hasbrouck Papers, Report of Headquarters, First U.S. Army, Office of the A.C. of S., G-2, Interview with Colonel B.A. Dickson, dated 17 April 1945. "He made a present of his Golden Kreuz and stated that he had never worn it and never would. It was in a cellophane package when it was handed over." Note: Bayerlein did wear it upon numerous occasions, as evidenced by photographs.

[4] The photo was taken with Bayerlein's Leica. Evidently, Bayerlein gave the photo to Hartdegen. Mr. Hartdegen's daughters loaned the photograph to the authors for exclusive use in General Bayerlein's Afrikakorps photograph book.

[5] Per Dal McGuirk, New Zealand.

[6] Per correspondence with Dolores and Ivana Hartdegen.

CHAPTER FOUR

[1] This photo from Bayerlein's apartment has been published before, it is included here as part of his personal collection.

[2] Per author Dal McGuirk.

[3] According to Rex Trye.

[4] Per Dal McGuirk.

[5] Another photo in Bayerlein's apartment that has been previously published. It is unknown if he was the original source.

CHAPTER FIVE

[1] Dal McGuirk, author of *Rommel's Army in Africa*, by Motorbooks International Publishers, aided the authors greatly in identifying Bayerlein's uncaptioned photographs.

[2] Per consultation with Dal McGuirk.

[3] Kühn, Volkmar, *Rommel in the Desert, Victories and Defeat of the Afrika-Korps 1941-1943*, Translated from the German by David Johnston, Schiffer Military History, Atglen PA., 1991. p.135.

[4] Per consultation with Dal McGuirk.

[5] Per Dal McGuirk.

[6] Per Dal McGuirk.

CHAPTER SIX

[1] Per consultation with Dal McGuirk.

CHAPTER SEVEN

[1] Liddell-Hart, *The Rommel Papers*, 282, 290, 371.

CHAPTER EIGHT

[1] Consultation between P. Spayd and author, Rex Trye of New Zealand.

[2] Per Dal McGuirk.

[3] Analysis per Dal McGuirk.

CHAPTER NINE

[1] Liddell-Hart, *Rommel Papers*, 383.
[2] Per consultation with Rex Trye.
[3] Liddell-Hart, *Rommel Papers*, 383.
[4] Ibid.
[5] Ibid.
[6] Ibid.
[7] Ibid.

CHAPTER TEN

[1] Per consultation with Thomas Jentz by author P. Spayd. Mr. Jentz has written many excellent books on Panzers, and some are provided in the bibliography.
[2] "The Rommel Collection," T84, Rolls 272-276, on file at the Microfilm Branch, National Archives and Records Administration II (NARA), in College Park, Maryland also has an identical photo. It appears that Bayerlein and Rommel periodically exchanged photographs.
[3] Caption written by Mr. Jentz.
[4] Ibid.
[5] Ibid.

CHAPTER ELEVEN

[1] Liddell-Hart, *Rommel Papers*, 292-293.
[2] Per author, Dal McGuirk.
[3] Per author, Dal McGuirk.
[4] Per author, Dal McGuirk.

CHAPTER TWELVE

[1] Per Dal McGuirk.
[2] Per Dal McGuirk.
[3] Per Dal McGuirk.
[4] Consultation with Rex Trye.
[5] Per Dal McGuirk.
[6] Per Dal McGuirk.

CHAPTER THIRTEEN

[1] Combat unit formed to protect Corps Headquarters. Liddell-Hart, *Rommel Papers*, 324.
[2] Liddell-Hart, *Rommel Papers*, 324-325.
[3] Per Gary Wilkins.
[4] Per Dal McGuirk.

CHAPTER FOURTEEN

[1] Spayd, *Bayerlein*, 25-27.
[2] General Robert W. Hasbrouck Papers, Carlisle Barracks: Report of Headquarters, First U.S. Army, Office of the A.C. of S., G-2, dated 17 April, 1945. B.A. Dickson, Colonel, G.S.C. Report stated that Bayerlein, "was outspoken in his denunciation of the Nazi Party and said he had no use for the Waffen-SS. He made a present of the Golden Kreuz and stated that he had never worn it and never would. It was in a cellophane package when it was handed over."
[3] Per handwritten note written by Bayerlein on the photograph.
[4] Personal correspondence between Rommel and Bayerlein, dated 31 May, 1943, provided to author P. Spayd by Mr. Manfred Rommel.
[5] Imperial War Museum, London, EDS 1907/2: *Kriegstagbuch* (KTB) AOK1, Daily Reports from 8 March - 5 May 1943. Report dated May 5 1943, Nr 202/43. Note: Bayerlein at his own initiative changed his duty from Chief of Staff (*der Deutsche Chef*) to the German commander (*Befehlshaber*).
[6] Descriptive duties per Gary Wilkins.
[7] Hauptmann Alexander Hartdegen's Personalakte, National Archives and Records Administation, Microfilm records file.

CHAPTER FIFTEEN

[1] Spayd, *Bayerlein*, 201, 208, 211, 223

BIBLIOGRAPHY

Bender, Roger James and Law, Richard D., *Uniforms, Organization and History of the Afrikakorps*, R. James Bender Publishing, San Jose, California, 1973.

Heckmann, Wolf, *Rommel's War in Africa*, Gustav Lubbe Verlag, 1981, translated by Doubleday & Company, Inc.

Kurowski, Franz, *Knight's Cross Holders of the Afrikakorps*, Schiffer Publishing, Ltd, Atglen, PA., 1996.

— *Der Afrika Feldzug, Rommel's Wüstenkrieg 1941-1943*, Volker Hennig Verlag

Herausgegeben vom Generalkommando des Deutschen Afrikakorps, *Marsch und Kampf, Des Deutschen Afrikakorps 1941*, Verlag E.S. Mittler & Son, Berlin, 1994.

Jentz, Thomas L. (edited by), *Panzertruppen, The Complete Guide to the Creation & Combat Employment of Germany's Tank Force 1933-1942,* Schiffer Publishing, Ltd., Atglen, PA., 1996.

— *Panzertruppen, The Complete Guide to the Creation & Combat Employment of Germany's Tank Force 1943-1945*, Schiffer Publishing, Ltd., Atglen, PA., 1996.

Liddell-Hart, B.H. (edited by) *The Rommel Papers*, Harcourt Brace, New York, 1953.

Lande, D.A., *Rommel in North Africa*, Motorbooks International, Osceola WI, USA. 1999.

McGuirk, Dal, *Rommel's Army in Africa*, Motorbooks International, Osceola WI, USA, 1993.

— *AFRIKAKORPS Self Portrait*, Airlife Publishing, Shrewsbury, Shropshire, England, 1992

Piekalkiewicz, Janusz, translation by Edward Force, *Rommel and the Secret War in North Africa, 1941-1943*, Schiffer Military History, Atglen, PA.

Spayd, P. A. (edited and written by), *Bayerlein, from Afrikakorps to Panzer Lehr: the Life of Rommel's Chief of Staff, Generalleutnant Fritz Bayerlein*, Schiffer Publishing, Ltd., 2003.

Trye, Rex. *Mussolini's Soldiers*, Airlife Publishing, England. 1995.

— *Mussolini's Afrika Korps - The Italian Army in North Africa 1940-1943*, Axis Europa Publishing, New York, 1999.

Volkmar Kühn, *Mit Rommel in der Wüste, Kampf und Untergang des Deutschen Afrika-Korps 1941-1943.* Motorbuch Verlag Stuttgart, 1992.

Wilkins, Gary, *The Collector's Guide to Cloth Third Reich Military Headgear*, Schiffer Publishing, Atglen, PA., 2002.

Also from the Publisher

GENERALFELDMARSCHALL FEDOR VON BOCK
The War Diary 1939-1945
Klaus Gerbert

The Von Bock memoirs allow the reader to see the entire drama of the Second World War through the eyes of one of Germany's most important military commanders. After the attacks on Poland and Western Europe, von Bock became Commander-in-Chief of Army Group Center that carried out the main drive on Moscow during Operation Barbarossa and brought the Red Army to the verge of collapse in the great battles of encirclement. This book allows us to reassess Fedor von Bock, whose complex personality is revealed by his diary entries, and by the biographical sketches by editor Klaus Gerbet.
Size: 6"x9" • 62 b/w photographs • 640 pp.
ISBN: 0-7643-0075-X • hard cover • $39.95

SCORCHED EARTH
The Russian-German War 1943-1944
Paul Carell

The classic! This new edition of Paul Carell's eastern front study picks up where *Hitler Moves East* left off. Beginning with the battle of Kursk in July 1943, Carell traverses the vast expanse of the Russian War, from the siege of Leningrad and the fierce battles of the norther front, to the fourth battle of Kharkov, and the evacuation of the Crimea, a withdrawal forbidden by Hitler. The book ends in June of 1944 when the Soviet Armies reach the East Prussian frontier. Hundreds of photographs, situation and campaign maps, complete index, and comprehensive bibliography, add to this impressive account. This edition includes a new preface by the author.
Size: 6"x9" • b/w photographs, maps • 600 pp.
ISBN: 0-88740-598-3 • hard cover • $39.95

FOXES OF THE DESERT
The Story of the Afrikakorps
Paul Carell

Here for the first time from the German viewpoint and with a great deal of hitherto unpublished material is the complete story of one of the most bitterly fought, exciting campaigns in modern warfare. As a result of personal interviews with over a thousand combatants, tireless reading, and painstaking research, Paul Carell has skillfully blended a mass of new and exciting information into a dramatic and completely authentic narrative. As a story of strategy and battle, *Foxes of the Desert* is both exhaustive and engrossing, and, as an authorative history, it cannot be overlooked by anyone wishing a full understanding of World War II.
Size: 5 3/4"x8 1/2" • b/w photographs, maps • 370 pp.
ISBN: 0-88740-659-9 • hard cover • $29.95

GERMAN PANZERS ON THE OFFENSIVE
Russian Front • North Africa 1941-1942
R.H.S. Stolfi

The German Army conducted offensive military operations more effectively than any other in the twentieth century. The acknowledged superiority of the German Army in battle fighting, however, is exemplified by the offensives of 1939-1942, and this book combines description and interpretation of the advances of nine German panzer divisions to reveal extraordinary details of the great victories. Based almost entirely on the division war diaries, this book is able to take the reader aboard the command and combat vehicles, escort him through the fighting, and extract reasons for German success in offensive maneuver war. The interpretation is constructed in enough detail to be a realistic basis for improvement of present-day military operations by the professional and to fascinate and inform the general reader.
Size: 6"x9" • eight b/w photos, maps • 224 pp.
ISBN: 0-7643-1770-9 • hard cover • $35.00

LAST VICTORY IN RUSSIA
The SS-Panzerkorps and Manstein's Kharkov Counteroffensive
February-March 1943
George M. Nipe, Jr.

The first detailed and comprehensive account of the Kharkov counteroffensive, the operations of the SS divisions and the supporting actions of *Armeeabteilung Fretter-Pico* and *1. Panzerarmee*. Hausser has been accused of disregarding his instructions from superior officers and throwing his divisions into costly combat in the city for reasons of personal and SS prestige, in order to regain Hitler's favor. This study has found that the records of the *SS-Panzerkorps* and *4. Panzerarmee* provide a different explanation for Hausser's actions.
Size: 8 1/2"x11" • over 210 b/w photographs • 368 pp.
ISBN: 0-7643-1186-7 • hard cover • $59.95

GERMAN BATTLE TACTICS ON THE RUSSIAN FRONT
1941-1945
Steven Newton

The tenacity of the German Army in Russia from 1941-1945, fighting against overwhelming odds but refusing to disintegrate, has fascinated readers for decades. Professor Newton has retrieved, retranslated, and annotated the detailed tactical accounts of combat in Russia that German officers provided their American captors after the war. In one controversial document in the early cold war included within these ten essays, the last commander of Army Group South recalls his futile attempt to interest General Patton in assisting him against the Soviets.
Size: 6"x9" • 320 pp.
ISBN: 0-88740-582-7 • hard cover • $24.95